Derek Taylor: For Your Radioactive Children...

'Days In The Life Of The Beatles' Spin-Doctor...'

Andrew Darlington

sonicbondpublishing.com

Sonicbond Publishing Limited
www.sonicbondpublishing.co.uk
Email: info@sonicbondpublishing.co.uk

First Published in the United Kingdom 2020
First Published in the United States 2021

British Library Cataloguing in Publication Data:
A Catalogue record for this book is available from the British Library

Copyright Andrew Darlington 2020

ISBN 978-1-78952-038-5

Typeset in ITC Garamond & ITC Avant Garde
Printed and bound in England

Graphic design and typesetting: Full Moon Media

Derek Taylor: For Your Radioactive Children...

Contents

For Stephen

Chapter One: Pre-Flyte

there are places in my memory…

Beatles for sale

You can buy this album – you probably have, unless you're just browsing, in which case don't leave any dirty thumbprints on the sleeve!

There's priceless history between these covers. None of us is getting any younger. When, in a generation or so, a radio-active cigar-smoking child, picnicking on Saturn, asks you what the Beatle affair was all about – 'Did you actually know them?' – don't try to explain all about the long hair and the screams! Just play the child a few tracks from this album and he'll probably understand what it was all about. The kids of AD2000 will draw from the music much the same sense of wellbeing and warmth as we do today.

Derek Taylor (liner-notes to *Beatles for Sale*, 1964)

Beatles historians argue about a lot of things. Like academics in any discipline, they dispute facts and interpretations of facts. But there's one thing beyond dispute. Derek Taylor's urbane charm. His easy intelligence, and the value of his contribution to The Beatles' collective story. And the stories that lie beyond it… if you know what I mean? Derek Taylor lived a charmed life. One that describes a fiery arc that goes all the way from 02:00 am, Saturday, 7 May 1932, in the Liverpool 17 suburb of Toxteth Park South, into being a writer best known as the press agent for The Beatles. He became The Beatles' friend and intimate across a span of thirty years, or – as it's blurbed on the paperback edition of his fragmented memoirs *As Time Goes By* (1973), 'journalist, publicist and honorary Beatle'. There's no shortage of claimants to the 'honorary' or 'fifth Beatle' status. Starting off with those who were, even for a short while, Beatles themselves. The late Stuart Sutcliffe – who rejoins them for the sleeve-collage of *Sgt. Pepper's Lonely Hearts Club Band*, drummer Pete Best, or even Ringo's temporary replacement Jimmie Nicol. And that's before you get to Brian Epstein. But Derek's claim to 'honorary Beatledom' is more valid than most.

In 1964 he co-wrote *A Cellarful of Noise*, the best-selling autobiography of Brian Epstein. Soon after, he became Epstein's personal assistant and Beatles press agent. Derek Taylor put spin on stories decades before the term Spin Doctor was concocted, with his droll, idiosyncratic way of speaking. In 1965 he moved to Los Angeles where he started his own public relations company, managing PR for bands like Paul Revere & The Raiders, the Byrds, and the Beach Boys. Brian Wilson called him a 'PR whiz' and 'a colourful slick-talking Brit'. But he could also be a 'theatrical, slightly conspiratorial man' according to Ray Coleman. Derek was co-creator and producer of the historic *Monterey pop Festival* in 1967. He's there in song when John rhymes 'Derek Taylor' with 'Norman Mailer' in 'Give Peace a Chance'. Then spool forward a few years, to when Derek returned to England to work for The Beatles again as the press officer for the newly created Apple Corps.

He had a deep capacity for friendship. If there were people who disliked him, I haven't discovered one. The thread running through the various aspects of this remarkable career is his easy personal charm, his ability to create a sense of delightful complicity. A glittering web of friendships through the austerity of the fifties, the hairstyles of the sixties, into the high decadence of the seventies. His own writing can be flip, humorous, spontaneous, wilfully infuriatingly imprecise when it's exact detail you're looking for. *As Time Goes By* seems to be an episodic collection of essays and sketches doodled as the mood takes him between appointments. When names elude him, or perhaps when the possibility of litigation intrudes, he substitutes them for play-names that could have been culled from the John Lennon mindset of *A Spaniard in the Works* (1965). A legal partnership called Absalom, Bollocks, Profit and Motive Ltd. Based in New Ponce Street, Mayfair. Or Victor Vagina Associates. Another called A Associate & Associates in Fellatio Drive. Easy to see why he became an intimate of the magic sixties circle, but maddening for academics hunting clues.

Derek Taylor died of cancer at his home in Suffolk on 8 September 1997, after a long illness. He was sixty-five years old.

There are a million stories that take place within the arc of Derek Taylor's life. I sometimes feel I have lived the entirety of my own life within them. I've spent many hundreds of hours discussing and teasing out details of that time, both in direct relation to and around the events within which he lived his life. I talked to the late Gene Clark of the Byrds, Dave Davies of the Kinks, Rick Parfitt and Francis Rossi of Status Quo, Grace Slick, Sid Griffin, Mick Fleetwood, Donovan Leitch, Graham Nash, Joe Brown, Sam Moore, 'Country' Joe Mcdonald. To my great regret, I've acceded to the few sources with first-hand knowledge of Derek's personal and musical life who specifically request anonymity. However, to such people, I'm indebted for their insight and contributions. A person's inclusion or exclusion from a sequence does not necessarily infer that that person has contributed to this book.

I've also conducted research through countless books, magazines and websites and have gratefully given credit accordingly. However, I apologise for those instances where I've been unable to correctly attribute quotes, despite my most exhaustive attempts to do so. I invite corrections to such omissions, which will be rectified in future editions. When it comes to sixties history, the forbidding tower of books and perilous mounds of newspaper cuttings, CDs and DVDs, that should be consulted before tackling the project, you wonder, with a doomy sense of futility in the deepest pit of your gut, how it will ever be possible to scratch your way through the veneers of other people's words and get down a few of your own. When it comes to Beatles-related tales, try to suck any of it into a novel, try and invent it, and chances are you might be gripped and amused, but you'd not be believed. And there are those who find the truth stranger than fiction, but still plump for the fiction. To Derek, 'I don't think that if you have a tidy mind, you will find this book easy to follow. But who needs a tidy mind? Who has one? No-one I know.'

Chapter Two: Dear Sir Or Madam, Won't You Read My Book?

Well, she was just seventeen, you know what I mean...

Cellars-full Of Noise...

The eighty-nine-word two-paragraph 'Prologue' to *A Cellarful of Noise* describes how, on Saturday, 28 October 1961, eighteen-year-old Raymond Jones walked up to the record-store counter of NEMS in Whitechapel, Liverpool, and asked for a record called 'My Bonnie' by a group called The Beatles. Brian Epstein, the store manager, didn't have the record, but politely promised to investigate... If that moment has since become an iconic one in Beatles history – and it has – it's because Derek Taylor chose it to be. In his own words, he was the third presence, the 'journalist sitting nearby, eavesdropping as journalists do.' Sifting through transcription-pages of the interview-tapes he and Brian had made together in the Torquay hotel, arranging and editing them into a coherent narrative, it was Derek who selected that pivotal moment to open Brian Epstein's ghosted autobiography. It was Raymond Jones' casual enquiry that set in chain a sequence of events that would transfigure the second half of the century. No – that's not too great an estimation. It's the encounter that set the twenty-seven-year-old record-store manager scurrying off to track down the group with the strange name for the irksome record he was unable to supply.

The accuracy of the event has since been called into question. In his book *With The Beatles* (2003, John Blake Publishing), Alistair Taylor rubbishes the story – and, as Brian's colleague at the time of the alleged incident, he's in a position to know. He even claims that it was he who fabricated a teenager called 'Raymond Jones' to justify the NEMS store ordering copies of 'My Bonnie' from its German Polydor distributor. Nevertheless, at some point, something pretty much like it may very well have occurred. Even though the veracity of its precise detail – clear down to fixing the time 'at about three o'clock' – seems to lean more on journalistic invention than on the notorious deceptions of memory. What if it didn't occur exactly like that? Not at that exact time. Perhaps 'Raymond Jones' was not 'wearing jeans and a black leather jacket' – isn't that just a little too contrived-cool? Perhaps the memory was, in fact, a virtual reconstruction conflated from a number of prior clues or intimations, an event razored down to simplify it for reasons of dramatic purpose? Countless other Beatles-related histories have worked their way around that incident, delving into it, researching it, drawing up theories. But Derek's account was the first. All the subsequent revisions have to begin from that point. It is Derek's version of events that have passed into history, and his version that other pop-historians have to contend with.

Writers writing biographies of other wordsmiths often start out by deploring the tendency to deduce details of character, values and curriculum vitae from their subject's writing, then proceed to do just that. I'm no different. Derek Taylor was a journalist. He knew how to structure a trickle of prose to maximum effect. Whatever the precise truth may be, he identified that 'Raymond Jones' moment as representing the pivotal equation in all of their lives. Without Brian Epstein, no Beatles. Without Beatles, no Brian Epstein. And also, without Brian Epstein and The Beatles, no Derek Taylor either. He drew that equation down into two sparsely effective paragraphs, extracted and focussed on it, and by doing so, made the incident a crucial part of the legend. But elsewhere he adds a cautionary note about the limits of what biography can achieve, asking 'who the hell are any of us to write about the rest of us? And I would ask all of you to take all of this with a pinch of rock salt.' Be warned.

Liverpool, Derek's 'raw seaport on the edge of England,' was a different place back then. You catch glimpses of it in the movie *Ferry Cross the Mersey* (1965), the skyline where those famous sculpted Liver-birds keep their eternal stone vigil over the dark water from their high perch on the Royal Liver Building on the city's Pier Head. It's claimed the fabled creatures will flap their wings if ever a virtuous woman passes through its polished revolving doors. They're actually meant to be cormorants, and they're the work of Carl Bernard Bartels, a German, but no matter. There's the stench of oil and mud as the ferry itself churns away from where the jetty stands 'dangling her landing stage in the water.' And you hear something of what it must have been like in Gerry Marsden's title song for the film. Back then, with its strong maritime heritage, the Merseyside Riviera was still an important berth with its notoriously dangerous nighttime dock-front areas skirting along the river. A place where nocturnal revellers would round off a fumbled back-alley knee-trembler with a drag on a Senior Service. Where tarts went down on furtive married men in Morris Minors and sometimes lifted their wallet on the way up.

Born in 121 Ashbourne Road, following an 'inexpensive confinement' at his maternal Granny's redbrick terrace house, Derek Wyn Taylor took his first breath in Liverpool, a 'hop skip and jump' from the Mersey. George Harrison jokes that Derek 'is one of those privileged people born in the 1930s, the decade of Cab Calloway and Hitler – and with two main influences as diverse as that in his formative years, what else would you expect?' Today, driving towards the Liverpool John Lennon Airport, Ashbourne Road is a right-hand turn away. There were – and are, herring-bone rows of terraced houses spiking out in grids, with *Coronation Street* entries to the rear. Built for the upper working class in the nineteenth century, it's a place fondly recalled where 'people around every corner, they seem to smile and say, we don't care what your name is, boy, we'll never send you away.'

But although he was born there, Derek was raised 'over the water' in West Kirby, a 'small seaside town' on a shoreline of vast sandbanks on the north-west tip of the Wirral peninsula. In what poet Roger McGough calls 'the smugness of the Wirral'. In his autobiographical *Fifty Years Adrift* (1983), Derek describes a childhood spent growing up in 'nice little middle-class houses' in this 'exclusive dormitory town'. If you travel further down the A540 south from West Kirby, it takes you through Thurnaston, and Heswall where Paul McCartney was to buy father Jim a mock-Tudor house called 'Rembrandt' – where Paul wrote 'Golden Slumbers', drive further and you reach the seabird-stalked Parkgate reserve on the Dee Estuary where clouds of waders and wildfowl, shellduck, oystercatchers and kestrels can be observed.

Or instead, you could go back up to Birkenhead then over the ferry to Liverpool itself. For although West Kirby was a quiet resort, it's just a ten-mile Corporation bus-ride out to the city centre on one of Liverpool's double-decker 'big green jobs', where the conductor punches neat round holes in your orange return ticket. Or the Merseyrail Wirral line rail-link to Liverpool terminates in West Kirby. As Derek recalls, 'if you can live in West Kirby you can live anywhere.' Visionary Science Fiction pioneer Olaf Stapledon was a former resident of West Kirby. So was former Chancellor Selwyn Lloyd. Glenda Jackson attended West Kirby Girl's Grammar School, founded in 1636 by William Glegg, gentleman. It was a secure and solid place compared to the unknown, anxious uncertainties of his parent's world. Neatly bringing together Scouse wit and sentimentality, Derek saw himself 'sitting up in his pram before Hitler came to power, before Roosevelt's first term, and before the then Prince of Wales realised that Mrs Simpson was Mrs Right,' blissfully immune to those innumerable crises and summit conferences that seemed so important to his parents.

In the coincidental web of future relationships, less than a year after Derek's birth – 18 February 1933, Yoko Ono was born on the other side of the planet, in Tokyo, the eldest child of a union between two prominent Japanese families. Her mother Isoko, was a Yasuda, founder of a merchant bank, and father Yeisuke Ono, of the highly educated aristos who married into business, and eventually ran the Bank of Tokyo. Then, some twenty-eight months after Derek's birth – on the 19 September 1934, future 'nemporor' Brian Epstein was born on Yom Kippur into a prosperous Jewish family. The son of a department store manager, he grew up in 197 Queens Drive opposite open fields, in the Childwall Five-ways, one of the smarter Liverpool suburbs.

George Harrison claims 'Derek Taylor is slightly Welsh'. In fact, Derek's father, George Wyn Taylor, was the fifth child of professional-class Welsh parents, brought up in Wrexham. He was twenty years older than Vera Marjorie née Hartley, Derek's mother, who came from the rather more working-class Aigburth L17 area of south Liverpool. His parents, plus the aunts and uncles on both sides of the extended family, instilled in young Derek a 'sure sense of self that no amount of wartime deprivation and hardship was to eradicate.' They were 'clever' parents but in different ways. His father, although domestically impractical and proud of it, was literate and articulate, amusing and amused, with a bristling moustache that eventually expanded to fully cover his upper lip. A headmaster – of sorts – he taught unemployed youths in adult education classes, such skills as 'trying to make a dovetail joint' in woodwork. 'My father's trick lay in attracting people to him, adding younger and younger sets so that by the time he was old... he would still have friends young enough to keep him alive,' a talent at which Derek seemed equally adept. Whereas Mummy's 'genius was in organisation and in keeping things clean. They were good parents.'

They started married life in cheerful little Monument Cottage on the steep uphill climb of Village Road in the shadow of wild and gorse-tangled Caldy Hill crested by a nineteenth-century sandstone marine monument called The Beacon', and hard by 'The Ringers' – the *Ring O'Bells Hotel* which would become Derek's favourite pub, and a meandering stroll down to the sands. In 1935, with the addition of Derek's younger brother, Bryan, they moved to rock Mount, a bungalow in the downsloping Grammar School Lane, which was still a lane in the sense of it being unsurfaced. Derek's first reclaimable memories were of watching, and being befriended by the workmen who transformed it with pavements, gutters and sizzling tarmac 'as smooth as treacle'. A little while later, when Derek was seven, the family upgraded further to 27 Grafton Walk, a bigger semi-detached property set at the end of a quiet dogleg cul-de-sac off Black Horse Hill. All three addresses lie within mere minutes walking distance of each other.

Derek's mental map extended little beyond West Kirby, the first twenty-six years of his life were played out within its boundaries. It's a template he took with him. A town where milk-bottles were delivered every morning from a horse-drawn float. Where the grocery arrived on the Co-op truck drawn by a horse, which – he noted – occasionally sported an impressive erection. There was a thatched house opposite the mock-Tudor timbered exterior of the *Black Horse*, or the rival attractions of the since-demolished *West Kirby Hotel*. For those not old enough to enjoy their hospitality, there was the Marine Lake. From its bordering sea wall, you could 'stand on the edge of the sands… and look over the estuary' to glimpse the coast of north Wales. Or looking right, across the stretch of enclosed water to Red rocks, and then on to the Hoylake township where, as Derek joked, 'Selwyn Lloyd and I were brought up, separately'.

Derek was 'a scrap of humanity… adrift in an open-necked shirt', a 'tiny chap with legs like a sparrow' wearing 'a Christopher Robin sun-hat against the glare', looking down from Grange Hill where gulls ride the thermals, rising to kiss the sun, out beyond the sea wall and the promenade, where the little town slept through its golden summer days. Here and there, along the beach, people lay at rest, drowsy with heat and lulled by the murmur of the waves. During the long hot summer holidays, a boy in Clarks sandals could squelch out between trapped saltwater-pools and moist seaweed beds across the wet sand at low tide out towards the 'Little Eye' of Hilbre (pronounced 'Hillberry') Island, 'this precious stone set in the silver Dee,' one of the smallest inhabited islands in the UK, with traces of Neolithic occupation through to the more-recent telegraph station. Maybe Atlantic grey seal-spotting. 'Were those the days, my friend?' he asks rhetorically, 'I thought they'd never end.'

In his introduction to *Fifty Years Adrift*, George Harrison writes about how Derek 'had a good solid upbringing between the two wars in that relatively happy era when they invented toasters and other things those of us born in World War II were not to enjoy for many a long year.' Derek was observant. He learned the minute details of class differences in this 'lovely village where only man is vile.' Wondered why it was deemed notable that the butcher's boy said 'ta-ra' instead of the more correct 'goodbye'. Why the gardener ate 'dinner' instead of 'lunch'. Derek suspected such distinctions were absurd, a suspicion The Beatles would confirm. He was a child filled with morbid anxieties, scared of dogs, bats, dead birds, people wearing masks and people who talk to themselves. There were also 'so many strange people to stare at and assimilate and imitate,' something which continued to be his 'favourite recreation'. But first, he attended Miss Tod's private infant's school, on Mostyn Avenue adjoining the Promenade, which had two play-areas, one for boys where they kick a ball around, shoving and mock-fighting, and one for girls where they set up the long skipping rope clear across the asphalt so five or six girls at a time can jump in, in immaculate choreography, before jumping out again just as precisely. They wore neat fawn-and-scarlet uniforms.

Derek was dark-haired and small for his age, not a Mickey Rooney smallness he stresses, although maybe a Donald O'Connor smallness – referring to the singing-dancing 'Make 'Em Laugh' child star. At home, the serials he read in *Boys Own Paper* were all 'well-intentioned morality stories' of the 'play up and play the game' genre, with no place for a 'bony boy who smoked and stole and lied and cheated.' He could be quiet and unsure when the mood took him, but with an equally well-developed sense of humour. Derek's own memories in *Fifty Years Adrift* form a vividly tactile, strangely touching mix of anecdotes and wistful nostalgia. Of Everton, piano lessons, asthma attacks, and twice-weekly choir practice. He laughed along to *ITMA* – the radio sitcom starring Sam Costa, Jack Train and Tommy Handley, populated by absurd characters such as Colonel Humphrey Chinstrap, the Minister of Aggravation and the Office of Twerps. Further along the radio dial, there were cliff-hanger espionage thrills with *Dick Barton: Special Agent* – the Light Programme radio detective, first played by Noel Johnson. And when the radio was turned off, Derek enjoyed Dudley Watkin's 'Jimmy And His Magic Patch' in the *Beano* – a picture-strip in which a schoolboy time-travels to significant moments from history through the Tardis-device of a trouser-patch fashioned from a piece of a gipsy's magic carpet to comic effect. Through such fantasies, he learned how words have the potential to bend and imaginatively reshape time too.

But Liverpool – that 'lovely ageing and battered seaport' – was a 'magic city where all things were possible.' Liverpudlians have always been traders, not manufacturers. As traders, wealth came into the city, they extracted their share, and they passed it on. The Beatles 'Penny Lane' was significant, claims Liverpool poet Roger McGough, because it was the first time pop iconography exploited an English, rather than an American, landmark. But there's a darker side to Paul McCartney's cheerful paean to suburbia – oddly, it now seems the inspirational street has unfortunate connections with Liverpool's eighteenth-century slave trade, named after James Penny, a slave ship owner of those dark days…

London and Bristol also had lively slave trades, but Liverpool made the dreadful commerce in human cargoes its own. In October 1699, a ship called the 'Liverpool Merchant' sailed out of the Mersey bound for what a contemporary map calls 'Negroland', thus becoming the first identifiable slave ship – although the discreditable honour of being the very first slave trader may be attributed to Captain John Hawkins who 'stole' three-hundred West Africans as early as 1562. Nevertheless, Liverpool has always been a terminus. The railway and the roads stop here. Liverpool has no rush hour through-traffic. The port is a geographically isolated west-facing city-state. It looks west to Ireland and America, the sources of its social character and its musical style. The factors that at once made it a vital link in the slave trade, a major European port and the second city of the Empire, also facilitated its cosmopolitan mix of Irish, black and Chinese communities. The famous waterfront is like nowhere else in Britain, with an entirely transatlantic feel. Liverpudlians form their own racial minority even within their own county, looking out across the sea, rather than inland towards boring Lancashire. Liverpool is a Celtic city. Manchester is Anglo-Saxon.

During the years Derek was growing up, Liverpool's economic decline was accelerating, its docks losing out to Southampton or Manchester. Across the space of half a century, one of the country's richest cities became one of its most depressed. Yet the geographical advantage originally responsible for its rise still made it a strategic destination for Atlantic convoys. It was also a base for Naval operations during the Battle of the Atlantic, when 'Hitler, who had become rather a nuisance, launched a sustained attempt to destroy Liverpool.' The city received the full fury of the Luftwaffe blitzkrieg intent on firming the stranglehold blockade on besieged Britain. Derek had just turned seven when, issued with gas-masks and identity-labels, some 95,000 youngsters were pre-emptively evacuated from Merseyside at the outset of hostilities. The tougher kids regarded it as a great adventure; they felt themselves impervious to the hazards of falling bombs. Others were not so sure.

Some families closed up their homes in vulnerable target areas and moved away completely. The Epstein family moved to the sedate seaside resort of Southport at the outbreak of the war, where young Brian attended Southport College to become 'one of those out-of-sorts boys who never quite fit. Who are ragged, nagged and bullied and beloved of neither boys nor masters.' As he'd later confide to Derek, he was 'not the best of sons and I was certainly the worst of pupils.' Cynthia Powell's mother was evacuated to Blackpool in 1939, where

the future Mrs Lennon was born. Others moved across the Mersey
to the sanctuary of the Wirral peninsula. Meanwhile, the Ono family
moved between Japan and the USA, settling back in Tokyo in 1941.
Yoko's father was transferred to Hanoi where he was interned, while
the family stayed in Tokyo until the fire-bombing of 9 March 1945.

By the time Derek was nervously swotting for his entrance
examination, a certain Richard Starkey was being born on 7 July 1940,
and the city had become a nightly target for Luftwaffe blanket-bombing.
Early targets of heavy and sustained bombing included Walton Jail,
where twenty-two prisoners were killed, and the Anglican Cathedral
which was damaged when caught in fusillades of stray blasts. The
Bentinck Street railway arches collapsed onto the people who huddled
beneath, who were using it as a makeshift air-raid shelter. In the midst
of it all, Derek learned he'd passed the exam, which determined he
got to go up to Calday Grange Boy's Grammar, commencing with the
September 1940 term, the 'smallest of the eighteen newcomers.' It
was a traditional 'big school' with a dozen eccentric but well-qualified
masters who 'smelled of tobacco'. Daniel 'James Bond' Craig was
another alumni. 'There was a war on outside; there was also a long
battle for survival raging inside this traditional boys' school.'

During a lull in a particularly violent raid, 'when the nasties were still
booming us,' at 6:30 pm on 9 October 1940, Julia Lennon gave birth
to her first child in a second-floor ward of the Oxford Street Maternity
Home, while husband Freddie was away at sea. Patriotically she named
her son John Winston. Paul would not be born until 18 June 1942
– in Walton Hospital where his mother's position as Nursing Sister
meant she got a private room. His father, Jim McCartney was there as
a wartime firewatcher on the docks when 365 people died over three
nights in the 'Christmas Raids'. In a typical Derek Taylor interjection,
'what, you may ask, has this all to do with the price of fish?' to which I
reply, nothing, I just thought I'd mention it. Except that the following
year Derek spent his ninth birthday – 7 May 1941, during the 'May Blitz'
– sheltering with Mummy and brother Bryan beneath the stairs reading
his main birthday present, Daniel Defoe's *The Life of Robinson Crusoe*.
The raid formed the devastating peak of the campaign when 681
bombers dropped 2,315 high explosive bombs and 119 incendiaries
on the wounded city below, killing 741. No bombs fell on Hoylake, but
waking the following morning, they could see a blood-red sky hanging
over burning Liverpool.

The cargo-ship SS *Malakand*, loaded with over a thousand tons of
explosives, was hit as it rode its berth in the Huskisson Dock, and

detonated spectacularly across the night sky. Half of the docks were put out of action as Liverpool earned the dubious distinction of becoming the most heavily targeted area in the UK, outside of London. Until, by an odd twist of fate, one of the final air-raids took place on 10 January 1942, destroying 102 Upper Stanhope Street, the birthplace of Adolf Hitler's nephew, William Patrick Hitler. According to his Irish sister-in-law, Adolf himself was reputed to have stayed over there in 1912-13. The crater was allowed to remain a bomb-site, among many other areas of wasteland rubble, a legacy of the blitz, visible in many northern cities through the 1950s and well into the 1960s. There were other ways lives were disrupted. Although aged fifty, Derek's father felt moved to volunteer for the war effort, was recommissioned by his old World War I regiment, the Royal Welch Fusiliers, and was gone for three years. The family even travelled by train to see him off from Birmingham; then he was away guarding Italian pows in Kenya. There were other fathers who also went away for years on end, returning as strangers with dark secrets they were unable to speak of. No counselling. No compensation claims. They got their demob suit and were turned out onto a civvy street still in the grip of austerity and rationing. They'd done with great events and global convulsions.

George Harrison was born 25 February 1943 – 'deep in Liverpool and deep in winter.' Around the time Derek was graduating from short trousers, into long trousers. School uniform too. A school where 'I was bullied a lot, but I was quick and unpredictable and I got by.' Mornings began with assembly, a hymn and a pious message. Derek was 'very good at English', learning spelling by rote and repetition the rules of punctuation, nouns and adjectives. He was taught not to start a sentence with an adjunct, or end one with a preposition. But he was not taught the keyboard skills that might have benefited his writing; they were taught – if at all – to girls destined for the office typing pool. Nevertheless, in an early adventure into print, he had a poem accepted for the *Mickey Mouse Weekly*. The war ended the month Derek entered his teens, the uneasy transition from twelve to thirteen. To his disgust, although Germany surrendered on his birthday, 7 May 1945, VE Day was declared the day after. His father, who returned in August, was a member of the West Kirby Sailing Club and played billiards in the clubhouse. Derek met champion golfer Dai Rees there and came away with his autograph. It was his first encounter with celebrity.

He was aged fourteen-and-half in January 1947, the coldest winter in half-a-century. The blizzards began to fall on West Kirby on 20 January, and snow stayed on the ground for fifty-three days, until 14 March.

It was a world of epic melancholy, bleached of colour, as drained
of extremes as the frosty wastes of Narnia, and as frozen in time. A
monochrome movie the shades of nicotine and dirty snow. The black
& white television images that survive seem appropriate. Life was grey,
as Minister 'Manny' Shinwell presided over a season of fuel starvation,
electricity power-cuts, falling gas pressure and no petrol on the garage
forecourts. And post-war rationing continued. Derek had his flimsy
green cardboard ration book. A passport to another age.

As George Martin recalls, it was a country 'still marred by the war,
and still paying for it.' When the thaw set in, with temperatures soaring
to 65F by the end of March, there was flooding. And the summer that
followed peaked into the 80F's and 90F's helping people to forget
the shortages, even as post-war reconstruction continued. Derek
daydreamed through adolescence, falling short of his earlier academic
promise by failing the School Certificate exam in 1947, despite passes
in English Language and Literature – and Scripture. He re-sat the exam
a year later as a sixth-former and passed. In January 1948 Brian Epstein
attended Wrekin College. Cynthia Powell was growing up in a two-
bedroom semi-detached in the middle-class suburb of Hoylake. She
would return there, with Julian, following her divorce from John in 1968.

In the oddly deflated mindset of the war-victorious England, where
Britain had resisted subjugation by fascist dictatorship, it fell to
bureaucracy. Its people were bored, not bombed into submission. To
Derek, it was just adult stuff. The world doing what the world does.
To his parents' generation, especially those of a timidly traditional bias
who watched it happen, it must have seemed like the long-threatened
Socialist Revolution, with the nationalisation of railways, coal and
steel production, the NHS – State Central Planning, taking place here,
transfiguring England's green and pleasant land with bold new plans
for social reconstruction.

Yet, as Clement Atlee's revolutionary socialist reforms fell apart
over the divisive issues of re-armament and NHS charges, even the
Conservative right-wing – sensing that such drastic measures were
essential to rebuild the bankrupt war-levelled nation – were reconciled
to preside over the new settlement. Once returned to power, with
ageing relic Winston Churchill eased back into government in the 1956
election, it feared to reverse Atlee's changes, and instead entered the
long period of 'consensus politics', successive governments accepting
the mixed-economy welfare state that would continue, until Thatcherist
'Punk' Monetarism ripped it all to pieces. But first, the Suez shambles
cruelly exposed the decline that the victory of 1945 had masked.

While an establishment of upper-class prigs and hurrumphing old fools established the decades of relative social stability that would define the arc of Derek's life. And for a long repetitive process of nothing, in particular, Britain slept drearily through the decade... even though, as Derek recalls, 'the story of the four most famous and musical young men on earth began in Harold Macmillan's "never had it so good" fifties Britain'.

In the midst of it all, Derek was spewed out of the education system, 'slightly shy and slightly ambitious'. But despite his English Lit and Language leanings, journalism was not the first career choice imposed upon him. His father encouraged an interview with the Midland Bank, and applications for positions as a Shipping Clerk (at Cayzer Irvine) or a Bookseller (at Charles Wilson). Fortunately, it was his mother who pushed for journalism. The editorial office of the small local weekly *Hoylake and West Kirby Advertiser* was at no.28 Grange Road, one floor above Lloyds Bank, overlooking the central Hoylake roundabout – 'the Piccadilly Circus of West Kirby' – and close on the Railway Station for Liverpool. Derek climbed the stairs, was checked out by editor Harold Higginbottom, and was offered a trial, stepping in for another staffer who was being called up for National Service. So Derek put his talents to practical use by becoming an indentured apprentice reporter, starting there on Monday, 31 January 1949, taking home a princely wage of 30s (£1.50). The newspaper appeared every Friday. He would stay there until September 1952.

He learned shorthand, given private lessons by a Miss FM Arthur of Brookfield Gardens, but never quite mastered touch-typing. Cautioned 'never write anything unless you have first established the answers to the questions: is it true? Is it necessary and is it too kind to do so?', three rules he would carry with him, recalling 'Apple, for me, began in West Kirby in 1949.' Early in his journalistic career, Len Hutton – 'the cricketing hero of my boyhood and beyond' – visited Calday to talk to masters and address the boys. In 'a surreal experience', Derek was assigned to cover the event, returning to his old school just eight months after leaving it. Then there was a local buzz that young actor Richard Attenborough had called off in the village to spend time with his aunt. On his own initiative, Derek plucked up courage, tracked him down, spoke to the aunt, and earned his first fumbling interview with a star name.

Later, Danny Kaye danced into Hoylake to play a round at the Royal Liverpool Golf Course. Danny had memorably portrayed Walter Mitty in the 1947 film version of James Thurber's story. And as Keith

Waterhouse wrote in *Billy Liar* – the more north-of-England variant
to which *Walter Mitty* was a precursor – 'he scribbled a few notes on
the back of a used envelope,' and Derek and a girl reporter named
Dorothy promptly star-chased Kaye, pausing only to loan box-cameras
from Wilson's the Chemist. Arriving out of breath at the golf course,
they agreed to split, taking half the course each. She managed to get
snatched photos; he got none – although twenty years later he got to
meet the star in Hollywood, and was able to tell him how he'd queued
for *Danny Kaye Show* tickets outside the Liverpool Empire in 1949.
Among the first records Derek ever bought, at Harold Ormrod's electric
shop, was Danny Kaye's *Ballin' the Jack*.

There were other compensations. He got to meet a young Sheila
Hancock when she appeared as part of 'The Spring Players' at the local
Tudor Theatre. He promptly fell under her spell; she was 'tall, fair,
brilliant, unpretentious and funny.' They became, and remained friends.
She visited the Taylor family on the 1952 Christmas Day, shocking
aunts with her bohemian shoelessness. And later he would write her
letters from his army bunk. Meanwhile, apprentice reporters might
occasionally be rewarded with the opportunity to 'travel to the big city'
for press receptions. On such an assignment, Derek got to meet singer
Elton Hayes, a regular on radio's *In Town Tonight* who 'sang to a Small
Guitar', doing his version of Edward Lear's 'The Owl and the Pussycat',
or his 'The Whistling Gypsy'. Elton also played Alan-a-Dale in the 1952
Disney version of *Robin Hood*, starring Richard Todd – not Richard
Greene, as Derek misremembers it. As Todd himself had more important
commitments, it fell to Hayes to make the long journey north to
Liverpool for the provincial film launch. For Derek, it constituted a small
step in showbusiness connections, but much more was to come.

From early 1949 he'd begun 'stringing' for the sports editions of
the *Liverpool Echo* and *Express* in Liverpool, a position farmed out to
him by the local postman, Albert E Booth. Phoned in from the local
butcher's shop – 'the only owner of a phone in that part of the village'
– it was paid on linage according to number of lines printed. After all,
writing for the print-and-publishing industry is a noble profession,
is it not? Wasn't print the first craft in the world to be mechanised
into achieving mass-production? Sure it was. A subversive liberating
medium, pouring out incendiary leaflets, booklets and hardback tomes
that first broke the tyrannical power of the medieval church by making
its mystical texts universally available, but also one that empowered the
spread of literacy, and with it, ideas that challenged the absolute power
of monarchy, the tyranny of the state, the social status quo between rich

and poor, men and women, citizens and slaves. A medium that enabled great poetry, literature, and ideas to find expression, to reach out and touch the masses. What new frontiers were there yet to be crossed by its experts-textperts, what new causes to be championed?

To Derek, 'when it was easy, I enjoyed doing it. When it was difficult, I didn't enjoy doing it'. Yet the daily grind of hackwork proved to be nothing like such inspirational ideas had led him to believe. As part of the press-gang, Derek found himself delegated such notable early chores as covering tedious council meetings. Phoning undertakers on Monday morning to enquire if any reportable local notables had died over the weekend. There was also 'Guessing the Weight of the Cake… Cake kindly donated by Mrs F.S.E Bardsley-Powell, won by Miss Alison Christian-Jones, runner-up Lady Cosmo Smallpiece-Hallmark.' He answered the 'ping' of the handbell on the counter and took notices for the sale or bereaved small-ads. 'It was crucial that I mix freely with the locals, but I was sometimes insecure and nervous of the self-assurance of the Rotarians, Freemasons, sporting hearties, and apparently powerful worthies who ran the town. It was a great relief to find that, the very first time I drank it, alcohol made me feel more confident. Nothing had ever worked like that before.' And the *Royal Hotel* was a 'beautifully shabby stylish hangout for blazered rugger types, leavened by an eccentric or two or three' in the former port of Hoylake on the edge of the Dee.

Some elements of the 1940s seemed to drag on through the fifties and endure into the sixties. Women in headscarves and curlers still trundling babies in battleship prams. Floods of identical men in long macs and flat-caps flowing through football turnstiles. Kids in short-trousers playing hopscotch on grubby pavements. Making do and keeping going, despite it all. Little had changed. Sometimes nothing. At home, the sugar and tea were stored in cream-coloured 'Royal Wedding' tins embellished with a royal crown and the initials of the new Queen, Elizabeth II. Despite his avowed socialism, Derek harboured an affection for 'the anachronistic and colourful theatre of the absolutely absurd' monarchy. At the local flicks, he watched Jane Russell, Abbott & Costello, Errol Flynn, and a merchant-marine wartime propaganda potboiler *Action in the North Atlantic* (1943) with Humphrey Bogart and Raymond Massey. At the end of each cinema programme, the audience stood to attention for the national anthem.

In the Saturday-night dancehalls, they were 'dancing to the hokey-cokey and the Gay Gordons. Ah, they could write music in those days.' On the radio, Derek listened to the pop-songs of the day. Glenn Miller, who's 'American Patrol' would be one of the featured 'samples' fed into the extended fade of 'All You Need Is Love'. And Vera Lynn, Derek little realising that at some unimaginable point in the distant future, he would be sitting in the Los Angels sunshine typing out the sleeve-notes for a Byrds album which included her song, writing about how 'they took a sentimental British keep-your-chin-up-and-your-upper-lip-stiff war song ('We'll Meet Again') and by investing it with a beautiful blend of barely discernible humour and Byrds harmony, produced a wonderfully fresh interpretation.'

And there were hesitant encounters with girls; Shelagh whose father drove a taxi, Pat who had 'enormous breasts', Pam Goldsmith who he met while cycling to the affluent Upton suburb of Birkenhead, and Joy Restall with whom he enjoyed a sunny Hilbre Island picnic. 'What larks!' He went out with Maureen Corlett for 'three or more years'. They even visit the 'Festival of Britain' together in the 'wet and windy summer of 1951.' There was an understanding that they would marry. But they didn't.

More immediately – September 1952, National Service was a two-year rite of passage. Derek's position on the paper had only been made possible because Walter Richardson, another former 'Old Calday' pupil, eighteen months ahead of him, had been called up. Conscripts went in at seventeen, maybe eighteen. They enter as a boy, to come back at twenty, a man. Supposedly. It's a shared bonding experience that unites us. Supposedly. We laugh along with the hapless squaddies in ITV's weekly sitcom *The Army Game*, or visit the local fleapit to enjoy the comic escapades of Bob Monkhouse and William Hartnell in *Carry On Sergeant* (1958) because we've also been there. For the generation that came before package holidays to the Costa's, never mind gap-year backpacking to Goa, when a works outing to Blackpool or a week at Butlins' was the high-point of the summer, the compulsory conscription years were your first time away from home, your first extended period away from your home town, perhaps your first glimpse of abroad too, if you happened to be stationed at a 'trouble-spot'.

Derek avoided such adventures. Declining deferment, he arrived at Gough Barracks in Armagh, Northern Ireland, to be given a document in a brown waterproof slip-jacket – his pay book. Beginning with name and number, it formed part identity card, part pay documentation, part record of shooting skills. This latter section was preceded by the statement 'Your Weapons Are Given To You To Kill The Enemy'. Fortunately, he was never called upon to perform the patriotic duty of 'meeting interesting strangers and killing them.' Instead, following

Boot Camp induction, the unlikely Royal Irish Regiment fusilier was transferred to a Nissen hut in Beaconsfield, Buckinghamshire. Within its 'pleasant shambles' he first suffered the 'terrible deprivation' of being confined to barracks for several days under a Section 40 misdemeanour, following the mess that resulted from an unfortunate assignment to assist 'a middle-aged cove with a club foot' and his daughter, distributing 'wheelbarrows full of heavy khaki greatcoats' through the snow. The recipients took advantage of Derek's easygoing gullibility to demand 'a plethora of alternations' that were impossible to deliver in time for the inspection parade. Yet, despite such mishaps, he worked his way up to become a Sergeant Instructor in the Royal Army Educational Corps – teaching Current Affairs, Business Letters and Job Applications, 'during, but not in, the Korean War'.

He assisted during storm damage, digging and filling sandbags to defend 'Blighty's coast against the brutal forces of Nature.' Yet the army was 'drudgery, drinking, raucous laughter and broken dreams' where, as he recalled later, 'I established a much-admired reputation as a heavy drinker.' For his next posting, with the Fifty-Ninth Regiment at Carlisle's Durranhill Heavy Ack-Ack (Anti-Aircraft Artillery), the mess where he also served as bartender was nicknamed *The Golden Slipper Club*. Once there, 'if alcohol be the food of friendship… the first two drinks demanded company, and they were rarely denied a party. A couple of anything were no use to me, not from 1950 onwards.' It went 'first to beer every day, then to spirits at weekends, and – in the army – to spirits every day. These were unenlightened times. It suited me very well to become "one of the lads" by drinking. It was so much easier and quicker than becoming good at any other recreation.' And Taylor D.W. 22728976 valued his reputation 'greatly, treasuring it above all other "values"'. It was a rite of passage, you come back a man, after all. For young men of Derek's generation, your army-number is something you never, ever forget.

He left the army in October 1954 with a 'huge drunken going-away bash' and – much to his own surprise – a glowing testimonial; 'he is keen, intelligent, has varied interests, and always aims at high standards.' While brother Bryan took it a step further by becoming a regular soldier, graduating as an officer in the King's Own Royal Regiment. Nevertheless, return to the stiflingly dull routine of West Kirby was not an exciting prospect, although he had met, and become engaged to social worker Shiela MacLellan. The engagement did not survive. After all, he was 'too young, too busy, too broke and too drunk' to marry.

Brian Epstein, an introverted, intelligent but distant young man, was 'called-up' for basic training at the Royal Army Service Corps in Aldershot on 9 December 1952, before being stationed as a documentation clerk at Regent's Park Barracks, until his military career came to a premature end after just ten months. The self-proclaimed 'lousiest soldier in the world', he was discharged on 'medical grounds', specified as emotionally and mentally unfit – a euphemism for 'gay'. He left the army on 27 January 1954. He was not the only one; others failed to make it through. It broke proto-rock Star Terry Dene and set his fledgeling career into a tailspin from which it never recovered. While, coming some few years later, the various members of The Beatles narrowly missed out on 'doing their bit'. George's elder brother Harry did National Service, and drummer Norman Chapman – who filled The Beatles drum-chair for three dates during July 1960, was unable to perform that function further when he was 'called up' barely months before the last national serviceman was conscripted that same December (although for some, deferred conscription dragged on until May 1963).

The end of National Service coincided with the rise of pop Culture, which precipitated much reactionary debate about 'falling standards' and 'long-haired louts'. The Barron Knights 1964 comedy hit 'Call Up the Groups' conjectured what might have happened if the Merseybeat stars had been called up. The Searchers stationed in Algiers, Freddie & the Dreamers in Cyprus, the rolling Stones in the navy, The Beatles having problems with their weapons-training to a parody of 'Twist and Shout'. 'Anybody older than us had been in the army', explains Pete Townshend. After his truncated army stint, Brian Epstein took charge of the Wirral furniture-retailing branch of his father's store in comparatively affluent Hoylake, adjoining West Kirby. History doesn't tell us whether the Taylor family visited the store. But Brian visited the Hoylake swimming pool and walked along the sandy beach.

All the while, during those years that pop singles were shrinking from ten to seven inches, the soporifically conformist 1950s were enlivened by the BBC Light Programme, although radio in the fifties had little patience for innovation. It was conservative in an almost tragic sense. 'One man, one wife, one love through life', hymned Dean Martin on 'Memories Are Made of This'. 'I've got to take you for my wife, so the story of my life, will start and end with you', confirmed Michael Holiday ('The Story of My Life'), promoting a monogamous domesticity that goes on forever. Radio carried no hope of change, only momentary respite. As American writer Greil Marcus wrote about its American country equivalent, the 'music was all limits'. Daphne Oxenford's authentic received pronunciation came from the beige plastic wireless set inviting children to *Listen With Mother* every afternoon. 'Are you sitting comfortably?', she would enquire, 'then I'll begin...' If you were older, there was the indecipherable – at least to adults – surreal humour of the Goons. Derek heard their 78rpm single 'The Ying-Tong Song' on the wireless, a record that actually made an unlikely entry into the Top Ten, with Spike Milligan, Peter Sellers and Harry Secombe at their most playfully absurdist, utilising bizarre sound effects, explosions, and eccentric recording techniques. It's a record that still sounds crazy across the decades, and for those who care to look, there are producer links to a young George Martin, who would play a not-entirely peripheral part in Derek's later life. In another future-connection, Richard Lester – who would enter The Beatles story with *A Hard Day's Night* – tried-out by directing the Goons eleven-minute *The Running Jumping Standing-Still Film* (1959).

Adult audiences tuned into *Life With the Lyons*, a cosy domestic sitcom portraying the warm, mildly amusing antics of 'Hollywood's Happiest Married Couple'. John Lennon would much later appropriate and parody its title for an experimental album with Yoko. Featuring Ben Lyon and his real-life scripter-wife Bebe Daniels, as well as their children, plus comic-character interruptions from Molly 'Aggie' Weir as their Scottish housekeeper and nosy neighbour Doris 'Florrie' Rogers, the radio series debuted 11 February 1955 (until 1 May 1966). It translated to movies via the Hammer studio, and television (5 November 1950-1962), in the days when TV was still a single-channel rarity. On its monochrome screen, you might also glimpse somnambulistic radio crooners Ronnie Hilton, Dickie Valentine or Liverpool's Frankie Vaughan, with their hummable whistleable tunefulness, undistracted by any disturbing element of threat.

Poet Adrian Henri took a series of black-and-white photographs from the Liverpool of this period which record scruffy street urchins playing around abandoned tyres on bombsites between rows of terraces, cheeky waifs who could have been snatched from some kind of Dickensian Victorian deprivation. It's possible to sit in as Adrian conjectures a trip into that Liverpool, like 'Marcel Proust in the Kardomah eating Madeleine butties dipped in tea.' Translated into 'eating hot Eccles-cakes at the Pierhead.'

Derek took weekend trips across the slate-grey 'River Arse' where the chill breeze comes in off the water, into the 'pool. Liverpool is beautiful and ugly, proud and wanton, impressive and dismaying, romantic and crass. It is not a city to feel neutral about. To Derek, 'in Liverpool, all department stores are landmarks and have a personality, character, ranking and joke-quotient of their own.' A place somewhere between heaven and Woolworths. The stores are all long aisles of glass-fronted counters. No self-service. You identify the item you want by pointing through the glass, and the assistant gets it for you. A store 'where you can get low-priced copies of the pops on the counter next to the cold-creams and curling pins and the ice-cream.' He's talking here about the racks of 'Embassy' records. Cheap facsimile sound-alike covers of current hits that no self-respecting music fan would ever even consider buying, with unknown singers, exclusive to Woolworths – although one of the vocalists proved to be Elvis Costello's father!

As the pop lyricists and Mersey poets discovered, the Scoucers of Liverpool are attuned to imagist language. 'Getting off at Edge Hill' is Liverpudlian for coitus interruptus, Edge Hill being the penultimate stop before the train reaches its destination at Lime Street. A characteristically Liverpudlian expression since it combines a coarse practicality with a touching sensitivity about place. As Paul du Noyer explains in his book about its music, *Liverpool: Wondrous Place* (2002, Virgin Books), a sort of pop surrealism was in the air. 'A hard day's night' was not brilliant poetic invention. Just the way they talk. While all around him, although he didn't know it, other disconnected fragments of Derek's collective story were coming together in random configurations, like a rear-projected movie background.

Brian Epstein was not seduced by the pop music of the day. He preferred Sibelius. Derek also developed a taste for Opera. In the late-fifties and early-sixties there wasn't much pop he could relate to. While in the Armagh barrack-room he'd listened to the 'one absolutely reliable treat' that was the Radio Luxembourg Top Twenty show. But perhaps he was also already too old to fall for the relentlessly teen-angled juvenile fumblings of 'American pop singers called either Johnny or Bobby,' as Harry Nilsson observed. Through Epstein, he writes 'they were no part of my life, because I was out of the age-group, also because I had been too busy.' The word 'adolescence' – although devised by American psychologist G Stanley Hall – evokes a kind of European functionalism. They were the product of social dislocation, whereas 'teenagers' were the vanguard consumers of the bright new material world still under urgent construction. The word 'teenager' – which only entered mass currency as recently as 1944 – presented a more positive face of all-American optimism. Of course, it was also a marketing invention to define a new demographic with its own accelerating spending power. A new definition of 'cool' through which to celebrate young freedom from the restraints of the stoic adult world. Music was the marker to define the chasm between generations.

Although Derek – and Brian Epstein – had fallen into the chasm between definitions, no longer either adolescents or teenagers, for Brian it was necessary to take an interest in what pop records were selling, to enable him to efficiently stock the demands of his customers at NEMS in Whitechapel. So, with more professionalism than enthusiasm, he monitored the home-grown variant of rock 'n' roll as it evolved through a slow and flawed process. As entrepreneur Larry Parnes learned from the overnight success of Lonnie Donegan, Terry Dene and especially Tommy Steele – the first British recognisably 'rock' performers. Parnes exploited the resource of the famous Soho *Two I's* coffee bar on O'Connell Street, to recruit his biddable stable of prettily photogenic teen pin-up boys with their atmospherically outrageous aliases – Marty Wilde, Vince Eager, Billy Fury, Duffy Power, Johnny Gentle.

'Mr Parnes Shillings & Pence' then opportunistically linked up with Jack Good's TV-exposure through newly-launched independent television's Saturday evening *Oh Boy* show – directly scheduled to follow the *Flash Gordon* serial, to reach susceptible teenage record-buyers with meagre but up-for-grabs disposable incomes. Outside the Parnes stable, Joe Meek created his own parallel independent brand, while Johnny Kidd and the Pirates, and Emile Ford and the Checkmates also broke through against the odds to top the charts. But in a complacent pop environment equally prone to Trad Jazz and novelty records, most tentative limited-ambition low-achievement forays into 'rock' leaned exclusively on imperfectly-apeing trans-Atlantic originals, taking and note-for-note replicating every detail of American hits, then playing to the slight margin of release time-lag, and staying safely within whatever radio or TV exposure they could garner to gain a toe-hold of advantage over the original. An approach entirely content to stay within the small enclosed world of the domestic market. With little scope to excite Brian's interest.

1956 was the wettest year on record. Derek turned twenty-four. And it was the year of Skiffle. The Quarrymen were John Lennon's teenage skiffle group, named for the school they attended. Like Derek before him, he'd passed his eleven-plus, which enabled his Aunt Mimi to get him from Dovedale Primary School into the solid grammar Quarry Bank High in September 1952, cycling the mile from Menlove Avenue in his black uniform blazer with its shiny buttons and red-and-gold stag's head motif emblazoned on the breast pocket. The result of an odd educational experiment that began when an errant Eton master persuaded Liverpool Education Authority to try to see it his way, the masters wore mortar-boards and handed out reprimands in Latin. Pupils had a tuck shop, did 'prep' and some learned Greek. Alumni included architect James Stirling, Labour Cabinet Minister Peter Shore, and Liberal Democrat politician Bill Rodgers.

John was easily distracted from his academic tasks, his 1955 school report, reproduced in *Lennon Legend: An Illustrated Life of John Lennon* (2003, Weidenfeld & Nicolson), comments on an 'attitude most unsatisfactory' as regards religious instruction. Instead, he'd discovered guitar and rock 'n' roll around the time he was discovering masturbation, as he grew out of Richmal (*'Just William'*) Crompton into Lewis Carroll, and preferred to channel his energies into those activities. The Quarrymen were little better but no worse than a hundred other groups that sprang up overnight in the do-it-yourself wake of Lonnie Donegan's success, playing with more energy than skill, and unburdened by expertise. In the fade of John's *Double Fantasy* (1980) track 'I'm Losing You' he inserts a quote from 'Long Long Lost John' – a Lonnie Donegan song borrowed from Woody Guthrie.

The original four were members of the same school 'house'. John Lennon and Eric Ronald Griffiths, who had learned guitar together. Banjoist Rod Davis – the school's milk monitor who quit the group in January 1959 when he opted to stay on into the sixth form, and John's long-time friend Pete Shotton who couldn't play an instrument but helped out on washboard. Pete claims to have contrived the group name, spelt variously the 'Quarry Men', or the 'Quarrymen'. Others dispute that claim. And friends come and go, Bill Smith – then Len Garry who replaced him. Nigel Whalley who played tea-chest bass in the first Summer 1956 line-up, but later acted as the group's 'manager'. Griffiths brought in Colin Hanton, whose main qualification for joining was that he owned a proper drumkit. The Quarrymen entered, but lost out in the finals of a 'Carroll Levis Discoveries' Skiffle Contest, for which they played the Vipers hit 'Worried Man Blues'. In a web of coincidence, it was George Martin who signed the Vipers Skiffle Group to Parlophone in 1956, with Wally Whyton as one of their three strong vocalists. They rewarded George's faith with the 78rpm hit record 'Don't You rock Me Daddy-O'. The Quarrymen were allowed to play at the school's sixth form dance in July 1957. They also played at the Cavern Jazz Club (7 August 1957), a set that included Elvis Presley's 'Don't Be Cruel', much to the displeasure of Trad purists.

This is the history Derek would help write. The familiar legend his PR skills would help build and embellish. To Derek, writing the CD liner note inserts for the first of *The Beatles Anthology* series (in 1995), the start of the narrative really begins here, that same month, when the sixteen-year-old John Lennon meets Paul McCartney in the leafy grounds of St. Peter's Parish Church where The Quarrymen were playing the annual Woolton Village Fete. For Derek, 'the Twentieth Century's greatest romance' began when they met and 'clicked'. That Sunday – 7 July 1957 – is one of those fateful dates that has since assumed epic world-shaping significance, but at the time meant precisely nothing to anyone. Not even to the participants. Yet unlike other early incidents in the story, each detail of it is sharp and largely uncontested. The Quarrymen had already gone through a shifting line-up. Now, apart from John, there was Eric Griffiths, Colin Hanton and Rod Davis. Len Garry was on tea-chest bass, and Pete Shotton was in the process of quitting, but remained John's friend, and would re-enter the story later. To Derek – 'rose-coloured, with long and loving hindsight' – the powerful narrative that grows out of the events of this singular day, events that would envelop and change the world, 'is so far-fetched that it needs the power of a song punctuating every page to remind you with a joyous jolt that it was all true.' At the time, of course, it was nothing of the sort. Admission was six predecimal pence, three for kids. Events include a Police Dog Display, the Crowning of the Rose Queen, and the George Edwards Band, as well as 'The Quarry Men Skiffle Group'. And 'Love Me Do' was still five long years ahead.

There's a hissy barely-audible Grundig TK8 reel-to-reel tape, recorded at a follow-up dance the same day in the Church Hall. Admission was two shiny shillings. The group can be heard playing Lonnie's 'Putting on the Style', a version of 'Maggie May' – a memory they'd briefly reprise on 'Let It Be' – and Elvis Presley's 'Baby Let's Play House' – which includes the lyrics 'I'd rather see you dead, little girl, than to be with another man', which John would lift intact to open his 'Run For Your Life' on *Rubber Soul*. A 'chubby-faced' fifteen-year-old Paul arrived at the fete on his bicycle. Lennon was a year older, sporting the best sideburns for miles around. Paul recalls they were doing a version of the Del-Viking's 'Come Go With Me' on stage, with John adapting, or making up the lyrics as they go along. Paul hung around afterwards. Former Quarryman bassist Ivan Vaughan introduced the two. It was a shy and awkward meeting. John noted that he could play guitar, upside-down, pretty good for a left-hander. Paul knew his way around the chords of some American rock 'n' roll, he sang Eddie Cochran's

'Twenty Flight rock'. That was worth knowing. 'John looking at me, like wow!' as Paul remembered it. They'd forged a useful connection. Little more. A fortnight later Shotton acted as intermediary, inviting Paul to join, although he didn't appear on-stage as a Quarryman until 18 October (1957). It's only hindsight that fixes that as the day everything began to germinate.

Of more immediate significance was the road accident that killed Julia, John Lennon's mother, on the 15 July 1958. A psychic landmark that left a profound and lasting scar. In the town where he was born, lived a man who sailed the sea. Waywardly rebellious, high-spirited, with a bohemian streak, auburn-haired Julia 'Judy' Stanley had married Alf 'Freddie' Lennon on 3 December 1938. In defiance of convention, and in spite of family opposition, she had actually proposed to the charming, feckless rogue. Incurably unreliable, he worked the passenger liners as steward, from Liverpool as far as the West Indies. Both were impulsive, they share a ready wit, and both harbour unrealised musical and showbusiness aspirations. With the outbreak of hostilities there are stories Freddie was working as a merchant seaman on troop-transports, others that he jumped ship in New York, and later served time in a North African British Military Prison for desertion. His visits home were rare, increasingly infrequent, then ceased altogether.

Although still technically married to the absent Freddie, they never actually divorced, she bore a daughter, Victoria, who was adopted. Then, while working as a waitress in a café, Julia met John Dykins. They set up home together – and she had two further daughters with him. John proved inconvenient. So, at the age of five, he was farmed-out and subsequently reared by Julia's childless elder sister, Aunt Mimi. He moved into 251 Menlove Avenue – 'Mendips' – in 1945, in the pleasant middle-class Woolton suburb three miles from the city centre, 'a nice semi-detached place with a small garden, and doctors and lawyers and their ilk living around – not the poor, slummy kind of image that was projected in all The Beatles stories' as John himself admits. He would stay there until 1963.

Contemporaries continue to refer to the young Lennon as a 'rebel'. Talking about Sam Taylor-Wood's film *Nowhere Boy* (2009) which documents those years, he is routinely described in that way, which is deceiving. Rebel is now the default setting. For an adolescent not to rebel is now in some way, unnatural. It was not so in that conformist time. Elvis might have been perceived as a rebellious force, but at heart, he was a patriotic God-fearing American good ole country boy. Lennon saw him at his most surly in *Jailhouse rock* (1957) at the Palais de Luxe with early girlfriend, Thelma Pickles. Cliff Richard might have been briefly a disruptive rocker, but he was into showbiz, not rebellion.

Derek Taylor was no rebel either. To be the rebel then was not a marketable pose, it was to be the marginalised outsider — a trouble-maker, out of step with society. For Lennon to be a rebel was to mark him out as different. Eventually, Julia began to visit him at Mendips, acting more as an older sister than a mother. Although buttoned-up prim-and-proper Mimi was less indulgent, it was Julia, the mother he'd only recently rediscovered, who not only bought him his first guitar – at £10/9s/6d – but taught him the basic banjo-chords that enabled him to start practising. 'In Freudian terms', explains Philip French, 'the stern Mimi, a practitioner of what we now call "tough love", is at work on John's super-ego, while the rebellious Julia, offering unconditional love, is exciting his id. In religious terms, they're his good and bad angels.' The *Observer* film critic goes on to misquote Philip Larkin to the effect that 'they fuck you up, your Mum and Aunt, they do not mean to, but they do.' Until the road accident that ends Julia's life. Leaving 'Mendips' after an evening visit, around 9:30 pm, she was crossing the road towards her bus-stop, stepping out from the central reservation, when she was hit by a car driven by an off-duty policeman. For John, her death constituted a second abandonment at an impressionable age, as if there's an age that is not impressionable for maternal abandonment.

If, as he would later claim, genius is pain, this where the pain begins. John Lennon had 'a chip on his shoulder that was bigger than his feet.' Years into the future – in January 1971, after the Passing Show that was the entire Beatles story had ultimately unravelled to its end 'in high dudgeon in high-end London' – the extreme pain of that bereavement would still be there as John recorded 'Mother', opening the track with the mournful sound of a tolling bell. By turn, wilful and truculent, complicated, flawed and clever, possessed of a savage wit that could reduce those closest to him to tears, this was the well-spring anger he never really processed. Through Doctor Arthur Janov's Primal Scream Therapy programme – based around the concept that adult behavioural problems are rooted in childhood trauma, and that the trauma must be re-enacted, 'screamed out' to exorcise its malign influence – he recorded the *Plastic Ono Band* (December 1970) album as therapy to free himself from the anguished legacy of that July 1958 day. To listen to 'Mother' is to hear the adolescent John Lennon screaming out the pain and confusion of separation, isolation and loss, crying out for his dead mother. And it's possibly his finest ever artistic achievement, for this is an album that retains its ability to provoke highly unsettling reactions in its audience.

Although in many ways a contrasting personality, the fact that Paul had also recently lost his mother, she died of breast cancer in 1956, formed a bond. As John would write 'Julia' for *The White Album* (and call his first son Julia-n), so Paul would reference his loss, and admit 'when I find myself in times of trouble, mother Mary comes to me' in 'Let It Be'. Through the shared experience as motherless children, their differing temperaments complemented each other, as fully interlocking as Lego bricks.

Chapter Three: 1961: Those Savage Young Beatles

It did happen. The whole wonderful thing did happen,
A long time ago, on the Mersey…
Derek Taylor notes to *The Beatles Anthology: 1*

It was the best of times, it was the worst of times… in 1959
(Patti Smith)

Within months of joining the group, Paul was linking his friend George
Harrison into The Quarrymen. George had also attended Dovedale
Road Infants and Junior School, a place so Dickensian that Dickens
himself had once taught there, before going up to Liverpool Institute
For Boys from 1954-1959. His bus from Speke estate to the 'Big School'
took an hour – an hour there, and an hour back. And it was on the
bus along Dovedale Road, near Penny Lane that he met Paul. Although
he was a year older, Paul had stayed at school longer to get better
qualified. They wore the same uniform and were travelling the same
route. So they started hanging out together.

Around the same time, Derek was going through that different set
of complicated social rituals known as 'courting'. According to poet
Philip Larkin, 'sexual intercourse' began in 1963, between the end of
the *Lady Chatterley* ban, and The Beatles' first LP. He was wrong, of
course. It happens in every life around the time raging hormones go
into meltdown. And for Derek, it arrived a little earlier than Larkin's
estimation. Although 'rationed by the purse', Derek 'drank only at
weekends, strictly beer, and I made a lot of friends of all ages, felt more
at home with girls, discovered the joys of pubs and pub people.' It was
at the *Riverside Restaurant* – a 'raffish and quite smart hangout' in
New Brighton, that he met the 'slim, tall and beautiful' Joan Doughty,
who would become his life-partner. It was 1956. She was a clerk at the
Prudential Assurance Company office on North John Street, her hair
immobilised by aerosol spray. In her words, 'when I was seventeen, I
fell in love, at first sight, with the man who became my husband.'

He was a twenty-three-year-old Wirral Reporter who had graduated by
a 'logical progression' in January 1955 to the *Liverpool Echo and Daily
Post* (circulation 350,000 a day), and doing well. The 'wonderful rosy
glow' of good draught bitter lubricated his sociability in every sphere
and his pleasurable consumption escalated. To Joan, 'in the early years
of our relationship, it was fun to be around him. He was full of good-

humoured energy, and I enjoyed going to pubs and parties with him.'
She ensured that wherever they went together, his pockets were 'bulging
with a couple of hundred old pennies in readiness for my calls via old-
fashioned coinbox telephone' with last-minute stories to Welsh news
editor W. Glyn Rees about 'fires, lifeboat rescues, heads stuck in railings.'

Although she was still underage for drinking, by a few months, one of
the places the couple discovered, 'after trial and error in the lanes and
byways of Drinker's Liverpool,' was the *Basnett Bar*. A 'snug and slim...
little jewel of a place' in Liverpool's Basnett Street, it was 'an extremely
pleasant pub, long and narrow with a marble counter' downstairs,
and a small restaurant above that served a decent plate of seafood or
beef grills, chops or ham-and-eggs for a shilling or two. A special place
with an Edwardian feel that fitted the couple like a glove, they soon
became familiar figures to barmaids Ada and Barbara, sharing time
there until it became their 'second home'. Together they were earning
£1,000 a year, and 'heaven was the *Basnett Bar* with Joan on paynight.'
Frequented by pressmen, critics, show-offs and wits, oddly, there were
other significant habitués. In fact, it was 'a glue-pot for people whose
lives would become inextricably intertwined.' George Melly was a
cheery visitor. Because it was 'a stage-whisper away from the Liverpool
Playhouse', a dapper Brian Epstein called in 'to hang out with young
actors, to talk business or pleasure.' As a furniture-salesman in the
family business, it was at the *Basnett Bar* that Brian first blurted out his
theatrical ambitions, to actor Brian Bedford who suggested he apply
to RADA. Peter Brown, 'a pink-faced young shop assistant', was there
too. While a 'brisk and amiable' Neil Aspinall, fresh out of Liverpool
Institute, even audited the books. Of course, they were all unknown to
each other. Related maybe, by sight and habit. Small world.

As the gregariously classless clients emerged from the *Basnett*,
they found themselves facing fashionable Bon Marché and the wide
windows of the great department store George Henry Lees, where
soon Derek and Joan were buying things for their 'bottomdrawer'.
Looking back on their 'Panglossian optimism' Derek concedes that
'the passage of years may have lent those days a serenity they didn't
possess, but it was certainly wonderful... and things were getting better
all the time.' Engaged on St David's Day, 1 March 1957, they married
exactly one year later. Joan resumes 'we married when I was twenty',
at St. Andrew's Church in Bebington, the Wirral. The newly-weds
honeymooned at the *Bell Inn* in Aston Clinton, then moved into a West
Kirby ground floor flat, close by the promenade, owned by landlords
Pip and Paddy Rae. 'Our first child was born a year later,' with Timothy

arriving 28 February 1959.

One night they'd gone over to Hilbre Island with a group of 'pop' fans and heard 'All Shook Up' being played on a portable record player as they shared a sleeping bag. Joan loved the music, 'but it made me uneasy,' adding 'I was so much older then – I'm younger than that now…' pop music was still 'Cool For Cats', and the cultivated tones of David Jacobs introducing BBC TV's *Juke Box Jury*. At the time, Derek never got to hear – and David Jacobs certainly never got to play – The Quarrymen's privately-recorded one-off 'vanity-disc' version of 'That'll Be the Day' c/w 'In Spite of All the Danger'. Elvis Presley had famously kick-started his career by privately paying to record a version of 'My Happiness' as a gift for his mother. In much the same way, one day in spring, or perhaps it was the summer of 1958, memories are understandably blurred, The Quarrymen decided to do the same. Percy F. Phillips had a small monophonic recording and mastering facility set-up in the front room of his Victorian terraced house at Number 38 Kensington. A modest affair, even by the standards of his Memphis name-alike, Sam Phillips' Sun Studio.

Around the same time – in May 1958 – a young Ronald Wycherley from Dingle (later Billy Fury) used the same Liverpool address to record a set of early demos, including his versions of 'Playing for Keeps', 'Have I Told You Lately', and his own self-penned 'Love's A-Callin''. Then The Quarrymen scraped together the 17s 6d fee necessary. Eric Griffith had joined the Merchant Navy soon after George phased himself into the group around February 1958, which meant that John, Paul – who had replaced Rod Davis – and George, all played guitars. There was also John Charles 'Duff' Lowe who played piano. Drummer Colin Hanton on drums did not participate. They all took their cramped places in Phillips Sound Recording Service, around the single microphone, and they played. Many years later, Derek would be instrumental in assembling the first *The Beatles Anthology* CD-set which would digitally-enhance, clean-up the crackles, and bring this long-lost single-sided ten-inch 78rpm track onto the market.

They'd seen Buddy Holly on *Sunday Night at the London Palladium* on 2 March, during his 1958 tour. 'We were all learning guitar on the back of the skiffle craze', explained Paul, 'so the fact that Buddy played, stood up and played, and sang was a major factor.' They learned the song from a record by the Crickets on the black Coral label, its title inspired by a quote from John Wayne in his Western movie *The Searchers* (1956) – which also provides another Liverpool band with its name. The Crickets' record had entered the UK charts on 28 September

1957, and by 2 November it had risen to hold the no.1 spot for three weeks, keeping Elvis Presley's 'Party' off the top position. It soon became part of The Quarrymen's set. 'We picked apart his records', continued Paul, 'it took us ages to get the opening riff of "That'll Be the Day"', but when we cracked it, it was like the bush drums. "I've got it, I've got it". "He's got it! He's got it!"' It became the first of a clutch of Buddy Holly songs they would record, including 'Words of Love' and 'Crying Waiting Hoping'. But 'That'll Be the Day' marks the first-ever real audio evidence of the group that would change the sound of the world. As track three on CD1, the spectral echo and eerily ragged harmonies of that proto-Beatles 'That'll Be the Day', warping in and out of focus through tape-hiss, seem to be tuning in through some space-time distortion from another distant age. It forms a direct bridge from 1958 to 1995, to now. While, although John and Paul had begun to write songs together, 'In Spite of All the Danger' is a Paul and George composition.

Although the group nucleus was now essentially intact, and all they needed was a drummer, everything was not well with the proto-Beatles. By this time, the other members of The Quarrymen had gone their separate ways. The band lapsed, played sporadically. From January to August (1959), due to their fragmentation and inactivity, George even began moonlighting with the Les Stewart Quartet. When the Les Stewart Quartet fell out prior to a *Casbah Coffee Club* engagement, George phoned his friends in, which inadvertently led to the stalled line-up reconvening. The *Casbah* was run by Mona Best, mother of Pete, who's group, The Black Jacks played there on occasions – Ken Brown, who was briefly a Quarryman, later joined the Black Jacks. Whatever, a copy of the *West Derby Reporter* from September 1959 runs the first-published photos of The Beatles, taken at the *Casbah* the day of that gig, 29 August.

Nevertheless, reduced to the John, Paul and George line-up they played the regional finals of the *Carroll Levis TV Star-Search* at the Manchester Hippodrome on Monday 24 November (1959), as Johnny and the Moondogs. Graham Nash and Alan Clarke, later of the Hollies, were among the dozens of other competing bands. Graham recalls the excitement and expectations running rife that night. 'Yes, we first played there in 1959', Nash tells me, 'we went down to where we were due to play, it was a place where I'd first been to see movies and stuff as a kid.' Neither group won. But Lennon came away with a stolen guitar. Meanwhile, John had completed his GCEs and, with some contrivance from headmaster William Pobjoy, secured a place at Liverpool College of Art from September 1957, where he met Cynthia Powell. And he met charismatic artist Stuart Sutcliffe. Stu was the first person to influence, confront and seriously alter John's consciousness. Opening him up from his earlier roughneck Teddy-Boy sense of style to the Continental Nouvelle Vague cool and James Dean hipness. The next influence in his life to be as powerful would be Yoko One. Although he was a non-musician, John insisted Stu become part of the group anyway. By January 1960 he was in.

With the Quarry Hill connection no longer relevant, some claim the origins of the name-change from Quarrymen to Beatles can be found in the insectoid designation of Buddy Holly's group. Hunter Davies relates another version of the tale, which he got from Derek, that it was Stuart Sutcliffe who suggested naming the group the Beetles through another movie connections, after the black-leather biker gang led by Chino (Lee Marvin) in Marlon Brando's *The Wild Ones* (1953). With John Lennon merely adding the spelling alteration. Derek, in his *Fifty Years Adrift*, tells the tale of Stu creatively mishearing the movie dialogue. George confirms – and may have been the original source of the story. And it's a nice story. But again, Bill Harry scuttles it by pointing out that the controversial movie was actually banned in the UK, and not publicly screened here until the late sixties. So if the tale is true, where or how did they get to see it?

Further along the *The Beatles Anthology* CD there are later tapes recorded in rehearsal in Paul McCartney's front room on a big borrowed Grundig open-top reel-to-reel tape recorder 'with the little green eye', dated to Spring… or possibly early summer 1960. They play Eddie Cochran's then-recent chart-version of Ray Charles' 'Hallelujah, I Love Her So' – 'because I had the Eddie Cochran record', says Paul. The spoof harmonies of 'You'll Be Mine' display early examples of Lennon's absurdist silly voice humour, alongside a Paul-composed instrumental called 'Cayenne'. With the group in uneasy flux, these are tapes that feature not only John, Paul and George – but the only existing known recordings made with Stuart.

By May the renamed Silver Beatles were on a short tour in Scotland. They'd approached Larry Parnes with the intention of backing Billy Fury. John Lennon got as far as asking Fury for his autograph. Parnes was less than impressed. They fail the audition and wind up playing behind Johnny Gentle instead, another – lesser – part of Parnes' stable. Together they perform seven dates from The Town Hall at Marsh Hill Alloa, in Clackmananshire (20 May), to The Rescue Hall on Peterhead's Prince Street in Aberdeenshire (28 May), enduring the roar of the crowd, the smell of the Thames van. Temporary drummer Tommy

Moore stepped in for the tour. By June he'd quit. They were booked for their first Hamburg trip by local promoter Alan Williams but still needed a drummer. So Pete Best tried out for a 12 August gig. Much to his family's disapproval, George absented himself from his 'thirty-bob-a-week' job at local department store Blacklers, and they embark together on the sixteenth. Sailing into legend.

Whether Derek noticed it or not, Liverpool was becoming the nucleus of an amazing outburst of youth culture. As local writer Bill Harry recalls, 'in the late 1950s groups began to thrive.' To Gerry Marsden, in Liverpool, 'if you didn't box, you started a band' – but they were still 'groups', for they were not yet called 'bands'. And they play in the 'jive hives', ballrooms and town halls booked by enterprising local promoters such as Brian Kelly, Doug Martin, Wally Hill, Vic Anton, Dave Foreshaw, Les Dodd, and Charlie mcbain. They remain among the unsung heroes of the Mersey scene. They promoted music-nights regularly at venues such as the Grosvenor Ballroom, Wilson Hall, Hambleton Hall, Aintree Institute, Blain Hall, Litherland Town Hall, St. John's Hall, Alexandra Hall, Lathom Hall, Mossway Hall, Knotty Ash Village Hall and New Clubmoor Hall. And 'it was the youth of Merseyside who crowded the venues, where only soft drinks were available. They went because they loved the music.'

Joe Brown's movie *What A Crazy World* (1963) is located some years later, and in London, but when young rocker Joe goes to a local gig, which happens to have Freddie and the Dreamers on-stage, it's amusing but a quaintly forgotten element of the time that they're served only weak coffee in Duralex cups. Yet The Quarrymen also venture into licenced premises with a booking at the Speke Bus Depot Social Club. While Gerry Marsden and Ringo Starr also do Working Men's Club appearances, at the Pitt Street Labour Club. But the music scene was not just rock 'n' roll. Different cultural influences had led to the multiple development of a wide range of live DIY music, from pub sing-alongs to sea shanties and Irish Folk songs. It's largely forgotten now that Liverpool was also the 'Nashville of the North' because it could boast the largest Country & Western music scene in Europe with its own annual 'Grand Ole Opry' held at the Philharmonic Hall.

Nevertheless, the common influences were American. Britain was still a predominantly insular nation, with little evidence of multiculturalism. But it was the port cities, such a Liverpool, that were more at ease with incomers than most. According to pop mythology, passed from insiders to journalists, these tales have entered music folklore. That, just as Liverpool had been an important access-point for wartime convoys, now – although the docks were in long decline – local seamen were returning from New York with exotic brands of ciggies, comic books, and the latest pop and R&B records, bringing sounds which filtered into the repertoires of local musicians. Bill Harry disagrees with this thesis, he suggests that, like Derek's convenient invention of 'Raymond Jones', the 'Cunard Yank' theory 'sounds nice, but it's not true.' That although, for example, Searcher John McNally had merchant seamen brothers who brought records back from their overseas trips, the majority of music in circulation could be picked up cheaply in second-hand stores or flea-markets, to those with the discrimination to seek them out. There's a suggestion that Bob Wooller, the *Cavern* DJ, acted as the sole 'Cunard Yank' cypher. By selecting American R&B to play at his *Cavern* sessions, he brought those rarities to the attention of the group members in the audience. The other element was the NEMS store – the early Beatles went and listened to elusive American records in Brian Epstein's sound-booths. Even if they seldom had the cash to buy them.

Oddly enough, the Liverpool groups, for whatever reason – partially at least, in those pre-motorway years, due to geographical isolation – stood aside from the entire slowly-evolving British 'rock' variant. It was even behind the times, out of step with the rest of the country. Vince Taylor ('Brand New Cadillac'), Billy Fury (on his ten-inch self-written LP), or even Screaming Lord Sutch and the Savages (with a line-up including many future star musicians) could all be impressively raw live. Those Larry Parnes 'stars' and the other more muscular mainstream acts were equally based around imported carefully-copied America hits, black R&B or rockabilly, many of which could as easily have been potential targets for Mersey group covers. 'A Shot of Rhythm and Blues' – used by a number of Liverpool groups and eventually recorded by Gerry and the Pacemakers, had already been done by Johnny Kidd and the Pirates.

Yet in some ways, Liverpool stayed where it had all begun, around the formative 1956 Skiffle boom. Learning how to pick out the three essential chord-shapes from Bert Weedon's *Play In A Day* guitar-tutor. While they stayed in awe of the by-then unfashionable first great wave of original rockers – Little Richard in particular, Chuck Berry of course, but Carl Perkins and Gene Vincent too, pre-army Elvis, Buddy Holly, Larry Williams, the Coasters, Billy Lee Riley, Frankie Ford, Johnny Burnette, Eddie Cochran… they all stubbornly retained a currency in Liverpool while national radio and the music press had moved on into smoother, more inoffensive recent American stylists. When a mystified Cliff Richard protested to *The Daily Mirror* about the advent of The Beatles, that 'all they've done is revert to rock 'n' roll', he was absolutely correct. Liverpool groups shared a common root system. Although it was less the sound of the future, as an enclave of the late 1950s that refused to be pacified into lucrative showbiz convention.

It's fair to say that none of the eventual Merseybeat bands were impressed by, or wanted to be Cliff Richard and the Shadows. And yet, and yet, on the extended *Get Back* rehearsal tapes, circulated in bootleg form, John Lennon improvises a 'Shaking in the Sixties' medley to which Paul contributes a respectable take on 'Move It'. And while Cliff would never repeat the incandescent adolescent fire of 'Move It' or 'Mean Streak', hits such as 'Please Don't Tease', 'Nine Times Out of Ten' or 'Gee Whiz It's You' were more slickly effective packages of Brit-rock than, say, Billy J Kramer would later achieve. The Shadows' February 1959 single 'Feeling Fine', written by former member Ian Samwell who'd penned 'Move It', is a prescient example of raw Beat-Boom rock 'n' roll, complete with Beatles-style yells in the instrumental break. If it had been issued in late-1963, it would have passed for contemporary.

Cliff Richard and the Shadows may have begun by taking the cover version route, but also generated their own material, or at least drew from a pool of British writers to distance themselves from the competitor-pack. 'We came into showbusiness', as Bruce Welch explained, 'we didn't come into the music industry.' 'Living Doll' even peaked at a Billboard no.30 during 1959 and Cliff writes about enduring an unrewarding American promotional tour, enlivened only by finding his own song included on a big chrome drugstore rockola jukebox. By January 1962, 'The Young Ones' was not only his twentieth UK chart hit but the defining sound of that summer. That it failed to cross over the Atlantic and find comparable success in the land that Derek Taylor described as 'the heart and soul of popular music' must remain one of the random inconsistencies that make music history so inexplicable. Its clean Hank Marvin guitar figures, Cliff's flexibly appealing voice and pin-up looks, powered by the radio-friendly generational message en-vinyl-ised all the vital ingredients that could easily have connected with stateside jukebox teens. But it missed out.

Although Cliff Richard was a big star across most of the English-speaking world, with hits and tours in Australia, South Africa, and across Europe, the birthplace of rock 'n' roll was caught up in its own playlists, and unsupported by radio airtime, the single failed to chart. George Martin, kicking his heels over at EMI's minor subsidiary Parlophone, jealously watched the continuing success of Norrie Paramor – producer for Cliff, the Shadows and Helen Shapiro. Paramor drove an E-type Jaguar. George was impatiently awaiting his own opportunity.

As Derek noted, America was always 'aware' of gently fading Britain as something vaguely 'interesting', and actors aplenty possessed a certain quality of elegance – Ronald Colman, David Niven, Leslie Howard, Cary Grant, Alec Guinness, Vivien Leigh, Basil Rathbone, Charles Laughton, enough to earn them elevation into the Tinseltown pantheon. And it's far from true that The Beatles were the first to make that pop breakthrough. Joe Meek's 'Telstar' – appropriately named for the first trans-Atlantic communication satellite – did defeat the odds stacked against British product by actually topping the Billboard chart in 1962 – over a year before The Beatles. It was only through a combination of petulance and incompetence that the hit remained an isolated freak event. Meek failed to capitalise on its success when proposed tie-in appearances foundered on the Tornado's touring commitments with Billy Fury. So, a one-off – that is, apart from Mr Acker Bilk's equally instrumental TV-theme 'Stranger on the Shore', an American no.1 six months earlier, or Kenny Ball's 'Midnight in Moscow' which made it as high as no.2 that same year. Or even Lonnie Donegan as long ago as 1956, who scored an American no.8 with 'rock Island Line'.

Each of those records 'made it' through their own unique novelty value. In this strange interregnum, they came, they saw, and then they went back home again. After all, what could the Brits bring to the rock 'n' roll feast that couldn't be cooked even better in America? Unlike The Beatles invasion that was still a couple of slender years away, there was no sense that they were part of any cultural or teen subcultural movement. There was no sense that England was Swinging, yet – or that the 'British Were Coming'. 'Always America seemed too big, too vast, too remote, and too American', as Brian Epstein explained in *A Cellarful of Noise*, and 'for years The Beatles, like every other British artist, watched the American charts with remote envy. The American charts were unobtainable. Only Stateside artistes ever made any imprint.'

To Derek, 'pop music throughout the world was limp and lame and meandering. There was no known direction for the tired stragglers from the rock 'n' roll race of the 1950s.' Kids 'looked at the old fifties styles and shuddered that the sixties might be more of the same.' Yet, although he was blithely unaware of it, on Saturday, 28 October 1961, eighteen-year-old 'Raymond Jones' walked up to the record-store counter of NEMS and asked for a record called 'My Bonnie' by a group called The Beatles, recorded during their second Hamburg trip. And – if only apocryphally – ignited the fire.

Meanwhile, there were decisive changes taking place at the *Liverpool Daily Post and Echo*. It was closed for long weeks due to a print strike. Derek was caught up in the dispute. As a staunch member of the NUJ, subject to a 'solidarity clause', he 'was out on strike in a trice' – only to be summarily dismissed by the management who contended that the agreement didn't apply to him. Championed and supported by the union, who considered him 'victimised', he drew strike pay, but when management, along with 'union members who had stayed at work in clear breach of all the movement stood for', produced a 'black' edition, Derek handed in his letter of resignation. 'I left with much sadness, leavened by a degree of self-righteousness.' With a young family to support, Derek temporarily freelanced with the North West News agency, 'in fact, the strike had done me an enormous favour' because 'by the end of 1959, I was telephoning stories to every newspaper and TV station in north Britain, without fear or favour.'

Derek was writing his way up through the press scrimmage of such now-lost titles as the *News Chronicle* – a long-lived Liberal paper formed in 1930 by the merger of the *Daily Chronicle* and *The Daily News*. It not so much ceased production as merged with *The Daily Mail*. Then there was Associated Newspaper's *Sunday Dispatch*. Previously the *Weekly Dispatch*, but acquired from Newnes to become part of Lord Rothermere's stable of titles, the long-running *Dispatch* had an unfortunate pre-war policy of supporting the fascist black-shirt movement. By the 1950s it was better known for incurring establishment displeasure by its eccentric coverage of the UFO phenomenon – running extracts from Frank Scully's *Behind the Flying Saucers* and Donald Keyhoe's *The Flying Saucers are Real*, declaring this extra-terrestrial threat 'bigger than the Atom Bomb' during a period when the government was furtively striving to suppress such Cold War scare-mongering. Ursula Bloom was an occasional contributor around the time Derek was doing the same. Until that title closed too.

But Derek was ready to move on. 'Joan and I drifted away from Merseyside early in our marriage, together seeking a different world.' At a bizarre and brief career tangent, his foray into freelancing involved twice-weekly trips to the Manchester Granada TV studios where he was hired by producer Tim Hewat of *People and Places*, a regional news show presided over by Bill Grundy. Derek's role was to 'interview guests who had either recorded a 'pop song' or swum in the Manchester Ship Canal.' He even got to present the weather forecast, using a blackboard, before closing the bulletin by flicking the chalk at the cameraman. From Liverpool to Manchester is now a 25-minute trip on the M62. Then it was a single train ticket through the barrier from Lime Street to Manchester Victoria, in a carriage that reeked of stale Players and Capstan smoke, following the path of the world's first-ever passenger train service. But 'after a few weeks, Tim Hewat was replaced as producer by Josephine Douglas, who quickly fired me'!

'All of which combined to propel me into Beaverbrook Newspapers whose policies, in general, were attractive to few of us, but whose status and rewards were appreciably higher than most others in Manchester. Anyway, a job was a job.' Joining the northern edition of *The Sunday Express* based in Manchester, he'd later reflect that 'his happiest working days' had been spent at the *Liverpool Post*, while his political differences with the Beaverbrook Press meant he would grow to 'hate its attitudes and stinking bigotry with fierce passion.' Yet their son Gerard was born in Manchester, on 3 September 1960. 'As more children came along, going out together wasn't very easy', explained Joan. 'Sometimes he went out, and I stayed at home, but that seemed the natural order of things in the north of England in the early 1960s.'

Nevertheless, by 1962, as Derek turned thirty, he was upgraded from on-the-ground reporting to become a feature columnist under editor Howard Bygrave. Of course, newspapers looked different then. *The Daily Express* was broadsheet size, as was *The Daily Mail*. In fact, the only tabloids around were *The Daily Mirror* and the now-lost *Daily Sketch*. *The Daily Herald* alone was an odd oblong shape unique to itself. They were all black-and-white too. No colour. And, by today's standards, they were insubstantial, slim, no pull-out sections or supplements.

Newspaper offices were inhabited by a race of grim-faced tobacco-smelling men with nicotine moustaches, who wore dandruff-strewn suits while telling each other rambling old stories — a predominantly male culture. What was important was listening properly – more muck-raking than ruck-making – while being meticulous about facts and quotes. Typing skills. The rules of punctuation. And, according to tradition, journalists saved their talent for writing and their genius for expenses. It was a drinking culture. Booze tended to figure, directly or indirectly, on those expenses. As Joan remembers, there were 'good baby-sitters', and 'after I put the children to bed, I would often catch a bus into Manchester and meet my husband in the pub near his newspaper office. I enjoyed the company and would drink halves of bitter with his colleagues; it was fun. We returned home by cab as neither of us drove a car then.'

After what he called the 'thirteen wasted years' of Tory misrule, Harold Wilson ousted aristocratic Old Etonian Alec Douglas-Home. And, working from his Liverpool constituency, he set about inaugurating the 'white heat of technological revolution' and coincidentally launching the sixties. In Liverpool, for those who cared to look, there were signs of another burgeoning revolution altogether. Glance at the *Liverpool Echo* dated Friday, 11 January 1963. There's a panel-advert for the NEMS electrical store at 62-72 Walton Road. The January Sale boasts savings of £19.19s on a Burco Twin-Tub Washer, savings of £31.10s on an Ace Stereophonic Radiogram, and a £17.17s allowance on your old TV against a new nineteen-inch Herald TV for 49 guineas. Delve further into the classifieds and you notice an abundance of live music events. *The Cavern* at 10 Mathew Street (off North John Street) announces The Four Mosts, plus Gerry and the Pacemakers. To-morrow (Saturday) there's Johnny Sandon and the Remo Four. Sunday there's The Swinging Bluegenes. Among next week's lunchtime sessions, for Thursday, there's The Beatles. Billy Kramer – not yet accessorised with the 'J' – is also listed. Meanwhile, a headline announces that Merseyside is suffering the 'Longest Cold Spell Since 1947 – And The Thaw Isn't Yet In Sight'.

Among the vinyl archaeology collected onto *The Beatles Anthology: 1* is their original studio demo of 'How Do You Do It?', recorded on 4 September 1962. Unconvinced by the Beatle's own unpromisingly ragged material, George Martin persuades them to work out a version of this new song, written by Mitch Murray. They try it out. But it's obvious they're performing it reluctantly, and deliberately badly, so George abandons the attempt, climbs down and allows them to get down to what they were really there to do, to work on their own songs. But even then, Paul McCartney explains how 'Please Please Me' was originally conceived as a slow-build ballad modelled on Roy Orbison's 'Running Scared'. It was only at George Martin's insistence that they open with the chorus, then accelerate it faster, faster, then faster still, to take on the defining features of what was to become 'Merseybeat'.

Derek's career as a newspaper reporter was by now fairly well-established, routine stuff, with only occasional opportunities for rewarding creative input, but with a solidly secure future in a reliable profession. 'Ah, the press... the Gentlemen of the Press', Derek rhapsodised, 'a gentleman of the press once was I, believing it to be my life's work and a Duty... Your newspaper reporter lives in a strange and frightening world, oversimplified by the need to write in baby-talk, over-complicated because the reporter is never told the whole truth. It is a world where human torches run down streets of fear in villages of wagging tongues, where police battle, where tracker dogs hunt, where judges lash rapists and governments are flayed by the opposition, where tug-of-love babies wrench heartstrings, where men fall hundreds of feet and live/die, where mayhem, murder, fire and drowning haunt families of eight, where teenage couples elope and stars confess they have been fools and spent all on the champagne life, where chess players wreak havoc and unions hold the country to ransom, where women weep and children play happily among swirling, poisonous fumes,' scribble scribble scribble. There's an old pressman's adage that says 'when it bleeds, it leads'. The story with pain, injury, or bereavement carries a greater circulation-charge than stories without. Hence, that's the story to chase. To Derek, 'for a week or two, it is OK, even exciting. After fifteen years, which is how long I lived in it, it becomes a pain.'

There are ways of anaesthetising that pain. To Joan 'he was sometimes unreliable and I didn't like it much when he was drunk, but that didn't often happen when he was with me.' But newspaper culture was a booze-fuelled laddish environment where only bloke's blokes survive, and as a product of it, 'he developed into a "big drinker". This caused arguments and resentments between us as his behaviour became more and more unreliable.' To Derek, 'in my twenties, I started having what I now know as blackouts, but which were then "can't remember a thing about last night, after ten o'clock…"' 'From my own family background I had come to believe that alcohol played an important part in "having a good time"', continued Joan, and 'after each upset we would try and bury our differences and get back to a loving relationship. I hoped that things would be different, but I had no idea how to set about making them so.'

To Derek, responsible parenthood provided an unbeatable motivation to combine earnings with art, or ambition. See the photos of him from the time. Wearing a conventional white shirt with neatly knotted black 'James Bond' knitted tie. Tie-clip and cuff-links. Formally cut light navy-blue suit with polished patent-leather shoes. He's clean-shaven with short, disciplined hair combed and Brylcremed into a frozen Lawrence Harvey quiff. The way everyone looked at the time. Brian Epstein wore a more exquisitely tailored, more expensive version of that same suit. No betraying hints of bohemian tendencies or sartorial frivolity. Little to indicate what was to come. But there were gradual steps.

The Taylor family were on holiday in the Isle of Man in summer 1962, having taken the ferry across to Douglas. It was a family holiday, based in the Carrick Bay Hotel. One evening, sharing a drink in the hotel bar,

Derek and Joan were approached by a local man who enjoyed regaling holidaymakers with tales. As their conversation became increasingly informal, he leaned forward and confided to Derek, 'I like wearing moleskin gloves, you know?' with a sense of innuendo, 'it gives me a little bit of an unusual sensation when I'm out with my girlfriend', adding, with a knowing nudge-nudge wink, 'I don't want to go into details.' So they didn't. But the curious conversation teased Derek's journalistic imagination so that many years later, the memory would surface in a vastly different context. He suggested the story to John Lennon, who reshaped it into the lyric 'she's well-acquainted with the touch of the velvet hand...'

There was another consequence of the holiday. Derek's *Sunday Express* editor phoned the hotel. Summoned from the beach to take the call, with a sense of foreboding, his editor informed him that Arthur Brittenden, editor of the *Daily Express*, was interested in taking him on as regular showbusiness correspondent, and regional theatre critic. 'My qualifications were that I was a trained newspaperman who knew more about showbusiness than anyone else on either the *Sunday Express* or the *Daily Express* in Manchester, which was saying very little...' Howard Bygrave would not oppose the posting, and to Derek, the opportunity seemed like 'a very good break'.

The first 'decent-sized' by-lined feature to come from his new promotion was about Frank Ifield, then enjoying a run of three consecutive UK no.1s with the million-selling 'I Remember You', the old Hank Williams' song 'Lovesick Blues', and 'Wayward Wind', recorded at Abbey Road Studios. Making every word count, Derek described the Australian yodeller as having 'a smile as wide and as white as Sydney Harbour Bridge', a bridge he'd never seen and, when he finally did get to see it on his first Beatles tour, turned out to be neither white nor very wide. Nevertheless, the achievement was vindicated when his coveted writer's credit – 'that's ME there, ME in print!' – came adorned by a 'faggish' photo of a smirking Derek in neat Double-2 shirt. Flushed with success, he followed it by travelling up to Blackpool to interview husband-and-wife duo Nina & Frederick, whose sweetly inoffensive 'Little Donkey' was a parentally-approved Christmas hit. He met blonde, aristocratic Nina in her demurely flared dress, and Frederick – bearded in acceptably Nordic well-trimmed fashion. The *Daily Express* was then an important mass-circulation title. Getting the journalist on-side was something worth cultivating, and in that less-spun world, Nina and Frederick were media-savvy. Although their current record was 'Sucu Sucu', theme-song for TV espionage thriller *Top Secret*, they opened the conversation by complimenting him on the Ifield piece. Derek warmly responded by wording an approving article about the Danish Folk-calypso duo.

Tellingly, he describes the feature as something 'I thought they would like' – an approach that immediately drew a reprimand from Bygraves who explained that criticism needs 'a little acid' to give it bite, that he should 'write up to the edge of libel'. Dutifully, the following Monday, Derek brought the advice to bear on a play he was assigned to review at the Manchester Opera House. The cast included forties heavyweight actors Derek Bond, who had played Captain Oates in *Scott of the Antarctic* (1948), Jean Kent, a former *Windmill Theatre* dancer and movie star of *The Browning Version* (1951), and veteran Shakespearian Griffith Jones. The appearance of his review the following day would 'bring the unhappy cast no joy', although he continued by spacing his enthusiasm with similarly negative pieces over the following two years. He always felt ill-at-ease with such demolition-jobs, considering himself inadequately qualified to judge the finer points of such productions. Combined with an element of guilt about so casually destroying a work that the writers, cast and production team had sweated to stage – drawing on his own experience of amateur theatrics as part of the Hoylake Operatic and Dramatic Society, while thereby discouraging a potential audience who might have derived pleasure from their efforts. 'Do you know what goes into the making of your morning paper?' he asks, 'it is much the same as what goes into the making of your morning bacon. A lot of flesh gets ripped off…!' It's an attitude that demonstrates two key elements that would form a continuity in his life and career. The desire to please others and gain their approval. And a natural inclination to up-beat positivism.

There were occasional flashpoints that disrupt this apparently conventional domestic life. Addressing himself in mock-Shakespearian, he wrote 'alas, poor Derek, I knew him well in his blue raincoat smelling horribly of beer and doing his best for his paper and for himself and for his contacts and so compromising all along the line that it is a wonder he can still look his clippings full in the fading typeface…' With bitter, self-deprecating humour, he later reflects 'how many heavy Fridays had there been? Maybe 1,250 since I had first started drinking, rarely a dry Friday since Attlee was Prime Minister.' 'I remember one particular night', adds Joan, 'after I had put our three small children to bed and was preparing dinner, he arrived home drunk. As soon as I opened the front door, he saw the disappointment on my face. In a typical pre-emptive strike he accused me of causing his condition... I was to be accused of being the cause of his drunkenness many, many times in the future... I was baffled by his behaviour. I asked myself over and over, how could he be drunk again?' It was a 'predictable co-dependent's pattern'. But all marriages have problems, don't they? All lives go through rough patches. There was nothing to mark Derek out as different. Nothing, that was, until he first encountered The Beatles.

But this was a time when extraordinary things were happening to ordinary people. On 30 May 1963 – three weeks after his thirty-first birthday, 'in the fourteenth year of a comfortable career as a newspaperman headed for Fleet Street' – Derek was assigned to cover a Beatles concert. He was young, too, only in a relativistic way. And his story, his history, takes its spin from this moment. The same week that The Beatles were no.1 with 'From Me To You' – their meteoric third single. They were due to play as a one-night stop-over at the Manchester Odeon, on the London Road, as part of a tour which had begun 18 May, alongside Roy Orbison, and Gerry and the Pacemakers.

Derek was briefed to bring back a sneeringly negative story. He went with Joan. 'Joan had seen The Beatles on television and liked them very much. I had not seen them but, although word took a long time to reach newspapermen, I had heard of them and we both thought it would be a good night out.' After all, they were a four-piece combo from his hometown, dismissively referred to as the 'mop-tops'. Although objectively, their hair was no longer than anyone else's, just combed forward into a pudding-bowl fringe just long enough to push your fingers through. Nothing much more radical than Adam Faith had flaunted a scant few years before. But that was more than enough to mark them out. Particularly to the conformist establishment represented by *The Daily Express* demographic.

Derek and Joan were seated on the front row, and 'on first sighting... I knew my life should be inextricably entwined with The Beatles... the(ir) sense of overwhelming cheerful confidence was too glad to be allowed to escape.' Like arriving in Oz, suddenly, the world was in colour. His review was not meant to be positive. Two hours after the concert he was dictating his prose over the telephone, without notes, 'just as it came'. And in the next day's edition, readers found he'd praised instead of damning them. 'The Liverpool Sound came to Manchester last night, and I thought it was magnificent...' he enthused, 'the spectacle of these fresh, cheeky, sharp, young entertainers in opposition to the shiny-eyed teenage idolaters is as good as a rejuvenating drug for the jaded adult.'

Retrospecting in his *Fifty Years Adrift*, Derek recalls 'I have never seen anything like it. Nor heard any noise to approximate the ceaseless, frantic hysterical scream which met The Beatles when they took the stage after what seemed a hundred years of earlier acts. All very good, all marking time, because no-one had come for anything other than The Beatles. Then the theatre went wild. First Aid men and police – men in the stalls, women mainly in the balcony – taut and anxious, patrolled the aisles, one to every three rows. Many girls fainted. Thirty were gently carried out, protesting in their hysteria, forlorn and wretched in their unrequited love for four lads who might have lived next door. The stalls were like a nightmare 'March Fair'. No-one could remain seated. Clutching each other, hurling jelly-babies at the stage, beating their brows, the youth of Britain's second city surrendered themselves totally...' There was not another group like them. Not here. Not there. Not anywhere. Not in a generation. And not for the generations to come. So 'the man from the press said we wish you success'.

Inevitably, the review came to the attention of both the band and their manager, winning their favour. Brian Epstein was scrupulous in his impeccably coordinated marketing. He singled out and took note of potentially useful allies. Especially when they occurred in the unlikeliest of places. The teenage press had already been won over. And Brian was drawing up strategies for the next phase and kept files of possible fifth columnists.

The Beatles returned to Manchester on 20 November, topping the bill at the Ardwick Apollo over Peter Jay and the Jaywalkers, and smiling Everly-clones The Brook Brothers. By then, everything had changed. It was just twelve short months since the release of 'Love Me Do' – which had modestly announced, not only the coming of The Beatles, but the arrival of the entire 1960s proper, emerging as if it was a sound from another planet. And by then the rest of the press had been forced to concede defeat. Respected journalist Donald Zec devoted a lavish *Daily Mirror* two-page spread (Tuesday, 10 September 1963) to the boys with the 'stone-age hair-cuts'. He opens by describing them as 'Four Frenzied Little Lord Fauntleroy's who are earning £500 a week,' then admitted they're 'as nice a group of well-mannered music makers as you'll find perforating the eardrums anywhere.' Within a month they topped the bill at ITV's *Sunday Night at the London Palladium* (13 October 1963) over Brook Benton, Des O'Connor, and compere Bruce Forsyth. They contribute a fifteen-minute five-song set, including 'All My Loving', and closing with 'Twist and Shout', as upwards of two-thousand girls riot outside the venue. The following Monday's *Daily*

5

Mirror wrote itself into history when Don Short covered a concert in sedate Cheltenham, reporting the story with a single-word headline – 'BEATLEMANIA'.

And by then, Derek had moved decisively into the Brian Epstein orbit. The four 'long-haired lads from Liverpool' 'were a dream worth harnessing…'

This is the story of Derek Taylor. You could accuse that it's also a story that uses Derek Taylor as a lens through which to write about some great bands and wonderful music – yeah, yeah, yeah. That's true as well. But portrayal need not be betrayal. Biography can never precisely capture real life. It selectively follows an imaginative arc that condenses or expands time and events. If this is a group biography of interconnected contemporary luminaries, with Derek's life as the armature on which it's built, then it's an interconnected biography of parallel, and occasionally intersecting lives. And those events don't always happen in strict sequence. Things occur to participants separately, yet simultaneously, the significances of which only reveal themselves later in other contexts. Moving in concentric circles, with one starting as another ends, the serial narrative turns back on itself in a looped-tape, or a biographical version of an MC Escher staircase, rewound or fast-forwarded. So there's some temporal-sliding, some manipulation of timelines, some re-crossing of events from alternate viewpoints to extract different but equally valid perspectives. Go with it.

For example – simultaneous to these events, 15 September 1961, on America's west coast, Brian Wilson and Mike Love were signing a songwriter's contract with Guild Music Publishing, breaking into what was known as 'discdom'. 'Surfin'' was issued as a single by the Candix indie label on 8 December, and crept its way into the national chart. Then, elsewhere in America, during the final months of 1962, a twenty-year-old Jim McGuinn was playing back-up at upmarket cabaret dates with Bobby Darin's group, while (Harold Eugene) 'Gene' Clark was being recruited into the New Christy Minstrels. Coming across the Atlantic, during the freezing winter of 1962-'63, the twenty-one-year-old Bob Dylan made his first stop-over trip to London, arriving 18 December, as 'Britain was slowed to a standstill' by the coldest snap since 1740. He became a familiar figure on the Folk scene, hung out with Martin Carthy, and added the first-ever commercial performance of the as-yet unrecorded 'Blowin' in the Wind' to the BBC play *The Madhouse on Castle Street*. Derek might have flicked pages through the issue, and paused to speed-read the less than enthusiastic *Daily Express* review about Dylan's 'nasal' performance. Or perhaps he didn't even notice it.

Either way, all those incidents, happening miles away and halfway around the world, would eventually interact with Derek's life. As Derek phrased it, 'all these and many more were drawn towards each other's tribe in strange ways, as if on threads. Each didn't know what the others were up to, but hey! Maybe something would come of it.' It's only in the rage of changes, that sense emerges collectively, or sometimes not at all. That's the nub. But grok it this way. Derek is a journalist filing columns for some pretty major newsprint titles. He's an intelligent, sparky, perceptive, likeable guy. A married man just turning thirty, but that story has a strictly limited appeal. Then he sees The Beatles. And it's the key to the wardrobe that takes the Pevensie children into Narnia. The twister that takes little Dorothy and Toto over the rainbow to put them on the Yellow Brick Road to the Emerald City. The rabbit-warren that Alice falls down into; yeah, yeah, yeah – enough of the over-the-top metaphors already. But you get the picture? Chronologically, the story could be said to start around that point. Without that magical connection, Derek's life would have been different. All the incidents that transfigure and shape his subsequent life flow from that moment.

He goes around the world with the Fab Four – for him 'The Beatles were part of the shrinking of the world, as much as jet travel,' he crossed what he called 'the decreasing divide between America and Britain' to set up shop in Hollywood, California, as publicist to many of the major rock stars of the sixties, returning to England in 1968 to resume as Beatles' publicist through its most outlandish period of Apple, Bed-Ins and the Plastic Ono Band. They 'broadened my vision... loosened my tie... hastened my classlessness, turned me on and inside out, literally put acid in my tea...' Most of us could never dream of getting that close.

But just as precisely, that's also the story of everyone who went through that generational experience. Derek's connection was amplified, but we all went through something similar. As Brian prophetically observed in *A Cellarful of Noise*, The Beatles were a group 'who have directly altered the lives of hundreds, even thousands of people, who have affected the entire balance of the entertainment industry, who have kicked up so much dust that in all our lifetimes, it will not completely settle.' All lives were changed. All destinies were altered. 'The magic of The Beatles is, I suspect, timeless and ageless. It has broken all frontiers and barriers. It has cut through differences of race, age and class. It is adored by the world.' The Beatles were a generational lightning rod, a phenomenon that 'millions of us were to pick up on and feed off and feed and feed off in one great seven-year feast.' The events of 1963 in Britain, and across the world the following year, sent a jolt of voltage around a generation. They created a sense of what was possible. By example: You no longer had to accept what is. You could change it. As they had. 'If they didn't see themselves like that...' if The Beatles didn't see themselves as leaders, which they didn't, 'that isn't to say we didn't follow them anyhow.'

If Derek functions as a cypher in other people's lives, that's because it was a shared thing. Was he, as in Fellini's *La Dolce Vita*, the would-be serious writer who betrayed his talent to work in celebrity journalism? If so, there's no evidence of it in his work. He enjoyed his times, and enjoyed his contribution to them...

You think you know something...

You know nothing. LSD is pounds, shillings and pence. Not yet lysergic acid. Not yet Lucy in the Sky with Diamonds. A pound note is large and green. A ten-shilling note is smaller, half the pound's value, and red. A fiver – a five-pound note, is scarce, and blue. It's a big deal. Kids had little disposable cash; hence they weren't seen as a demographic worth targeting. Teenage marketing was in its infancy. A 45rpm single costs six shillings and ninepence, which is roughly the price of a gallon of petrol. It comes without a picture jacket. Instead, each label has its own distinctive uniform sleeve livery-design, although some stores also have unique branded card covers and all target on the circle-opening where you can read the title as you flip through the racks. The first edition of 'Love Me Do' arrived in a now highly-collectable red label and matching sleeve. By the time of 'Please Please Me', the label was hard, no-nonsense black emblazoned with a '£'-sign logo – a trademark which to Brian Epstein 'was to become a symbol of unbelievable wealth.' The Parlophone sleeves were green. But watch the label at the disk's centre, Pye was a lurid tasteless pink. RCA had a geometrical red zig-zag connecting the logo roundels. Philips were rich blue. CBS – still associated with boring lounge-core Andy Williams or smooch-along couple Steve Lawrence & Edie Gorme – was orange.

'Strawberry Fields Forever' c/w 'Penny Lane' would be the first UK single with its own picture sleeve. Prior to that, if you really wanted picture sleeves, you answer the small-adverts in the music press or the fan-magazines and pay over the odds for expensive American imports.

By contrast – eps, extended plays, were neat little seven-inch four-track packages that came in miniature laminated sleeves complete with photo-covers and liner-notes. Slightly more expensive – costing a significant twelve shillings and sixpence – they made a more considered investment, and hence rarely register on the charts – and actually only qualify for inclusion in the *New Musical Express* Top Thirty anyway. Elvis had done it with his *Follow That Dream* and *Kid Galahad* movie mini-albums. But 'Twist and Shout' was the first to go top-three, selling 650,000 copies as it did so, establishing a new benchmark for bands to aim at. The Searchers' 'Ain't Gonna Kiss Ya' EP. The rolling Stones 'Five by Five'.

Albums, cover 'laminated in Clarifoil', cost 32s 6d, which translates to around £1.75p – a lot when your take-home pay at the end of the week might total something like £8. So you think twice about making that purchase. 'Twist and Shout' is a good illustration of the price-scale. A cover of the Isley Brothers original American routine, it became the stand-out finale track to The Beatles first album, powered by energetic live performances and TV. Nonsense lyrics about an obsolete dance-craze, but massive with raw energy, positioned at the album climax-point, later to be occupied by 'Money', 'Tomorrow Never Knows'... 'A Day in the Life'. But albums were expensive. So the label spun-off four of the titles onto the more economical format of an EP, headlined by 'Twist and Shout'. By 10 August 1963, it climbed as high as number four on the singles chart. But even eps don't come cheap. So, sensing a hit-opportunity, Decca rush-release a bland cover single by Brian Poole and the Tremeloes – you remember them? The band Decca had signed while rejecting The Beatles. It's fair to say that no-one actually preferred their version, even to suggest as much was to invite hoots of derision. But it came significantly cheaper. So it got to no.4 during that same month. Incidentally, the Isley Brothers' year-old single also sold in sufficient numbers to chart its way into the Top Thirty.

While a nation's teenagers were listening with ears cupped to imperfectly-tuned transistor radios, plugging into an otherworldly beyond or playing their collection of singles, pausing only to blow some fluff off the stylus.

Chapter Four: 1962: What The Papers Say

roll over Beethoven, and tell Tchaikovsky the news...

The Beatles and The Stones, made it good to be alone...
(House of Love)

The Beatles were special. We'd seen them earlier on Granada TV's *People and Places*, doing 'Some Other Guy' live from *The Cavern*, introduced by Bill Grundy on 17 October 1962. Derek had briefly appeared on *People and Places* too. Grundy would later interview another newer spikier Fab Four. The Beatles were brought back to the Granada studio another eleven times between April and December 1963. We'd bought the singles. The albums. Charted them up and down the Top Twenty. Knew each track beat-for-beat. Loyalty to Elvis persisted. The rolling Stones and the Animals play with a far purer undiluted rawness. But The Beatles were special. I'd been turned seventeen for less than a month, been employed as a print apprentice at Henry Booth's (Park Avenue) for roughly the same period. I was wearing acne, a pale blue knitted tie, and Chelsea boots with Cuban heels. Roy Orbison's 'It's Over' was no.1 on the chart, while the first black-and-white episode of Gerry Anderson's Supermarionation *Stingray* introduced Troy Tempest to ITV viewers.

Two Big Bangs in the life-history of one universe is not bad going. Professor Stephen Hawking can tell you about the first. And the second – John, Paul, George and Ringo... live, I saw them on the chilly Friday evening of 16 October 1964. The venue was the grey Regal cinema, Hull, later reduced by expansion into the ABC Multiplex, now totally erased to make way for the newly integrated Ferensway Transport Hub. There were two houses, 6:15 and 8:30 pm. It was what they used to call a 'Package Tour'. On 'Package Tours', each act was allocated something like twenty minutes for a hit, a B-side, and a cover-version. Topliners would get perhaps – what, forty-five minutes? Sounds Incorporated open with a rousing instrumental solo set, and then provide across-the-board backing. The Rustiks were no-hopers signed by Brian Epstein and never heard of again. Tommy Quickly had cut 'Tip of My Tongue', a Lennon-McCartney song not subsequently sighted on vinyl since. And hence highly collectable. Mary Wells – Motown's 'Little Miss Hitmaker' – was special guest, with 'My Guy' and 'Two Lovers'. There were also make-weights in the modest form of Bob Bain and The Remo Four.

Then The Beatles themselves were practically inaudible behind a tactile wall of hormone-propelled screams and a multi-hued hail of hurled jelly-babies. Although they hardly move on stage, they colourise the greyness with new energies. Paul and George move heads-in close, sharing the left-hand mike. Someone throws an orange that hits George on the head. Lennon boots it with 'Roy of the Rovers' skill back into an audience he probably can't even see. Someone remarks that Paul looks like 'Doctor Moon' – as played by John Alderton, on ITV's new Soap *Emergency Ward Ten*. They play 'A Hard Day's Night', George concentrating on his fingering as he picks out the chiming solo. They close with 'Twist and Shout', John standing splay-legged for emphasis, guitar high. No encores, this was 1964. And the colour switches off. Everything downgrades back to monochrome. We know that, like us, The Beatles are Northern. Working Class. That although they love R&B and rock 'n' roll as we do, they've already gone way beyond yesterday, and this night it doesn't matter if they've got no tomorrow. They are NOW!!!

It was all part of growing up in an extraordinary time. Coming out, the second house is queuing to go in. 'What're they like?' they plead. 'Brilliant', I say. Then, conscious of my cred, 'but wait till you see the rolling Stones!'

Derek Taylor saw The Beatles during the same time-span. And it changed his life. Could it really have happened that easily? Yes. And no. Could it have happened like that for me? Could I exchange what I have to have been where Derek Taylor was? Yet to have been what Derek Taylor was is to have been Derek Taylor, and to have been Derek Taylor is to have been Derek Taylor in his darker years, and to have paid his dues, been born in his place, and that was not an option available to anyone but Derek Taylor. Plus – Derek had fifteen years start on me. He knew what he was doing. He modestly defined his own talent as simply 'energy'. But there was more; it was also necessary to have the ability, the genius, a facility for word-spinning, swilling vocabulary around, plus the charm, something else too. He was attuned to The Beatles. He identified something in them that others didn't. It's obvious now; it wasn't so obvious then.

Now we know how The Beatles would both charm and disarm the establishment; how Paul McCartney's melodies would be likened to Schubert; how William Mann, music critic of *The Times*, would compare elements of *Revolver* (1966) to Mahler's *Song of the Earth* with 'major tonic sevenths and ninths built into their tunes, and the flat submediant key switches, so natural in the Aeolian cadences at the end,' baffling The Beatles themselves. The all-conquering success of The Beatles put an end to the days when working-class culture was viewed with condescension. But all that was yet to come. When I saw The Beatles, and when Derek Taylor saw them, it was still the early days. 'pop' was still an irrelevance aimed at kids, a silly frivolity you'd grow out of. Pop records and pop stars were not something worthy of serious critical consideration. But Derek was sharp enough to see beyond that. He knew there was something significant happening. Afterwards he 'followed, noted and reported every scintilla of their progress every single day.' He was hungry to be a part of it.

Not a difficult equation, surely? Except, of course, it wasn't quite so obvious then. Now we take the story for granted, we've seen *Backbeat* (1994), watched the *A Hard Day's Night* TV re-runs and read the endless regurgitations of the story. The Fabs. Their Mop-Top conquest of the world. History, through over-familiarity, assumes its own inevitability. Hindsight is the dry-rot of writing about past-time, and one of the tricks it plays is to turn the incredible into the inevitable. It could have happened no other way. It was preordained. But at the time, nothing was certain. Everything was up for grabs. And everything could be lost, the next day, the day after tomorrow.

Earlier than that, we take for granted that the executive at the Decca auditions who sidelined The Beatles in favour of Brian Poole and the Tremeloes was some variety of loser. That he – Mike Smith, a new A&R man – delegated the task by Dick Rowe – was too blind and cloth-eared to recognise the biggest franchise in pop history. How could he fail to have heard it? But listen to those New Year's Day 1962 'Decca audition' tapes again. And they're doing jokey stuff like 'The Sheik Of Araby' – with silly 'not 'arf' voices, and a comedy routine 'Three Cool Cats', which Cliff Richard had dueted with Marty Wilde and Duffy Power on the ITV *Oh Boy* show a few short years earlier... listen, and try to make that decision again, without foreknowledge. It's not quite so easy. There's nothing here to remotely suggest the potential for 'Twist and Shout' or 'She Loves You'. The only original material is 'Hello Little Girl' – supposedly John Lennon's first composition, later a hit for Fourmost – 'Like Dreamers Do' (the Applejacks), and Paul's 'Love of the Loved' (Cilla Black).

Yet Mike Smith had actually seen The Beatles before, in their natural environment. Brian had lured him down to the *Cavern* in December, where he was sufficiently impressed to secure the studio try-out. In mitigation, after a two-hundred-mile drive down from Liverpool through blizzards and heavy rain – New Year's Day was not yet a public holiday – the four Beatles arrive too late to get a decent evening meal or a good night's sleep at their 27/- a night overnight B&B put-up at the *Royal Hotel* in Woburn Place. Then they report, cold and miserable 'in a thin bleak wind, with snow and ice afoot', at Decca's Broadhurst Gardens, West Hampstead NW6 studio where – on Epstein's recommendation – they deliberately play-down their wilder material, going for a softer, more conventionally acceptable angle. It was an uncharacteristic loss of nerve. A failure of self-belief on their behalf. And if so, the approach misfired. There's a sense of delayed revenge when, 30 January 1969, The Beatles close their rooftop set on 3 Savile Row with 'Get Back', and John jibes 'I'd like to say thank you on behalf of the group and ourselves, and I hope we passed the audition.'

When people talk of destiny, they invoke a past in which things could never have turned out otherwise, but what then becomes of choice, randomness, and free-will? Because Brian returned to Decca in March, where Dick Rowe – 'a short plump man' – told him, 'not to mince words, Mr Epstein, we don't like your boys. Groups of guitarists are on the way out.' After some haggling, Rowe grudgingly extends the offer of a further session, with Tony Meehan presiding, if Mr Epstein was prepared to stump up £100 for studio time? After some consideration, Brian decides he was not so prepared. He recalls the time through the pages of his Derek Taylor-ghosted autobiography. A failed actor himself, Brian even recorded prose-extracts with George Martin (in the London EMI studios, 13 October 1964) with the intention of producing a kind of audio-book album version of the book. Although the project was never completed at least one sequence survives to be included on *The Beatles Anthology* CD-set. It constitutes the brief track 14 on CD1, with Brian's precise enunciation reciting Derek's prose.

Even later, for the first EMI recording sessions, nothing was finalised. The 'Mersey Sound' was still in evolution, still being invented. But surely there were portents for those able to see them? Now, pop endlessly eats and regurgitates its past in resampled configurations in ways that the invisible presence of pop-Art prophets Andy Warhol or Roy Lichtenstein could scarcely have imagined. Now, in the twenty-first century, we squat upon an accumulated mound of cultural detrition that makes post-modernism not only inevitable but unavoidable. In the 1950s, it was different. Everything was broken. It was a cultural Year-Zero. It's true that each generation finds its own newness. That's the nature of growing into awareness. Perhaps music-fans with the benefit of another ten years growth could see through to the black roots of Elvis Presley, then identify the rolling Stones first album as a mere compilation of familiar R&B covers. After all, there were progenitors even for that first wave of rock 'n' roll, of course there were. Even Bing Crosby had been jazz-literate, and then there was Hank Williams. Perhaps a little innocence was required not to penetrate too far beneath the sixties sheen of newness. Yet the new music was unprecedented. White artists, white British groups replicating R&B, were culturally unprecedented in ways that nothing that has happened since could ever be again. But back then, at the time of The Beatles' Decca audition, great change was about to happen. But it had not yet happened.

The Beatles represented a paradigm shift in popular music. One of the reasons they had difficulty getting signed was that the industry was looking elsewhere for its model. It was still mind-fixed on an earlier template, on the malleable pin-up cute teen pretty-boys with quaffed-back hair, onto which soppy-catchy love songs from the Brill Building machine could be attached. The industry was structured around that workable format. Recent UK stars such as Eden Kane replicated and continued it. It wasn't bust, so there was no inclination to tamper with it. In Francis Ford Coppola's *Peggy Sue Got Married* (1986), Peggy Sue (played by Kathleen Turner) body-switches back in time to 1960. Once there, she gifts wannabe pop-singer boyfriend Charlie (Nicolas Cage) 'She Loves You', which he immediately reconfigures into 1950s Doo-Wop style. That's how it worked. 1963 changed all that. Forever. Once the paradigm shifted, once The Beatles had dislodged that immense complacent inertia, every music agent was looking to sign beat-groups. Arguably, despite the advent of electro-Dance and Rap-Urban-hip-hop, that paradigm has not shifted since. Stone Roses, Oasis, Brit-pop, even Punk continued that self-sufficient four-five-piece group format. As Derek typed his copy for the next edition, time was caught on the awkward cusp between the last gasp of the old post-war order – that old road that was rapidly ageing – and the imminent seismic shifts of the sixties proper. A strange interregnum.

Meanwhile, in Liverpool life goes on day after day, hearts torn in every way. Penny Lane was still just Penny Lane, a roundabout, a fire station, a barber's shop. Strawberry Field(s) was still just the thickly-wooded grounds of the Salvation Army children's home. Brian Epstein later reminisced in a letter to Derek that 'John tells me (that Strawberry Fields) is between Menlove Avenue and Beaconsfield Road.' Menlove Avenue, a long, mainly residential thoroughfare in South Liverpool where he lived until 1963, gave its name to John's posthumous 1986 album, a collection of out-takes from previous album-session. Part of the ring road, it is also a primary route – the A562, through the Woolton area. Cynthia, who worked at Woolworths, moved into 'Mendips' as a lodger for a while. Then – as in the Carla Lane sit-com set in Liverpool, first screened by BBC-TV in 1969 – she lived the flat-share *Liver Birds* life, at 93 Garmoyle Road with Paul's girlfriend, Dot Rhone.

And Liverpool was not yet a significant fixture on the showbiz map. The city's first music star to top the chart had been the Ted Heath Band's torch-singer Lita Roza in April 1953, although she refused to perform her embarrassingly cute novelty-hit 'How Much is That Doggie in the Window' as part of her shows. After that, the biggest pop star to come out of Liverpool was Billy Fury, a former deckhand on Mersey tugs who became one of the strongest rockabilly rockers on the early British scene – admittedly, not a hotly contested title, but at least he started out by writing his own material, including all of the tracks on his now highly-collectable *The Sound of Fury* (1960) ten-inch album. In 1961, a twenty-seven-year-old Brian Epstein betrayed his showbusiness ambitions by blagging his way backstage at the Liverpool Empire in an attempt to meet teen-tycoon Larry Parnes. Parnes obligingly introduced him to his bill-topping artists, Marty Wilde… and Billy Fury. Epstein was duly impressed. Persistent rumours claim that at one point he even offered to manage Billy Fury, but Fury preferred Parnes, who helped consolidate his moody image by guiding him into success with a series of big romantic ballads.

There was also tattyfilarious music-hall style comedian Ken Dodd whose mythological interpretation of real Liverpool locations such as Knotty Ash ensured him showbiz longevity into the present day, following a tradition of Merseyside comedy that includes Ted Ray, Arthur Askey and Tommy Handley. Yet on the brink of the sixties, unbeknown to the rest of the world, the local Liverpool music scene was booming as never before. The compact Merseyside scene was unique for its time. It is not a large city, yet an estimated 350 groups were operating within the area. Overnight, underground clubs were mysteriously opening up in cramped sweatbox dives, or overground in rooms behind grubby pubs. Bands were lugging their rudimentary gear into coffee bars or decked-over swimming pools, the wannabes, would-bes and never-would-bes, playing social clubs or ballrooms; rehearsing in caffeine-fuelled youth clubs, church halls, synagogues and village halls. 'It's Always A1 at the A1 – Your Weekend Dances', boasts the Aintree Institute ticket advertising the 'Great Boppin'' Beatles plus Johnny Sandon and the Searchers'. The St Patrick's Night rock Gala at the Knotty Ash Hall at the junction of Easton Road and East Prescot Road (Saturday, 17 March 1962) announces The Beatles, Rory Storm and the Hurricanes, a buffet, novelties and prizes, all for 5/- at the door.

To Derek, 'the pop fringe is a strange piece of fabric, it is woven by many hands, not all of them skilled, but to the last tattered strand, it involves only the dedicated, and many of the people without a specific role have a far warmer sensitivity to the pulse of the lifestyle of the artists than the men who claim a knowing and important role – the bookers, the entrepreneurs, the agents, the impresarios, the press.' Everyone, in other words, plays their part in evolving a 'scene'. *The Cavern* had been a Trad Jazz cellar located beneath a Victorian fruit warehouse. It sold only hot-dogs and coke. According to Bill Harry, they once refused George Harrison admission for wearing jeans. And Rory Storm – with Ringo drumming – was fined £5 for playing rock 'n' roll there. But by then it was a venue for raw local rock groups, a 'lovely grubby haunt of bubbling Mersey youth' or, to Gerry Marsden, 'the black hole of Calcutta, in Liverpool'. The Beatles played their first appearance there lunchtime 9 February 1961, counting in the numbers by clicking their Cuban heels on the hollow stage-boards. Others played at *The Jacaranda*, *The Iron Door*, *The Beachcomber*, or larger venues such as *The Tower*, *The Locarno Ballroom*, or *Litherland Town Hall*, which counted audiences in their thousands. The punters 'bodies pressed into dresses or sweaters, lavender at *The Cavern* or pink at *The Sink*', according to Adrian Henri. Local promoter Sam Leach explains conspiratorially how 'the world never saw The Beatles as we saw them.'

The Hamburg story is too familiar to require re-telling. We all know how it all came together. We've watched tele-documentaries and read countless accounts of the trips. The 1994 *Backbeat* movie catches something of it. After so many years, so many rewrites, all that myth-making, elaboration, and those faulty memories, this is possibly the closest we can ever now get to understanding it. John and Paul already bonded. Paul a little in awe of Lennon's acerbic wit, yet asserting his own agenda, for collaboration is also competition. The young George already vitally integrated because of his fingering dexterity. Stuart Sutcliffe – like Sid Vicious would be with the Sex Pistols – a non-musician who fitted in because of his mindset, and his intense friendship with the group's nominal leader.

There was precious little rock 'n' roll in Hamburg when The Beatles first fetched up there in August (through to December) 1960. They found it wasn't a city like Liverpool where thousands of beat-hungry teens were cramming venues to hear hundreds of groups. In fact, there were just three clubs, all within walking distance of each other within the notorious red-light district stretching from the Reeperbahn to St Pauli, the cramped *Indra* ('Star') *Club* (their first residency), the *Kaiserkeller* (which survived for just over a year), and the *Top Ten Club*. There was no regular audience, either. The only rockers to precede them to Hamburg had been Tony Sheridan and Howie Casey – both recruited from the famous *Two I's* in Soho, then beat-groups the Jets, and Derry and the Seniors. The Beatles had to fight for their audience. Had to learn how to hold a crowd by grabbing them by the throat and making them dance, then doing it 'noch ein mal' ('one more time'). Despite Epstein's assertion in the Derek-ghosted *A Cellarful of Noise*, that 'audience response is their only stimulant drug', Preludin was a fuel more chemical by nature that enabled them to do that and to stay awake. Roger McGuinn would later call 'speed' 'artificial energies', like Dexamyl – the triangular blue tablet marketed initially for neurosis and obesity – or Dinaml – purple hearts.

Their first stint, arranged through club-owner Bruno Koschmider, ended when a routine police inspection showed seventeen-year-old George's work permit was invalid, he was under-age and deported. Paul and Pete were simultaneously charged with attempting to torch Koschmider's cinema and were also deported. Further, the group returned minus Stu, who decided to stay over with German girlfriend Astrid Kirchherr and reimmerse himself in his original love of art. He studied in Hamburg under Eduardo Paolozzi, only for his ambitions to be cruelly cut short by the brain haemorrhage that killed him aged just twenty-one, on 10 April 1962. He rejoined The Beatles, if only in effigy form, for the cover collage of *Seargent Pepper's Lonely Hearts Club Band*.

In the *Backbeat* movie, Pete Best is already portrayed as the taciturn outsider who just doesn't get it. He would remain a Beatle for the two years from August 1960 – almost to the day. He was there when they returned to the Hamburg Top Ten Club in April 1961. And he was there for The Beatles final Hamburg engagements 13 April–31 May 1962, at the *Star Club*. During that residency Ted 'Kingsize' Taylor – also over from Liverpool with his group the Dominoes – recorded some twenty-six songs on a mono domestic tape machine, which would later be issued as *The Beatles Live! At The Star Club in Hamburg, Germany: 1962* (Lingasong Records, 1977). By then Paul had taken over the vacated bass role, the sleeve notes claim Ringo 'happened to be sitting in' for Pete Best, and they were infiltrating their own material – 'I Saw Her Standing There' and 'Ask Me Why', alongside the regular rock 'n' roll covers, and pre-Abbey Road EMI material, 'Twist and Shout', 'roll Over Beethoven', 'Matchbox' and 'Long Tall Sally'.

To Derek, it was 'in Germany where fame, that dangerous bird, had first brushed their cheek.' Yet, as Bill Harry points out, although Hamburg was an important rite of passage for them, which made them a better group than they'd previously been, 'it was their battles with the other bands in Liverpool over the following two years that gave them their edge.' There were further forays outside Liverpool too. During 1960 comedian Bernard Manning booked them into his *Embassy Club*, a rundown former billiards hall that he'd opened in 1959 in Westbourne Grove, off the A664 Rochdale Road in the Harpurhey district of Manchester. 'They were fourteen-quid, and they just did a one-off show', recalled their controversial host. 'All nice boys, got there dressed, went on and did the show and then buggered off. That John Lennon drove me potty because he wanted a dressing room with a washbasin. What did he want that for? You come here to work, not to wash!'

Private Eye is often quoted as being the first British 'underground magazine'. Yet *Mersey Beat*, a highly-regional community indie-press paper serving a well-defined music-based audience, also carries many of the necessary credentials. And it grew out of what Liverpool-born Bill Harry calls 'arguably the first major youth movement in the British Isles.' There had been jazz, Beatniks, and the Beat Generation all present at the early stirrings of the CND Aldermaston marches. Young British writers, freed up by the American Beat Poets, were evolving the first British counter-culture, if you were hep enough to know where to find it – writers such as Michael Horovitz, Jeff Nuttall, Adrian Henri, Pete Brown, Jim Burns, and Dave Cunliffe. There were other pioneering Blues-influenced musicians working from identical templates in Newcastle, Manchester, and Richmond too. But Bill happened to be in Liverpool. An early SF, enthusiast he'd started out by joining the Liverpool Science Fiction Society and producing his own fanzine, *Biped*, which led to a correspondence with an equally precocious teenage fantasist, Michael Moorcock. By the time he'd become a student at the Liverpool College of Art in 1958, he was on good drinking terms with first Stuart Sutcliffe, who then introduces him to another Art School contact, John Lennon. And he'd begun thinking in terms of taking his dabbling in publishing to a more advanced level. After watching poet Royston Ellis at Liverpool University, they found themselves rapping about Beat Poetry in a pub called *Ye Cracke*. John Lennon was often there with girlfriend Cynthia Powell. At Bill's insistence, Lennon showed him some of his own poems.

They hung out together in a coffee bar called *The Jacaranda* where Stu had painted the murals. Bill tried out with a magazine called

Premier, then moved on to produce a hip Bebop jazz journal simply called *Jazz*. While the as-yet-unnamed Beatles 'all grew guitars and formed a noise', according to Lennon. Joined by Paul McCartney, George Harrison and Pete Best, they were soon rehearsing in the cellar beneath *The Jacaranda*. So skint they couldn't afford microphone stands, they attached the big old-fashioned mikes to broom handles held by their girlfriends. As a member of the Student Union committee, Bill Harry was running the film society, screening Jean Cocteau's *Orphée* (1950) and Luis Bunuel's surrealist classic *L'Age D'or* (1930). Then he and Stuart proposed and seconded a motion that the Union donate funds to buy amplifiers for the 'college band'. The band, by then called The Beatles, took that equipment to Hamburg with them, and the college never got to see it again.

Around this time it dawned on Bill that what was happening around him was 'as unique as what had happened in New Orleans at the turn of the century, but with rock 'n' roll groups instead of jazz.' This, he realised, was what he should be writing about. So he switched focus accordingly. With a £50 loan and his girlfriend Virginia (later his wife) as a £2/10s a week typist, he rented a tiny attic above a wine merchant's shop in Renshaw Street. The rent was £20 a month. He survived on his scholarship allowance. Operating out of this office he launched *Mersey Beat* (no.1 dated 6 July 1961). The title, he explained, was more to do with a patrolling policeman's 'beat' than it was a reference to rhythm, but it was more than just a 'What's On' events guide. Remembering the uniqueness of John Lennon's poetry, he solicited a contribution. Hence its lead feature was the article 'On The Dubious Origins of Beatles: Translated From the John Lennon' which John handed to him as soon as he returned from Hamburg. Published unedited, word-for-word, but for the Bill Harry-devised title, the group-origins concern the dream of the 'man on a flaming pie' who said 'you are Beatles with an "a"', a brainwave Derek would allude to, and quote on a 1995 CD-insert, which Paul would recall for the title of his 1997 LP *Flaming Pie*. Meanwhile, that first issue with its archive of historic photos claimed a fully sold-out print-run of 5,000. It's an accepted law of publishing that you always exaggerate your sales figures. That's as true of the mainstream press as it is of the indies. But there can be no exaggerating the long-term significance of this launch issue. Or the ones that follow.

Derek Taylor never contributed to *Mersey Beat*. There's no real evidence that he ever got to read it, or even wanted to. Yet it's an integral part of his story, and an integral part of the book he would later write with star-maker Brian Epstein, covering – and sometimes perhaps misinterpreting – the events chronicled in those issues. Derek Taylor never called around Renshaw Street. But the office soon became a hang-out for the visiting group members he'd wind up acting as press officer for. 'Even Ringo used to drop in when he was visiting the nearby dole office', adds Bill Harry.

Mersey Beat no.13, 'Liverpool's own music journal created by Bill Harry', published its 4 January 1962 poll. The front page was taken up with a Beatles photo by Albert Marrion. The same photo, in their black leathers that would be used for the Hamburg-era *The Early Years: The Beatles featuring Tony Sheridan* Contour-label album. Paul's name is miss-spelt 'Mcartney'. The poll listing goes: (1) Beatles, (2) Gerry and the Pacemakers, (3) Remo Four, (4) Rory Storm and the Hurricanes, (5) Kingsize Taylor and the Dominoes, (6) The Big Three. Actually, Rory Storm and the Hurricanes had polled higher, but suspecting fraud, a large bundle of votes 'in the same handwriting in green ink and posted from the same area at the same time' was disqualified. Shoving The Beatles, who'd also multiply-voted, to the top position. In the top-right corner of the page, there's a box-ad for NEMS of Whitechapel and Great Charlotte Street, boasting 'the finest record selection in the North.'

As 'Love Me Do' charted at year's end, John Lennon was mildly annoyed. He'd expected the keening harmonica-riff, or 'mouth-organ' as it was called at the time, to be an innovative sound, but Texan white blues singer Bruce Channel had already anticipated them by some six months with his no.2 hit 'Hey Baby'. The Beatles had even supported Channel on 21 July 1962 at an Epstein-promoted concert at the Tower Ballroom, New Brighton. Backstage, Lennon briefly met Channel's harmonica-player Delbert McClinton. Rumours persist from that moment on that John learned how to play the instrument from Delbert. That's untrue. He'd been playing for some time already. But it's teasing to conjecture that they perhaps traded tips in harmonica-technique. Around the same time, with a synchronicity that would only become apparent later, across the Atlantic, the Beach Boys' first national release through Capitol records, 'Surfin' Safari', was climbing the chart. Issued on 4 June 1962, it finally peaked at *Billboard*'s no.14 during October. For the early sixties, according to Greil Marcus, 'rock 'n' roll was a waiting game'.

The Beatles play a short tour of Scotland, from Elgin *Two Red Shoes* (3 January 1963), the Dingwall Town Hall (4), the Bridge of Allan Museum (5), and Aberdeen's *Beach Ballroom* (January 6). The year starts out with the Top Twenty safely topped by Cliff Richard ('The Next Time' c/w 'Bachelor Boy'), unseated by his backing group The Shadows

('Dance On'), then by ex-Shadows duo Jet Harris and Tony Meehan ('Diamonds'). But by the year's mid-point, everything has changed, irrevocably, forever. Overnight, established chart stars were rendered obsolete. Since 'Move It' in 1958, and since 'Apache' in 1960, Cliff Richard and the Shadows had dominated the UK pop scene. Suddenly – although The Beatles were similar ages, and two of The Beatles were actually older than they were – Cliff and the Shadows were suddenly out-moded, relegated to the past. Their talent and ambition ensured they'd continue having hits, and maintain an audience, virtually through to the present day, but never again, after 'Please Please Me', would they be the happening thing.

'Please Please Me' was not a great tune, admits Brian in *A Cellarful of Noise*, 'but it was an exciting new sound.' At the time, there were something like three different pop charts published simultaneously, and Derek describes the problems of accurately determining the true chart position in a feature for *KRLA Beat* (14 April 1965). As he points out, there was a chart in *Melody Maker*, another in *New Musical Express*, and a third in *Record Mirror*. They didn't always tally. In fact, they seldom agreed. Sometimes a favourable placing could depend on the advertising spend the label devoted to the paper in question. It was far from an exact science. And it leads to complications on 'pop Quiz' pub nights. Some, the *NME* for example, claim 'Please Please Me' was the first Beatles no.1. *The Record Retailer* chart – also used by *Record Mirror*, and subsequently the database for the compilation of the various Guinness chart books – says differently. It records that 'Please Please Me' peaks at no.2 (28 February 1963), one place behind Frank Ifield's yodelling 'Wayward Wind'. Which means that, according to that version of history, a few months later, EMI's second Epstein group, Gerry and the Pacemakers' version of that same rejected 'How Do You Do It?' significantly out-sold The Beatles. Gerry knew exactly how to exploit the song's innuendoes all the way up all three charts, beating The Beatles by becoming the first 'Mersey' disc to actually reach the no.1 position (4 April). Lennon 'was pleased, and a bit annoyed', insists Gerry cheerfully.

Others smartly jump the trend for beat-groups. Adam Faith recruited The Roulettes – who include a future member of Argent – to provide his backing, then discovered talented new songwriter Chris Andrews, and managed to extract another year of hits from the formula. Johnny Kidd and the Pirates, who had once recorded the classic slice of British rock 'n' roll 'Shakin' All Over' but had been virtually hitless ever since, happened across the beat-styled writing of Gordon Mills and found themselves returned to the Top Ten, while the original Mersey star, Billy

Fury, adopted a strident guitar figure for his 'Do You Really Love Me Too (Fool's Errand)' hit, with more than a hint of Billy J Kramer about it.

On 22 January 1963, The Beatles studio-record their *Saturday Club* debut at the London *Playhouse Theatre*. A long-running radio institution chaired by a very dignified, immaculately precise Brian Matthews. It was broadcast four days later. Among the songs they chose was Gerry Goffin and Carole King's 'Keep Your Hands Off My Baby', a recent hit for Little Eva. The track eventually turned up three decades later on *The Beatles: Live At The BBC* (1994) double CD, for which Derek Taylor would write the insert booklet notes. There are sixty-nine tracks in total spread across the two CDs, showing the full range of material the group could spontaneously draw upon.

Like student painters, they'd spent years copying the early masters and learning their craft before attempting to write songs of their own. And some of those original songs were here, including ones that they never actually got around to recording themselves, such as 'I'll Be On My Way', previously only a B-side for Billy J Kramer and the Dakotas. But there was also a host of old rock 'n' roll covers, from Elvis ('That's All Right Mama' and 'I'm Gonna Sit Right Down and Cry Over You'), Chuck Berry of course ('Carol' and 'Too Much Monkey Business'), The Shirelles ('Baby It's You'), Buddy Holly and the Crickets, The Coasters, Arthur Alexander, Carl Perkins, Little Richard... an amazing breadth of material. A pool of songs built up over the years working raucous Reeperbahn bars and rowdy Liverpool clubs, but a repertoire they could draw on in a moment. 'I've been playing "roll Over Beethoven" for twenty-eight years', George tells Alan Freeman on-air. Many of those songs were held in common by the Mersey groups. 'Some Other Guy', done by The Beatles, was also a favourite by the Big Three and recorded by the Searchers and Freddie and the Dreamers. A precise 1:40-minute version of 'Hippy Hippy Shake', done here by The Beatles, was also recorded by Billy Fury, and taken high into the charts by the Swinging Blue Jeans. According to legend, group leader Ray Ennis sent his friend Sue Johnston into NEMS to buy a copy of the 1959 Chad Romero original so they could sit around the record-player and learn the lyrics. The same Sue who would later appear as an actress in *Brookside* and *The Royale Family*. The lyrics, once they'd studied and memorised them, were nonsensical. Contrived to catch yet another fleeting dance-craze. Not that it matters. The lyrics to 'Twist and Shout' were just as silly. All that was required was that they convey a level of unrestrained excitement. It was only later that lyrical content would assume any degree of meaning.

An Arthur Howes-promoted package-tour opened on 2 February 1963 with teenage star Helen Shapiro topping the bill. Danny Williams and Kenny Lynch were also listed on the posters. The Beatles play the opening support slot. Rock history tells us that The Beatles introduced the British audiences to American R&B and Motown, yet Helen had beaten them to it by covering the Miracles' Smokey Robinson hit 'Shop Around' before The Beatles had even tried out for Decca. The Beatles originally wrote 'Misery' – a track on their debut album – as a song for Helen to cover. After her producer Norrie Paramour turned it down on her behalf, Kenny Lynch, who had taken note of the song during the shows, cut his own version, taking the liberty of lyric-changing it into a more personal expression. For Kenny, 'I've lost her now for sure, I won't see her no more' becomes 'I've lost you now for sure, I won't see you no more.' He'd already scored chart hits with 'Mountain of Love' (1960), 'Puff' (1962), his cover of The Drifters' 'Up on the Roof' (1962), and 'You Can Never Stop Me Loving You' (1963). His amended version of 'Misery' became the first A-side cover of a Lennon-McCartney song, although it didn't chart. Kenny went on to become a significant writer, for the Small Faces, among others, and as a popular comedian.

But acts that Brian Epstein had signed now dominated the charts, and had switched around the very concept of what a pop star looked like, sounded like, acted like. The Beatles, of course. But also Gerry And The Pacemakers, bagging three consecutive no.1s at nose-bleed inducing speed with their first three singles. Billy J Kramer with The Dakotas, three number ones, two of them Lennon-McCartney compositions. I was one of six-million viewers to tune into ABC-TV's *Thank Your Lucky Stars: Summer Spin Liverpool Special* at 06:05 on Saturday, 29 June to celebrate the triumph of the Epstein stable with The Beatles, Gerry and the Pacemakers, The Big Three, and Billy J Kramer with The Dakotas, as well as other Merseysiders Lee Curtis, Kenneth Cope and the Breakaways, and the Vernon Girls.

With obvious pride, Brian Epstein writes about Gerry Marsden as a singer 'with a smile as wide as he was short, a huge generous personality and a fascinating voice full of melody and feeling.' George Martin had travelled up to Liverpool on 12 December 1962, to follow up on Brian's enthusiasm. He saw Gerry performing at an under-fifteens dance at the Birkenhead *Majestic Ballroom*, his guitar played chest-high, enabling him to simultaneously watch his fingering, and maintain eye-level contact with his audience. George was suitably impressed.

Gerry Marsden was born 24 September 1942, and with drumming older brother Freddie (born 23 October 1940) came up through the usual Skiffle route. They formed The Mars Bars – Mars as in Marsden – in the naive expectation of acquiring sponsorship from the confectionary company, only to receive warnings of litigation instead! Nevertheless, they play the *Wallasey Grosvenor Ballroom* alongside the Silver Beatles as early as 6 June 1960 and go on to serve the Hamburg apprenticeship circuit. They recruit solid ex-bank clerk John 'Les' Chadwick on bass. Then, to provide the Fats Domino-Jerry Lee Lewis rock 'n' roll keyboard authenticity, pianist Les Maguire joined. He might look one straight-clean step on from smiling Russ Conway, but together, they became Gerry and the Pacemakers. Not only performing regularly on bills with The Beatles at all of the legendary Liverpool haunts but, in June 1962, becoming the second signing to NEMS. Unlike just about every other act in the Epstein stable, Gerry never filched from Lennon-McCartney, although – according to Gerry himself, his pal John offered him 'Hello Little Girl', which he turned down. For Gerry, the only real Mop-Top's song-connection lay in The Beatles' rejected studio demo of 'How Do You Do It?'.

Passed over by The Beatles, Brian gave Mitch Murray's chart-topper-to-be to Gerry. Although their debut album-title *How Do You Like It?* (1963) conflates the titles of Gerry and the Pacemakers' first two no.1s – the second being 'I Like It' – the album itself features neither of them and only contains a trial run for their third, the anthemic 'You'll Never Walk Alone'. With one eye on the pre-Beatles logic of expanding your career into adult-friendly all-round entertainment, Gerry had gone back to the 1940s song which had already been translated into a rock-era context by Gene Vincent, Conway Twitty, Roy Hamilton and Johnny Preston. The Broadway show-tune had been a Pacemakers' stage crowd-pleaser for a number of years, but it was following the song's favourable reception while touring that they re-record it more ambitiously. In a three-way dialogue between Gerry, Epstein and George Martin, the strings were added.

The rest of the album (with its carefully-posed fun-cover of Gerry using his guitar to tug-of-war with the Pacemakers) consists of a mildly toe-tapping grab-bag of then-current pop-rock covers, the best being 'The Wrong Yo-Yo' and 'Chills'. The album was followed by Gerry's time-capsule soundtrack for *Ferry 'Cross the Mersey* (1965), the movie created from a story by Tony Warren (who devised *Coronation Street*), and the cinematographer Gilbert Taylor (who Richard Lester had used for *A Hard Day's Night*). Derek filed an affectionate report on the film for *KRLA Beat* (10 March 1965). The full twenty-six song soundtrack listing was pumped up by including a guest-contribution from Cilla

Black ('Is It Love?')... and one from the Fourmost ('I Love You Too'). With an ear-to-ear grin, Gerry had broken through with catchy pure pop, but on album tracks such as the group's version of the Johnny Kidd and the Pirates' speciality 'A Shot of Rhythm and Blues', they prove they can do raucous too, while Gerry's ability to perform poignant ballads such as 'I'll Be There' indicated there was more to come. Asked by a BBC-TV interviewer 'what has Brian Epstein meant to you?' Gerry promptly replied 'Money'... before hastily adding a more tactful qualification.

Then there's Billy J Kramer with the Dakotas. They, again through the George Martin catalyst, take the languidly slow 'Do You Want To Know A Secret?' from that first Beatles album, speed it up, cutely shape it into a more pop-friendly artefact, and it charts all the way up to no.2 (30 May), one place below 'From Me To You', which – on this chart at least – is now The Beatles own first chart-topper. Elsewhere, as if to iron out these irritating inconsistencies, at the rival *New Musical Express* chart-desk, both 'Please Please Me' (2 March) and 'Do You Want To Know A Secret?' (1/8 June) take it all the way to the no.1 slot. But try explaining that to your pub pop Quiz host. Yet the fact is – The Beatles, they're still on a learning curve. They're still noting what George Martin had done. Tightening. Accelerating. And how the sales figures were responding.

Epstein also had the Fourmost, and Cilla Black (previously Priscilla Maria Veronica White of Liverpool's notorious Scotland Road), all charting strongly. A 'stable' of stars even more successful than Larry Parnes had been able to assemble. Bigger than Jack Good who controlled ITV's pop-music content through his *Oh Boy* show. Bigger than Joe Meek's eccentric DIY record-industry. During these early months, Brian Epstein never took a wrong step. Smarter than Colonel Tom Parker would ever be, he controlled what needed to be controlled contractually, legally, through merchandising and promotion, so creating a firm environment in which the group could simply concentrate on absolute creative freedom. Through Derek's writing, Brian explained how 'The Beatles have always been happy to leave timings, plots, plans, schemes and the development of their careers to me because they were good enough to trust me.'

Even the Searchers, a Liverpool four-piece from outside the enchanted Brian Epstein circle, were up there scoring a no.1 with 'Sweets For My Sweet', a speed-version of the old Coasters hit. In *Fabulous* magazine, 25 January 1964, Brian Epstein considered his achievements so far and mused that if he could retrace his steps and add just one more Liverpool group to his stable, it would be the

Searchers. Their no.1 was dislodged in turn – in a kind of Liverpudlian pass-me-on – by 'Bad To Me', another Beatles composition, by Billy J Kramer with the Dakotas. Stack up seven 45rpm singles onto your Dansette autoplay, flip the arm across to hold them in place on the central spindle, watch them drop one-by-one onto the turn-table below, the stylus arcing across to fall gently onto the play-in groove. There's the anticipatory electro-crackle. Each of these singles are recent purchases. Each of them from new northern bands; if it's not the Swinging Blue Jeans or the Merseybeats, it's the manically prancing Freddie and the Dreamers.

Complacent London showbusiness moguls, the baffled record industry old guard who had been contentedly serving up a smug diet of safe American-sourced pop music, where shaken rigid by this Northern Uproar, led by the suave elegant unlikely manager with his penchant for silk scarves and cashmere overcoats. Suddenly, industry talent-scouts, scheming agents, money-making showbiz czars and venal opportunistic spivs who yesterday would be pushed to be able to locate Liverpool on the map were booking their train tickets and heading north. As well as Epstein's Big Three, Decca signed the Clayton Squares, Lee Curtis and the All-Stars, Freddie Starr and the Midnighters, and the Dennisons. Philips or its subsidiary Fontana grabbed the Merseybeats, Earl Preston and the TT's, Ian and the Zodiacs. While, as well as the Searchers, Pye signed the Undertakers, Johnny Sandon and the Remo Four, plus black vocal group the Chants.

Some two-hundred singles would be unleashed from Liverpool 'popular Beat Combos' over the next few years, most of which would stiff, and the groups would be dropped as quickly as they were signed. There's a pervasive myth that, somehow, The Beatles created the Mersey scene. That it was only in the wake of their phenomenal success that other Liverpool groups began to come together and form beat combos, eager to replicate their national breakthrough. Numerous writers have taken and reinforced that line. Yet the opposite is true. The phenomenon known as 'Merseybeat' had always been essentially a live thing. Captured on the Big Three's *Live at the Cavern* EP, it snares something of the atmosphere. Or by a series of opportunistic recordings made by the small Oriole label done at the Cavern under live conditions (1963), later salvaged onto the Edsel *This Is Mersey Beat* (1989) CD compilation.

As with any 'movement', the closer you examine its supposed participants the less they admit to a shared aesthetic or seem to have much in common. At its best, it was a furious collision of naïve enthusiasm for imported American R&B and early rock 'n' roll, performed with more energy than their fairly inept technique. Predominantly four-piece – bass, rhythm, lead and drums – The Beatles were able to utilise Paul's left-handed guitar to create a unique visual effect the others couldn't imitate. Yet, as Bill Harry points out, 'this image tends to make people forget just how extensive the range of the music scene in Liverpool was, there were duos, trios, quintets, and groups with pianos and saxophones in their line-ups. Girl-groups too, such as the Liverbirds.'

Technology and economics play their part. A beat-group is a self-contained entity. Amplification – albeit crude compared with what was to come – enabled the four-piece line-up to operate viably. Drums, rhythm guitar, lead and vocal harmonies, offer sufficient scope for depth and variation to enable a repertoire of numbers. It became a highly mobile unit conveyable from engagement to engagement – from gig to gig, in a Thames van, the forerunner of the Transit, in ways that the cumbersomely expensive Big Swing Bands never could. When songwriting became the norm, as it did over the following few years, operating in-house on The Beatles' model, it completed the evolution. The movement even had its own vocabulary. Pop groups became 'Beat Groups'. They played 'Beat Sessions' at 'Beat Clubs'. Once it went national, the press adopted the title of Bill Harry's fortnightly paper for its generic name. Once a scene has a label, it fundamentally changes. A label limits what's happening deems some people in and others out, alerts the money-minded to the idea that there's cash to be made, tells the mainstream that something's happening it should know about. And – just like that, the scene is invaded, changes, moves on, and eventually dies. But briefly, with a dazzling incandescence, Mersey Beat held youth transfixed. Yet it was an unstable compound, never integrated enough not to disintegrate.

Television – a medium only a few years older than rock 'n' roll itself – still insisted on treating pop music and its followers like unwanted children. But, irritatingly for the hierarchy, it was popular, so there were audiences to be won – so long as its stars watched their mouths. Like an over-protective parent, TV was super-moralistic, behind the times to the point of being reactionary… but omnipresent. It couldn't risk causing offence. So The Beatles guest on the 16 May 1963 edition of the children's *pops and Lenny* show, broadcast live from the Shepherd's Bush Empire, compered by ventriloquist Terry Hall and his loveably floppy puppet Lenny the Lion. Lenny was an unlikely lion insofar as his stage persona was shy, gentle and lisping with a high-pitched voice and a slight speech impediment. His catch-phrase 'Aw, don't embawass me' was delivered with a cutesy paw covering his face, endearing him to audiences. The Beatles perform 'From Me To You' and 'Please Please Me' before joining the hosts for a raggedly 'embawassing' rendition of 'After You've Gone' (The Beatles were not alone in colluding with the TV 'variety' format, the rolling Stones perform their Arthur Alexander cover 'You'd Better Move On' on a February 1964 *Arthur Haynes Show*). Over on BBC-TV, Lance Percival and Kenneth Cope fronted what might have been the first-ever Beatles spoof on Saturday night satire show *That Was the Week That Was*, a re-worded 'From Me To You'. Even Bob Monkhouse, in his BBC-TV sitcom series as a rather desperate media hustler, feels the need to satirise the Beat Boom. He asks a morose northern group, meant to be representative of the new thing, 'What have you got in the Top Ten?' 'The top nine' comes the laconic reply. It even infiltrates TV soapland, as a *Coronation Street* plot-line has Dennis Tanner becoming manager of failed beat-style rocker 'Brett Falcon'. The spin-off single, 'Not Too Little, Not Too Much' by Chris Sandford, makes the charts as high as no.17 in December 1963.

By September, all these elements come together into one furiously contagious single – 'She Loves You', a song sketched out in a Newcastle hotel room and demoed acoustically to George Martin, who had doubts about what he considered to be the 'old-fashioned' high-point 'yeah-yeah-yeah' harmony-split. I remember the first time I heard it. Hunched up into a listening booth in an electrical retail store off King Street in Cottingham. From that first pounding drum intro, it is incontrovertibly evident that this is a moment to equal the assassination of some sleazy Archduke in Sarajevo, or the Presidential motorcade winding through Dallas towards its appointment with destiny at the grassy knoll, this is Hiroshima Moon-Landing stuff, both the Berlin Wall going up – and then being torn down – in one seven-inch vinyl disc. This is history in the making; this is the very stench of all things future revolving at 45rpm.

Through the medium of the book Derek ghost-wrote for him – *A Cellarful of Noise* – Brian Epstein pinpoints the date precisely to 31 October 1963, with The Beatles flying in, to an ecstatic welcome home from a five-day promotional trip to Sweden. For Brian, it was his moment of realisation just how big the thing had become. 'Beatlemania descended on the British Isles in October 1963. It happened suddenly and dramatically and we weren't prepared for it.' The statistics of it all, even today, remain staggering. That's when they'd gone from playing ballrooms for comparatively small fees, when it was still possible to watch them without fighting your way through tides of screaming girls.

The Beatles had earned £3 ($9) for each of their *Cavern* appearances. That's £3 divided between the four of them. It eventually rose to 75/-. Elsewhere they might score as high as a collective £15 for a gig. And then suddenly, their UK record revenue for the first sixth months of 1963 topped £6 million, with seven-million records sold throughout the year. Sales of their sheet-music topped its respective chart for nineteen weeks, copyrights that earned Dick James and Northern Songs Ltd over a million pounds ($4 million) during 1964. For the first time, the mainstream press was all over them. For the first time, they'd ceased to be just another pop group, and become a phenomenon. A household word in everyone's household.

Welcome, to the greatest rock 'n' roll story ever told...

Chapter Five: 1963: With The Beatles

I Read The News Today, Oh Boy...

Words. Derek grows them for a living. He was, above all else, a hack at heart, ink swilling in his veins. It is not necessarily a glamorous profession. What a writer leaves is their words. What that comes down to is books that remain in print, are read, reviewed, discussed and argued about, for a number of months, or perhaps years if they're fortunate. And can then only be located through the dusty shelves of secondhand bookshops, or through online book-search agencies. Or mouldering mounds of yellowing magazine back-issues, most of them binned within a week, some carefully hoarded by obsessive collectors, others shrink-wrapped at an escalating price-tag by specialist dealers. The crisp new smell of ink on paper. Then the aroma of ageing newsprint.

Southern writer William Faulkner wrote 'the past is not dead. In fact, it's not even past'. Afterwards, even decades afterwards, critics, musical and social historians, TV documentaries and nostalgia retrospectives construct earnest and meaningful theses on what all these events mean, what it was all about, where it came from, what its origins were, what it represented in this, that, or the other sense. Then, there was no self-knowledge; no self-awareness of place or history. There was only instinct. There was only the immediate potential of a now that might not last, could all end tomorrow, and had to be seized while it lasted. Nothing else mattered. The Beatles became teenagers when the teenager was suddenly something to be, when teenage emancipation was big news. They had their heroes, Little Richard, Jerry Lee Lewis, Chuck Berry, Lonnie Donegan, Elvis Presley, Smokey Robinson, equally inarticulate performers who offered their own version of escape into a more intuitive place.

Brian Epstein had his opera and classical music. Derek also liked opera, visited classical concerts at the Liverpool Philharmonic Hall, and owned 78rpms of Italian castrati singers. In a later retrospective he claimed, prior to that eventful June 1963 concert, that he'd never even heard of Roy Orbison (in *KRLA Beat*, 9 June 1965), which seems difficult to believe. But with a wider perspective, 'it doesn't matter whether it's The Beatles or Ibsen or Gilbert & Sullivan or Pinter or Mahler... I think it is absolutely vital for our survival that we have this great well of music and drama and laughter and song to fill our boots, to wash away our pain, to renew our psyche.'

The fans screamed because there was no other way to articulate what they were feeling. Just as the equally dumbfounded journalists had yet to formulate a vocabulary sufficient to deal with it. When it came to polite family entertainers or even deconstructing the complexities of a jazz solo, they had an established critical thesaurus to draw upon. But rock 'n' roll was different. Even the supposedly specialist music press was forced to fall back on inept clichés of 'swinging beat' or 'rock-a-ballad'. Writers with the one-note perception and empathy to see, and identify with what was happening, and with the skills to express it in print were few and far between. But even for 'one-note' actors, there's always someone out there looking for that one note.

Derek Taylor was one such writer. He was sharp enough to see what was happening. And perhaps even something of where it could lead. Within a brief but seismic twelve-month period, Brian Epstein had become the most important figure, not only on the British music scene but in the history of the British Music Scene. NEMS represented a big deal, with a string of noughts attached to it. His stable of acts now dominated the domestic market, a status that had satisfied the limited-ambition low-achievement aspirations of previous management teams, but Epstein believed – firmly and absolutely – that his artists had the potential for more. As Derek would explain in *A Cellarful of Noise*, Brian regarded the careers of 'me and my Beatles' as a series of stages. First, the recording contract – 'this, to us, was the greatest thing that could happen.' Then the first record. Followed by the first no.1 – 'there could be, we believed then, nothing more important or dramatic or thrilling than to be number one in the British record charts.' Each achievement opened up the next level of expectation. Brian was not prepared to accept any restrictions whatsoever. And he was soon to translate those ambitions into global dimensions. To Tony Barrow, Epstein's 'approach to business was scrupulously open and painstakingly meticulous. He looked after the interests of his singers and musicians to the best of his ability and with complete honesty. Being a workaholic with no romantic relationship to steer him off course he devoted his entire attention to looking after the acts on his management roster and providing them with the best possible environment in which to enhance their careers.'

Yet conversely, back in Liverpool, the pop Gold-Rush was already over. Far from igniting an explosion in the number of Merseyside bands, the success of the Epstein stable more likely resulted in a near-extinction event. The Beatles themselves had already polarised opinion by what was locally perceived as their three betrayals; they'd dumped their leathers for smart suits at Epstein's behest, they dumped Pete Best for Ringo Starr, and they'd more or less deserted their regular venues for the national big-time. 3 August 1963 marked the last of their 274 gigs at *the Cavern*. Then, after the 1964 high-water mark, new groups from Liverpool – no matter how good – had become personae non-gratae. But as the first wave of Liverpool beat groups was losing its pop momentum, an overspill effect from the Mersey Sound was inaugurating a make-over renaissance of the city's image and culture. If Billy Fury had once sought to disguise his warm treacle-thick scouse accent, The Beatles had made it 'fab'. Overnight, it had become trendy. And talent in the city didn't so much dry up, as mutate.

On 1 January 1962, BBC-TV launched its new weekly cop series – *Z-Cars*, a gritty evolution on the cosy old *Dixon of Dock Green* model, and the Ford Zephyrs that furnish its identity call-sign cruise around the suburbs and council estates of Seaport and Kirby Newton on a thinly disguised Merseyside. 'We were as famous as The Beatles, we were', insists Brian Blessed (PC 'Fancy' Smith). The series' strongly northern documentary-realist true-to-life dialogue was scripted by the likes of Alan Plater. The Swinging Blue Jeans make a guest appearance in one *Z-Cars* episode. Strange, too, to consider that before embracing a viciously right-wing Thatcherism, cocky former Dovedale Primary School pupil comedian Jimmy 'Tatty 'Ead' Tarbuck was seen as part of the vibrantly emerging Merseyside sub-culture. He wore a Beatles fringe and used cheeky Beat-Club sketches – 'You dancin'?', 'You askin'?', 'Then I'm dancin'!' – delivered with sharp regionally observed put-downs – 'Who knitted your face and dropped a stitch?' Madcap hamster-eating Freddie Starr also started out singing for the Merseybeat group Freddie Starr and the Midnighters.

While poets Brian Patten, Adrian Henri and Roger McGough were figure-heading a live poetry revival that happened between the beat clubs, the *Streates Club* or the *Crane Theatre*. Their Penguin anthology prominently name-checked 'The Mersey Sound', while adding its own distinctive voice to its collective experience, its red-drenched collage cover juxtaposing images of pop-screaming girl-fans with dock-fronts and Liverpool city landmarks. Their lyrics were pop-friendly in a way that poetry had never been before, and perhaps never has been since. As Patten says, 'when in public, poetry should take off its clothes and wave to the nearest person in sight.' Theirs is a poetry that does exactly that, and was fine-tuned to a pop-Art awareness of advertising, comicbook, and TV-culture, colloquially integrating it all with perceptive scouse wit, street-romance, and surreal absurdism.

'Angel-headed' Brian Patten had quit school at fourteen to work for his local newspaper. Adrian Henri, born in Birkenhead, wrote 'Mrs Albion You've Got A Lovely Daughter' in a mangled Allen Ginsberg tribute, including lines about those 'beautiful boys with bright red guitars, in the space between the stars'. An artist too, he wrote verses in which 'white birds would wrench themselves free from my paintings and fly off dripping blood into the night.'

And while Adrian Henri's Liverpool Scene albums achieve a degree of subcultural presence, Roger McGough – who's poetry already looked forward to a time when he would be 'one-hundred-&-four/ and banned from *the Cavern*' – took it further into Henri's dream of 'poets (who) get their poems in the Top 20.' By joining forces with Mike (McGeer) McCartney to form the Scaffold performance group, they not only escalate into the charts in their own right but provide the scally-anthem for Carla Lane's TV debut *The Liver Birds* (from 14 April 1969). Again, the setting is Liverpool, with girls-about-town Beryl and Dawn's – later replaced by Sandra's – flat-share located on Huskisson Street in Liverpool. Carla goes on to also locate her next project, *Bread*, on Merseyside, initially provoking some local enmity with its portrayal of the Scoucer Boswell family, Catholic DHSS scroungers, before it too works its way into the nation's affections. Paul and Linda McCartney guest in a series four episode broadcast on 30 October 1988.

Others became unwitting beneficiaries of the realignment. John Buchanan succeeds Arthur Brittenden as editor of *The Daily Express* and quickly realises the paper was onto a good thing. It might be a temporary fad, but the 'Liverpool Sound' constituted very much a geographical switch, shifting the nation's cultural centre-of-gravity decisively away from London. Towards the north. And Derek's near-Liverpool origins make him its natural ally. There was a strong northern angle that he's uniquely positioned to exploit. So when the press become curious about the enigmatic former-retailer behind the mop-top haircuts, and begin seeking exclusives, when Derek lobbied to do a story on Brian Epstein, Buchanan further indulged his showbiz correspondent.

They meet and talk, with Derek as warm and chatty as ever. The interview extended, at some considerable length. The interview was published, to Epstein's immense approval, taking Derek another vital step into The Beatles' enchanted circle. There had been an immediate mutual respect. And rapport. Derek's first impressions were that 'were it not for his buckled shoes and the royal blue initials on his shirt,' Brian 'could be in shipping or cotton.' He playfully extends the idea.

Brian could be working in a 'bank, with an eye on the managership.' But within a notoriously tacky industry rife with what Epstein calls 'jealousy, dissatisfaction, sharp practice', his honesty of purpose is clear. He tells Derek that 'I want none of it.' The favourable profile closes with Derek quoting Brian's appraisal that 'whatever happens to popular music, whatever happens to beat groups, The Beatles are in the business for life.'

Newspaper offices were different creatures in 1963. You catch a glimpse of what it must have been like to work at *The Daily Express* offices in Val Guest's impressive fantasy movie *The Day the Earth Caught Fire* (1961), in which its journalists report the on-coming heat-death of the world due to unwise nuclear testing that has altered the Earth's orbital path. It was shot in the paper's actual Fleet Street HQ with former editor Arthur Christiansen playing himself, with Leo McKern and Janet Munro, plus a brief cameo from Michael Caine as a policeman ushering crowds out of the city. You enter the *Daily Express* offices, across the mosaic crusader-logo on the foyer floor. As the journalists write-up their stories, there are no terminals or flat-screens. Instead, you clack-click-clack your copy in with a heavy Remington typewriter. No Tipex. You make an error you use the eraser, or you xxxxx it out for speed. At the end of each line, the carriage pings, and you yank the return lever back. The paper you wind into the platen, or the rejected sheet you crumple into a ball and lob at your colleague at the next desk, is not A4, but strange shapes with names like Foolscap, Crown or Imperial. You use crinkled blue carbon-paper if you need a copy, with the mildly intoxicating spirit-duplicator aroma wafting from the hand-crank Gestetner in the corner.

Overhead there's a sign with a prompt-list – 'IMPACT: Get It In Your First Sentence! Get It In Your Headline! And In Pictures – Most Of All!!!' The copy you've typed bearing these guidelines in mind is subbed down and flecked with proof-reader marks by the sub-editor, then carried physically downstairs to the composing room where compositors in khaki overalls transpose it into lead type. Either nimble-fingering it from open font-trays into 'sticks' with justifying lead spaces. Into neat rows in galleys of grey type. Or keyed into Linotype slugs from where it becomes the curved lead rotary formes for printing on the huge presses that smell of grease and printing inks.

During September 1963, some time before The Beatles first American trip, George Harrison used his new-found cash flow to visit his sister in Benton, Illinois, bringing back 'stories that made the mind leap of the size and scale of the place, the fast-food and the drive-in movies.'

Louise had married an American in July 1954. So it was a useful double-opportunity to renew his long-distance family connection. And to reconnoitre the American market. He found it not encouraging. In November, Brian Epstein took Billy J Kramer to New York on a further exploratory foray into the American market. As Derek's *A Cellarful of Noise* tells, they were received as 'people of no great importance,' and Brian was reduced to chasing up vague industry contacts as 'in the early days, as in London in 1962.' He sought out the Vee-Jay record label because they'd done a reasonably good job promoting Frank Ifield. He had more success with TV talk show host Ed Sullivan, who had happened to witness Beatlemania first-hand while his flight home was held over in London. Aware of the scale of what was happening outside America, he was more open to persuasion. All that was necessary was to haggle over the billing, Brian holding out for – and eventually getting – the top guest-slot on Sullivan's top-rated show.

Before their first American trip, The Beatles were booked for a series of shows in Paris, a one-off at the Versailles' *Cinema Cyrano*, followed by a residency at the *Olympia Theatre*, commencing 16 January through to 4 February. It was another market that had yet to yield to their charm. A vast UK press-raft crossed the channel to write-up this imminent cultural collision. But *The Daily Express* had a head start on the opposition. Derek had been following the group's explosive ascent since that first encounter had jolted them into his consciousness. Following a number of subsequent exclusive interviews and concert reports, he'd built up a closer relationship with them. For Brian Epstein, Derek's status as drama critic, as well as his Italianate good looks, provided a further catalyst. The rapport he built up with Brian during this period would later stand him in good stead.

John Buchanan hatched an idea. Why not push Derek's tentative contacts further? Why not introduce a Beatles guest column into the Friday edition? A guest column Derek could write? The project was an enticing one, although Derek little realised where it would lead. But which Beatle? Derek suggested George. The group's 'Dark Horse'. So 'Buchanan and I proceeded to draw up a draft proposition,' and scheduled a meeting to put it to NEMS.

Situated in Liverpool's Moorfields, 'a charming little street near Exchange Station,' Brian's office was located above a novelty magic shop called *The Wizard's Den* where you could buy everything from 'a horror-mask to a joke spider'. Once there, the two newspapermen explained they were inviting a Beatle to 'write' a running 'diary' for their northern edition, or rather, the Beatle would lend his name to the regular weekly column. Only a Beatle would not write it. Derek would write it. 'Oh, why?' asked Brian. 'Because Derek knows what the reader wants', argued Buchanan. 'Eppy' accepted the logic, he thought it was a useful idea; he was already drawing up marketing strategies for his charges next career-phase. The 'diary' would provide a deliberate opportunity for George to grab his share of the limelight.

'It will be nice for George', Brian told Derek. 'John and Paul have their songwriting and Ringo is – ah – rather new.' And he'd remembered the name of the *Express* journalist who had written that very positive review from Manchester some six months earlier. The journalist who had conducted the flattering interview published shortly afterwards. Brian had singled out the name and kept it on file. As a potential ally within the national press. So yes, Derek Taylor could ghost-write 'George's Column'. All that remained was to talk terms. Brian laid down the ground rules. They haggle over the fee. Buchanan bid £50 – more than Derek earned for a week's graft. Brian grudgingly countered £100 (although it was subsequently renegotiated up to £150).

The original intention was for George to read through whatever Derek had already prepared, with the right to approve or disapprove as he felt appropriate. Something deemed perfectly OK for most ghosted showbiz columns. To this end, Derek set to work on a closely-typed two-page draft article. He wrote it in 'Articulate Scouse As She Is Spoke' with 'motives tossed in from a newspaperman's ragbag of stereotypes.' He talked over some general background with George, did a little research, but wrote it 'without consulting him much about the content.' Discovering that George's father had been a Liverpool bus-driver, he started out by using the routine journalistic enlivening-technique of fabricating an imaginary conversation in which father-Harrison tells his son 'don't worry about me, son, you stick to your guitar and I'll carry on driving the big green job.' It was a perfectly acceptable invention in the usual star biographies of the time, adding a personal family-touch to the story; the kind of 'Raymond Jones' device that crystalises and focuses a rather more drawn-out process.

Once typed-out and read-through, Derek took the train down to London to deliver it to Brian's Belgravia flat at Whaddon House. Again, there are differing accounts of what happened next. In the first, Derek was invited to read it out loud to the assembled Beatles themselves. An intimidating proposition. But after he'd 'passed the test' by reacting well to the resulting laughter, George's thorough critique of that first column turned it into a collaborative effort between the two. In Derek's account (in *I, Me, Mine*), George merely read through the typescript, quoting bits out loud, commenting encouragingly 'that it wasn't all bad, but there were ways of putting it right, for instance… and another thing, and then this and that.' And it developed into a collaboration from that point. George providing the stories, Derek polishing and structuring the prose. That degree of hands-on involvement says something. First, what was fine for other showbiz columns, was not fine for The Beatles. They cared about what went out bearing their names. Secondly, 'if a chord is struck between two people, then you soon find out if you both know the same tune', according to George. The column launched at the end of 1963 when The Beatles were already two albums and five singles into their career. It was also the beginning of an enduring relationship between George and Derek that would continue through The Beatles story, and into the years beyond.

He got to know them before the global madness and its attendant security requirements took over. And coincidentally, around the same time, Derek was becoming a little restless with his career, as he wrote, he was 'no longer a watchdog, and lacking the curiosity and fear of failure which prompted him once to kick doors down, he would be a useless man to any newsdesk nowadays…'

Andrew Loog Oldham also claimed a walk-on PR role in The Beatles story around this time, before transferring his attentions to the rival attractions of the rolling Stones. An ambitious nineteen-year-old hustler of Anglo-Dutch parentage, he'd already served time with Larry Parnes and boasted names like Don Arden and Mary Quant prominently – if dubiously – on his CV. A self-proclaimed 'terrible user and a thief', he happened to meet Epstein on the lavish Birmingham set of ABC-TV's *Thank Your Lucky Stars* (13 January 1963) – a weekly pop showcase introduced by Brian Matthew (The Beatles' second-ever national TV performance had been on a *Tuesday Rendezvous* edition of the same show broadcast on 4 December 1962). They were telerecording an edition of the show that would be broadcast on 19 January, miming to what would constitute the TV premiere of 'Please Please Me'. But Billy Fury was the show's star, performing his dramatic single 'Like I've Never Been Gone', and Oldham was there promoting the current hit 'Go Away Little Girl' by his client, winsome balladeer Mark Wynter. Yet when he saw The Beatles, he instantly recognised career-advancement potential. And instead, he seized the opportunity of gaining access to them. He wangled his way to meet Epstein in the dressing room throng, speed-jived him and managed to extract a £25-a-month retainer as NEMS auxiliary publicist, envisaging unlimited one-to-oneing with what was already becoming the biggest act in the biz.

But Brian had other ideas. Oldham found himself relegated to working for Gerry and the Pacemakers and Billy J Kramer; not quite what he'd had in mind, but he hung around long enough to establish his credentials, and when a journalist's tip-off led him to the Station Hotel in Richmond where he witnessed an altogether darker and more intense R&B, he recognised the distinctive scent of the next big thing. The rolling Stones. There are tales that he took his find to Epstein to work out some kind of funding sponsorship. But Brian wasn't interested. He had enough on his mind already.

So Oldham gambled on going it solo while covering himself by luring The Beatles down to bestow their seal of approval to his find. The scam succeeded better than he could have envisaged. To Derek, The Beatles 'gave a sparc hit to the rolling Stones.' With the Stones' big-lipped skinny-hipped artful gawkiness and strategic moodiness applied to a barely-completed sketch of a new song – 'I Wanna Be Your Man', giving it a hard, aggressive guitar-driven treatment that took the band into the Top Twenty for the first time (their debut single, covering Chuck Berry's 'C'Mon', had stalled at no.21). Ringo's version of 'I Wanna Be Your Man' on *With The Beatles* (November 1963) is an altogether more easy-going jog-along affair. The link was both invaluable in granting the Stones that first step into commercial consciousness, and an enduring source of vexation to Mick Jagger across the years. The fact that the Stones needed to be the recipient of such a helping hand from what they considered their equals, their rivals. In the spoof documentary *The Rutles: All You Need is Cash* (1978) some decades later, Jagger cameos knowingly about how the fictional Rutles came down to see the early formative Stones, and how they'd offer him a song. With smirking relish, he grins, 'it was rubbish'. It was revenge at last. Oldham already saw the Stones as the anti-Beatles. If Epstein could make a million by taking four scruffy ruffians and turning them into nice 'safely dangerous' guys, if he could take four horny louts and disguise them as pretty friendly boys in cute tight trousers, Oldham could do the same by taking four (or five) nice guys and turning them into loutish ruffians.

Meanwhile, at precisely 18:36 the evening of New Year's Day from 1963 into 1964, disc-jockey Jimmy Savile introduced the first-ever edition of BBC-TV's new music programme *Top of the pops*, broadcast from a converted church on Dickenson Road in Manchester. The first band on-screen were the rolling Stones, kicking off proceedings by playing their new hit 'I Wanna Be Your Man', which stood at no.15. The show closed with a film-clip – the precursor to the pop video – of the week's no.1, 'I Want to Hold Your Hand' c/w 'This Boy', issued with UK advance sales of 950,000. It eventually became Britain's best-ever world seller with ten-million copies sold globally. But The Beatles were also at no.3 with 'She Loves You'. Other Brian Epstein acts on the charts that same week included Gerry and the Pacemakers ('You'll Never Walk Alone' at no.16), Billy J Kramer ('I'll Keep You Satisfied' at no.21), and the Fourmost ('I'm In Love' at no.32). In addition, the novelty record 'All I Want for Christmas is a Beatle' by comedienne Dora Bryan hovered at no.24, while Bern Elliott and The Fenmen's version of 'Money', powered by the song's inclusion on the *With The Beatles* album, was at no.19...

Yet some remained unconvinced. There was a large mocking single-panel Giles cartoon in a January 1964 issue of that same *Daily Express* showing excited teens queuing to see the new kids on the block, the Dave Clark Five, the new faddy sensation with what they were calling 'The Tottenham Sound'. The punchline was that The Beatles were already overtaken in teen-taste terms, already has-beens, over the hill, with the old collarless Beatle jackets already relegated to trend-history. To some, The Beatles-boom was a fad that wouldn't survive the transition of the year. For teenagers, lacking such a parental perspective, today was the only present that mattered.

Meanwhile, Brian had neglected to pick up the option on the rolling Stones, not that it mattered. He already had more wealth and social status than he'd ever dreamed of, to indulge his extravagant taste for suites at the best hotels, gourmet food and wines, and clothes from the finest Savile Row tailors. While Andrew Loog Oldham went on to style himself the 'Godfather of Hype'. To Derek, writing later in his weekly column for *Disc*, it's 'nice to see Andrew Oldham still reserves the right to speak his mind. I agree with most of his views. Like Brian Epstein – and unlike the bulk of the malevolent men behind the pop scene – he knows precisely what's going on and why...'

'Only A Northern Song...'

In his excellent and densely-researched history *Shout* (1981, Pan MacMillan), Philip Norman states that The Beatles were 'not in any sense political or subversive', which has to be disingenuous. They were northern, perceived as working-class, with a playfully irreverent attitude to the very idea of authority. After all, the scouse gene is something you carry with you. It may not have been their intention to be political, but they were. Theirs was a mocking disrespect, rather than outright hostility. But their active years together covered a spontaneous combustion of British society, and the effects of that conflagration are still smouldering, still very much with us. Those years – what Derek called 'the noisiest interlude in the history of entertainment' – altered the social fabric of the nation. Politicians argue the blame and the benefits of its legacy. For those years, The Beatles, above all other names, symbolise those changes. The Beatles were together seven years; less time than U2 or REM. Oasis was a performing and recording unit for longer than The Beatles. The Bootleg Beatles tribute band was working for twice as long as their template's entire career. It was a way-briefer time-span than Elton John or Rod Stewart. Yet seismic years.

Timothy Leary claimed that the first nuclear tests form a firebreak in history, a quantum leap in the nature of the human culture. Those born after the detonations are different from those born before. He had a point. But perhaps it was the social convulsions of World War II itself that formed the watershed, culminating with Hiroshima? Whatever, when people agonised over what they defined as the irreconcilable generation gap, that's what they meant. There had been the Beat Generation, the bebop-fuelled Beatnik hepcats of the late-forties into early-fifties. An American import to be hunted out in obscure bookshops and specialist record shops by cognoscenti. Then there were the Angry Young Men, insurrectionary writers, regional, largely northern and perceived as working-class.

The 1950s north you read about in Stan Barstow's novel *A Kind of Loving* (1960), or see in Karel Reisz's movie adaptation of Alan Sillitoe's dirt-real *Saturday Night and Sunday Morning* (1961) portrays the limited life and random loves of Vic Brown in fictional Yorkshire and frustrated Nottingham factory worker Arthur Seaton. Reviewing the premiere of John Osborne's *Look Back in Anger* (in *The Observer*, 13 May 1956), critic Kenneth Tynan says it 'presents post-war youth as it really is... all the qualities are there, qualities one had despaired of ever seeing on stage – the drift towards anarchy, the instinctive leftishness, the automatic rejection of "official" attitudes, the surrealist sense of humour... the casual promiscuity, the sense of lacking a crusade worth fighting for.' He closes by declaring of this new breed, 'they are classless, and they are also leaderless.' Their shock-effect permeates literature, movies, and infects styles of TV drama, breaking down conventional formality and deference. The Angry Young Men are poised between conflict and consumerism, with a high degree of intuitive left-political awareness – but also lured by the frivolous desire to flood the dance halls and espresso bars.

Billy Liar (1959) was a novel created by another provincial journalist,

Keith Waterhouse of the *Yorkshire Evening Post*. Taken from its West End play adaptation, the 1963 movie stars Tom Courtenay as the 'Walter Mitty'-style Daydream Believer Billy Fisher, who uses his vivid power-fantasies to escape the claustrophobic dullness of his northern life, and talks of moving to London to take up a job offer writing scripts for comedian Danny Boon. As the film closes, he gets the chance of realising his dreams by heading south with his ambitious girlfriend Liz – played by Julie Christie. But at the last moment, on the rail-station platform, he chickens out. She goes to London. He stays with his parents in their terraced house in fictional Stradhoughton – which is actually Bradford. Not that Derek Taylor was ever a *Billy Liar* character. Even in West Kirby he was 'dreaming of the great beckonings beyond and the Big Time beloved of so many provincial imaginations.' But like the groups of the Epstein stable, when his own decisive moment on the rail-station platform arrived, he didn't flunk the opportunity. He slipped the surly bonds of provincial journalism with scarcely a backward glance.

Mersey Beat had made Liverpool, in a phrase Derek borrowed from Allen Ginsberg, 'the centre of consciousness of the human universe,' which couldn't help but take on political dimensions. After decades of BBC 'presenters' with plummy accents, to hear voices on the radio or TV with northern accents was, in itself, a thrilling shock. Like some teenbeat replay of the 'Fall of the Roman Empire', it saw the northern barbarians storming the gates of soft southern over-civilised London. When Brian asserts – in *A Cellarful of Noise* – that Cilla Black 'is warm and natural and frank and this may be far more important than protocol', he's saying what we now take for granted. Not so back then, when the tiresome demands of protocol persisted.

Derek Taylor, who recorded the quote for Brian, was part of that northern eruption, part of the working-class inundation trashing the citadel of the established order. He might not have considered himself that way, but as he travelled south to participate in the phenomenon, that was exactly what he was. The metropolitan intellectual self-styled elite who ran the London literary scene treated the northern uproar as a strange new species. Something to lionise, and patronise. Humphrey Lyttelton lamented that once The Beatles headed south down the motorway, it signalled the final nail in the moribund coffin of trad jazz as the teenage music of choice. Failing to notice that its transition merely shifted the focus from the authentic replication of one style of black American music – Dixieland – for another – R&B.

It's also easy to forget just how resented The Beatles were, in certain circles. How despised. There was a time, lest we forget, when pop was trivial low-brow music for empty-headed teens, it was not 'serious' music worth serious consideration, when the mere mention of The Beatles could send the most eminent classical and/or cultural critic into paroxysms of despair at the state of the world. Back then, the reliably curmudgeonly Paul Johnson wrote of 'the bottomless chasm of vacuity' revealed by The Beatles, with the barely disguised disdain of those who mistake their own dull prejudices for cultural superiority, and described their fans as 'the least fortunate of their generation, the dull, the idle, the failures...' This was nothing less than a cultural, and generational war.

There's a comic confrontation in *A Hard Day's Night* as The Beatles share a train-compartment with cantankerous old duffer Richard Vernon – as the ex-officer named in the script as 'Johnson'. Ringo turns on his transistor radio. Johnson angrily turns it off. During the argument that ensues, Johnson protests 'I fought the war for your sort...'. Ringo retorts, 'bet you're sorry you won!' He may well have been correct. But overnight the city-gent and his value-system had become an anachronism. This was a meeting of mutual incomprehension between two irreconcilably ruptured generations. The soporific singalong sentimentality of Dame Vera Lynn, the reverence for Churchill, the tragedy of a khaki generation whose defining moments were the Blitz and forgotten campaigns with irrelevant names like 'Anzio' and the 'Dardenelles', had seemingly been reduced down to comic-strips and monochrome films for light entertainment. In opposition to the insolent shrug of a generation who cared little or nothing for the tragic sacrifice and loss of their desperate crusade against the most monstrous forces of tyranny in history. All their greatest fears reduced to comic cliché.

Ringo might not have written the riposte. The script was by Liverpool playwright Alun Owen – who had already written *The Ruffians* (BBC-TV, 1960) and *No Trams to Lime Street* (ABC-TV, 1959, with the musical remake in 1970). But it catches the attitude exactly, The Beatles' nasal vocals, their sharp scally quips. The values of patriotism, deference, respect, have become legitimate targets. What Edward Heath, from the Tory side of the opposition benches, wistfully called the 'death of deference'. Everything the Angry Young Men had threatened to be, but with catchy hooks and a radio-friendly backbeat. Labour Prime Minister Harold Wilson may have claimed The Beatles as his 'secret weapon', but their effect was more fundamental than that.

While the effect of the movie was setting up new equations. Johnny Rogan, in his epic *The Byrds: Timeless Flight* (1980), writes about how

Jim McGuinn, Gene Clark, Michael Clarke and David Crosby, by then collectively known as The Jet Set, religiously attend a screening (of *A Hard Day's Night*), and how it shocked them into the realisation that 'hard rock could have style'. They even 'took careful note of the instruments that The Beatles played.' David Crosby recalls a vision of the future unfolding before their eyes, and how he came out of the movie-house so enthused and energised by it he found himself swinging around a lamppost at arm's length shouting 'YES!' And McGuinn traded in his banjo for a twelve-string electric guitar the following day, a move spoofed in his own 'So You Wanna Be a rock 'n' roll Star' step-by-step guide as 'just get an electric guitar, and take some time, and learn how to play.' Elsewhere the fast-cut movie sequences were rewriting the visual grammar of pop. The promo film-clip, predecessor to the video, would never again be a static thing performed by a group line-up to camera. And the entire career of the Monkees has its origins here. Presiding over their madcap TV-capers were what Micky Dolenz called 'the four kings of EMI sitting stately on the stair' (in his Monkees-song 'Alternate Title')…

Chapter Six: 1964: Eight Days A Week

Beatles For Sale...

The Beatles are history. Quite literally. The incidents we are talking about happened decades ago. That's a galaxy a long, long time away. Generations have been born and matured during the period between, technologies have created lifestyle revolutions, and then been superseded. Yet the basic four-piece rock band template has not varied a great deal, and what The Beatles created has retained a contemporary ever-renewing relevance through each of those decades. Of course, The Beatles didn't invent the four-piece rock-band line-up, the amplified self-contained songwriting/performing unit. But they made it obligatory. We take this for granted. The fact that anti-musicians are still going around posing rock as a revolutionary stance, as if it were still alive, must be one of the great curiosities of our age.

It wasn't always so. The main justification for a biographer recovering what has already been so thoroughly covered is the 'telescope effect'. Look through the instrument one way, and the subject under examination is so close you feel you can touch it – but you can't see it whole. Spin the telescope around, and it's crystal-clear but distant. Passing time has much the same effect. Being up close to your subject can be a liability for a biographer. Has there ever been a good biography written by a spouse? But distance, in time as well as place, adds useful perspective.

Bookmark that date when Derek Taylor first saw The Beatles – May 1963. And instead of projecting forwards towards today, project it back across that same space of time. Use 1963 not as a full-stop, not as punctuation, but as a pivot. A mere ten years before he saw The Beatles – in 1953 – there was no such thing as rock 'n' roll at all. The term had yet to be minted. There were black 'Race' records sounding something very similar, there was Fats Domino in New Orleans, there were Country Music outfits with a rockabilly backbeat, and there was Hank Williams, but the final fusion – and the seismic catalyst of Elvis Presley – had yet to happen. Only ten short years. But a different world.

Take it back further... two decades this time, to 1943, and it's an even stranger world. A planet consumed by the flames of global war. With nothing remotely resembling the rock 'n' roll format. Big Swing Bands feature smooth crooning vocalists, with sweet close-harmony vocal groups. There was radio, although even rock's technological support-structure – amp systems, electric guitar, multi-track recording – had yet to be devised. TV was so scarce it was a science fiction concept. Yet all those changes had happened across just twenty years.

In 2003, we were four decades on from 'She Loves You', but if we go back an equal slab of time – to forty years before that date – to 1923, the entire music industry as we now accept it, did not exist. Jazz was making its upstart presence felt. There were big pizza-sized 78rpm shellac records, but the biggest-selling consumer-format was sheet-music, scores you play yourself. It's all a matter of scale. Because this is the length of time, we're dealing with. At the turn of the millennium, into the twenty-first century, the fact that the complete Beatles CD back-catalogue was there at Borders, HMV and Virgin megastore – and had never been out of print – was something weird. That it's now less than a click away, is something we take for granted.

In 1963, it seemed that everything that mattered about music began with rock 'n' roll. Nothing of any interest had occurred in music before Elvis walked into the Sun Records studio and cut 'That's Alright Mama'. That was year zero. That's when history began. Yet now we happily listen to, and replicate variations of music that not only our parents, but our grandparents grooved along to; is that curious, or is that curious?

9 May 1963, American falsetto star Del Shannon played the Royal Albert Hall on a bill with The Beatles. He was already a big star. He'd been having major hits since, topping the trans-Atlantic charts with 'Runaway'. A big guy, with vaguely Vulcan ears, he was intrigued to find that the UK music scene had been transfigured in the brief period since his last promotional visit. And he was smart enough to see that there's something real going on here. He sought them out. Allowed them to persuade him to record a Lennon-McCartney song. Back in the States, Del's version of 'From Me to You' achieved the first chart-placing for a Beatles song, making the Hot 100 as high as no.77 in July.

With his 'George Harrison' column running in *The Daily Express*, Derek Taylor was in Paris on 16 January 1964 as part of the contingent of British journalists. But the response was muted the morning following The Beatles' debut at the Olympia. Hispanic singer Trini Lopez was also on the bill. His drummer – Mickey Jones – would later play with Bob Dylan's electric band on the legendary 'Judas' tour. And wherever he toured, Mickey took home movies. He was sufficiently impressed to grab colour footage of The Beatles' performance. Silent, but it catches some of the atmosphere. George Martin and future-wife Judy were there, he oversaw the recording of 'She Loves You' and 'I Want to Hold Your Hand' in German. Later, eating lunch in a discrete restaurant with photographer

Dezo Hoffman and Derek Taylor, they got a buzz from Brian Epstein. They promptly return to the George V hotel, near the Champs Elysee, where the entire contingent had taken up residence.

'Brian was there', Hoffman recalled to Philip Norman. 'He was sitting on a chair and The Beatles were sitting on the floor around him. He said the news had come through that "I Want to Hold Your Hand" was number one in the *Cashbox* American Top Hundred. The Beatles couldn't even speak – not even John Lennon. They just sat on the floor like kittens at Brian's feet.' The celebrations that followed were unprecedented, photographer Harry Benson snapped The Beatles' triumphant pillow-fight, and Brian Epstein celebrated to the extent of allowing himself to be photographed with a chamber-pot on his head!

Although it wasn't necessarily planned that way, to be caught up in such phenomenal events was to prove significant for Derek. He was getting to be known and trusted. The bond with George had been instant, and would prove to be enduring; he was 'elder brotherly' to George. 'France was always a curious market for you', he observed to George. Yes, but it has 'always been a strange market for pop', emphasised George, 'they're very fond of their own artists.' But 'you did pretty well at the Olympia', Derek counters, 'I remember it was quite wild there.'

John, wearing his thick hornrimmed glasses offstage, was wary, initially more suspicious, 'caustic John, who was really nothing of the sort.' Derek soon observed The Beatles were 'late risers and late to bed', and it was during a drunken evening together that the issue with John was explained and resolved. Derek details the story in *Anthology*, about how they were in the bar together, 'just him and me,' the last of the entourage still up, and naturally they'd already had a few drinks when the conversation took a difficult turn. John accused Derek: 'Are you pretending to be from Liverpool or something?' Derek parried, it's true his family had moved to Manchester, but 'I don't know about pretending, I am from Liverpool.' John persisted, 'yeah, born in Manchester.' 'Well, that's a narrow way of looking at it. At the moment I live in Manchester. A lot of people are not born where they happen to live later. I was born in Liverpool, lived in West Kirby, my wife's from Birkenhead.' Once it was firmly established that he wasn't from Manchester 'and therefore useless', once that misunderstanding was out of the way, the conversation unravelled in a variety of pleasant directions 'in an extremely wholesome sort of way... none of which I remember, because we did get very drunk together.' 'I enjoyed that night a lot', he concludes.

Now accepted by John too, more togetherness sessions follow. They would 'stay up on pills and drink.' It was, as Derek explained, 'the kind of friendship that men have when they are drinking together, whatever that means!' Paul still stood politely back a little – 'suspicious of journalists', although 'we have a lot in common, both Merseyside grammar school boys, different ages, but we sort of fitted. Later, Derek would send Paul press primer bulletins headlined 'Stray Thoughts And Trivia from Fleet Street's Finest.' 'Isn't life great?' – in Derek's own words. 'Yes. Sometimes it really is.' As yet, he didn't know Ringo at all. Ringo was 'smoking a great deal, saying very little.'

1964 seems as long ago as 1864. But this is the day the Earth really caught fire. Nothing that happened subsequently could ever equal the events of these few months. These moments would never resonate again. Not in the same way. Because it was happening for the first time. Each new generation would still push their pop stars up the charts with their own unique excitements. But the first time only ever happens once. A few weeks later, on Friday, 7 February, the four-cornered unit that was The Beatles boarded PanAm flight 101 from Heathrow to New York. Despite the growing bond he was developing with the group, *The Daily Express* didn't send Derek with them – Paris was one thing, but there were budgets to consider, and they already had a correspondent out there, David English.

So Derek stayed home and watched the events unfold on TV. They were inescapable. At Kennedy International Airport, George emerged from the plane first, then John, and Paul, with Ringo bringing up the rear. They were stepping into bedlam. And into history. This should not be important. It was a pop group. Although The Beatles didn't look like any pop stars American girls had ever seen. There were more significant events happening on that day All those screaming girls would soon just as enthusiastically be screaming for the rolling Stones, Herman's Hermits, and the Dave Clark Five. But yes, of course, it's important. Those black-&-white newsreel images would be re-screened so frequently, recycled at every flashback opportunity, that they've become iconic. So familiar they've become cliché. So of course, yes, it was important. To Derek, The Beatles 'painted a new rainbow right across the world, with crocks of gold at each end, and some...' This was the beginning of that rainbow. These were events that overnight ratcheted pop celebrity up to another, higher level of cultural awareness. One that had not existed before, but which would become inescapable from this moment on.

Although they were technically part of the same EMI family, Parlophone and US Capitol shared little synergy. The complacent American label had no great enthusiasm, or even awareness, of what they had. After all, their music industry existed to shift product to the world through its global subsidiaries, not the other way around. History passes down a general impression that The Beatles heroically triumphed against the entrenched forces of a massively insular American music industry. One which makes the US success of 'I Want to Hold Your Hand' c/w 'I Saw Her Standing There' – with sales of 4,900,000 – revelationary on every level. But this is not an idea exactly borne out by a little research. The year immediately prior to The Beatles' break-out saw the *Billboard* charts topped by the Japanese-language Kyu Sakamoto in June, and the Belgian French-language Soeur Sourire, The Singing Nun in December. Neither of them could be considered obvious hit contenders; both were foreign acts who won out against home-grown opposition.

But what The Beatles brought was more than just a catchy one-off hit-tune such as 'Sukiyaki' or 'Dominique'. What they brought was an entire package of music, style, fashion, lifestyle and attitude. Fortuitously, that package extended to include other music apparatchiks who shared its defining characteristics. Including PR men. The Beatles follow-up visit, on a ten-day turn-around, led off with three loss-leading coast-to-coast telecasts on Ed Sullivan's Sunday-evening TV-show – going out live on 9 and 16 February. Unsmiling Ed Sullivan – a Richard Nixon look-alike, had already proved himself a sympathetic pop host, vital in launching Elvis nation-wide. He would later do the same for the Byrds, the rolling Stones, The Mamas and the Papas, Sly and the Family Stone, and the Doors. But his Beatles trilogy of shows would go down in history, as a planet-shifting event. The first one attracted 73-million viewers. Georgia Brown and Tessie O'Shea – also on the bill – were virtually overlooked. Most of the audience-tickets went to the kids of TV bigwigs, but the Broadway cast of *Oliver* were studio guests, ironically including 'Artful Dodger' Davy Jones, who had transferred from the West End production and would later replicate Beatlemania as part of the Monkees. The Beatles performed an opening set in the first half – 'All My Loving', 'Til There Was You' and 'She Loves You'. Then a reprise of 'I Want to Hold Your Hand'.

The Maysles Brothers' docu-DVD *The Beatles: The First US Visit* (1991) catches all the fine details of the tour. As the shockwaves spread, The Beatles travel by train up to Washington DC for a show 'in the round' at the Coliseum (Tuesday, 11 February). Snow is on the streets. There's a photo-opportunity in Central Park. Paul does his 'it's wonderful to be here, it's certainly a thrill' stage announcements, using his funny accents – northern gruff or pseudo-nob. Ringo is filmed dancing at the *Peppermint Lounge*. New York WINS deejay Murray 'the K' Kaufman gatecrashes the party as the self-styled 'fifth Beatle' ('Do you remember Murray the K, Alan Freed and high-energy?' ask the Ramones many years later on 'Do You Remember rock 'n' roll Radio?'). There is looning in the Plaza hotel, and antics on the train which were recognisably the same as those scripted for them for *A Hard Day's Night*. While George improvises an acoustic 'Blowin' In The Wind' Dylan-pastiche along the lines of 'Singing Guitar Blues'. Through to what Brian – through Derek's words – called the 'sprawling appalling' Embassy reception in Washington.

And – unseen on-screen – Cynthia Lennon travelled with them, for the first and last time. She phoned home every day to enquire about baby Julian, still less than a year old. The second Sullivan show was an on-location special coming from the Miami Deauville Hotel – where they got to meet Muhammad Ali (who was still Cassius Clay) for a celebrity photo-shoot, with Harry Benson snapping them being KO'd by the champ in domino effect, and they perform 'From Me to You', 'This Boy' and 'All My Loving'. Finally, back up in New York, from CBS-TV's Broadway Studio 50, drawing 150-million viewers, they were watched across America doing 'Twist and Shout', 'Please Please Me' and 'I Want to Hold Your Hand'. They were unleashing the tsunami of Beatlemania, from a local into a global phenomenon.

Other singles rapidly follow the breakthrough – via labels Brian had hopefully negotiated one-off deals with. 'Twist and Shout' c/w 'There's A Place' (on Tollie), 'Please Please Me' c/w 'From Me to You' (Vee-Jay), which had initially been ignored. By 4 April, The Beatles held the top five positions on the US chart. They also had fifteen discs in the Top 100, while 60% of all discs played on the US airwaves were by The Beatles. By January 1966 – in little over two-and-a-half years – they had total global sales of 150-million singles (counting an LP as six singles). This constitutes the biggest sales for any artist in history over such a comparable period. Brian Epstein's vision had been vindicated, beyond his wildest dream, even if – for the first time – he sometimes feared he was losing control of the situation. For the first time in a generation, Britain was the best at something. Cricket Sonny Curtis humorously suggested, on his single 'A Beatle I Want to Be', that they'd conquered America because their fringes meant people couldn't see the whites of their eyes!

By the time The Beatles left the States on 21 February, heading for a mob-welcome in London, and for seven concentrated weeks of filming, they had irrevocably altered the rules of the rock 'n' roll game. As a jobbing Folkie, 'Papa' John Phillips recalled 'by February the music industry was jolted by a sound – a force – that would alter all of our careers. It was a song called "I Want To Hold Your Hand". With little more than two minutes of electric rock music, The Beatles had virtually ended the era of commercial acoustic folk music.' In another part of town, Jim McGuinn began singing Beatles songs at *The Troubadour*. Bob Dylan was taking note too, to him 'they were doing things nobody else was doing. Their chords were outrageous, just outrageous, and their harmonies made it all valid.' To poet Philip Larkin, The Beatles had become 'unreachable, frozen, fabulous...', entering generational mythology. Steven Spielberg produced a 1978 movie called *I Wanna Hold Your Hand* – the directorial debut of his protégé Robert Zemeckis – using an affectionate comic eye to follow some New Jersey high-school kids coming up to New York to grab a glimpse of The Beatles as they visit for *The Ed Sullivan Show*. Although this delightful evocation of Beatlemania bombed at the box office, it led to Zemeckis going on to success with *Forrest Gump* (1994).

Beatlemania. To Derek 'it spread – and quickly – from the screams at Kennedy Airport into every State of the Union and into almost every state of mind.' And, a matter of months later, Derek became the natural choice to assist Epstein when the deadline approached to deliver on an agreement he'd made to write his autobiography for Souvenir Press. So ghost-writing *A Cellarful of Noise* became Derek's first commission for NEMS, even before he had technically left Fleet Street – in the days when Fleet Street was still Fleet Street, the undisputed centre of the newspaper realm. By now his conflicting loyalties – to the *Express*, and to The Beatles – were stretched to breaking point.

There was the earlier example of Ernest Hecht, a Czech-born publisher sharp enough to capitalise on the teen-explosion of the pop market. Where others still denigrated its ephemeral sub-literate frivolity, he'd made a killing by bringing John Kennedy's Tommy Steele biography into print, and followed it with *It's Great to Be Young* (1961), the Cliff Richard life-story, while simultaneously ensuring a wide readership-spread by controlling spin-off serialisations and foreign rights. Impressed by Hecht's efficient persistence, and seeing a genuine opportunity to enhance himself into a more durable form of history, Brian accepted a £2,000 advance to be the subject of the Souvenir Press' third title. After all, Brian Epstein was an extraordinary phenomenon in his own right, the elusive Svengali and arch-manipulator of the greatest movement in rock 'n' roll. Surely he had a remarkable tale to tell? Yet Brian had then prevaricated for months before taking the project on to its next stage.

Partly, this delay was due to work pressure, but also due to the sensitive question of lining up a suitable ghost-writer. Someone not only with the correct literary skills but also attuned to the required mindset. Various names had been considered and rejected – Godfrey Winn, Tony Barrow, Tony Stratton-Smith or perhaps even Beverley Nichols? Then – on inspiration, why not Derek Taylor? He had no previous experience writing to book-length, but there are other, more important factors. There was mutual trust. So Brian extracted a sheet of NEMS notepaper, headed 'The Finest And Most Efficient Management / Direction Of Artistes in The World', and made out an offer to Derek of £900 – with £250 of it as an up-front advance. This would all come out of the total £2,000 advance Brian received from Hecht. But time was still at a premium. Access would be limited.

Brian began by attending a Cilla Black recording session. He'd found a song for her to follow-up the no.1 success of 'Anyone Who Had A Heart'. He sat in as she worked her way through the early takes of 'You're My World'. Then he met up with Derek. Together they drove down to the Associated-Rediffusion studio set to watch from the side of the soundstage as a slick Billy J Kramer with the Dakotas ran through a session for TV's *Ready Steady Go*. The easy swing of 'Little Children'. When they were whisked from the studio there was a chauffeur-driven car waiting for them, to take them down the A38 to the hotel.

The process began – from Friday 3 to the 8 April, with Derek interviewing Epstein as they were holed up over a single weekend at the Imperial Hotel in the posh resort of Torquay, spooling it all into a big Grundig reel-to-reel tape recorder. The tapes became the basis for the book, which Derek later 'refined' into print over a few frantic weeks, working on the run, adding linking passages imitating Epstein's own voice. Diana Vero Palmer, Brian's secretary, recalls how she 'worked with him [Derek] closely during April 1964, typing while Derek dictates.' The book succeeds in maintaining an equilibrium that is both reticent about Brian's sexuality, while also forming a strangely honest self-portrait of a complex and enigmatic figure.

In the prologue, Brian (through Derek's ventriloquism) considers, 'it occurs to me that I'm going to be asked why in the midst of a busy life I should take time off from the personal management of my artistes to whom, after all, I have signed myself, to write my own autobiography when I'm not yet thirty. It is simply that I wanted to put down at an early stage an accurate account of the emergence of The Beatles and other artistes from my own point of view. So much has been said that is exaggerated, inaccurate, extravagant, and open to misinterpretation that I thought that a detailed account could only help and, I hope, prove of considerable public interest.' A later paperback edition was star-blurbed 'The One Essential Beatles Book' and, if anything, it's that which tends to unbalance the slim 119-pages. Something equally true of much of Derek's own subsequent writing.

Derek Taylor was never the central character of his own writing. He wrote about the stars, the artists, the creative people in whose orbits he moved. He made them the focal point. Seeking a glimpse of Derek himself, it is necessary to peer between the lines of text to find the writer. So does that mean he lived his life in shadows? He is the 'Zelig'- character, who can be glimpsed standing behind The Beatles when they do a press conference; he's momentarily there in a Beach Boys video; he's the presence behind the Byrds; the ghost behind Brian Epstein. He provides the thread of continuity, the link between the scenes, reflecting back the times. But if he existed in their shadows, everyone who grew through that era did so within those same giant shadows. He was merely closer than most. He – and Brian – obviously identified The Beatles-connection as the book's major selling point, and stress that connection to the detriment of any other factor. There's plenty about the group, and perhaps not enough background material on Brian Epstein himself. Something that is equally true, in his later works, about Derek. It's as though they feel that the reader's attention can only be maintained by returning to The Beatles on a regular basis. This is an accusation that is apparent all the way from *A Cellarful of Noise*.

To the furtherance of such ends, what Derek calls his 'pot-boiler' opens with 'Chapter One: Beatles USA', before doubling back to 'Chapter Two: Beginnings', drawing on the open and candid conversations in Torquay to paint an affectionately sympathetic portrayal of this most mercurial of interlopers, the most vital influence on the first formative phases of The Beatles story. Taking it from Brian's shy and withdrawn middle-class childhood, through his troubled school years. Relating how he was a reluctant scholar at seven schools, and 'had a rotten time in all of them.' At Beaconsfield, a Jewish Prep School near Tunbridge Wells, he made friends with a little horse called Amber 'who got on very well with Jews,' but academically excelled only in art and drama.

On 10 September 1950, Brian reluctantly reported for duty at the family furniture store in Walton for £5 a week, channelling his design ambitions into window-dressing. He took career-breaks for the army,

and – as the original 'Cracked Actor' – spent three terms at the Royal
Academy of Dramatic Art in London, but – repelled by its phoniness
and hypocrisy – he retreated to the safe haven of Liverpool. In 1957,
aged 23, he reimmersed himself in the family business, arranging
for singing star Anne Shelton to open the record department of its
new city-centre Charlotte Street branch. The sales performance of
Harry Belafonte's 'Mary's Boy Child', the year's massive Christmas
seller, got the department off to a runaway success. He got Anthony
Newley to open a second branch of North End Music Stores (NEMS),
in Liverpool's Whitechapel in 1959. It's here the narrative picks
up momentum, with an intensification of the rhythms of daily life,
conjuring seductive myth from the solid foundations of history.

By way of comparison, Sam Phillips was deliberately looking for
Elvis Presley. Even before he had ever heard him sing, long before he
had clapped eyes on him for the first time, he had the idea of 'Elvis
Presley' in mind. He already had the exact specification, the 'if I could
find a white man who had the negro sound and the negro feel, I could
make a billion dollars.' Elvis was simply the fulfilment made flesh of his
preconception. Brian Epstein was not like that. He knew that his life
was incomplete. He knew that he was restless, dissatisfied. He knew he
was looking for… something. But he never imagined for a moment that
his deliverance would come in the form of four disreputably charming
louts with more ambition than skills.

Socially ill at ease, the young Brian had made the Whitechapel
venture a surprise success, until the department was (according to
A Cellarful of Noise) 'running like an eighteen-jewelled watch', at
least in part due to his pride in delivering on customer enquiries.
Destiny intercedes when Brian follows one such enquiry made by the
mythic eighteen-year-old from Huyton. Unable to locate the German
import 'disk' by that curiously named group, he notes on his pad 'The
Beatles. My Bonnie. Check on Monday'. Tracking the record down
to its German distributor he rapidly sold out every copy he bought-
in. Intrigued, his further investigations led him to the *Cavern Club* in
nearby Mathew Street, Liverpool 2 – the titular 'Cellarful of Noise' –
which was less than a hundred yards from his store. Just 250-footsteps.
The Beatles happen to be playing a lunchtime session.

It was just after 12:30 pm on 9 November 1961. Brian took his
assistant Alistair Taylor with him. Alistair (no relation!) Had joined
NEMS in response to a 1960 ad in *The Liverpool Echo*, and would
continue to be a long-term part of The Beatles' story. They paid their
one shilling entrance fee and descended the eighteen steps into

the dank basement club, an 'unpleasant dungeon… black as a deep grave, dark and damp and smelly.' The Beatles were on stage; John Lennon (then aged 21), Pete Best (20), Paul McCartney (19), and George Harrison (18). Later, two of the Merseybeats who happened to be there – Tony Crane and Billy Kinsley – recalled how much older Brian seemed than the rest of the crowd. Epstein was 27. And he was transfixed by the four 'ill-presented, unkempt youths with untidy hair,' the hair that reminded him of the Peter Pan statue in Sefton Park – and his life was transfigured. Just five songs were enough – including 'Shout' and 'Hello Little Girl' – to convince him of their 'very considerable magnetism.' The first Beatle he spoke to was George. Alistair and Brian then retreated to the more civilised *Peacocks* where they talked over what they'd seen. And the possibilities. This is the primal detonation out of which would coalesce all of those shining new galaxies and bright constellations of vivid supernova stars. And yet all of this has occupied *A Cellarful of Noise* only up to page 47, across the space of a mere two chapters…

And Bill Harry also contests even this neatly concise interpretation, contradicting the version that Derek's writing has bequeathed to rock history. Instead, Harry recalls how, months before these events, NEMS had agreed to stock the debut issue of *Mersey Beat*, and how Brian took a personal interest in the paper from the very start. How the second issue (dated 20 July 1961) devoted its entire front page to The Beatles' Hamburg recordings with Tony Sheridan for Bert Kaempfert, under the splash-headline 'Beatles Sign Recording Contract!' with an accompanying group photo inside taken by Astrid Kirchherr. Brian had bought advertising space and even got himself appointed the paper's record reviewer.

From issue no.3 (dated 3 August 1961) he contributed a column headed 'Stop The World – And Listen To Everything In It', with the by-line 'Brian Epstein of NEMS'. His first column talks about the musical *The Music Man* (which includes Paul's solo *With The Beatles* track 'Till There Was You'), and Anthony Newley's 'Stop the World, I Want to Get Off' (the same Newley who had guest-opened Brian's store). His second column extends the scope into covering more mainstream chart music with Elvis, Chubby Checker and Acker Bilk. With these articles and reviews sharing pages with Beatles stories in subsequent issues. During one of Bill Harry's product drop-off visits, Brian even commented favourably on one feature penned by Bob Wooler in the 31 August issue. Yet in *A Cellarful of Noise*, Brian claims 'I had never given a thought to any of the Liverpool Beat groups then up and coming in cellar clubs. They were not part of my life.' How could Brian not have been aware of The Beatles? Paul McCartney, in his *Many Years From Now* autobiography, supports Bill Harry's alternative version of events.

Yet it seems the story Derek wrote is so neat and precise that other writers since, faced with choosing between the truth and the legend, opt to go with the legend. 'My Bonnie', with 'Ain't She Sweet' and a batch of other songs had been recorded during the same 22 June 1961 session with producer Bert Kaempfert at the Hamburg Friedrich-Ebert Halle – producing a single, eventually issued in the UK by Polydor 5 January 1962. Cut for a one-off payment, yet the tracks would return to haunt The Beatles across the years. With Polydor subsequently finding themselves with the rights to rare masters by the biggest band in the world, they rush out 'My Bonnie' as by Tony Sheridan & The Beat Brothers c/w 'The Saints' – which had previously been available only in Germany. It reached a UK no.48 (6 June 1963). Then 'Ain't She Sweet' c/w 'Nobody's Child' – the B-side of which doesn't even feature The Beatles, and neither side available previously anywhere. It equalled its predecessor's success in reaching no.48 (11 June 1964). The American market proved even more responsive with 'My Bonnie' reaching no.26 (7 March 1964), and 'Ain't She Sweet' – with its strong John Lennon lead vocal – climbing all the way to no.19 (1 August 1964).

Tony Sheridan (Andrew Esmond Sheridan McGinnity) was an ex-*Oh Boy* rocker who found himself playing the Hamburg clubs with The Beatles standing in as his occasional back-up band. The potential of the combination was brought to the attention of Kaempfert who set up the recording session, resulting in the strange trove of titles. There were two further singles taken from the sessions, 'Sweet Georgia Brown' (which may or may not feature The Beatles) c/w 'Take Out Some Insurance on Me, Baby' (which certainly does). Then 'Why' – Tony with The Beatles – c/w Paul and George's intriguing composition 'Cry For A Shadow', with Beatlesque screams submerged in an otherwise Shadowsesque instrumental. These, with the addition of other titles of disputed provenance, would be issued in various formats across the following decades.

Eventually, three of the tracks – including the punning Hank B Marvin-parody – would be ushered into the official Beatles canon, with the release of the first *The Beatles Anthology* CD. The group had been, according to Derek's liner notes, 'four teenagers with no more than eight O-levels between them, running and biking and busing and busking all over Liverpool in search of new chords and old guitars, a half-decent drum-kit and any gig at all.' All of which prompts the question, why – with the group's extensive repertoire of American Blues and R&B, not to mention the first clutch of original compositions – they should opt for such strange material to record at their first opportunity in a genuine studio? 'My Bonnie' is a Scottish folk song, probably dating back to the Bonnie Prince Charlie campaigns of 1745. It made no.5 on the German Top Ten, claims Paul brightly, if a little inaccurately, but 'Achtung! Didn't do a thing over here.' Yet.

While 'Ain't She Sweet' was written in 1927 by the team responsible for 'Happy Days are Here Again' – Milton Ager (who wrote it for his daughter Shana Ager) with lyricist Jack Yellen. 'Ain't She Sweet' was originally premiered by Paul Ash and his Orchestra, after which it rapidly became the kind of smash hit that typifies the Roaring Twenties, graduating into a Tin Pan Alley standard. Other versions follow, by Eddie Cantor, Erroll Garner, Frank Sinatra, and 'Paul McCartney's favourite American group', Sophie Tucker. So why choose a song that was a hit before your mother was born...? Why not a neglected Chuck Berry or Little Richard cover? A Carl Perkins, or Larry Williams? Perhaps The Beatles' early vision was not quite as clear as we like to imagine? Perhaps they were using the Gene Vincent version of 'Ain't She Sweet' as a template? Perhaps they'd heard Johnny Kidd and the Pirates doing their version of the song?

But after all, at that time, the rock 'n' roll song-reservoir available to draw upon was not extensive. Looking back from the perspective of a half-century, it's difficult to envisage such a state of musical infancy. But it was only six years since Elvis Presley's first record. You can take the genre back through Fats Domino, or to Ike Turner's 'rocket 88', but whichever way you date it, not a great deal of time had elapsed in which to build up a back-catalogue of original material. And in England – even in Liverpool where the stories of the 'Cunard Yank' importing rare R&B are more apocryphal than most histories assume – it was easier to fall back on pre-rock material, with the strategic addition of a frantic backbeat. Radical reworkings of alleged 'standards' provided an acceptable alternative to the scarcity of new songs – Elvis had done Rodgers and Hart's 1934 'Blue Moon', an original hit for the Casa Loma Orchestra, and more recently he'd done Al Jolson's 1926 Roy Turk song, 'Are You Lonesome Tonight'. The Everly Brothers topped the chart with Arthur Freed's 'Temptation', following it with 'Don't Blame Me', both carrying a Bing Crosby pedigree all the way back to 1933. Even Little Richard had his biggest UK hit with a turbo-charged rebranding of Al Jolson's 1926 song 'Baby Face'. But whatever the motivations, and whatever the exact sequence of events, it was these

Beatles' recording sessions with Tony Sheridan that provided the
physical plastic link to Brian Epstein.

Epstein was humorously christened the 'Nemperor' by *Cavern* DJ
Bob Wooler. Brian accepted the term as a compliment. He was never
less than expensively groomed, with slightly wavy hair, polished and
manicured fingernails, claiming 'I found little pleasure in accepting
less than the best.' He spoke in superior smoothly-modulated
Oxbridge tones without a trace of Scouse, more similar, in fact, to
the contemporary BBC announcers on the radio. Yet there was a
hole of dissatisfaction at the centre of his life. This is the man who,
on Wednesday 3 December 1961, first met The Beatles. Soon after
4:30 pm in his NEMS Whitechapel office he, The Beatles and, on their
behalf, Bob Wooler, warily came face-to-face. Checking each other out.
In a sense, the participants were all discontented misfits who'd fallen
together – fortuitously, into something amazing – something that was
more bohemian than it was commerce. More of need than calculation.
To Derek, in Liverpool, 'there was a drifting together of people of like
mind which had in it something of pubs, something of poetry and
Folk-song, something of art-school.' A process of which The Beatles
were a part, and in which they 'were a catalyst and levellers, bringing
everyone together.' Despite advice from the gregarious Alan Williams
(who ran the *Jacaranda* coffee bar – as well as the *Blue Angel Club* –
and who had previously functioned as their manager) that The Beatles
were 'unreliable', and despite Brian's own serious lack of showbusiness
managerial experience, he signed them soon after.

They signed their first contract together on 24 January 1962 in Pete
Best's West Derby living room, over the *Casbah* basement club. And
the first booking Brian arranged for The Beatles in his new managerial
capacity, oddly enough, was at the *Thistle Café*, 'a genteel little spot on
the sea-front at West Kirby' (1 February 1962), although Rory Storm is
said to have stood in for an absent John Lennon. They were paid £18.
Derek was not there, but he knew the café, he'd bought ice-cream floats
there. On 26 June, NEMS Enterprises Ltd was launched, making Brian
an impresario, after which a second more binding five-year contract was
signed (1 October 1962). After Brian signed them, he redesigned them
into a more marketable commodity and became increasingly obsessive
about his 'boys'. He cajoled them out of leathers and into smartly-
tailored suits, contriving the make-over aura around their mop-top
image. The process that Astrid Kirchherr had begun, he completed.
But as Derek's text points out, Brian Epstein's evolving relationship
with his charges was never that of the traditional artist-manager.

Which meant, unlike virtually every other management structure in sixties pop, 'there is no room in our relationship for contract-slavery.' Although he often made what – by traditional rationales of business strategy – were inept decisions, his strength lay in his absolute conviction, his loyalty and his vision. He lived through his acts. His restless hedonism was sublimated into finding vicarious expression through this surrogate family. And with sense and sensitivity, Derek goes on to carefully chart his way around the minefield of Brian's sexuality, admitting that the Epstein family considered his 'boyhood dreams of dress-designing' and his acting ambitions to be 'unmanly', while avoiding mention of Brian's penchant for rough trade gay sex, or the homoerotic overtones behind his initial attraction to the 'boys' on stage, especially John Lennon. A sanitising duplicity not only adopted for morality or marketing purposes but because homosexual acts were still, in those unenlightened times, imprisonable offences. Although he was personally at ease in his body, and with his sexuality, Brian was nonetheless compelled into troubling subterfuge by its repressive illegality. True – he held himself and the immaculately blemish-free respectability of his reputation in high esteem while fighting an uneven war with the demons that gnawed at the dark side of his prim and dapper facade. His was an exquisite anguish of unhappy longings for love and companionship, offset by a self-disgust at his own urges.

These ground-rules were established early on during the taped conversations in the Imperial Hotel. Ray Coleman recreates the scene in his *Brian Epstein: The Man Who Made The Beatles* (1989, Viking). 'Brian felt uneasy about not mentioning his homosexuality. It was a barrier that had to be crossed before it impeded progress with the interviewing process. He was conscious of saying to Derek: 'There was the girl…' when he should have said 'boy'. Over lunch, Epstein came out with it. 'Did you know that I was queer?' Derek said 'No'. As a journalist, he was not easily surprised, and his quiet understanding relaxed Brian. 'It had become inconvenient for him to lie; he was not a deceitful man, but brutally frank. Until that moment he was very cagey. There was no in-between situation. He was cautious and careful until he knew it was going to be OK. Then it was right out in the open. I didn't find him sly except that he wasn't going to tell all to a *Daily Express* reporter on first meeting. I found him extremely vulnerable, sensitive and really rather sweet.' From the moment of confession, Brian became totally free. He said he had nothing to hide. He said he was glad Derek was not a homosexual, since that made the working relationship much easier.

Derek was two years older than Epstein, but 'he was a fellow you'd want to father.' Taylor detected a man who 'liked a good time in many different ways.' The best way above all was taking care of The Beatles; it was 'his primary need throughout his life; all he wanted in the end.' Once he had broken the ice about his homosexuality, Brian talked about it jocularly. 'I found him very easy and amusing on the subject', Derek says. 'He was very free with all sorts of jokes. I already then had three children and here was quite a lofty young man, who, however, was very vulnerable. But he was not a very camp man...'

Derek doubts if Epstein would have mentioned his sexual preferences in his book even if the climate had been more liberal. 'He would have had to ask permission of people; he was a consulter of people. I don't think he would have made any kind of public statement without asking everybody, not only The Beatles but the Rustiks (a group he signed later) and the Fourmost. And a lot of them would have been very cross if he had not asked them because if he hadn't, it might have been assumed that he was somehow involved with them. Among acts, it wasn't talked about much...' Subsequent biographers would be less reticent. There's a claim in Jonathan Gould's *Can't Buy Me Love* (2007, Three Rivers Press) that Epstein propositioned Pete Best in Spring 1962. But 'to characterise his (Brian's) sudden interest in managing a pop group as narrowly sexual, emotional or entrepreneurial is to simplify. Epstein's attraction to The Beatles was all of these things combined, and it was precisely their ability to provide him with an all-purpose outlet for his energy and creativity that led him to state that truly "everything" about The Beatles was right for him.'

However, supposedly talking about the fireside chairs he sold in the family furniture store, Brian, through Derek, admits 'I was very keen on splayed legs', adding, 'suddenly, there were splayed legs! I was entranced by the possibilities.' Just possibly, Derek was making a camp tease at Brian's expense? He is more forthright in denouncing the anti-Semitism that Brian first encountered at the Liverpool College, from which he was expelled. Yet Derek's account can be factually misleading, or at least economical with the truth, as it simplifies Epstein's account of his subsequent travails at securing a record deal. Epstein's only industry contacts, as a retailer, were through the regional sales and marketing departments of labels through which he'd order stock for the NEMS outlets. But he embellished those contacts, lubricating them with his persuasive charm and enthusiasm to make up for whatever deficit he had when it came to managerial experience. To this end, he tracked down 'Disker', and added him to his networking address-book.

To make your fortunes, you must go to London. There were no real studios in the north. The Decca audition was rightly described as a setback. But each subsequent 'disk company' in turn also knocked him back – Philips, Oriole, Pye, without a Beatles Chelsea-booted foot, ever crossing the studio threshold. With John and Paul waiting in the *Punch And Judy* Coffee Bar near Lime Street Station for Brian to get back from London Euston with the news. After the latest rejection, 'John picked up a tea-spoon, flicked it high into the air and said "Right, try Embassy"', his jibe referring to Woolworth's cheapo label. In 1962 there were no Indie labels. The record industry was locked up tight by a self-satisfied cabal of London-based apparatchiks who controlled total access to magic vinyl and had no intention of relinquishing that lazy monopoly. In the face of inertia and deliberate disinterest, Brian – a northern incomer with no managerial contacts and limited experience – had nothing going for him but his energy, enthusiasm, and his absolutely unshakeable belief in his artists. In *A Cellarful of Noise*, he shows obvious irritation when he complains, 'my Beatles were overlooked in 1962 by people who should have known better but didn't.'

Brian had hit rock bottom. His father, chafing at his errant son's neglect of the family business, gave him a twenty-four-hour make-or-break ultimatum to conclude his crazy Beatles project. So, in a convoluted tale, Brian booked into the Green Park Hotel and then called off at 363 Oxford Street – the HMV music store – to network with Kenneth Boast, 'an exceedingly pleasant executive', manager and a former acquaintance. It was February 1962. They arrange to transfer a couple of Beatles songs from the Decca audition tape onto a rough 'acetone' disk. During the transfer, the in-store disc-cutter, Jim Foy, was sufficiently impressed with what he heard to casually suggest Brian should check out Sid Coleman, head of EMI's music-publishing arm Ardmore & Beechwood. Sid might be interested in the group's original songs. Brian's entreaties had already been politely rejected by EMI A&R departments, so he strategically switched from vinyl potential to attempts at interesting Coleman – less in the group, more in some Lennon-McCartney compositions instead. Fortuitously, Sid listened, liked, and more, he provided the nudge that contrived the situation where The Beatles got to meet George Martin, through George's secretary Judy Lockhart-Smith (they would marry on 24 June 1966), even though she wrote 'Bernard Epstein' in his appointment book! And once together – 4 June 1962, at EMI's Manchester Square 'office block' – there was an immediate chemistry.

A formal audition and test recording were arranged for 6 June at Abbey Road's Number Three studio. Norman 'Hurricane' Smith was assigned studio-engineer for the try-out session. Listening to the playback, he told tape-operator Chris Neal, 'go and pick up George from the canteen, and see what he thinks of this.' 'George', of course, was George Martin. In *A Cellarful of Noise*, Brian describes the gentlemanly Martin as 'a tall, thin, elegant man with the air of a stern but fair-minded housemaster.' It seems to have been the consensus opinion. Bernard Cribbins – beneficiary of his production skills for comedy hit records 'Right Said Fred' and 'Hole in the Ground', commends his 'air of serenity and authority'. To Cilla Black, who would also chart with George Martin productions, he was 'suave and sophisticated'.

Always suited, George Martin was the EMI A&R man who would 'in less than two years produce sixteen no.1 disks by my artists.' In return, Martin was impressed by Epstein's obvious sincerity and slowly came to recognise something of The Beatles' potential too. At first, he wondered, which is the frontman singer? Before deciding there is no frontman. After the first playback Martin invited comments. George Harrison laconically responded that he didn't like Martin's tie. It broke the ice. George Martin commended George's guitar, the 'commercial' qualities of Paul's voice, and even expressed a liking for their song 'Hello Little Girl'. The Beatles respected George Martin's track-record. Recording Spike Milligan with The Goons made him immediately cool in their eyes. Paul loved the *Songs for Swingin' Sellers* (1959) album. George had also produced the *Beyond The Fringe* satirical revue album for Parlophone, with the team of Peter Cooke, Dudley Moore, Alan Bennett and Jonathan Miller. To Derek, 'his ability was somehow the right shape', while Epstein considered Martin's old-school professionalism as a 'safe pair of hands' for his charges.

It was then down to Epstein to help manoeuvre Pete Best out of the drum-chair and Ringo into it (16 August 1962) – to complete the 'globe-shattering union'. According to *A Cellarful of Noise*, it was The Beatles – against Brian's wishes – who wanted Pete out, and Ringo in. Alistair Taylor relates an anecdote in which John Lennon explained to him, 'Pete Best was a good drummer. Ringo Starr is a good Beatle.' Some months earlier – 5 February 1962, when Pete was unwell – Ringo had actually stepped in as a temporary Beatle for the afternoon *Cavern* set, and at the Southport Kingsway Club that same evening. But during the long summer, Ringo was playing the Skegness Butlins Holiday Camp with Rory Storm. His first 'official' date as a Beatle was

18 August, at Hulme Hall, Port Sunlight, Birkenhead. And then... 'Love Me Do'. During their first studio session together, Ringo sat quietly in the corner and said very little. At Martin's instigation, it was session-drummer Andy White who played on the re-recorded *Please Please Me* album version, while Ringo beat time on a tambourine. Although the 4 September version, issued as the single – and later collected onto the *Past Masters* (1988) album – features Ringo.

After they'd cut the single, they flew out to Hamburg 'for a further stint behind the vulgar neon of the Reeperbahn,' while Brian kicked his heels back at the NEMS store. In July, he cabled Germany with the news that Parlophone had signed them on a one-penny-per-disc-sold basis, although that would be renegotiated once they charted. They return to Liverpool high on expectations in September. From then on, Brian would supervise their early group-bonding tours where his meticulous attention to detail and his protectiveness would prove so invaluable. While – years later, at the height of The Beatles' power, and as the news of Epstein's death was breaking – the *Sunday Express* ran a story about how Pete Best was by then working in a bakery for £18 a week.

Other significant incidents are given scant mention in *A Cellarful of Noise*. Such as Epstein's obvious displeasure when Lennon married Cynthia. Despite being in many ways the rebel, when she became pregnant, John still felt compelled to 'do the right thing' by Cyn. Looking for circumstantial evidence, Brian would have found it useful to read Stan Barstow's *A Kind of Loving*, which came out of very much the same mindset. Describing the fall-out of the late-fifties culture of shame – before the advent of the more 'permissive society' – Barstow's protagonist, Vic Brown, gets local girl Ingrid pregnant, although he's not sure he loves her, he chucks away his ambitions, and opts to stand by her, to make an honest woman of her. It would be pretty much the last moment that such social strictures applied, either in Barstow's fictional 'Cressley' northern England, or Lennon's Merseyside. During the build-up to the release of 'Love Me Do', John and Cynthia married on Wednesday, 23 August 1962 at Mount Pleasant Registry Office. Aunt Mimi didn't approve. So Brian Epstein was not only the best man, but he paid for the reception too. As her pregnancy progressed, and as The Beatles career escalated, the couple secretively use Brian's flat at 36 Faulkner Street.

Accepted opinion dictated that married pop stars were no longer regarded as 'available' by fans. It was widely perceived that marriage had sent rocker Marty Wilde's chart career into a terminal tailspin. So the marital situation was deliberately suppressed. Their son Julian

was born on 8 April 1963 in Sefton General Hospital – while John was
out promoting 'Please Please Me'. Brian became godfather while the
single was still inside the Top Thirty. Just twenty days later, as Paul,
George and Ringo recuperate in Tenerife, John and Brian flew off to
Barcelona together for a much-discussed much-mythologised twelve-
day holiday. Pete Shotton, Lennon's friend, wrote about it in his book
The Beatles, Lennon and Me (1984, Stein & Day), and Christopher
Munch fabricated a film around it, *The Hour and Times* (1991). Was
there intimacy? Apparently, John later confided to Shotton that yes,
he had given in to Brian, but 'I let him toss me off, and that was it.'
Explanations were not always so casual. At Paul's twenty-first birthday
party in Liverpool (June 1963) Cavern DJ Bob Wooler teased John
about Brian's predatory attentions during the Catalan break. Drunk and
confrontational, John retaliated by beating him up so badly Wooler was
hospitalised. Yet if certain interpretations of 'You've Got to Hide Your
Love Away' are correct, he was also capable of more sensitive responses
to Brian's clandestine sexuality. By September 1963, The Beatles were
living collectively in Flat L on the fourth floor of 57 Green Street in W1
– 'London was where they wanted to be and where they had to go in
order to make it.' This was until news of John's secret wife and child
broke during December 1963.

All of this also provided a primer for what Derek could expect over
the coming months of working closely with Epstein, as he moved the
Taylor family down to London, and as the phenomenon went global. It
was a role that combined the warring aspects within himself, his sense
of Celtic excitement conflicting his English detachment, his desire to
keep close to home conflicting his urge to discover the 'Big Time'.
Was he a complex man? We all have our complexities. Derek was not
complex in the way that John Lennon was complex. Or the way that
Brian Epstein was. Without the fortuitous Beatles connections that
knocked his life off course, which knocked the world off its orbit, he
may well have remained a mid-tier journalist. A modestly successful
family man. Content with his lot, with only the occasional burn of
unvoiced ambition.

Yet, he muses, 'the music industry may be written off as "cruel" and
"a jungle" by journalists far beyond the fringe, is not really cruel at all
– as businesses go, but rather an amiable and friendly milieu', adding
'at least, that is how I find it.' Absolute real lives will always ultimately
escape biographies – that's as true of Derek Taylor writing about Brian
Epstein as it is about biographers attempts to record Taylor's own life.
The complexities of real lives smash biographer's perceived plans,

puncture theories and assumptions while unearthing the true, troubled turbulence of the time. What we get are edited approximations. Selected quotes from interviews that are muddied with inconsistencies, denials, forgetfulness and the different perspective-interpretations that language-transcripts can't always decipher. When Epstein, supposedly writing his foreword in Belgravia August 1964, refers to what has been 'exaggerated, inaccurate, extravagant and open to misinterpretation', is it Brian – or is it Derek documenting the failings of his own profession? When Epstein claims that 'enjoyment' is 'the essence of a creation, be it a book, a disc or a live stage performance', it could equally be Derek's opinion about the book, expressed through, and selected for emphasis, from what Brian had told him.

Casting around for a suitable title for his completed book, John Lennon's razor-sharp wit helpfully suggested either 'Queer Jew', or 'Cellarful of Boys'. Nevertheless, launched with a prominent display-ad in *NME* and an Epstein interview on Granada-TV from Manchester, the book – published by Souvenir Press, 2 October 1964 (with a first paperback edition through New English Libraries, October 1965) – was generally well-received by both critics and the general public. There were even serialised extracts in *The News of the World*. Picked up by Doubleday in the USA, its high-profile success was repeated there. As he accompanied The Beatles around Britain on their current tour, Brian stopped off at each city's leading book-stores to check out window-displays and monitor sales of 'his' book. Songwriter Tony Hatch later gave the book a knowing wink by working its title into the lyrics of Petula Clark's hit 'I Know A Place'.

Epstein's next biographer, Ray Coleman, considers that *A Cellarful of Noise* was, 'even in 1964 when pop people were never projected abrasively, a vapid autobiography. It bore signs of being hurled together too quickly and prematurely, with no real depths attached to Brian's life and prodigious work pattern.' Coleman nevertheless accepts that 'its attribute was a touching sincerity, a true reflection of Epstein's faith in his artists and dedication to work.' Tony Barrow observes how Epstein 'bathed in the reflected glory of The Beatles and his eyes shone with sheer love-light whenever he stood in the wings watching the Fab Four perform.' Derek observed the same thing. 'I saw him with tears in his eyes when he saw the Fab Four a lot, but those were tears of joy. I don't want to be coy, but he always looked like a chap crying on the inside. He always looked, despite his radiance, a sensitive man. He would say things like: "Never mind that – we're going to have a lovely party. Let's sit down and plan it." He did pride himself on being a good judge of people. That was a fair self-assessment. In terms of business relationships, he sometimes made mistakes and they could be costly...'

And if journalism is the first draft of history, then *A Cellarful of Noise* functions perfectly. Written to a punishing deadline, while the story was still very much happening all around him, with the full facts either unclear, or deliberately smudged for reasons of propriety, and with the sad outcome as yet undecided, Derek had indeed produced a 'first draft' of Brian Epstein's life. He catches the precision of Brian's exaggerated phrasing – 'the answer can be manifold' – so that the reader hears his voice. While he also finds space to quote from Vance Packard's analysis of the psychological and sociological implications of Beatlemania from the pages of the American *Saturday Evening Post*. The book closes with an unnamed journalist – who might be Derek – asking if Brian would ever sell The Beatles. And his moral dilemma of whether to do so, in the face of an offer he was contemplating. The Beatles might indeed be better off with a more experienced management team behind them. And the global expansion of his responsibilities was putting unfair stress and pressure on Brian. Perhaps some kind of deal was the answer? Putting the question to the 'boys' themselves, John said 'get stuffed'. Paul said 'something similar, though less polite.' With his confidence restored, Brian looks forward to the future, 'I think the sun will shine tomorrow.' Later biographers, with the luxury of more leisurely research time, a freer moral agenda, and with the benefit of hindsight, would add further volumes to the story, correcting or amending aspects of Derek's outline. But if the project was seen by Brian Epstein as some kind of initiation, a test of his competency and reliability, then Derek had passed.

The writing flows. He gushes prose in an easy-on-the-eye journalistic joining-up, where others faff. Yet when he talks, he is fastidious in his phrasing, making it difficult to prize behind the flip-prose and detect Derek Taylor beyond. There is less candour than there is style. Derek worked, as journalists tend to, with a tumbler of Bell's Whisky and a Marlborough ciggie, through the prism of other's lives. His own life was entangled with the social changes that occurred over that most innovative of decades, his writing providing its quote and punctuation marks. But he was, superficially at least, not a rebel in a time when heroes were expected to be rebels. His writing did not proselytise, lobby or campaign. It was always subservient to and functioned in the service of, the artist he was writing about. If there are glimpses of Derek's attitudes, opinions, or tastes, they are filtered through those of his subjects; Brian Epstein, Michelle Phillips, George Harrison. The insatiable need is to put it down in words, but not necessarily his own, more in reflection, by selection, or emphasis. The preparatory interviews with Brian were not necessarily a transaction of ideas, but its reportage can be slanted and skewed by interpretation.

Events were happening fast; everything was accelerating, too fast to over-think through. Derek became Brian Epstein's personal assistant and scriptwriter, a position made official from Monday, 20 April 1964. He was a sparky guy, but 'I suppose it was because he fancied me that I got the job', Derek conjectures, more than a little tongue-in-cheek (to Philip Norman), 'even though, in all the time I knew him, he never so much as laid a finger on my knee.' He might have missed out on the American breakthrough, but Derek travelled the world for six months with Brian as part of The Beatles' 1964 world tour entourage. Between completing *A Hard Day's Night* at the end of April, and its release in July, The Beatles took a month-long vacation before embarking on the tour. Then, as the mania kicked off in earnest, he was on the road with them.

And Derek was experiencing the fan-mania of the Australian jaunt, through an incredible mid-June. Even when their plane made an unscheduled 2:00 am refuelling stop at Darwin in Northern Australia, some four-hundred screaming fans materialised as if from nowhere to greet them. Derek unleashed his satiric wit about the Australian 1964 tour in a *Saturday Evening Post* interview, 'the routes were lined solid, cripples threw away their sticks, sick people rushed up to the car as if a touch from one of the boys would make them well again... the only thing left for The Beatles is to go on a healing tour.' Developing the theme elsewhere by adding the 'Australians turned out for The Beatles the way a Latin American country might turn out for the pope.'

Derek was also observing the work of Tony Barrow, The Beatles' Press Officer. From Crosby in north Liverpool, Tony Barrow was still a seventeen-year-old sixth-former at Merchant Taylor's School when he initially landed a job writing a weekly record review column – 'Off the Record' – for the Saturday magazine section of the *Liverpool Evening Echo*, under the pseudonym 'Disker'. He never looked back. And it was 1961 when Brian Epstein first contacted him to write about this new group he was representing, hoping to drum up interest. 'He was hoping to get something in the paper through me to show the lads. He then came to see me at Decca in London where I was working writing record sleeves and brought me a demo disc that he had made in *the Cavern*. He apologised for the poor quality of the disc that he said was from a Granada documentary, but it turned out later that this business about the disc being poor quality was a white lie. Brian had actually held up a microphone to record it.' Working freelance, Barrow was by then in London, with writer-connections to Decca. Record-collectors might have noticed his sleeve-notes on the reverse of the 1962 EP *Billy Fury Hits*, praising this 'quartet of recordings' in 'a 45rpm nutshell.'

As if it was yesterday, Tony adds 'I could not hear The Beatles, but I could hear the excitement and the electricity.' Unfortunately, although he liked what he heard, and shoved local bands whenever he could, his remit didn't extend to reviewing tapes. He told Epstein that because it wasn't a professionally recorded single, he couldn't help. Although he wrote later that 'my natural home-town interest in the group prevented me taking a totally unbiased view.' He was aware that Brian had no real creative input to offer, but he was known to the industry as the owner of the North End Music Store (NEMS), a major outlet for selling 'plastic ware'. So there was enough prestige invested there to pacify him at least to the extent of securing an audition for his unlikely clients. 'Once he left my office, I got in touch with the marketing people in Decca and told them about Brian Epstein and when they realised it was NEMS they said he was a big customer, so we had to audition them. That was the basis on which The Beatles did the audition.' Tony goes on to write his own entertaining memoirs – *John, Paul, George, Ringo and Me* (2006, Andre Deutsch) – recording his own spoken-word CD version.

While still technically employed by Decca, Tony was induced to write the 'press-pack' for rival EMI's release of the 'Love Me Do' single. Columbia was EMI's main label, with a top star roster boasting Cliff Richard, the Shadows, and Helen Shapiro. Parlophone was a less prestigious subsidiary, it had hits with Adam Faith, but was known primarily for its comedy output. Tony was compensating for its low-key, low-priority promotion with Epstein's more focussed approach. A young Max Clifford claimed to have worked on The Beatles' behalf at EMI. For NEMS, all of the protagonists involved were on a sharply ascending learning curve.

The second single, 'Please Please Me' was recorded on 26 November 1962 at Studio Two in EMI's Abbey Road Complex in St John's Wood, north London. To be issued on 11 January 1963. By February it was charting – entering at no.33 (24 January), with the Shadows' 'Dance On' at no.1, replacing Cliff Richard and the Shadows double-sided movie hit 'The Next Time' c/w 'Bachelor Boy' now at no.2, and former Shadows Jet Harris and Tony Meehan at no.3 with 'Diamonds'. The following week, as Jet and Tony took over the top slot, 'Please Please Me' was up to no.16, as girl's fan-mag *Boyfriend* was describing The

Beatles as 'even more modern than modern.' Then it was into the top three, at three.

Photographer Michael Ward travelled up from London to catch The Beatles as their single peaked on Thursday the nineteenth. 'I wasn't interested in them', Michael recalled much later, 'I didn't know who they were.' In the lull before Beatlemania, in their hometown, they were free to stroll unmolested, for perhaps the last time in their lives. In a forerunner of the iconic *Abbey Road* cover-shot, Michael photographed them crossing a rather ill-kempt zebra, although Paul is eclipsed behind Ringo, and it was too cold to go for a re-shoot. Together they make their way to Epstein's office in Whitechapel where Ward continued to snap informal black-and-white shots. Then on to a session at The Cavern. They'd play their last gig there in a few tumultuous months, on 3 August, following a set by the Merseybeats. After the first number, the lights fused. In the enveloping unamplified darkness, the audience heard Paul singing lines from a previously unheard song. They'd not hear the full 'When I'm Sixty-Four' until *Sgt. Pepper's Lonely Hearts Club Band*, many years from now.

Meantime, it was also Tony Barrow who penned the lively sleeve-notes for the *Please Please Me* album (issued 22 March 1963), helpfully pointing out who sang what with whom, emphasising that 'they write their own lyrics, design and eventually build their own instrumental backdrops and work out their own vocal arrangements', precisely because no other groups of the time did that. Although it's now taken for granted, their self-contained 'do-it-yourself angle' was in itself hugely innovative.

Meanwhile, The Beatles played a gig in Sheffield. An aspiring entrepreneur called Peter Stringfellow had inked the original booking in October 1962 for *The Black Cat Club* that he'd opened in the St Aidan's Church Hall. Then *Please Please Me* hit, Epstein cranked up the fee from £65 to £90, and Stringfellow switched the venue, upgrading it to the *Azena Ballroom* in White Lane in the Gleadless area on the city (it has since been converted into a supermarket!). For the night of the appearance, 12 February, Stringfellow sold 1,200 six-shilling tickets for a venue with an 850-capacity, and a thousand more turned up ticketless on the night. The Beatles arrived after having already played a gig in Oldham the same day.

Intriguingly, there's some mystery element concerning subsequent merchandising of the event's posters, which show the famous 'dropped T' logo used for the group-name – although they supposedly didn't start using it until May. According to the official histories, they used the 'bugs' logo, until Ivor Arbitor supposedly designed the new device for display on Ringo's drumkit in April. A tempting explanation for the anomaly is suggested by another aspect of the poster. The day specified is Saturday. But 12 February was a Tuesday. Although a little cash-in replication after the event makes the authenticity of the merchandising dubious, the gig would nevertheless have featured songs from the forthcoming debut LP. Famously, with Parlophone unwilling to devote too much expenditure on their newest signings, the remaining ten tracks for the album were recorded within a single day – 11 February 1963, in three three-hour sessions. 'pop picking is a fast 'n' furious business these days', according to Barrow. In fact, they'd ducked out of a single date on their Helen Shapiro tour to create the time-space to do it.

But Peterborough's loss resulted in an album of fourteen tracks, involving both sides of the first two singles, plus the four tracks from the 'Twist and Shout' EP. It broke down as eight original compositions from 'their own built-in tunesmith team', each of them credited – presumably to Paul's subsequent satisfaction, as 'McCartney-Lennon'. Opening with the frequently covered 'I Saw Her Standing There' which – titled 'Seventeen' until the last moment – which acts as a manifesto for a new pop age. No pizzicato strings or shrill female backing-vocals here, just tough, guitar-driven rock 'n' roll and sharp colloquial lyrics. 'She was just seventeen', adding with a knowing nudge, 'you know what I mean'. Yes, we know. George takes vocals for their own first take on 'Do You Want to Know a Secret'. Then Ringo sings the 'fast rocker' 'Boys'; John takes impassioned soul vocals for Arthur Alexander's 'Anna', there's Goffin-King (the Cookies' 'Chains'), Bacharach-David (the Shirelles' 'Baby It's You'), and Paul's 'trick duet' double-tracked lead for the show-tune 'A Taste of Honey'. Taking its three-word title from a line in the *West Side Story* song 'somewhere, there's a place for us', they form another Beatles-lyric ('There's A Place') unconsciously mimicked very soon after by Brian Wilson – 'there's a place where I can go' for 'In My Room'.

George and Ringo made important contributions to the group-image and sound, but even recently Tony Barrow has repeated his assertion that he considered The Beatles as primarily a launch-vehicle for Lennon-McCartney songs. At the time, asked how long The Beatles career-trajectory would last – John guessed at five years. And what would they do once it was all over? Paul seriously speculated that he and John would continue to write material for other artists, as a kind of Lieber-Stoller, Goffin-King team, while Ringo planned to open a string of women's hairdressers. But before that eventuality, Brian designed, and Tony wrote the NEMS hand-out promoting the 'From Me to You' single (issued 12 April) which was mailed out to every national and regional newspaper in the UK. It quotes Brian Matthew to the effect that The Beatles are 'visually and musically the most exciting group since the Shadows.'

By the time Tony Barrow was working with Gerry and the Pacemakers, and writing the press release for Cilla Black's debut single, 'Love of the Loved' (which had originally been intended for Liverpool's Beryl Marsden), NEMS had a London office. On 2 May 1963, Tony was installed in 'Service House', 13 Monmouth Street, London WC2 as their first full-time publicity officer, operating from a first-floor office located above a dubious bookshop imaginatively called 'The Bookshop' which sold soft-core sex-mags in a curtained-off back-room. While above it all, Tony was infiltrating trendy Mersey slang into the promotional prose – 'fab gear', 'fate' and 'endsville'. It was while abbreviating his own prose in that way that he coined the term 'The Fab Four'...

Chapter Seven: 1964: In My Life

Ringo Starr: The Best Drummer In The Beatles…?

Derek's first visible role as The Beatles' 'new press rep' was presiding over a press conference called on 20 May 1964 at NEMS' London office, for The Beatles to discuss their up-coming world tour. But the day before that tour began, Ringo collapsed during a photo session, and was rushed into University College Hospital. As George says in *A Hard Day's Night*, 'drums loom large in his legend.' But, hospitalised with tonsillitis, his Beatles-logo'd drum-seat was temporarily filled by stand-in drummer Jimmie Nicol for the first leg of the Europe-and-beyond tour (4 to 12 June 1964). That doesn't happen much these days. Now, they just cancel the tour. Eventually, Ringo flew out to Australia to reclaim his drum-stool. Returning to the hospital 2 to 16 December for the operation to remove those troublesome tonsils, posing for a *Melody Maker* cover-photo with a placard saying 'I Feel Fine', as his contribution to their current hit.

Derek Taylor was with them throughout the tour, telephoning reports back to NEMS from stop-offs at Denmark and the Netherlands, then Hong Kong, Australia and New Zealand. 'Busy days', he understates. It was going OK. Reactions were consistently good. Ringo's absence was not adversely affecting fan-hysteria, which was just as manic as it ever was. There's a clip from Dutch VARA-TV (5 June) – 'The Beatles in Nederland', filmed at the *Treslong* café-restaurant, of The Beatles miming to 'She Loves You' and 'Can't Buy Me Love' with Jimmie Nicol in the drum-chair, looking understandingly disconcerted, as Derek, Mal and Neil strive to keep the predominantly-male fans from mobbing the stage. In the chaotic scenes, as Brian notes in *A Cellarful of Noise*, 'in Holland the police took no chances and punched, swung and hurled my assistant Derek Taylor and road manager Neil Aspinall to the ground half-a-dozen times a day, because they thought they were trying to attack The Beatles'! After the show, The Beatles relax by taking a tour of the Amsterdam red-light district.

Of course, it was easy to write Ringo off as fame-by-association. He wasn't there for the *Backbeat*-period Hamburg group-bonding. He wasn't even there for the rejected Decca audition. Instead, he shaved off his beard and was drafted in last-minute for 'Love Me Do' as the acceptable fringe when Pete Best refused to sacrifice his quiff. Despite the personal account that Derek recorded in *A Cellarful of Noise*, it's said that he wasn't even the first-choice alternative and that Epstein offered The Beatles' drum-chair to Johnny Hutchinson of the Big

Three first. On such whims are history made. In some alternate time-stream could it have been John, Paul George... and Jimmie Nicol – or Pete Best, or Johnny 'Hutch'? If so, how would things have panned out differently? Ringo grew up in Liverpool 8, attended Dingle Vale Secondary School – which later became Shorefields Technology College. He played with the Eddie Clayton Skiffle Group from 1957 to 1958, then joined Rory Storm and the Hurricanes from 25 March 1959. As part of the group, he had his own featured vocal-spot for which he'd perform 'Boys' (later on the *Please Please Me* album) and his cover of Johnny Burnette's 'You're Sixteen' – which he'd record as part of his post-Beatles LP *Ringo*, from which it became a 1974 hit single in its own right. Meanwhile, when he became a Beatle 'I was an only child, and suddenly I had three brothers.'

With a nickname borrowed from John Wayne's character in John Ford's seminal Western *Stagecoach* (1939), Ringo was the jester, the good-guy, the cohesive force defusing the in-group tensions around him. To Brian, 'Ringo slotted into the curious chemical pattern and thus created the four-constituent formula.' Of course, that formula had started out with Lennon as the writer-leader. And although credited to Lennon-McCartney, most of the early hits they farmed out to other acts – to Billy J Kramer, the Fourmost, the Applejacks, or Peter & Gordon – were McCartney songs that Lennon considered not good enough for the Fabs. It was only after *A Hard Day's Night* – and 'Yesterday' – that Paul's equal-abilities could no longer be denied. Isn't that why Lennon singles out 'Yesterday' for particular abuse on 'How Do You Sleep'? After that, for every'"We Can Work it Out', Paul had a 'Day Tripper', for every 'Strawberry Fields' a 'Penny Lane', for 'All You Need is Love' a 'Hey Jude'. Lennon told Jan Wenner he especially resented his psychedelic meister-work 'I Am the Walrus' getting B-side relegation to Paul's relatively trite pop-catchy 'Hello Goodbye'. As the group went through the final phase of its painful disintegration, Paul gave away no.1 'Come and Get It' to Badfinger, which must surely have been a parting shot, a barely-coded message, an ultimatum aimed at his colleagues?

Meantime, Ringo's role throughout was not just to drum for both factions, but to arbitrate between their two warring poles. A demilitarized buffer zone. Alan Clayson uses meticulously exhaustive research to navigate his eventful career-path (in *Ringo Starr: Straight Man or Joker*, Sanctuary, 1997), the years that lead up to it – through Rory Storm and the Hurricanes, and the decades since. Ringo's mediocre solo albums, mildly entertaining movies, indulgences and rehab. And the long inactive spaces between. The Beatles may have started out as a lonely man's (Epstein's) fantasy group of imaginary friends, but it wound up as something still chockfull with secrets. Unvoiced through loyalties to the dead, or the living. But if Ringo won't write it, and McCartney must have untold stories he's never likely to divulge, Clayton's book is about the best we're likely to get. It is by turns sad, touching, comic, and never less than informative. But betrayingly – rather than checking out the 'Ringo' index-references, you tend to search out the more creatively-interesting names around it.

Yet Ringo Starr was Marge Simpson's favourite Beatle.

With The Beatles – with Tony Barrow's second stab as sleevenote scribe – impacted the stores on 22 November 1963. I remember the day clearly. Cycling into the village from school, lunchtime, seeing that iconic black-shadow Robert Freeman photo cover integrated into the store-front display, a shot that eerily recalls Astrid Kirchherr's Hamburg photos; speeding back to school to brag the first sighting. 'Two generously-filled sides', rather than a collection of recent A- and B-sides plus fillers, their albums run from twelve to fourteen top-quality tracks – no fillers. Fourteen pristine new tracks – when the industry norm was twelve, or sometimes as few as ten, no recycled or future singles this time. Seven Lennon-McCartney originals (including much-covered 'All My Loving', 'It Won't Be Long' and 'Not A Second Time'), plus George's composition 'Don't Bother Me', which he tells Derek is 'the first song I wrote' (in *I, Me, Mine*), presumably forgetting 'Cry for A Shadow' – or, perhaps because that's an instrumental, it doesn't count?

Ringo does vocals on their first take of 'I Wanna Be Your Man', and Paul contributes his skip-over show-tune '"Till There Was You' – the song that gains them grudging parental approval when they perform it as part of their televised London Palladium set. There's a generous shot of R&B and rock 'n' roll from Chuck Berry ('roll Over Beethoven'), from Smokey Robinson's 'rhythmic group' The Miracles ('You Really Got A Hold on Me'), plus more Motown (the Marvelettes' 'Please Mister Postman' and Berry Gordy's climax 'Money'). Beatles albums were already shaping up as events in their own right. And spawn a new onslaught of covers. Matt Munroe ('All My Loving'), Phil Spector's The Treasures ('Hold Me Tight'), while Jackie Lynton covers John's 'Little Child' for Pye – a survivor of Larry Parnes package tours and *Saturday Club* live-sessions. Adam Faith did a version of 'I Wanna Be Your Man', recorded live with the Roulettes, while there were numerous versions of 'Money', from the rolling Stones all the way to Bern Elliot and the Fenmen.

Some may recall the release date for other reasons. It was the day of the Kennedy assassination. John F Kennedy, whose voracious sexual adventures make the spurt-stains on Monica Lewinsky's dress seem like a mild flirtation and whose most high-profile moment comes out-facing the Soviet Union over their Cuba-based missiles. Fortunately, he comes up against Premier Khrushchev who was pragmatic enough to back down. Had he found himself eyeballing the more inflexible Stalin, or Brezhnev, the story might have turned out differently, and now we'd all be living in some mutant-crawling Mad Max post-holocaust nuclear wasteland. Yet Kennedy was at the forefront of the civil rights struggle, which shifts him onto the correct side of the equation, and his death equates the 'death of youth' that, some claim, left a need across America that only The Beatles could fill. Brian Epstein mused – in *A Cellarful of Noise* – that there must 'have been a basic longing to find something outside themselves and their experience, or Americans could never have taken to The Beatles in the way they did.'

It was also the day Aldous Huxley died. The novelist who, during his final decade, explored hallucinogenics and wrote *The Doors of Perception* (1954) which went on to become a sacred text for the psychedelic movement to come, and also, in that way, another direct influence on the course of Derek Taylor's life.

On 1 May 1963, Tony Barrow signed to NEMS, turning up to be welcomed by John Lennon's acidic greeting 'you're not queer and you're not Jewish, what are you doing coming to work for NEMS?' He'd agreed on a basic £36-a-week, double what he'd been earning freelancing for Decca or as 'Disker'. To justify that wage he first set about reorganising the out-of-control expansion of The Beatles' Fan Club. He divided it down into a northern region run by original organiser Freda Kelly, and a southern region set up for Bettina Rose, operating from the NEMS base at 13 Monmouth Street. To oversee the two entities he created a fictitious composite, 'Anne Collingham' (aka Mary Cockram), whose name would appear on Club literature. 'She' would become, to Fan Club members, a real person. Tony also originated the idea of The Beatles Christmas Record – free flexi-discs available to all fan-club members – as he was simultaneously spinning press-promotions for all of the NEMS acts.

But by now, Epstein's fast-moving stable of artists had mushroomed – with an according lapse in quality control – and the workload had become so unwieldy that some delegation had to take place. Tony was assigned to work across a stratum of non-Beatles-acts. Initially, the Epstein touch had guaranteed overnight stardom. But as the pop world absorbed the Mersey Beat innovations, and began to come up with a second wave of variations, that began to become more precarious. Now bands go away for three years to record their second album safe in the knowledge that nothing will have significantly changed by the time they return. Then, within the space of twelve months, the entire ground-rules had shifted. Hair was longer. Beats were rawer. The R&B had become more 'authentic'. It went from a Punk to a New Wave phase virtually overnight. Sharp suits and photo-shoots were no longer making it. And suddenly, around the time The Beatles were installed as the first pop stars ever to be displayed in Madame Tussauds (28 March 1964), Billy J's crooked matinee idol grin and Gerry Marsden's cheeky Tommy Steel chirpiness were embarrassingly retro; instead, there were newer musicians cropping up on the scenester radar.

Yet the man with a mile-wide grin and a cheeky double-entendre became the only male member of Epstein's sorry stable to still register a profile into the late eighties. Gerry survived long after their first run of hits as his own songwriting skills developed, with hits including 'Ferry Cross the Mersey' and 'Don't Let the Sun Catch You Crying'. But his eighth single glanced back to the formative days when DJ Bob Wooller would close sessions at *The Cavern* by spinning Bobby Darin's 'I'll Be There'. The song provided Gerry Marsden with his final top ten hit of the decade (in March 1965). From there, he moved effortlessly into stage musicals. Bizarrely, Gerry would return to the no.1 position during the 1980s fronting two chart-topping charity records, with The Crowd – including Paul McCartney, with Ringo's son Zack on drums – recording a benefit version of 'You'll Never Walk Alone' for victims of the Bradford City Football Club fire (no.1 on 15 June 1985), and doing much the same for the Christians' 'Ferry Cross the Mersey' – also featuring Paul McCartney (no.1 on 20 May 1989) for the victims of the Hillsborough football disaster. By then, long after the Pacemakers had ceased to exist as an active concern, drumming brother Freddie Marsden had become a telephone operator and a driving instructor. Yet when he died in December 2006, aged 66, he was able to leave a net estate worth £928,973.

Gerry Marsden's two late Top Ten entries are probably the equivalent of the nouveau TV-celebrity achieved by Cilla Black once she'd ditched NEMS for the Neighbourhood Witch Scheme. Cilla Black, the former clerk/typist with BICC, who signed to NEMS on 6 September 1963, was also developing into a major star, carefully nurtured by Brian's continuing enthusiasm and song-selection. Despite near-universal doubts, especially from a George Martin mystified by Brian's faith in his skinny raucous latest 'star', Epstein's long-term view was to be vindicated. We now know that 'Auntie Cilla' would graduate into a stalwart of Saturday night TV game-shows. But she'd always been a rough working-class riposte to the pearls, twin-set and evening-gown taste that defined light entertainment. When she sang the folk-song 'Liverpool Lullaby', written by Merseyside former CND-activist Stan Kelly, she could do the 'oh you are a mucky kid, dirty as a dustbin lid' with an unmatched raw authenticity. When her cover of 'Anyone Who Had A Heart' reached no.1 (12 March 1964) it was more than just another NEMS statistic, it was the first time in the history of the charts that the entire Top Thirteen was made up of British-based records. Epstein's Billy J was no.3 ('Little Children'), and Gerry at no.13 ('I'm The One'). Other northern groups were at no.6 ('Just One Look' by the Hollies), no.7 ('Needles and Pins' by the Searchers), and no.8 ('I Think of You' by the Merseybeats). Southern acts were at no.2 ('Bits and Pieces' by the Dave Clark Five), no.5 ('Not Fade Away' by the rolling Stones), and no.11 ('Candy Man' by Brian Poole and the Tremeloes). The other places were taken by the more retro voices of the Irish Bachelors (no.4 with 'Diane'), pre-Beatles heartthrob Eden Kane (no.9 with 'Boys Cry'), glamorous songstrel Kathy Kirby (no.10 with 'Let Me Go Lover') and Dusty Springfield (no.13 with 'Stay Awhile').

Despite appearances, Billy J Kramer with the Dakotas were already stumbling badly. Born William Ashton in Bootle, near Liverpool, in 1943, he was the youngest of seven children. 'But when I was twelve', he told *Eagle* (31 July 1965), 'my mother added enough to the little that I had managed to save for me to buy a £3 guitar. I then formed a skiffle group with some of my school-mates and we used to pound out a mixture of skiffle and rock 'n' roll. On leaving school, I became an indentured apprentice fitter with British Railways, and in the evenings, I used to play rhythm guitarist with a small combo called the Phantoms.' At the suggestion of Liverpool 'deejay' Bob Wooler, Billy began to play a larger part in the vocal side of things. Backed by a Merseyside group called the Coasters, Billy set aside his guitar to concentrate on singing – with almost immediate success. In the annual *Mersey Beat* popularity poll the group had come third, while Billy was named top semi-professional vocalist. He was presented the award by a young former record shop manager called Brian Epstein, who was starting to gain fame as the manager of a very promising beat group called The Beatles. Epstein had actually seen Billy Kramer and the Coasters before, sharing a bill with The Beatles at the Widnes Queen's Hall.

Brian saw a big future for Billy J – who he considered 'the best-looking pop-singer in the world', and, in January 1963, signed him

to an exclusive management contract. When the Coasters weren't
so keen to turn pro, Brian drafted in a top Manchester group called
the Dakotas, teaming them up into an uneasy alliance. There was a
Manchester club called *Three Coins* at 64 Fountain Street, off Market
Street. The posters called it 'The Show-Place of the Stars'. One
announced 'Billy J Cramer' – with a 'C'. Another announced Pete
MacLaine and the Dakotas. Together, they'd then been groomed by
Brian with the intention of becoming NEMS' version of Cliff Richard
and the Shadows. Billy became 'Billy J' – at John Lennon's suggestion
(the 'J' to stand for his new son Julian). Billy J's hair was not combed
forward into a fringe, but stayed in the traditional 'Mirabelle' pin-up
quiff, like the one glimpsed on the gravure-colour cover of 'Fabulous
208' in *A Hard Day's Night*. Once they have hits, the Dakotas were
spun-off into their own separate-but-connected career-path with the
first of their instrumental singles without Billy J, 'The Cruel Sea', which
predictably charted. Billy J Kramer with the Dakotas topped the bill
at The Daily Herald Beat Festival at the Stanley Stadium on Saturday
31 August 1963 at the peak of their success. 'Top Groups In The Top
Show!' announced the posters.

The summer very nearly belonged to Billy J Kramer. He was Epstein's
pretty puppet, a Mersey Beat Cliff Richard. And although *Listen...*
(1963), his debut album, obviously lifted its title from his first no.1,
oddly, neither 'Do You Want to Know A Secret' – a song loaned from
The Beatles first album – or any of his subsequent John-Paul-penned
hits made it onto this vinyl. Not the B-side 'I'll Be On My Way', a
charming and highly collectable Beatles song only eventually available
on the pared-back *Beatles Live at the Beeb* (November 1994) CD
collection. No 'Bad to Me', 'I'll Keep You Satisfied' or 'From A Window'.
In 1963 it was considered bad form, even immoral, to confuse singles
and albums markets with duplication or overlaps. But we do get a
serviceable 'I Call Your Name', a song later revived by its authors on
The Beatles 'Long Tall Sally' EP, and as a John Lennon tribute by The
Mamas and the Papas. There's also a standout 'Liverpool Sound' non-
Beatles song – 'Pride', which achieved a high-visibility popularity when
Billy J performed it with laid-back finger-popping ease on ITV's must-
see *Thank Your Lucky Stars*. And he's quite competent at such catchy
undemanding pop, but the inclusion of more ambitious material, such
as the standard 'The Twelfth of Never' or Presley's old B-side 'Anything
That's Part of You' severely exposes the limitations of his vocal range.
The first rupture occurred when they disagree over 'Little Children'.
Billy J was keen for the song to be his next single. Brian disagreed, he

preferred to stay with the winning Lennon-McCartney formula. When Billy J persisted – and worse still, when his view was vindicated as it became his biggest hit, much to Epstein's chagrin – their relationship never recovered. Cilla also defied Brian Epstein's opinion – just once, when she insisted against his advice that her version of Randy Newman's 'I've Been Wrong Before' should be her next single, but he was suitably mollified when it failed to equal the success of her previous hits, and stalled just outside the top ten (at no.17). She repented, conceded his correctness, and vowed to defer to Brian in future. While for Billy J, the stream of Lennon-McCartney songs ran out, he recorded Bacharach-David's 'Trains and Boats and Planes' before falling back on The Beatles again for 'From A Window', by which time even their magic failed to work.

Same with the Fourmost. Originally known as the Blue Jays, the Four Jays, then the Four Mosts, they'd actually debuted at *the Cavern* on 1 March 1961 – nearly three weeks before The Beatles. But the only other thing remotely noteworthy about these Liverpool likely lads is the way they benefited from their Epstein management connection by scraping crumbs from the Lennon-McCartney table, scoring chart placings with Beatle-compositions unavailable anywhere else. But neither 'Hello Little Girl' (no.9 in September 1963) nor 'I'm in Love' (no.17 in December 1963) appeared on *First and Fourmost* – their debut album (originally Parlophone PMC1259 in September 1965). From their earliest Liverpool days, they'd always featured a strong comedy-element in their set, so producer George Martin attempted to develop the group's negligible comedic talents by running them through Buzz Clifford's novelty hit 'Baby Sittin' Boogie', and adding his own post-Goons funny voices to Presley's movie theme 'Girls Girls Girls'.

But even more ludicrous is Epstein's Sounds Incorporated, infusing guest horns onto their inept retread of 'The In-Crowd'. Any less credibly 'in'-crowd of losers than the Fourmost is difficult to imagine. The basic track-list was expanded to twenty-eight for its July 1997 CD digital reissue, with the original cover-shot retained, showing the group cavorting astride a cannon overlooking the Thames. Perhaps the photo was meant as a metaphor for their slight part in the first wave of the Northern Beat Boom's total conquest of the pop scene during that far-off year of 1963? After their two Top Ten Beatles songs, they progressed to cover early Motown with the Four Tops' 'Baby I Need Your Lovin'', then reverted to a Beatles-cover, but even the magic bullet of 'Here, There and Everywhere' failed to revive their flagging career, or reverse their inevitable career decline. It's odd, Mersey Beat's place in the scheme of things was supposed to be as a primitivising agent, a refreshing blast of rawness, a pre-emptive Punk. But their pleasant, slick, occasionally bland records seem to beg some historical revision on that score. They also fell out of favour with Epstein following a series of disagreements in which they called his judgement into question. Never a good move. Despite management neglect and public indifference, they hung on. As late as February 1969 Paul produced their over-looked single 'Rosetta'.

But Brian Epstein was still out there compulsively signing new 'artistes', even though his quality-control instinct had stumbled into fault-mode, and once added to the roster those signings simmered there in resentful neglect. The strategy that once worked so spectacularly – neat suits, smart image, a strategic overspill of Beatles songs – failed to launch Tommy Quickly. Brian spotted Tommy Quigley doing an unpaid 'unknowns' slot with his group the Challengers, supporting The Beatles at the Majestic Ballroom in Birkenhead some time during the early months of 1963. The suitably renamed singer went into the studio that same August to cut 'Tip of My Tongue' c/w 'Heaven Only Knows' for the Piccadilly label. The A-side was a lost song The Beatles had recorded with George Martin on 26 November 1962, but never subsequently issued. Little more than an unfinished sketch of a song, it's possibly the poorest composition in the entire Lennon-McCartney portfolio, based around the idea of a tongue-tied boy unable to express his love, but who ultimately marries his girl anyway. Epstein arranged for a group called the Remo Four to be on hand to provide back-up, with curiously dated vocal accompaniment.

The Remo Four hung around to help Tommy promote the nearest thing Quickly came to a hit, when his 'Wild Side of Life' peaked at no.33 in October 1964. Next, he was given Lennon-McCartney's 'No Reply' and attempted seventeen takes before abandoning it. He couldn't hit the correct key. Despite Epstein's most fervent endeavours, the former telephone-fitter was NEMS' most expensive failure, and Quickly was dropped by Pye records (4 June 1965). After he failed to sign elsewhere, he was discreetly dropped from the NEMS roster, during a March 1966 reshuffle, along with other 'failed projects' the Rustiks and Michael Haslam. For the Remo Four, being signed by Epstein was also a long, frustrating and inconclusive time. During the fall-out period that followed, Wayne Bickerton and Tony Waddington from the group became part of the Pete Best Four. They worked with Billy Fury, and they played on George Harrison's *Wonderwall* (1968) soundtrack album. But they would have to wait a full ten years for their own big chart moment when they wrote and made a successful demo of a song called 'Sugar Baby Love', then formed a pick-up group called the Rubettes to record it. By 18 May 1974, it would be safely up there at the no.1 position, beginning a brief run of glitter-lite hits.

The Big Three, who had been Epstein's third signing, proved less pliable, less amenable than The Beatles (or Gerry) had been. They'd initially gone along with the Epstein programme, only dubiously. Signed to Decca, Leiber-Stoller's 'Some Other Guy' was selected as their launch single, a fall-back club standard also done on stage by The Beatles. They recorded it the day after they'd returned from an exhausting stint in Hamburg. Although Johnny Gustafson expressed dissatisfaction with his ragged vocals, the label vetoed a second session and Epstein agreed to the release of the version they'd done. Although his delivery is raw, this only adds to their air of rough 'n' ready rock. A quality they also catch to perfection on their highly-rated *Live at the Cavern* (1963) EP. In fact, their finest most-defining moment would not happen on the singles chart at all, but with this vinyl-verité mini-album that perfectly captures the spirit of the moment. With 'By The Way' they had a new Mitch Murray song – but despite an ingredient that had turned Gerry Marsden into a major pop star, it only achieved a low-chart entry. Then, with 'If You Ever Change Your Mind' ('Bring it on Home to Me') they not only pre-empted the Animals cover of Sam Cooke's great song but were promoted as the first Mersey group to add strings to the arrangement. Yet the major breakthrough never happened. Eventually, to Brian, they proved unmanageable, in *A Cellarful of Noise* he complains about a 'lack of discipline' that 'cannot be tolerated.' And he fired them.

These were the acts that Tony Barrow inherited. Because, initially, a man called Brian Sommerville worked exclusively on The Beatles' behalf, without the distraction of such lesser attractions. His one-man PR company was brought in at the time of The Beatles' winter 1963 tour. A pompous regimental man described by Philip Norman as a 'small plump, already balding' ex-Royal Navy Lieutenant Commander turned Fleet Street journalist, 'he had the aspect of a country squire and a quarterdeck brusqueness which did not at once endear him to his new charges.' His upper-class voice could command attention in those still class-respectful times. Lennon respected Sommerville's hard-headedness, in the same way that he'd later respect Allen Klein. He didn't much like him; he was not 'one of us', but he got the job done. He was a necessary evil. Paul was warily polite. George was outright hostile, the two of them even coming to blows during the famous incidents at the Paris *George Cinq Hotel*. But Sommerville set about screening journalists seeking interviews – deleting names from the list regardless of priorities (alienating a number of Tony Barrow's carefully cultivated contacts in the process), and easing tour-problems as they arose. Epstein – via Derek Taylor, relates how Sommervile told the Chief of Police, 'I am told in Miami you have the best police money can buy.' A statement, Brian considered, 'memorable for the innocence of its ambiguity.'

The uneasy situation persisted until – mid-point on the first American visit – Brian Epstein spectacularly took umbrage with Brian Sommerville. Tetchily jealous and possessive about his 'boys', Epstein bitterly resented the intervention of any closer association than his own. And when Sommerville's name appeared in a press-feature, contravening what he assumed to be the press officer's correct anonymity, Epstein furiously demanded assurances that the affront would never be allowed to happen again. Sommerville indignantly refused to appease him. That's it. He was out of the story before his contract had run its course. An interregnum period followed, during which Tony Barrow attempted to fill in, even as, on 9 March 1964, NEMS relocated from its original Monmouth Street offices to new premises on the fifth floor of Sutherland House, at 5-6 Argyll Street, next door to the city's most famous theatre. Brian 'just loved having offices next door to the London Palladium', recalled Derek, and NEMS would stay there through the 'white-heat of Beatlemania' until August 1967.

And it was a more than usually hectic time during which The Beatles complete the filming of *A Hard Day's Night* in just eight weeks – 'well, it was only black and white, of course', explains John. But to see them on the big screen for a full ninety minutes was an important event horizon to cross, picking up on their style quirks, individual mannerisms, facial expressions, all set in the real, recognisable world, making it suddenly accessible. Lennon even manages to promote his book of poems and random 'based on a novel by a man named Edward Lear' absurdities, *In His Own Write* (March 1964) – in part made up of writings compiled from John's pseudonymous 'Beatcomber' stories in *Mersey Beat*. The cover of the book is clearly displayed – as a kind of product placement – in the movie (his second book, *A Spaniard in the Works* (June 1965), achieves a similar presence in *Help!*).

Then there's the matter of recording a dozen original songs for the soundtrack, including its rush-released first single 'Can't Buy Me Love'. With the *A Hard Day's Night* (July 1964) album, pop Music was once again evolving before the listener's ears. If the first two albums – *Please*

Please Me and *With The Beatles* – created the template-style for the
first Mersey Beat deluge, this third album would have similarly wide-
reaching effects on the next wave of bands. There were a couple of
Beatles-by-numbers fillers – 'Tell Me Why' and 'I Should Have Known
Better' – the kind of tracks which were by now almost too easy to
produce, yet both were promptly covered by lesser entities (the
Naturals took the latter to a UK no.24 in August).

Mersey-style covers would continue to be part of the repertoire. With
the 'Long Tall Sally' EP, (with Little Richard's title-song, Larry Williams'
'Slow Down' and Carl Perkins' 'Matchbox'), more covers on *Beatles for
Sale* (Buddy Holly's 'Words of Love', Chuck Berry's 'rock 'n' roll Music',
Doctor Feelgood's 'Mr Moonlight', Little Richard again with 'Kansas
City' and two more Carl Perkins – 'Honey Don't' and 'Everybody's
Trying to be My Baby') and into *Help!* (Larry Williams' 'Dizzy Miss
Lizzy' and Buck Owen's 'Act Naturally'. Ringo would later record a
duet version of the same song with Buck himself in 1988). There was
another Larry Williams cover, 'Bad Boy', included on the June 1965
American album *Beatles VI* which only became available in the UK as
part of the November 1966 hits compilation *A Collection of Oldies...
But Goldies*.

Such material was familiar to first-generation children-of-the-bomb
rock 'n' roll. And although very soon, official albums would consist of
all-original songs, covers would remain staple studio warm-up fuel –
evidenced by the 'Rip It Up' (Little Richard), 'Shake Rattle and roll' (Big
Joe Turner), 'Blue Suede Shoes' (Carl Perkins) medley and 'Mailman,
Bring Me No More Blues' (Buddy Holly) collected onto *The Beatles
Anthology 3* from as late as the *Abby Road* sessions. There'd be a kind
of nostalgic return to their own early Mersey-period material with 'One
After 909' on *Let It Be* – and, of course, post-Beatles John would record
an entire album of *rock 'n' roll* favourites (in 1975).

But for the first time, with the thirteen newly-penned songs making
up the *A Hard Day's Night* soundtrack album, things were obviously
changing. Not only is this the first album entirely made up of original
material, but the only Beatles album ever completely consisting of
Lennon-McCartney songs. Although to Albert Grossman it is 'as close
to a solo album as John ever made with The Beatles, Paul's 'Things
We Said Today' and 'And I Love Her' were clearly and distinctively
drawing away from John's 'If I Fell' – what Grossman considers John's
first 'attempt to write a sentimental ballad.' While the title track alone
defines everything that's best, most imitated, and yet most inimitable
about the group. It has all the wildness of the first rock 'n' roll wave,

yet bound by tight harmonies and contra-harmonies. Those opposing energies, those contradicting impulses power its momentum, pulling against those restrictions with contagious urgency. From the crashing chord opening, through a compulsive melody and immaculately precise breaks, to the spangled Rickenbacker fade. With the kind of inevitability that had by now become expected, it simultaneously tops the charts of both sides of the Atlantic.

All of this highest-profile activity required close and carefully nurtured press liaisons... and this young guy Derek Taylor just happens to be conveniently available. 'I've had a lovely, lovely idea, Derek', said Brian, 'I want you to join us.' The job was his, if he wanted it.

Derek had spent half his working life as a jobbing journalist, chasing, researching and filing stories, annoyed when he finds his work-in-print has been snubbed-down, paragraphs deleted or phrases altered, when misspelling or wrong punctuations sneak uninvited into the text. Frustrated when favourite pieces get spiked for 'space' reasons or because of a new breaking higher-priority feature. It's time to move on. This is a now-or-never moment. He had a good job as a features writer and a life that was not without its comforts. He was an almost middle-class, middle-aged urban professional with plans and expectations, but, more than that, a growing sense of rootedness, social investment, almost – hush who dares, a kind of ominous contentment.

The challenges of change are riskier than the certainties of the status quo. It is in such conditions, of course, and at such times that a man – and particularly a man – can start to question himself and his purpose in life. If the midlife crisis is a figment of the psychiatric and literary imagination, it's a figment that has migrated into the male imagination at large. The option of fleeing one's responsibilities seems, paradoxically, to grow more appealing as the responsibilities themselves become more rewarding. As in the same counter-intuitive fashion, there is nothing like the arrival of new life to focus the mind on the proximity of death. You become more rounded, and simultaneously the ground becomes less steady.

Play it safe... or take this wildest of chances. 'I know what the time is', he mused, 'it is later than it was.' Did Derek hesitate? Did he agonise? Draw-back from the decision...? It was a hunch-based choice. There's a world to conquer out there. He'd turned thirty. Draw-back now, and the chance would never come again. So Derek became The Beatles' press agent at Brian Epstein's request. In Spring 1964, he moved the family down from Manchester to London, renting 5 The Village, North End Way in Hampstead – a property across the road from the renowned *Bull and Bush* public house. It would not prove to be a long-term address, but soon Paul was calling round to say 'hello'. And by the end of the year, Derek was buying a neat grey suit from the trendy *His Clothes* boutique in Carnaby Street, more in keeping with his new role. 'All our provincial lives were over. We had no choice and maybe, anyway, it was time to go crackers. Hold tight. Close your eyes...!'

To John Lennon, in *Anthology*, 'we've never had more than one PR fella with us, ever. Brian's only got one for each of his artists, and they don't work together. Derek we've known for about a year, but he's one of those people that clicks as soon as you meet him.' The Beatles were a self-contained club that took care of its member. And Derek had the club membership card.

'I joined them because I wanted to work for them, that was all', adds Derek. 'I had been working for *The Daily Express,* but you can only do that for so long without going mad...' then, he adds wryly, 'I went mad anyway.' As the sixties began he was 'uptight', career-focused, upwardly-mobile, on the make – and it was a soul-killing thing, 'we had no place to go but up, and up was really very down.' It was not always an easy transition. 1964 was 'a very hard and sometimes unhappy year.' But reflecting on the time later, it's apparent that 'working for The Beatles has affected all of us in different ways, but affected us it has and forever, come what may we will never be the same.' With the family now living in NW3, 'I was still a bit middle-class.' Working for Epstein, working with 'the best-dressed and, on a good day, quite the most captivating people anyone could remember,' he managed to avoid the strict timetable of office work, and could cultivate more eccentric habits.

The sixties had a similar effect on many, to a greater or lesser degree, in fact to the majority of the planet's population, using pretty much the same Beatles-shaped catalyst. Derek's close proximity to the eye of that generational storm just brings those changes into sharper focus. But if he was to get things done, he would still have to spend hours of each day hunched over a desk, writing his two-thousand words a day. The tedium of the writer's life means biographers either have to bore their readers senseless or fashion a 'myth' – exaggerating picturesque elements of the writer's personality, embroidering anecdotes and, in the end, rendering the writer as a fictional character. For every major literary figure, there are dozens of myths flying around. It's not necessary to manufacture myths about Derek Taylor. He was a writer, but he was living through mythic times, the picturesque anecdotes are all true.

He was part of a huge undercover operation that commenced 8 am on Saturday 2 May 1964, smuggling the disguised Beatles plus wife and girlfriends to a secret holiday in the Virgin Islands and Tahiti. The subterfuge was necessitated partly by unwelcome press attention, and also to avoid the moral censure of singletons holidaying together! John and Cynthia went as 'Mr and Mrs Leslie', with George and Patti Boyd under the aliases 'Mr Hargreaves and Miss Bond'. Another faction travelled by a separate route, with Derek incognito as 'Mr Tatlock' – named after the grumpy 'Uncle Albert' character from *Coronation Street*. He was with Paul, who was in blue-tinted shades and slim moustache, alias 'Mr Manning' with Jane Asher as 'Miss Ashcroft', and Ringo in black hat and drooping ginger moustache as 'Mr Stone' with Maureen as 'Miss Cockcroft'. From Luton Airport, they reached Paris uneventfully, then by Air France Caravelle to Lisbon, and from there to Puerto Rico where, despite such elaborate precautions, there was a huge fan reception waiting!

Then, for the 23 to 25 May Whitsun weekend, Brian Epstein holidayed more modestly within the tacky glamour of Blackpool. It was chill and windy, but as always, his attention was never far from his work. So while there, he took time out to travel to the White Hart Hotel in Bolton. In the car with him were journalist Godfrey Winn… and Derek Taylor. As always, Brian had a hidden agenda; he'd been tipped off by Winn to check out a twenty-four-year-old guitar-playing Lancashire balladeer called Michael Haslam, as a potential NEMS signing. After all, Brian had groups. He had a top female solo star with Cilla. But there was a gap in the spread of his roster for a top male solo star; a space for 'my first ballad-singer,' an answer to testosterone-fueled Tom Jones. They watched his set, after which Winn made introductions, and they wound up back at Haslam's home where Brian made his pitch. It was Derek's opportunity to watch the Nempror in action. With an ever-whirring tape-loop in his journalistic head telling him he was witnessing an unreal bizarre performance.

Once signed, Michael Haslam recorded a Proby-style 'Gotta Get a Hold of Myself', benefiting from a George Martin production and Johnnie Spence arrangement, yet was seldom heard of again (although sister Annie Haslam would later front Renaissance).

18 August 1964. Not only The Beatles' second US visit but the opening of their first full American tour, twenty-five cities in thirty-two days. Derek flew out with them to San Francisco, accompanied by Brian Epstein. Although Brian returned to England soon after, he rejoined the tour on 14 September to catch their final dates, until they all flew home together on 21 September.

By the time Derek assumed the role, the world had been conquered through its soft teenage underbelly. This tour was not conquest, but re-conquest, an exercise in solidifying and building on what had already been achieved. For the press office, much of the early groundbreaking work had already been done, by Tony Barrow. It was no longer a case of mailing out promotional material and chasing journalists in the desperate hope of soliciting a favourable mention. It was more about rationing access, selecting which writer or which magazine-title was to be bestowed the precious face-to-face audience with the 'boys'. Most of that had already been done. Derek's job would be of a different order. It was crisis-management — damage limitation.

He prepared for the trip by discussing media-strategy with Barrow. He listened well, as a good pupil should. Tony already had years of experience with the group, but this would be a sharp learning curve for Derek. 'I felt much more comfortable with Taylor than I had done with Sommerville', recalls Barrow, 'probably because of Derek's journalistic background, which made him sympathetic to the needs of the press on such a tour, but he was also diplomatic and benign in his handling of The Beatles.' Tony details his preferred approach to on-tour press relations. The role that Derek would have to assume. Firstly, there must be balance, there must be access to the 'boys', but to such an extent that access does not become too intolerably intrusive. So it's essential to arrange a limited number of daily one-to-one interviews with selected journalists and radio people who would be on the road with them as the tour moves from city to city. At the same time, there would be large press conferences – hurly-burly's of notebooks, flashbulbs, arms, legs and smouldering cigarette butts, to which the local promoters would invite their own selection of local media representatives. In his book, Barrow writes that 'we made The Beatles far more accessible than any comparable world-class superstar – Elvis Presley, for example – and this helped to maintain goodwill between the group and the media.' This way, he explains, both needs are accommodated.

Derek would be negotiating – no, tactfully demanding – front-page status as a condition of granting that precious interview, ensuring editorial control and veto over any related photo-content; Negotiating away negative or risqué stories by offering the inducement of a more powerfully upbeat 'exclusive'. Then he was arranging syndication to maximise the potential of each interview. The press was more compliant, more respectful then than it is now. And Derek, with his smooth, easy manner, was in an advantageous position. Everyone wanted The Beatles. And they were prepared to do anything they had to do to get them. Derek was good at coordinating press largely because he still saw things through a journalistic lens himself, and he 'wanted to give the boys and girls of the press what they wanted', even when the sheer scale of it was overwhelming. The pressures were more intensive than anything he'd ever envisaged, or could have prepared for. No less than 20,000 people phoned the switchboard of The Beatles' New York hotel! Fortunately, Derek was travelling with assistant press officer Bess Coleman. She'd been part of the original EMI press crew in London during the initial launch phase of The Beatles' career. Since then she'd transferred to New York. Hence she had an insider's knowledge both of The Beatles themselves, and also the way the American media worked. Curt Gunther was along as tour photographer. Support for the tour included Jackie De Shannon and the Righteous Brothers.

As The Beatles' Press Officer, for the first of his two interrupted spells, Derek was quick to realise that the PR role was as much about concealing as it was revealing. About managing details of The Beatles' emotional lives, and concealing the paternity suits that inevitably followed them. About Brian's homosexuality. Or when John's long-lost father Freddie suddenly turned up unannounced at NEMS in April 1964, showing previously unsuspected concern for his celebrity son. And about John's inconvenient marriage to Cynthia. The need for absolute subterfuge had been blasted to smithereens by the press revelation, so the Lennon's moved south, first registering under the name 'the Hadleys' for a three-bedroom flat at Emperor's Gate off London's Cromwell Road. But once there, fan harassment made life impossible, so they moved to a mock-Tudor mansion in Esher, Weybridge called Kenwood, in 1964. Paul, meanwhile, moved in with the family of his actress girlfriend Jane Asher in Wimpole Street. George and Ringo stay on at Green Street until Spring 1964.

Of course, the press was less intrusive then than it is now, less prepared to run fuck-and-tell revelations in the Sunday tabloids. The celebrity culture was less developed, less litigious. But few lives could have been more closely examined than The Beatles. And when slips unavoidably happen, the PR role was one of damage limitation. Spin. Derek was a good press officer. But the quotes he uses were theirs, 'and there is no comparison between a mouth and a mouthpiece.' 'I don't need to tell you what to say, and never did, do I, or did I?', Derek points out in conversation with Paul. 'No, of course you didn't', Paul confirms. And Derek could be tactful when required, telling John, 'I know you don't like the phrase "Beatlemania"', then apologising, 'if you'll forgive the phrase...?' when he inadvertently uses it.

Derek immediately discovered that his press title was less than clearly defined. He was now part of the Fabfourdom's 'Liverpool Mafia' – alongside quiet and suave Neil 'Nel' Aspinall. Neil had joined the trip in 1959, augmenting his £2.10s salary from a Liverpool firm of chartered accountants by driving The Beatles around the Mersey Beat circuit, collecting and counting the cash before they left each venue. He'd been with them through every stage since. Alongside Neil was another former habitué of the *Basnett Bar*, the 'tremendously smooth' Peter Brown. Derek recalls how, in their earlier lives, Peter would 'ease his way into a central spot (in the *Basnett*) and stand with his back to the wall, facing the marble counter to see who or what might turn up.' Now he was NEMS 'fixer supreme'. Then there was big bespectacled Liverpudlian Malcolm 'Mal' Evans, their equipment handler, Alistair Taylor, and Epstein himself. All had separate job-descriptions, but all were interchangeably fixers on twenty-four-hour call.

To Derek, 'we were there because we wanted to selflessly serve The Beatles.' And all were equally there to facilitate the real-life gig-by-gig subterfuge that had to be worked out with military precision. A vital part of Derek's remit was to arrange the group's exit strategy from each venue. Something of what he was faced with can be glimpsed in the opening newsreel-quality sequences of *A Hard Day's Night* as the group are pursued through Paddington Station by waves of relentless fans. In the States, if anything, that situation was amplified. Their set, as top-of-the-bill, consisted of just twelve numbers. It might last for thirty minutes. Sometimes a little less, rarely much more. And for Derek, even the pattern of audience-screams became predictable, as he told Gloria Steinem, the frenzy reaches a crescendo 'after one of them tosses his hair or lifts his guitar.' Then, when George hits the crashing suspended-G introductory chords to *A Hard Day's Night* on his new Rickenbacker twelve-string, that was Derek's signal to set things in motion. There would be a conspicuous 'decoy' limo out front to draw hysterical fans' attention away from what was happening just around the corner where The Beatles and their entourage would be climbing into an alternative getaway vehicle, an ambulance or a delivery van. They could then hopefully escape back to the hotel as inconspicuously as it was ever possible for a Beatle to be.

As Derek wrote, through the Michelle Phillips book, 'these were days and nights of enormous change.' It was an exhausting, exhilarating time, lived at the epicentre of a youthquake that was consuming the world. There had been screaming bobbysoxers and rock 'n' roll riots before this, and there would be periodic group-centred manias in the decades that follow, but nothing quite like this. There were dissenting voices. But they were first disarmed by the wit, charm, and sheer contagious energy of The Beatles, then drowned out by the sheer power of the global phenomenon they were unleashing. Theorists theorise about the reaction to the Kennedy assassination. Others about the carnival of youth on a rising wave of comparative affluence unleashing colour after the decades of austerity, drabness, shortages and moral conformity. All of which might be true. None of it compares to being there. 'It was, though there was then no sense of the phrase – "very sixties"', according to Michelle Phillips (through Derek's guiding pen), 'everyone aboard with no end in view, because why the hell not…?'

After they'd entered the USA 'by the back door' – that is, through San Francisco – touring America with The Beatles meant flying in 'the big grey job', a chartered American Flyers Airlines Lockheed Electra, dealing with unpleasant officials and self-important civic dignitaries demanding access to the 'long-haired louts… who had received so much money for a half-hour show which no-one could hear,' on behalf of the official's obnoxious kids.

And there were hazards, even for those caught up in the Press slipstream. It was Labour Day (30 August) in Atlantic City, mid-tour, and The Beatles' arrival unleashed a frenzied street-invasion that made a Presidential visit seem tame by comparison. Civic authorities had badly underestimated the crowd-control facilities. Inadequate numbers of cops attempted in vain to restrain crowds estimated at over 18,000; the Convention Hall was crammed for the performance itself while frenzied chaos was unleashed in the streets outside among those still waiting. Until, as the motorcade wound its slow way through, according to Derek's commentary, the police lines broke and the cars were swamped by hysterical fans. 'They broke into each of our vehicles one by one, attacking Bess Coleman among others. They didn't know who we were. The police rescued us, barely. Atlantic City may have seen some wild conventions in its time, but this was the biggest thing that ever happened. They're saying it's not like Sinatra, Presley or the late President Kennedy. It's The Beatles and it's without precedent.'

To be present at one of the concerts was to become inaudible behind solid sonic walls of screaming capable of stripping the paint off the theatre walls. Open-air venues were particularly prone to abrupt miniskirt break-outs and beehive hair-styled teen mob-surges over the barriers determinedly towards the stage, which security were totally incapable of controlling. Flipping cross-border into Canada, they play the Vancouver Empire Stadium on 22 August, broadcast live on local radio CKNW. They open tumultuously with 'Twist and Shout', then run through 'You Can't Do That', 'All My Loving' and 'She Loves You'. After George's 'roll Over Beethoven', the MC, Vancouver DJ Red Robeson, pleads for the audience to simmer down if the show is to continue. After Ringo's spot with 'Boys', Derek himself takes to the stage, addressing the crowd directly, informing the heaving crush of fans that they're 'very worried about the situation at the front.'

Then, at the Gator Bowl in Jacksonville, Florida (11 September), Derek ran into what *Florida Times-Union* reporter Larry Kane called 'quite a row' with newsreel and TV cameramen. Backstage, in the build-up towards the gig, Mal alerted Derek that there were 'cine cameramen, television men, mobile film units from Hollywood on the field ready to film The Beatles show, people who are anxious to make commercial capital out of filming The Beatles show.' Derek strongly disapproved. The Police were not anxious to entangle themselves, and the promoters were getting 'stroppy', suffering from inertia yet refusing to intervene. So, 'I went on and appealed to the kids.' Derek again went on stage demanding 'Do you want The Beatles on this stage?' – to an immense 'Yeah!'. 'Well then, do you want to get rid of the cameras?' – 'Yeah!' It was a bluff, except that it wasn't a bluff, because The Beatles refused to go on until the situation was resolved. There's a photo in *Anthology* of the moment, Derek is addressing the crowd, arms upraised, his shirt-sleeves rolled-up, cig in right hand, tie pulled askew.

High in the plane to the next venue in Boston, Derek apologetically explained to Larry Kane the stance he'd been forced into taking, revealing 'what I had to risk was that the kids wouldn't riot.' The interview-tape was fortunately retained and added to Derek's contentious *Here, There & Everywhere* CD. His first gut-instincts were with the press. At heart, he was still one of them. 'We are completely in favour of, and work very happily with legitimate news-gathering media, we like radio men, we like television men, and we very much like journalists, and we have quite a cross-section travelling with us on this plane.' But 'a Beatles show is the hottest thing in showbusiness, in history,' and unauthorised concert footage was a valuable commodity. Pirating of 'any moving film' by 'what we used to call in the old days "spivs"' was getting out of hand. At the Cleveland Public Hall (15 September), the fan-situation got so riotous cops stepped in to close the show for a ten-minute delay. Derek again attempted to cool things.

His controlled articulate English accent helped, and 'he didn't yell at them like the cops did.' Then for their concert at Kansas City on 17 September, The Beatles were paid $150,000 (£53,571), then the biggest fee ever paid for a single performance.

But history was already being almost innocently rewritten. In an early interview, a journalist suggests to Paul McCartney that the titles of The Beatles' first three singles are all built around the directly personalised 'you /me' – 'Love Me Do' c/w 'PS I Love You', 'Please Please Me' c/w 'Ask Me Why', 'From Me to You' c/w 'Thank You Girl'. Relating immediately to the target listener on the most basic of levels. Some time later, in another interview, Paul makes a point of mentioning this as though it had been a deliberate masterplan all along. A strategy they'd devised together as part of their blueprint for chart domination, not merely a happy accident. Myth and truth were already becoming indistinguishable, even to the participants.

Back in the hotel, John could be sullen and argumentative, with a verbal cruelty capable of reducing Brian Epstein to tears. Oddly, his caustic wit disguised an essential shyness around women. What he would later describe as being 'crippled inside'. By contrast, Paul was agreeable and bent on pleasing, affable to all who cross his path, while quietly – and sometimes deviously, pursuing his own agenda. Epstein observed that Paul could 'be temperamental and moody and difficult to deal with', while he was capable of turning on his charm to devastating effect when he wanted to manipulate rivals, colleagues… or women he fancied. He was the most adept at 'pulling birds', although George may have eventually overtaken him when it came to nubile groupies. George, who reacted badly to the rigours of touring, became tired and withdrawn. Ringo was 'as merry as a cockroach in a pantry,' while staying the least involved in the on-tour sexual shenanigans…

The 1964 world tour was described by a leering Lennon as 'Satyricon', with Derek getting his first taste of it in June during its Australian leg. Mal Evans would select suitably miniskirted screaming girls simply by pointing 'you, you… and you,' corraling them into an adjoining holding room where Neil Aspinall and Derek 'allocated a continual supply of carnal delight to the tour members,' under the careful scrutiny of Epstein; 'we were the link, the pipeline, the barrier, the obstacle course to be cleared to reach the big prize.' The fiercely protective Mal was scrupulously prudent in his selection, eliminating any obviously under-age girls who could prove litigious, but ushering others through, including 'Dragon Lady' Jennie Kee at the Sydney Sheraton Hotel. Sometimes even his filtering system failed. Derek found himself having to hastily improvise a cover story as soon as they hit America. The opening concert was at the San Francisco Cow Palace (19 August). From there they took a flight to Las Vegas to appear at the Convention Hall, staying over in a suite in its heavily securitised twenty-third floor. Derek, Mal and Neil found themselves working together to deflect a distraught mother looking for the twin under-age daughters who were in John's room... apparently 'watching television'.

As Derek found out, his new position had also placed him in an unexpectedly hazardous place. Brian Epstein was the honourable man who had taken The Beatles 'from Boys in Black Leather to Lords of the Earth'. But he could also be childishly defensive. Meticulous, both shyly polite and capricious. A misfit. And Derek soon found himself caught in the no-man's-land between The Beatles and Epstein's proprietorial obsession. And the nemperor's spurned-lover tantrums could be viciously spiteful. As Derek explained, 'I'd been told he could be cruel. I only realised it when I came to organise a Fab Four press conference. Brian didn't want it to work. If I made a mess of it, even though The Beatles would be in that mess, he'd be happy – because I'd gained no control over them. He said "Go ahead – but this is doomed. I look forward to speaking to you about it afterwards." I joined in April, here he was in May, treating me with massive cruelty.'

He'd had intimations of what was to come when Derek attended the premiere of *A Hard Day's Night*. He charged the limousine home that night to NEMS. Once Brian found out, he arbitrarily deducted the fare from Derek's salary. 'It was his method of making sure the staff didn't take advantage', Derek confided to Ray Coleman. 'But I didn't see myself as staff, rather one of the gang. He saw me as one of the gang emotionally and spiritually, but not when it came down to the books. That's why I saw him as a shop-keeper!'

Taking 'two small yellow Dexedrine tablets' became an essential part of Derek's tour routine. Crunching happy pills. Sleeping pills to slow him down. Stimulants to accelerate him. Crossing America on a blend of angry little pills and extreme logistical planning. As the tour wound down, before the final Paramount Theatre charity date (20 September), the entourage rested for an overnight break at the invitation of the Pigman Family in Arkansas. They flew out from Dallas where they'd played the Memorial Coliseum (18 September). They change at an intermediate airport, into a small private plane – 'so like Buddy Holly,' with the pilot navigating from a little map unfolded on his knee illuminated by a flashlight, flying through pitch darkness surrounded by looming mountains on all sides. Finally, landing in a field lit-up by blazing oil-barrels. Yet at the Pigman's ranch, rather than rest, they take stay-awake pills and play cards all night.

Tony Barrow explains that 'dry-humoured and affable, Derek got on exceedingly well with The Beatles, George in particular, but his fatal mistake was to get too chummy with them. He strove hard to be "one of the lads" and he succeeded in winning their affections, but in doing so he earned a hefty black mark from Brian Epstein. Brian's jealous, possessive nature made him mistrust the motives of anyone who developed a close personal relationship with his boys. This was something I realised very soon after I went to work with him. Derek was a good writer and a kind, considerate and even-tempered person, but he lost Epstein's support by taking too many matters into his own hands and failing to keep his boss posted on what he was doing. The friction between the two men grew hotter and their ferocious arguments became an everyday occurrence, witnessed by everyone from the boys themselves to the office clerks and receptionists. Eventually, both parties admitted that they could not go on working with one another and Taylor's professional connection with The Beatles was severed, although his friendship with them survived...'

To Philip Norman, 'Taylor proved to be a perfect fit' for the job. He shared with The Beatles the typical Merseysider's dry and cynical sense of humour. George reports a typically disconnected exchange between them; 'if I said something to Derek like "Hey, did you see the bit about when he walked on the water?" He would pull out a postcard of Bethnal Green and say "Have you seen this one, Hitler was only two foot three." "Yes, but Sri Yokteswar once wrote..." "Well do you ever remember this about A Hard Day's Night premier?" Well, that went on for years, but somehow it didn't matter. So thanks to him, I do now know a lot more about the Royal Family and Hitler.'

Derek wrote poetry too. Spontaneous prose-bursts for no particular purpose other than to amuse himself. Sometimes sound-verse such as 'grattig snalsog, shoghot binging, harold schwein...' relying on an onomatopoeic resonance. Or little droodles of verse that reconfigure the events of his life into comic absurdism. Something needing only the slightest of nudges. His poems lay somewhere between the Mersey Poets anthology, Adrian Henri, Spike Milligan, and – most obviously – John Lennon. While, to Derek, The Beatles were 'perfectly cast and dead on time for Marshall McLuhan's "Global Village", with electronic means of communication representing his notion – not, in my opinion, as specious as his detractors seek to prove – of an externalised nervous system.' 'Liverpudlians in exile tend to stick together', points out

Barrow, 'it's a survival thing.' The obvious conclusion is that this first tenure was brought to a premature close because he was too successful at his job. His bonding with his charges was so complete that it played on 'Eppy's jealous insecurities. If he'd been less good, less accepted into their enchanted inner circle, he might have lasted longer.

Epstein has been criticised for not maximising The Beatles' merchandising potential, for not taking up the countless opportunities available for exploiting their celebrity. He'd managed the electrical department of the Liverpool family business. Then he was manager of the biggest phenomenon in the world. He consulted with the best; he was learning the game. But at the same time, he had firm ideas about what he was doing. By setting quality standards, through protection and careful selection, and by limiting the overkill that devalued the Elvis product, he instead established a reputation for reliability and honesty that is more valuable for the long-term credibility of the brand. By sometimes deciding on the lower-yield high-prestige option, in favour of the smash-and-grab choice, he built a reputation for honesty and reliability. What had previously been thought of as a grubby exercise in extracting pocket-money from gullible and impressionable teens, Brian elevated into what he saw as the 'finest and most efficient management/direction of artists in the world.' He authorised the launch of a monthly magazine – *The Beatles Book* (no.1 dated August 1963) – edited by Sean O'Mahony (aka Johnny Dean). Priced at just seven-and-a-half old pence, but once assured of its integrity, Epstein adopted a policy of non-interference. Each issue retains an escalating collectors price tag.

Whereas Colonel Tom Parker's short-sighted, short-term acquisitiveness may have made instant killings by monopolising the market in both 'I Love Elvis' and 'I Hate Elvis' button-badges, he never outgrew that limited carnival huckster mindset. Epstein knew when to let go. Perhaps he had no choice? Perhaps letting go was only a grudging acceptance of what was already a reality? Tom Parker never did let go, even Elvis' death was a mere temporary interruption to the smooth marketing flow. The Beatles were a far less supine, far more strong-willed proposition. If Epstein got hurt in the process of separation, which he was, if he was a casualty of their growing autonomy, it was neither a hurt they deliberately sought nor was it something that concerned them greatly.

The Beatles' skill lies in the fact that they were never once wrong-footed by the fast-changing shifts in trend. They were outgrowing Epstein to navigate their own course. Already Andrew Loog Oldham was out there building his 'anti-Beatles'. As The Beatles were growing away from their reliance on cover versions, writing their own material, so Oldham was separating out Mick and Keith with instructions to write songs. They start hesitantly with their own B-sides, with a surprise hit for American star Gene Pitney ('That Girl Belongs to Yesterday'), and for their nymphet protégé Marianne Faithful, before daring to chance their own A-side. And if The Beatles were snapped by their 'official photographer' Dezo Hoffman frolicking on the Weston-super-Mare beach in Victorian bathing-wear for a summer special – which they were – Oldham ensured the Stones were photographed pissing up against a garage wall, and the photos made it into the shocked and outraged national press. Yet even the Stones were out-guessed by psychedelia with their sprawling *Their Satanic Majesties Request* (December 1967) album, their answer to *Sgt. Pepper*. It may be a wonderfully exotic curiosity, a gem of its curious era, but at the time it was largely perceived to have failed and derailed their irresistible rise.

Something that never once happened to The Beatles.

Brian's flaw was his inability to delegate – and his own self-belief in his grasp of media matters, which combined to undermine his press officer. When the mood took him, Brian took it upon himself to circumvent them, and deal directly with the press. When the group were on the road, incoming phone calls to rooms occupied by The Beatles were blocked, but the line to the PR suite was kept open so that essential matters could be sorted. That was part of the job description. But through Epstein's increasingly mercurial temperament, he also made a habit of stopping calls to his own suite too and re-routing them through PR. Barrow found this 'mildly annoying'. Derek Taylor inherited such annoyances.

To Tony Barrow, Brian Epstein's 'proud attachment to John, Paul, George and Ringo was passionate, fanatical, obsessive and all-pervading… He took responsibility for their every fresh achievement and adopted a ferociously possessive attitude when anyone got too close to the boys. At least one top NEMS executive, Derek Taylor… fell by the wayside solely because he became too friendly with the group for Epstein's liking.' Al Arowitz agrees. To him, 'the tighter Derek got with The Beatles, the more jealous The Beatles' moody and temperamental manager became. Until finally, Derek's relationship with Epstein blew up…'

The 1964 five-week USA tour had opened 19 August at the San Francisco Cow Palace. To say that the tour had been eventful is to state the obvious. Celebrities jostled to meet the Fab Four, everyone from

movie stars to politicians. There are tales that have acquired mythic
status, told and re-told with slight variations in numberless first-hand
memoirs and second-hand accounts. Crises happened, and they were
handled. 'Some months of some years stand out in the memory', wrote
Derek – through the ghosted voice of Michelle Phillips – 'and obviously,
for me', one such month in one such year was that August. At a press
conference prior to playing the *Hollywood Bowl*, The Beatles were
asked which Hollywood actress they'd most like to meet. Paul said
'Jayne Mansfield'. His wish was immediately granted the following
day when she was there at the *Whisky a Go Go* club, 8910 Sunset
Boulevard, for a charity-party held in their honour.

Derek was in attendance when George, less than pleased about
constant press harassment, threw his Scotch-and-Coke over a persistent
photographer. Then, after the Forest Hill concert (28 August), The
Beatles got to meet Bob Dylan at the Manhattan *Hotel Delmonico*, a
summit brokered by Alfred Aronowitz, a *New York Post* reporter who
had followed The Beatles from New York down to Miami during their
first trip. Al and Dylan – the 'ghost of electricity howling in the bones
of his face' – cruised up to the ritzy Park Avenue hotel in Dylan's blue
Ford station-wagon, chauffeured by Victor Maymudes. 'It was the usual
state of siege with the street-scene spilling into the hotel lobby and
armed guards everywhere. Pinkerton's and cops and plainclothesmen,
men with short-sleeved white shirts and thin grey ties and short-sleeved
white minds and thin grey thoughts, checking and re-checking passes
and authorisations.

Singled out by Mal Evans, Dylan's trio were escorted through the
melee, and into the 'holding room' of The Beatles' suite where Derek
was attempting to entertain hordes of photographers and journalists,
as well as Peter Paul & Mary and the Kingston Trio. Then Dylan was led
into The Beatles' presence, with Derek on hand to arbitrate. No need.
Everything is cool. Al gestured to Victor, who had a marijuana stash in
his pocket. Dylan rolls a joint and passes it around. He assumed they
were already familiar with it, after all, hadn't they been singing 'I get
high, I get high' in the chorus of 'I Want to Hold Your Hand'? Actually
no, the lyric is 'I can't hide, I can't hide' they explain. They'd been
doing a variety of pills since Hamburg. But not 'wacky-backy'. Not
until now. Dylan passed the joint to John... who warily passed it on to
Ringo. The effect was immediate. Soon everyone, including Derek and
Epstein, was high. Paul grabbed Derek by the arm, 'it's as if we're up
there', he burbled excitedly, indicating the ceiling, 'it's as if we're up
there. Up there, looking down on us.' It was an out-of-body experience

that shifted the group's orientation forever. By the time they were
filming *Help!* In the Bahamas, they were all openly smoking 'pot'.

For Derek, his simultaneous introduction to getting high was just
as much of a revelation. 'It was the marijuana which solidified my
friendship with Derek Taylor', recalled Aronowitz. 'As the man who had
turned him onto weed, I commanded a certain respect from Derek, just
as poets Michael McClure and Joanne Kyger plus painter Robert Lavigne
– the persons who gave me my first joint, still command a certain
respect from me. In the beginning, you can't help but look upon the
person who turned you on as an experienced old-timer, an expert who
can tell you much more about the ins and outs and ups and downs
of THC and the weed-world. Plus you can't help but feel a certain
gratitude towards that person for having given you a key to satori and
having opened the door for you to an expanding universe. By the last
time I saw Derek some years ago, he had turned into as much of a
pothead as I've ever been' (in his *The Blacklisted Journalist*).

Cannabis, chiefly marijuana, or 'grass' – 'a wonderful escape from
whatever reality is' – promised to be the magic potion to open an entire
generation's mind to new possibilities. As Paul observed to one of his
biographers, 'we'd met people like Dylan and we got into pot, like a lot
of people from our generation. And I suppose, in our way, we thought
this was a little more grown-up than perhaps the Scotch-and-Coke
we'd been into before then, so once pot was established as part of the
curriculum, you started to get a bit more surreal material coming from
us, a bit more abstract stuff.' In doing so, they were following earlier
converts, Beat writers such as Jack Kerouac, Allen Ginsberg and William
Burroughs, who extolled the virtues of what Derek dubbed 'the filthy
rotten mind-eroding devilweed' and helped consolidate its image as
a magic door to a world of new experiences. During the Vietnam war,
dope-smoking would assume a political dimension, a sign that its
users were at odds with a US government fighting an unpopular war.
Cannabis soon became a major ingredient of the West Coast counter-
culture, a facilitator of free love in a return to a more sybaritic era. All of
that was still to come.

The tour closed on 20 September with The Beatles making a charity
appearance on behalf of the United Cerebral Palsy Fund at the New
York *Paramount Theater*; 'An Evening with The Beatles' compered by
married lounge-core duo Steve Lawrence and Edie Gorme. Afterwards,
the end-of-tour party was held at the lavish *Riviera Motel* within sight
of the Boeing's taillights circling over JFK. Again, Bob Dylan turned
up for the event. The tour had been an unqualified success, no two

ways about that. But within the magic circle, all was less than well. As the tour wound down, Albert Grossman observed that 'by this time, Lennon's rage against the American public and press had focused to a laser-beam intensity... Derek Taylor, drew a telling picture of the scene at the *Delmonico Hotel* after a typically insomniac night, with the sycophants of the press corp sitting around stoned and Murray the K lying half-crocked on a cot – one filmy eye open, the other closed – as John Lennon poured contempt upon the whole retinue and, by extension, on Beatlemania'.

On this last night, the celebrations were further spoiled, at least among those who cared to know, by an uncharitable falling out between Derek and Brian Epstein. There's something about an argument with Brian about a limousine. Brian accused Derek of taking his limousine from outside the Paramount. Tony Barrow claims Derek 'made the big mistake of jumping into limousines with the boys ahead of Epstein.' Derek himself wrote of 'an over-hasty escape from the usual state of siege' in a courtyard of an Indianapolis motel. 'The Beatles had been rushed into their limousine, a bad case of over-haste by panicky officials, and I had waved the car away as an alternative to losing an arm or maybe a life, trying instead to climb in the front seat beside Brian Epstein who had been slammed in bodily.' So, Derek attempted to clamber into the front seat beside Brian. But Brian saw him coming and slammed the door 'bodily' to exclude him. Derek found himself abandoned and had to rely on a lift from a racist redneck who detoured him through what he calls 'Coonsville' towards the next connection at the Indiana State Fair. 'Catch one of them at night and put a scare in him and yes sir, there ain't a funnier sight in all the world than a frightened coon', commentated the redneck, while negotiating a favour-for-favour deal with Derek for his son to meet The Beatles.

Derek had been fired before. Since the earliest days of their association, there'd always been a stormy and precarious relationship between him and Brian. 'I still had an independent spirit. I knew about trade-union rights and holidays and speaking your mind and that sort of thing', he argued. But this time the resignation was absolute with no possibility of reconciliation. It came in train with the latest in a long line of explosive tiffs and flare-ups, and Derek phrased it bluntly. Epstein called him a swine. Derek replied in kind – and resigned. 'I'm not taking any more of this man's shit. I love The Beatles, but I'm not hanging around to be fired another hundred times, I'm off.' Those privy to the organisation's inner circle of aides, gofers, intimates, and associates got to know about the incident – first by rumours, then by the clear announcement that Derek had irrevocably quit, both as the group's press officer and as Epstein's personal assistant.

Derek Taylor. He resigned. His first Beatles tenure was over. From the time Brian Epstein initially noted down the name of the journalist responsible for *The Daily Express* review of the Manchester concert as a promising new contact ripe for cultivation, through to their irrevocable split in what Derek calls an American 'Something Hotel' beside JFK airport, was a period measured in months. Sixteen of them. His first spell of work with The Beatles – first unofficially, then as an official member of the entourage – had taken him through to the end of 1964, which had been their most explosive year yet. Just about the most explosive year in UK pop music, and possibly the most explosive months in twentieth-century music. Through an April in which they broke out across America and found themselves holding the top five positions in the US charts. Through the filming, and the premiere of *A Hard Day's Night* and its hit singles. Through the no.1 'I Feel Fine' c/w 'She's A Woman'. And during those months the world had shifted on its axis. And Derek's life had been transfigured out of all recognition. Nothing, literally, would ever be quite the same again. But Derek's break-point had been with Epstein... not with The Beatles themselves, even though a split with the former made a continuing working relationship with the latter difficult. At least for now...

Yet Brian insisted Derek work out his contractual notice, which extended through to immediately prior to Christmas. It was also a delaying tactic on Brian's part, allowing him time to hopefully talk Derek around. Sure, there was tension and stress; how could it be any other way? But when they work together, they work well. On the 25 November Brian, Derek and Tommy Quickly flew out to Los Angeles as part of a promotional push for Tommy's latest single, 'The Wild Side of Life' (Pye 7N 15708), which had just been picked up for release by the Liberty label. A lively version of the song written by William Warren and Arlie Carter, it had been a 1952 country hit for Hank Thompson, which had also been recorded by Bill Haley (1961), then by Jerry Lee Lewis (1965) and Conway Twitty (1966). But Brian Epstein had high hopes for the commercial potential of the jaunty Quickly version and led up the promo delegation to America. Tommy appeared on *Shindig!* With the Remo Four, where he sings 'I didn't know they made honky-tonk angels' with thumbs hooked casually into his belt. But for Brian, the jaunt was also a covert attempt at reconciliation with Derek. They were met at the airport by Lionel Bart. Brian hung around until 3 December while Derek and Tommy continued with what Derek called the 'torture' of promotional commitments.

Then into December 1964, with the release of The Beatles fourth
UK album. As perhaps a final inducement to stay, it has sleeve-notes by
Derek Taylor. Probably the most widely-read words he'll ever write. A
more widely read and more intensely-scrutinised prose than his books
or the words he wrote supposedly authored by George Harrison or
Brian Epstein. 'This is the fourth by the four. *Please Please Me, With
The Beatles, Hard Day's Night.* That's three. Now... *Beatles for Sale.*
The young men themselves aren't for sale. Money, noisy though it is,
doesn't talk that loud.'

Retitled *Beatles '65* in America, to Derek, 'this album has some lovely
samples of Beatle music. It has, for instance, eight new titles wrought
by the incomparable John Lennon and Paul McCartney, Marvellous.
Many hours and hard day's nights of devoted industry went into the
production of this album. It isn't a potboiling, quick-sale, any-old-thing-
will-do-for-Christmas mixture. As on other albums, The Beatles have
tossed in far more value than the market usually demands. Quite the
best of its kind in the world. There is little or nothing on the album
which cannot be reproduced on stage, which is, as students and critics
of pop-music know, not always the case. Here it is then. The best
album yet – quite definitely, says John, Paul, George and Ringo – full
of everything which made the four the biggest attraction the world
has ever known. Full of raw John and melodic Paul; a number from
George, and a bonus from Ringo. For those who like to know who does
precisely what, there are details alongside each title.'

There are still a clutch of covers, as though, having exhausted the
back-log of original songs and partial song-fragments they'd stored
away for later development since their pre-*Please Please Me* days,
they'd been forced to fall back on other's songs. As though the
demands of writing the full original score for *A Hard Day's Night* had
drained them? Circumstantial evidence suggests this was not the case.
After all, they still had songs to spare for Peter & Gordon's 'Nobody
I Know' or the Applejacks' 'Like Dreamers Do' which both charted
during the months the album was being prepared. Rather, in Derek's
words, 'there are six numbers culled from the rhythmic wealth of the
past extraordinary decade' included, 'mingling with the new'. 'Pieces
like "Kansas City", and "rock And roll Music"' – on which 'George
Martin joins John and Paul on one piano.' Plus two Carl Perkins songs
– George doing 'Everybody's Trying to be My Baby' and Ringo taking
his one-song-per-album vocals for 'Honey Don't' (he'd previously done
Perkins' 'Matchbox' on the 'Long Tall Sally' EP – a song already passably,

adequately covered by *6:5 Special* regular Terry Wayne). There was also a close-harmony arrangement of Buddy Holly's 'Words of Love' on which Derek reveals 'Ringo plays a packing case'.

But those covers were already overshadowed by their own writing, and there are telling evolutions apparent in the original songs. Derek points out that 'at least three of the Lennon-McCartney songs were seriously considered as single releases until John popped up with "I Feel Fine". These three were "Eight Days A Week", "No Reply", and "I'm a Loser". Each would have topped the charts, but as it is they are an adornment to this LP and a lesson to other artists.' In fact, opening side two, the swirling 'Eight Days A Week' was lifted off to become a no.1 American single in its own right. 'There are few gimmicks or recording tricks', Derek continues, 'though for effect, The Beatles and their recording manager George Martin, have slipped in some novelties. Like Paul on Hammond organ to introduce drama into "Mr Moonlight", which also, and for the first time, has George Harrison applying a thump to an elderly African drum because Ringo was busy elsewhere in the studio, playing bongos. George's thump remains on the track. The bongos were later dropped. Beyond this, it is straightforward 1964 disc-making.'

The folk-simple 'I'll Follow the Sun', and more significantly John's 'I'm a Loser' deliberately ape Bob Dylan's phrasing (like 'You've Got to Hide Your Love Away's 'gather round all you clowns') and even his nasal delivery and harmonica. Like 'Help!' and 'Nowhere Man', 'I'm a Loser' was a product of what Lennon termed his troubled 'fat Elvis' period, when his marriage was faring badly, and he was concerned about his weight gain. His darknesses hidden within the group's collective carefree image. As George confided to Derek, 'it would depend on what mood you were in how you behaved. That's why the fab four were good, because if one of us was in a bad mood, the others would cover. We protected each other' (in *I, Me, Mine*).

The inner gatefold photos by Robert Freeman line up a typical stage in-performance shot against a newer image of them posed against a collage of vintage movie-stills. The outer sleeve frames them starkly pastoral and simply wind-blown against yellowing fallen leaves – although snapped in Hyde Park close by the Royal Albert Hall, it was redolent with intimations of new sounds and the radical new directions that pop music would soon be taking... the implications of which are still very much with us...

It instantly replaced *A Hard Day's Night* at no.1 on the LP charts, yet it's already apparent that it's a different breed of record to its predecessor. The Beatles were changing. And Derek was going through his own changes. 'I've had a drink or two, and I don't care', sings John on 'I Don't Want to Spoil the Party'. Previously, in pop, boys cry, when no-one can see them. But they don't drink. And if they do, they don't own up to it. This lyric marks out a new maturity, a new casual honesty. The Beatnik hipster audience, previously the preserve of jazz or Bebop, were in the process of taking notice and shifting across to rock. They heard the December 1965 co-A-side of 'We Can Work it Out' / 'Day Tripper' and detected LSD-trip references.

Sometime during January 1965, in their Charles Street apartment in New York's Greenwich Village, Michelle Phillips met Cass Elliot for the first time. It was also the first time they took LSD-25. Derek Taylor would ghost-write each detail of the evening in Michelle's 'autobiography', about how, through the enhanced perception which the acid-impregnated sugar-cubes gifted them, 'we heard, we heard The Beatles for the first time. We had stereo 'phones, two sets of them, and we were just dumbfounded with the music of The Beatles, the energy and those tunes, and most important, they could sing. In that moment we knew that we, this group of people, whoever we were or would become, were going to make a transition in our music. We had to.'

Which Beatles album was it they were listening to? She doesn't say. But it was 1965. So the chances are it was *Beatles '65*, with its Derek Taylor-scripted liner text. And if so... what a box of frogs that presents. What force of predestination was at work that would determine that the same Derek Taylor would eventually be ghosting her own account of the evening's events, within his own ghost presence...?

Chapter Eight: 1965: So You Want To Be A rock 'N' roll Star?

I wore my fringe like Roger McGuinn's, I was hoping to impress...
('Consolation Prize' by Orange Juice/Edwyn Collins)

''65, '66, '67. These were the years of dash and daring', says Derek. These are stories that echo down through the years...

Music is not an exact science.

Nevertheless, for Derek Taylor, there was an invitation from Bob Eubanks for him to work as publicist for Los Angeles radio station KRLA. The actual terms of employment might be a little vague. But it provides an access point to new possibilities. A popular DJ, Eubanks would later become nationally famous as a TV game-show host for, among others, the 'awful' *Newlyweds Game* from 1966. 'Have you seen the Newly-Weds?' mocks Derek. The template for its UK equivalent *Mr & Mrs*. It is 'David and Julie, on toast. The aim is to find how much the newly-weds really know about each other, e.g., What would your husband say if he farted – (a) I regret farting, (b) I don't regret farting, (c) I guess I farted, or (d) who farted?' Eubanks was an ideal TV presenter, 'clean' and respectably suited.

But their first connection was that he was also the music promoter of 'clean clubs for teens' who was responsible for bringing The Beatles to the West Coast in 1964 – which he'd done by mortgaging his own house, for their Hollywood Bowl performance. Although Eubank had introduced them on-stage, Derek was never entirely convinced that he, bequiffed like a fifties Frankie Avalon, genuinely liked the group. Or whether he'd merely astutely spotted a perfect business opportunity for making money. 'Hell, he was getting rich.' But 'there were many other deals going. One of the drivers, after the first Bowl show, handed The Beatles towels to dry their sweat. He later cut up the towels, encased half-inch squares of towel in plastic, and sold them for five bucks each. The driver was really a radio station newsman.' It was during the turmoil of that Beatles west-coast visit in 1964 that Eubank's connection with Derek first happened. He said 'why doncher work for me buddy, we'll get rich?'

Now, for Derek, 'it wasn't only vibes, man, though they were crucial... it was also the weather, the media and the myth. The Sunshine State... the Golden Gate...'. Frank Lloyd Wright said, 'if you tip the world on its side, everything loose will end up in California.' The west coast has the sunshine, and the girls all get so tanned. And LA is the only place to be, where ambition and creativity walk hand in hand in hand, the 'land of tinsel, false idols and broken promises.' It was an opportunity to spend time in 'Hollywood, movie capital of the world', where he could expect the promised Hollywood salary – $215 a week with expenses. No more of Brian Epstein's hissy fits. Derek's life had never been exactly charmed, more self-sufficient. Until that first Beatles moment tipped his world on its side. That one opportunity. Now was the time for the second leap of faith – or at least, of self-belief. His life had come loose. So, taking what he'd learned from Brian and his Beatles experience, and flying by the seat of his very well-tailored razor-sharp suit, he made that Atlantic Crossing. He took up the lease on a house on Nichols Canyon Road, in what is now West Hollywood, and with his wife and children – Timothy, Gerard, Victoria and Vanessa, he moved to California.

'And why LA?', asks Derek. 'Well, of course, this is where they'd all gathered. This is where many folksingers finished up in those days. This is the end of the road because they had the *Troubadour* and the *Ash Grove* and they were near San Francisco and there were many other things they could do. And anyway, the sun was shining and those people that were starving were finding it easier to starve here, probably that's why. And then when it got what San Francisco would call glossy and shiny and over-commercialised, San Francisco said, "we'll make our own music now, we are ready. And we won't have any of that LA nonsense." Except that they do come to LA, I notice, for big advances from the capitalistic record companies. But it happens when it happens, if the right people meet at the right time…'

To paraphrase Derek, each chapter in this book is a story, but the overall story it tells is the best one of all. This was a transitional period. But all periods are transitional, from someplace to somewhere else. Travelling between places. Leaving everything old, with everything new lying ahead in wait. At one time, aspirant travellers would take with them 'letters of introduction' from important home contacts to influential dignitaries abroad. KRLA had hyped up an intense promo campaign in preparation for Derek's arrival, largely based around his Beatles connections. That, in itself, was all the recommendation he needs. It was enough. He needs only his fame-by-association. His Beatles back-story provides all the gold-card celebrity-endorsement 'letters of introduction' he could ever need.

That, and the fact that he's bright, urbane, a smooth talker, and a good sales-person with a warm outgoing personality. *KRLA Beat* was the station's four-page newssheet, upgraded from its former fanzine

status, selling at just ten cents, but growing with each issue. Vol.1 No.1
(dated 25 February 1965) leads off enthusiastically with the story of
Derek's arrival. 'I cannot describe the Californian experience. You just
have to go there and do it and rely on your ability to absorb it and
still stay alive and reasonably steady. If you can do it there, you can do
it anywhere. Do what? Do anything.' Yet so far there was no real job
there for him to do. And he wound up staying with KRLA – a Top Forty
station fronted by frenetic on-air personality Dick Bondi – for only a
few short weeks. He was given an office at 6290 Sunset Boulevard, as
what he termed 'puppet head' of Prestige Publicity. The office boasted
a suitably prestigious high-backed leather chair, and a couple of eager
on-the-make partners in the shape of Texans Gayle and Cecil Tuck.

In America, English was this year's colour. The tables had turned
massively. The Knickerbockers were scoring with two huge Beatles-
xeroxed hit singles that are still capable of fooling radio audiences.
Programme their 'Lies' or 'One-Track Heart' today, and check the
reaction. Other American bands were busy covering British hits, in a
neat reversal of everything that had previously been taken for granted
– the Cryan Shames covered the Searchers' 'Sugar and Spice'. Brenda
Lee went to London to record 'Is It True', specifically calculated
to get the 'British Sound' by using London studios and future Ivy
League songwriters John Carter and Ken Lewis. The Everly Brothers
– who'd already done the 'yeah yeah yeah' thing years earlier on their
'Temptation' hit – did the same, recording their London album and
scooping up original songs by the Hollies to get their share of the
'Beat Boom'. As Derek wrote, 'everybody wanted to go to England
and get to the clubs and sit in the *Ad Lib* with The Beatles and be
recognised and meet people in Carnaby Street and the King's Road.'
Simultaneously, young DJ John Peel was accelerating his American radio
career by playing off his Englishness, and more specifically, his Mersey
connections. Ian Whitcomb was making himself over into a professional
Englishman.

So how did that affect Derek Taylor? Brian comments in *A Cellarful
of Noise* that 'it is considered an asset to have some contact with
someone who knows The Beatles.' As an Englishman in the United
States – more, as an Englishman with genuine Merseyside origins and
bona fide Beatles connections – it was just about as good as you could
get. From the start, there had been offers and opportunities. Even as
he took over from Brian Sommerville the previous July he'd received a
cable – addressed via John Lennon, The Beatles, London – at his NEMS
Enterprises office, offering the 'music critics position' at Dallas KLIF

radio. But the time had never been so right before. Now Derek was expected to bring all of that kudos to KRLA, to amplify and perform the same function. He was uneasy with the unrealistically high level of their expectations – as The Beatles' publicist it was assumed he had the magic to make anyone famous, as though 'if you rolled me up and smoked me, you would be on *The Ed Sullivan Show* Independence Day.' But he allowed himself to be driven up and down the Boulevard by Bob Eubank, as if participating in some strange ticker-tape welcome, designed to draw attention to the station's latest Beatles-connected acquisition, 'like Tom Ewell did to Jayne Mansfield in *The Girl Can't Help It*.' And he was networked around the Hollywood media community, meeting the record industry movers and shakers, artist managers, TV people, and making useful introductions, supposedly for Prestige Publicity.

Another useful and gregarious contact was Jim Dickson, a freelance A&R man with connections to Jac Holzman's prestige-label Elektra. 'Bald, fair, tall, round' – once married to actress Diane Varsi, Dickson was a talent-scout, gadfly, producer, manager, all-round fixer, and whatever else he could turn his hand to. He was a smart cat who'd already worked with Dino Valenti – maverick Quicksilver Messenger Service member – the Dillards, Lord Buckley, and Hamilton Camp. In turn, Jim linked up with a guy called Eddie Tickner – 'dark, thin, more than 6ft tall, from Philadelphia' – bringing his knowledge of accounting and working with Odetta, to form the Tickson Music publishing imprint in late-1963. Together, they alchemised the Byrds project.

Take a bunch of Folk musicians. Fuse them to a Beatles backbeat, with Beatles styling. Add Dylan songs. And they were 'waiting there to sell plastic ware'. Plus, Dickson had heard about this new-guy-in-town, Derek Taylor – the name with The Beatles connections. He established the mutual link through photographer Curt Gunther who had also done work for The Beatles. The networking was kicking in. Derek was eking out his promotion work for KRLA when Dickson 'accosted' him with an advance acetate of 'Mr Tambourine Man'. Some time later Derek recounted the events to Johnny Rogan. It was Friday, 19 February. 'The Byrds came in off the street through Eddie (Tickner) and Jim (Dickson). It was those two and the acetate that convinced me. After hearing "Mr Tambourine Man" I had to get involved. I felt that enormous possessive sense that you did as a youth – somehow I must get involved in this thing.'

The next obvious step was to check out his new clients in their natural environment. So, within days of the initial encounter, Derek took up an invitation to see the Byrds play at their residency at *Ciro's*, just down from the hip *Whisky a Go Go*. Derek recalls that 'when we first turned up, there was hardly anyone there, literally about sixteen of us. From then on, through, it was always packed. The sound was new and exciting, McGuinn was terrific. He had a certain abstraction about him which was fascinating, and then there were those incredible dancers. I can vividly recall this young girl dancing on her own, wearing McGuinn's glasses. I was captivated...' It was almost a Manchester Odeon 30 May 1963 moment. Like the first time he'd seen The Beatles less than two years before. Only different. A different kind of revelatory experience. Intelligent and literate, poetry with a dance-beat. He also liked the fact that they performed Paul's 'Things We Said Today'. They also drew Chuck Berry's 'roll Over Beethoven' into their set, using the *With The Beatles* arrangement. *Ciro's Le Disc*, at 8433 Sunset Boulevard, was a former supper club. It had once headlined slick entertainers from an earlier era, names such as Peggy Lee, Sammy Davis Jr, and 'Rumba King' Xavier Cugat. After standing dark for some time, the Byrds had debuted there on Monday, 26 March 1965. Within a short space of time, they turned the place around. Soon, to Derek, 'the dance-floor was a madhouse. A hard-core of Byrds followers – wayward painters, disinherited sons and heirs, bearded sculptors, misty-eyed nymphs and assorted oddballs – suddenly taught Hollywood to dance again.' It was ground zero for the LA proto-hippie youth revolution, as the group became the motivating inspiration for the Turtles, Leaves, Love, the Seeds, Sonny & Cher. And it was the place where the scene-makers hung out; Sal Mineo, Steve mcqueen, Carol '*Five Easy Pieces*' Eastman, Peter Fonda, Lenny Bruce (whose mother got the Byrds their first paid gig, at East Los Angeles College, for $50), Barry McGuire... and Derek Taylor.

For Derek, 'I wanted it', this was 'the specific job for which God had sent me to LA.' It was only a matter of time before Derek moved out of Prestige Publicity, to set up his own public relations office down the strip apiece. That, after all, had been the long-term objective all along. A gamble, sure, but a calculated one. He'd been around the block a few times without securing a parking space. KRLA was a stop-gap, a foot in the door, a means to an end. It was time. The Byrds provided the push.

The drawback was that Dickson didn't have the available funds to pay the retainer that could be expected for the services of a prior Beatles PR, because his clients had no proven track record. So Dickson suggested a deal, dependent on a commission of the group's as-yet theoretical earnings, 'a tenuous offer of two-and-a-half percent of bugger all.' A loose arrangement, 'it wasn't even on paper', Dickson confided to Johnny Rogan. 'We never talked about it. It never came up.' But the relationship did become even closer. The duo had taken out an office on the eighth floor of the spanking-new skyscraper tower of the 9000 Building, Sunset Boulevard. A choice made, at least partly, because it stood directly across the road from Tickner's favourite delicatessen, the *Gaiety*. They'd moved in immediately prior to Derek joining them there. So Derek moved a few doors down the corridor, sharing not only the Byrds' office but a share of their secretary, Jackie, too. She was there from start to end.

The 9000 Building was a block seething with rock and showbiz management firms. Derek had his own 'nice little gimcrack' office-room there with a secretary, two desks, three chairs, a telephone, and two typewriters. Diana Vero Palmer, Brian Epstein's former secretary, was there to help, a familiar face in a new uncertain venture. She'd been there during the chaotic 1964 tour, they'd dined together in Frisco. On the www.abbeyrd website, she recalls how 'Derek was the reason I moved to Los Angeles in 1965. He was my American sponsor and I was supposed to have worked with him. I still remember him fondly from that crazy year, 1964, when we were all riding on the crest of a giant wave that we didn't even realise would be still going strong thirty years later…'. It was Diana who had typed out the text of *A Cellarful of Noise*. But the new arrangement proved to be a temporary one 'that didn't work out'.

Soon, Derek also found himself doing a lot of business in the *Gaiety*. The PR functions as a connector, spreading viral idea-epidemics. As well as the Byrds, another 'group were handed to me' as a parting gift by Bob Eubanks, the group was Paul Revere and the Raiders. They became Derek's first signing, he agreed to a fee of $350 a month, a reduction on their deal with Eubanks. In the history books of the American War of Independence, 'Paul Revere' is immortalised as the patriot who made the famous ride announcing 'The British are coming!' – now his namesake was performing the same function in rock 'n' roll, announcing his goal as to trounce 'the British dominance of the disc scene.' Derek worked for Paul Revere for two-and-a-half years, during which he estimated he must have written some 175,000-words about him, the equivalent of two full novels-worth of prose including features for *Teen*, *Flip*, *Teen Life*, *16* and *Tiger Beat* fan magazines. Derek was adept at hustling in the speedy Californian music scene. 'I became a publicist to dozens of very nice people in the music business… with mighty sixties pop stars on my books.'

The loosely-defined arrangement that united the Byrds, Derek Taylor, Eddie Tickner and Jim Dickson worked well. Although, as Derek observed, 'the group did it all themselves. The Tickner/Dickson thing was just right for the Byrds, just relaxed enough for them. Had they had an Elliot Roberts or Irv Azoff, it might have frightened them. They were so scruffy, and their attitude towards the audience was so blasé. They were often quite bad on stage, but they had this relaxed management who said "That's cool!". Dickson really knew what being laid-back meant. He was so laid-back himself – no middle-aged, middle-class hang-ups. Everything went with Dickson. His attitude was, "if David Crosby wants to do this, let him do it." Eddie curbed Jim's wilder instincts. It was a good partnership.' Although there were down-sides.

Derek signed the Beau Brummels, a chart-name, but made the mistake of taking them to see his even-newer signings, the Byrds. The Brummels immediately smelled what sounded like competition, and promptly fired Derek for divided loyalties. Tickner's wife, Rita Rendall, who had some prior experience of working with Albert Grossman, assumed the tedious responsibility of sorting out accounts. 'Rita didn't want any messing', Derek told Johnny Rogan. 'And with this thing we were in, it was all messing. She couldn't believe she was involved in such confusion. Bad Boys! Eddie getting involved with these teenagers and this piss-arsed Englishman who was so charming and unreliable and always late with his rent. Never mind!'

Rogan relates an anecdote about how – despite her reservations, Derek's 'laconic charm and eloquent prose often saved the Byrds during moments of minor crisis.' In a fit of truculence, the Byrds decided that they weren't going to honour an engagement booked for them in small LA club opposite *Ciro's* – it was around the time 'Mr Tambourine Man' was breaking big, and they felt they didn't need to work small-scale anymore. Which meant there was a minor problem with the contract. The club just might sue! Derek was assigned the task of fixer, and he went around to pacify the situation. Such were his powers of diplomacy that a couple of days later Jim Dickson was amazed by the arrival of a mysterious package at the Byrds office, within it was a home-made cake, iced with the words 'Get Well Soon Byrds', alongside the fragments of the ripped-apart contract. Dickson breathlessly commented that 'what Derek did blew my mind. He told them some story about the Byrds being sick and created so much sympathy that they not only dropped the contract, but actually baked a cake. They'd let us off the hook. That was Derek at his finest.'

Many US hits operate from strong regional identifications, they might be massive on the east coast, but less so on the west, huge on the west coast, but less so on the east. The chart position that results balances out those regional inconsistencies. But, issued on the 12 April, 'Mr Tambourine Man' happened simultaneously, everywhere, in the same way that 'I Want to Hold Your Hand' had happened simultaneously everywhere. By 2 June it entered the US Top Ten sandwiched between Herman's Hermits' 'Silhouettes' and Freddie and the Dreamers 'Do the Freddie'. A fortnight later 'Mr Tambourine Man' was No1. It repeated the feat, and became UK no.1 the week of 29 July – to be dislodged the following week by 'Help!'. So, within a matter of months, taking the pulse from the British invasion, but its romantic lyricism from Dylan, the Byrds hit massively on both sides of the Atlantic with one of the decade's most defining singles. Its jingle-jangle Rickenbacker play-in proved to be an instantaneous litmus identifier immaculately attuned to the precise moment. Michelle Phillips recalls – through the book Derek ghosted for her – turning on the radio and hearing 'the unmistakable sounds of success coming from our dearest friends in music. I remember hearing "Mister Tambourine Man" and saying "Shit man, McGuinn's got a hit."'

Success was immediate and overwhelming. 'McGuinn and (Barry) McGuire still a-gettin' higher, but that's what they were aimin' at', as John Phillips wrote it in 'Creeque Alley'. But, for the Byrds, the stakes were differently calibrated. Writing about Byrd Gene Clark, biographer John Einarson points out that 'at age twenty-one the world rested at his feet. He never fully recovered from that instant adulation and it shook his confidence the rest of his life.' If the Byrds were America's answer to The Beatles... what exactly was the question? If The Beatles began 'it', then the Byrds too began their own 'it'. Naturally, once the Byrds hit big, Derek's slight two-and-a-half per cent equalled something like $250 a week, until 'I guess when Derek left we never paid him anymore,' admits Dickson.

More Cellars-full of Noise...

Adam Faith stunned the establishment by debating intelligently on BBC-TV's *Face to Face* with incisive interrogator John Freeman. Not so much for what he said, which was pretty unexceptional, but for the fact that, in December 1960, a pretty-boy pop star pin-up was capable of basic joined-up articulacy at all. The same establishment mentality occurred, or was satirised, in the *A Hard Day's Night* sequence where George wanders into the fashion focus group. 'Can he read?' queries the director, regarding George as some kind of proletarian street-specimen for cautious examination. 'You don't have to do the old adenoidal glottal stop and carry on for our benefit', he tells the bemused Beatle. But checking his wall-chart for the next teenage craze anyway, the director is relieved to find that it was still safely three weeks away. It's difficult to envisage now, the social divisions of High and Low Culture, class and hierarchy that stratified all aspects of life in England back then. Flash forward a fistful of years, and whatever bishops might or might not have felt moved to say matters less than zero. Pop stars have become the Gurus...

So when did the sixties start swinging...? Some date it to as early as November 1960, just a year after Adam Faith's 'What Do You Want?' had become Parlophone's first-ever no.1 UK single, and when a jury at the Old Bailey trial of the long-banned *Lady Chatterley's Lover* decided that DH Lawrence's novel was not obscene. A few days later, John F Kennedy was elected President of the United States. The conjunction of those two events created a widespread feeling that a major, liberating change was in the air. That what, for better or worse, we now speak of as the sixties started that same week. Others say the sixties began the day Kennedy was gunned down in Dallas. Or when Cassius Clay defeated Sonny Liston in the ring. Or when Brigit Riley, Richard Hamilton and Peter Blake first put the 'pop' into pop-Art. When the Profumo scandal and BBC-TV's *That Was the Week That Was* accelerated the slow gradualist striptease of censorship liberalisation. In his sharp suits and slicked-back hair, Derek had followed the week-by-week breakouts of those revelations in the national dailies while he'd been employed in their north-westerly regional counterparts. Stories that were shaking the walls of the establishment to its deeply conservative roots. Little suspecting that he'd be a part of that establishment-shaking process within the space of years

Decades are irresistible divisions of experience, no matter how arbitrary. And like trains, decades seldom arrive on time. The actual 'Swinging Sixties' was short-lived, beginning symbolically with the free-spirited Julie Christie catching the midnight train from Yorkshire to London in *Billy Liar* in 1963. For pop music, it was certainly not during the decade's first few years, when the scene was still dominated by pouting pretty-boys with swept-back quiffs and twee teen ballads. If The Beatles' breakthrough in the UK in 1963, and in the States in 1964, were cusp years, certainly the ingredients were already there, and the pendulum primed. Musical tectonic plates were about to shift, with massive cultural fall-out in train. Time, previously so slow and incremental, was speeding up in a torrent of convulsive change.

In the realms above the world, the super-power confrontation was accelerating the Space Race into futuristic comic-strip dreams of 'Dan Dare', 'Jet-Ace Logan' and 'Captain Condor', albeit in the unfamiliar cosmonaut guises of Yuri Gagarin or Gherman Titov. And the Cold War was in the process of becoming hotter in Vietnam, Cuba and Berlin, validating the ideological context for 'James Bond' movies – the first, *Doctor No*, arriving towards the end of 1962 (with sneaking references infiltrated into the *Help!* Movie), and creating the delicious thrill of strangeness feeding post-apocalypse New Wave Science Fiction landscapes crawling with radioactive mutants.

Although the UK had nothing approaching the integration Civil Rights struggles ripping America apart, the *Empire Windrush* generation of immigrants, attracted to what they'd been taught to think of as the 'mother-country', were met by 'No Dogs, No Blacks, No Irish' signs outside properties. Racism? – Derek recalls, 'I hadn't heard the word ("coons") since the news editor of *The Liverpool Daily Post* had let it drop once, many years ago, explaining that he was only using it affectionately.' Yet the immigrant's cultural influence was almost immediately evident in thawing traditional British reserve. Although the first Blue-Beat hit single was by white copyists The Migil Five ('Mockingbird Hill', no.10 in March 1964), it was followed by Millie ('My Boy Lollipop', no.2 also March 1964), and soon no Mod's record collection could be considered complete without Ska/rock Steady from Prince Buster, the Ethiopians, Ezz Reco and the Launchers, the Skatalites, and eventually the immaculate Desmond Dekkar. While, as well as the highly-visible success of white R&B bands covering neglected American records, igniting an upsurge of interest in albums by the original artists, there was a surge of chart singles by 'Great Unknowns' – from Chuck Berry (no.6 in October 1963 with 'Memphis Tennessee'), Bo Diddley (no.34 in October 1963 with 'Pretty Thing'), John Lee Hooker (no.23 in June 1964 with 'Dimples'), and Little Richard (no.20 in June 1964 with 'Bama Lama Bama Loo').

Pirate radio, broadcasting from outside the reach of the law, brought Top 40-station presentational styles, catchy jingles and zany young djs to pop, championing obscure records by new artists on whim, availability, or because they genuinely felt strongly that they deserved to be heard. An irresistible gift to record-promoters and the PR industry hunting new angles. The pirates introduced a more directly personal way of addressing listeners, unlike the dreary po-faced BBC where presenters still employed a microphone-technique as if addressing a public meeting. Apart from exceptions such as the Light Programme's

Saturday Club or *Easy Beat* – their scarcity making such slots even more valuable to beat-starved ears – the formal BBC, restricted by Musician's Union needle-time agreements, just couldn't compete. Still time-warped in the fogey-attitudes of the sheet-music era, they couldn't quite comprehend why there should be any intrinsic difference between 'Day Tripper' as performed by the Northern Dance Orchestra, and 'Day Tripper' done by The Beatles. By the dying days of 1964 – nearly halfway through the decade now remembered as the high point of pop and youth culture – Radio Caroline was joined by the even more out-there hip Radio London to answer the neglected, if not actually forbidden hunger for exciting sounds. If you miss that elusive one-off radio play, you might never hear that record again. The pirates brought what Postmaster General Edward Short called 'chaos in the ether'.

rock was beginning to evolve out of pop, extending away from the hummable three-minute pop singles that had defined youth culture from 1963 to 1965, with lyrics rooted deeper than in the caprices of the teenage crush. To Derek, 'it was the end of the age of innocence in rock', nudging 'in a new and better direction.' rock had become the poetry of popular culture. And what was emerging was a strange elision of commerce and art, a union that also involved a piece of plastic-merchandise and a public-relations gimmick. 'A great record album is to the 1960s what a piece of sculpture was to the Middle Ages. Isn't it? The Byrds think it should be, and I agree with them because I agree with them on most things. So do The Beatles, by the way.' And it was in this time, when pop stars were still new and as powerful as gods, that the Byrds flew into London. 'The Byrds Is Coming' said the posters and press-ads, coming into what passed for the long-lensed paparazzi glare of expectation.

They arrive at Heathrow, from Chicago at 08:00hrs on a chilly Monday 2 August, for a tour agreed with the Musicians Union on the basis that the Dave Clark Five enjoyed a reciprocal trip to the States. Maybe Derek should have better-briefed his charges about the vagaries of English summer. Maybe they should have packed something warmer. Sure, they were young and good-looking, with 'their hair grown right and their pants worn tight.' They knew how to dress in the Anglocentric way, but they trouped shivering in their hip Californian gear through immigration, through customs, into the arrivals hall – to be greeted by hundreds of shrieking girls, and litigation from Ronnie Wood's English Birds. A legal case had been confected, a writ alledging name-theft that had more to do with staking out column inches than it was to do with legitimacy. McGuinn diplomatically defused the situation: 'I don't want

to compete with you, all I really want to do is be friends with you' –
craftily lifting the Dylan-lyrics of their latest single.

Ignited by early plays on the new Pirate radio stations illegally
broadcasting from outside UK territorial jurisdiction, 'Mr Tambourine
Man' had topped the chart. 'It's like a game of tennis' rationalised Jim
'Roger' McGuinn, peering over the rim of his granny glasses, beneath
his fringe of mop-top hair. 'The ball goes back and forth, across the
Atlantic.' What The Beatles had started had percolated out through the
music industry, through all levels of show business, across continents
setting up copyists, reactions, and replies. In Britain, The Beatles and
the rolling Stones faced the Beach Boys and the Byrds. Each of them
setting agendas that moved the thing forward incrementally. This way,
and that, across the Atlantic. McGuinn created the Byrds' guitar 'jingle-
jangle' in conscious imitation of George's 360/12 Rickenbacker. In 1965
it was David Crosby who first introduced George Harrison to the work
of Ravi Shankar. Then George requested Derek to convey a message
to McGuinn, that he'd borrowed bits from 'The Bells of Rhymney' and
'She Don't Care About Time' while arranging 'If I Needed Someone' for
Rubber Soul. And the girls on 'So You Want to Be a rock 'n' roll Star'
are not screaming for the Byrds, but for The Beatles. You can clearly
hear them calling out for 'Paul' (although the liner notes for the 1990
4-CD Box-Set claims Derek Taylor recorded the Byrd-screams at their
Bournemouth show on that 1965 tour).

Derek Taylor was an essential part of the Byrds package. He was
excited about taking the group to England, and had already networked
his UK media connections to spread what was already becoming known
as 'Byrdmania'. He knew the names of the right editors and had access
to the correct journalists to send his extravagant press-packs to, along
with those iconic photos. But he still harboured niggling reservations
about the promoter's intentions. 'What I brought to the Byrds was an
expertise from British newspapers', he rationalised, 'I'd come from Fleet
Street newspapers to The Beatles knowing nothing about the world
of rock 'n' roll. I didn't know anything about gigs or bookings, all that
was done for me. I was an innocent so I wasn't able to give the best
advice to (Byrds manager) Eddie Tickner about the halls they would be
playing. All I did know was that the correspondence from (promoter)
Mervyn Conn didn't assure me. It didn't seem like the world I'd left –
the Epstein world. I kept expressing doubts about the content of the
letter. There was something about the grammar. You know, "I'll give you
a deal" and "we'll get you some good gigs". The whole thing was very
much showbusiness, almost pantomime showbusiness.'

The Byrds play 'All I Really Want to Do' on *Ready Steady Go*, 6 August 1965. McGuinn in his quirky rectangular granny-glasses and jingle-jangle Rickenbacker. Crosby with his impish grin and suede cape. Gene Clark with his 'Prince Valiant' hair and Cuban-heeled boots, nonchalantly bashing a tambourine on his thigh. Yet they were generally judged to be static, uncoordinated and disappointing. Anticipations were set impossibly high. During the tie-in tour dates, they took five-or-seven minutes tuning up on stage, they didn't smile, didn't talk to the audience or announce song-titles, they appear aloof, detached. In some circles, they were resented as rivals to English hip supremacy. The English smirkers smirked. But the Byrds vagueness defined a new breed of cool. Theirs was not the cheerful cheek of a Gerry Marsden, more what Jim Morrison would call 'stoned immaculate', the new impenetrable hipness that Bob Dylan epitomised. To Johnny Rogan, the Byrds already possessed an 'otherworldly ambience and groomed prettiness… the combination of positivity and coolness made the Byrds seem unfathomable. Like Dylan, they gave the impression that they had discovered some great secret, which they were unwilling to impart to the uninitiated.' But Derek's misgivings were also realised.

The Byrds were never a garage-band. Nor school-friends. They all had careers, and recording histories, long before they even met. Their story had begun with Jim Dickson, who Derek called their 'manager and encourager'. Or maybe even, much earlier than that, with Chicago-born James Joseph McGuinn III. Jim was thirteen-going-on-fourteen when Elvis Presley's 'Heartbreak Hotel' shocked him into music. From there he played as the fourth member of the Chad Mitchell Trio, with Judy Collins, and with the Limeliters – he plays on their *Tonight: In Person* (1961) LP. He'd even auditioned for the New Christy Minstrels, but on 13 July 1962, his twentieth birthday, he got an offer from and toured with Bobby Darin instead. Back in New York, he started working Beatles songs into his Greenwich Village basket-house sets, to frequently purist-snobby unsympathetic reactions. To McGuinn, 'I was really enamoured with the sound of The Beatles. They were mixing elements of Folk and rock because they had been a skiffle band, but they were doing it kind of subconsciously. They were shooting for a 1950s rock style, but they were blending a lot of things together, sort of under the hood. I don't think they really knew what they were doing. Anyway, I picked up on it, and… I would take these songs apart in the coffeehouses and say, "Listen to this. They're doing fourth and fifth harmonies like bluegrass modal or Appalachian modal songs. This is

Above: Derek Taylor at Apple with George Harrison.

Below: Derek Taylor, both pensive... and mischievous.

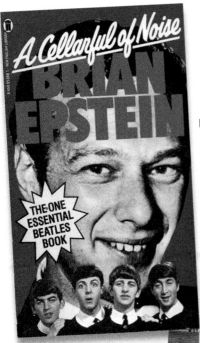

Left: *A Cellarful Of Noise* the book that Derek Taylor ghosted for Brian Epstein.

Right: The author at the Ring O' Bells Hotel, West Kirby. (*Andrew Darlington*)

Left: Derek Taylor's House, 27 Grafton Walk, West Kirby. (*Andrew Darlington*)

Right: John and Paul with The Quarrymen, when shoestring ties were all the rage.

Left: John Lennon with The Quarrymen.

Right: Beatles top the poll in *Mersey Beat* magazine, in January 1962.

Left: An early publicity shot of John, Paul, George... and Pete Best.

Right: *A Hard Days's Night.* The Beatles third studio album. (*Parlophone*)

Below: Wilfred Brambell was not really Paul's grandfather, but he was 'very clean'.

Right: Derek Taylor flies with the Beatles, 'man, I had a dreadful flight'.

Left: 'If the rain comes, they run and hide their heads'.

Right: Beatlemania USA on the *Ed Sullivan Show*.

Left: Some considered the cover of *With The Beatles* to be satanic.

Right: Inside the Abbey Road studio with George and George.

Left: The failed Beatles line-up with Jimmie Nicol on drums and Derek on vocals.

Right: Neil Aspinall hazardously comes between Brian and John.

Left: Brian Epstein confides, Derek Taylor listens.

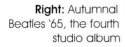

Right: Autumnal Beatles '65, the fourth studio album

Left: *Rubber Soul* has altered track-listing for the US edition. (*Parlophone*)

Right: The Byrds, the original 'Mr. Tambourine Men'.

Left: High-flying Byrds and their second album *Turn! Turn! Turn!*. (*Columbia*)

Right: Sonny and Cher, when all they really want is each other.

Below: *Help!* The semaphore actually spells 'NUJV' - not 'HELP'. (*Parlophone*)

THE BEATLES

PARLOPHONE EMI

Below: Beatles with a 'Ticket To Ride' from *Help!*

John and George in a scene from *Help!*

Right: Everybody's talkin' about a little touch of Schmilsson in the night. Harry Nilsson in the studio.

Left: The Beatles *Revolver* cover illustrated by Klaus Voorman. (*Parlophone*)

Right: *Pet Sounds* by The Beach Boys, proof of Brian Wilson as 'genius'.

Left: Brian Wilson - more comfortable away from the surf beach.

Right: *Sgt. Pepper's Lonely Hearts Club Band*. Aleister Crowley, Mae West, Lenny Bruce, Karlheinz Stockhausen, WC Fields, Carl Jung, Edgar Allan Poe, Bob Dylan, Aubrey Beardsley

... and the rest. (*Parlophone*)

Above: Jimi Hendrix ignites America from the Monterey stage.

Right: *The White Album*. The music of choice for the Charles Manson Family. (*Parlophone*)

The BEATLES

№ 9088627

Left: The Big 'Apple' logo.

Right: Derek Taylor arbitrates between John and Paul.

Left: John and Yoko. They look just like 'two gurus in drag', as 'The Ballad Of John And Yoko' suggested.

Below: 'Elementary penguins singing Hare Krishna', according to 'I Am The Walrus'.

Left: George, both magical and mysterious, from *Magical Mystery Tour*.

Right: 'Your Mother Should Know', from *Magical Mystery Tour*.

Left: 'Goo Goo G'Joob'. From *Magical Mystery Tour*.

Right: James Taylor, more 'rain' than 'fire' from Apple.

Left: The animated mop-tops from *Yellow Submarine*.

Right: *Abbey Road*. Will there be an opportunity for some future spoof photos here? (*Parlophone*)

Left: Allen Klein, in a reassuring 'safe pair of hands' sort of pose.

Right: Paul and the 'Lovely Linda'.

Left: Pete Best is neatly eclipsed by Ringo in the torn-collage *Anthology* artwork. (*Parlophone*)

really a cross between Folk and rock". So that's the origins of folk-rock really. It started in Greenwich Village.' By Spring 1964, McGuinn was opening for Roger Miller at the LA *Troubadour*. In the audience, Gene Clark was one of the few who recognised and appreciated what he was attempting to do.

Coming from a thirteen-child Catholic family with Irish and Cree Native American blood, Gene – from Tipton, Missouri – was rugged and athletic, but also intense and wired. A complex, insecure, troubled man, prone to swings in temperament that Einarson's investigations now interpret as evidence of a bipolar condition. His sister Bonnie recalls how his music began, 'after Gene saw Elvis, all he wanted to be was a rock star.' During his fresher year, he joined high-school band Joe Meyer and the Sharks, moving from there into the 'Michael Row the Boat Ashore' coffeehouse folk-thing with a doctored ID. By 12 August 1963, the eighteen-year-old Gene was recruited into the wholesome hit-making New Christy Minstrels alongside Barry McGuire. He cut records with them (the first called 'Saturday Night'), and appeared on *The Andy Williams Show*. They did a special White House performance for new President Lyndon Johnson in January, but to Gene, the group's cheerful family-friendly choreography was frustratingly 'square'. At around the same time, he heard The Beatles for the first time, on a jukebox in Norfolk, Virginia, and pumped nickels all night to hear them again. He was not only listening, but analysing their dynamics, how they did it, and why what they did worked so well. It was the catalyst he needed. He quit the Cristy's – before he was fired – and headed for LA.

Intending to work as a duo, McGuinn had the advantage of a few years over Clark, and a deeper aloof proto-hip die-hard folkie sensibility. He sought to blend his folk influences to a Beatles beat, not so much by copying The Beatles, as recognising in The Beatles' music some elements of his own evolving style. Gene's experience was more with commercial pop-Folk and he saw himself more as a Beatles-style writer. A marginal but significant distinction that introduced the spark of creative friction to what they envisaged as a folky duo along the lines of Peter & Gordon, who were topping the chart with Paul McCartney's 'A World Without Love', or Chad & Jeremy, charting soon after with 'Yesterday's Gone'. Instead, they added a third voice. In the *Folk Den* – a front annexe of the *Troubadour* – they were joined by David Crosby, an earlier acquaintance of McGuinn's.

David Van Cortlandt Crosby came from LA privilege, growing up in well-heeled Santa Barbara where his father was Academy Award-winning cinematographer Floyd Crosby. Expelled from private schools,

the some-time actor, part-time fun-burglar and spoiled-brat rich-kid
had dropped out to do the folk club circuit. He'd played Greenwich
Village, Florida's *Coconut Grove*, and he'd hung out with Dino Valenti,
David Freiberg and Paul Kantner in the embryonic San Francisco Bay
area. In 1963 he'd been a part of commercial folk group Les Baxter's
Balladeers, and recorded the album *Jack Linkletter Presents A Folk
Festival* (1963) with them. But McGuinn was wary. The incorrigible
Crosby was an upsetter, into his own mischievous alternate reality, but
in his favour, he had Jim Dickson's ear.

Jim was a useful guy to know. More, he had permission from Dick
Bock to use World Pacific studios at Hollywood's 8713 West Third Street
to record his 'discoveries' after hours. That made him an even more
useful guy to know. He'd already taken advantage of this free studio
access to try out some solo tapes with Crosby – including an early
demo of the classic *Younger Than Yesterday* Byrds song 'Everybody's
Been Burned', which hadn't attracted much positive response. Now he
set his sights on the group that had started out calling itself the Jet Set,
extending them a daily hamburger allowance, and encouraging them
to refine their material during unlimited nocturnal sessions. During
rehearsals, the trio expanded their sound by soliciting Michael James
Dick into the drum-chair. According to legend, they recruited him
because his long Beatles-style hair made him resemble Brian Jones.
But Crosby had noted him playing congas with Dino Valenti in Big Sur
some time before, and had been impressed by his beatnik sensibility.

Originally from Spokane, Washington, he assumed the name Michael
Clarke, and was reduced to thumping cardboard boxes on early
rehearsals, until an investment from art collector Naomi Hirshorn set
the group up with Roger's Rickenbacker twelve-string – like George
Harrison's – Gene's Gretsch Tennessean rhythm guitar, and Michael's
Ludwig drums – like Ringo. But there were dubious internal group
politics and ego-games. Jim McGuinn, Gene Clark, with David Crosby
were three strong-minded creative wills tied into uneasy compromise
and permanent simmering contention. They were still sounding each
other out, jostling for places. Initially – as the most prolific songwriter
– Clark was naturally seen as the vocal focal-point too. McGuinn
emerged as lead guitar, with his voice adding harmonies, and Crosby
contributing a harmony triad.

When Crosby flunked the Fender bass role, Jim Dickson brought
in Chris Hillman, from San Diego County, as a fifth member on $40
Japanese bass, freeing Crosby to concentrate on voice alone, something
he soon found uncomfortable on stage. But he could be relentlessly

and slyly manipulative. Until, as Tickner recalls, unhappy with his role, Crosby mounted a concerted campaign to wrest Gene Clark's rhythm guitar from him. 'Crosby made fun of Gene's playing', until Gene backed down, and became the tambourine man instead 'when they took the guitar out of his hands.'

Examples of the rehearsal material they worked on, charting their development, later emerged as *Preflyte* (1969), then in an expanded CD form as *In the Beginning* (1988). One of their first acoustic folk-trio collaborations, demo'd as the Jet Set, was the mid-tempo McGuinn/Crosby strum-along composition 'The Only Girl I Adore', an attractively stripped-down and roughly imprecise Everly-style work-tape. Another, an early Clark/McGuinn composition 'You Showed Me', with harmonies by then electrically-underpinned by McGuinn's twelve-string, eventually became a US Top Ten hit for the Turtles, and was later re-done by Lightning Seeds. Crosby sings 'Airport Song'.

Writing, warming up, with ideas distilling into songs, they were no longer a folk-group, with Gene already emerging as the strongest writer. 'You Movin'' is his most obviously Mersey-influenced song, about watching the 'little girl' dance. But 'I Knew I'd Want You' shows him drawing on the new vocabulary with 'you've had me on your trip, right from the start.' It and four other tentative works from the sessions would be carried over and reworked for the first official CBS album. But first, Lenny Bruce called round the rehearsals, and through his recommendation, the group played their debut live gig, at East Los Angeles City College. There was also a one-off single.

Dickson took a three-track work-in-progress tape to Jac Holzman of Elektra, who liked what he heard... up to a point. There was something there, even if he wasn't sure exactly what it was. He drafted in bassist Ray Pohlman, replaced Michael Clarke with session-drummer Earl Palmer, and assigned Paul Rothschild – who would later pilot Doors' sessions – to co-produce. So, essentially recorded as a four-piece 'Please Let Me Love You' was written by Clark and McGuinn with friend Harvey Gerst, Gene's lead vocals standing out from the plaintive harmonies and the strong jingle-jangle guitar figure, enhanced by a Beatles-referencing 'oh yeah, oh yeah'. Flipped with an early version of Roger and Harvey's 'It Won't Be Wrong' called 'Don't Be Long', the record formed an attractive proposition, not too dissimilar to the recent Beau Brummels' hits. It was issued 7 October 1964 under the alias of the English-referencing Beefeaters, so as not to compromise the chance of a CBS/Columbia deal. Even then, its unsupported hit-potential must have seemed doubtful. Although all the essential Byrds-ingredients were there, there's a lightness to the sessions, lacking the tight stridency, rhythmic kick and production sheen of their later CBS work.

It was Dickson who obtained an advance demo of Dylan's 'Mr Tambourine Man', after seeing him perform it at the 1964 Monterey Folk Festival. His history with Chris Hillman went back as far as 1963, when pre-Byrds Chris was mandolin-player with Vern and Rex Gosdin as the bluegrass and country Gosdin Brothers group. They metamorphosed into the Hillmen, whose album featured a cover of Dylan's 'When the Ship Comes In' (*The Hillmen* re-emerged in 1970). The Hillmen were also playing the Folk Festival, and Dickson happened to be there as part of the package. He was impressed when he heard the new, unissued Dylan song. On 9 June, he managed to obtain an acetate of Dylan with Jack Elliott providing shambling harmonies, but the Jet Set were initially unimpressed. An early, uninspired take of what was to be their defining song was later included on *In The Beginning*.

As with The Beatles grudgingly trying out 'How Do You Do It?', while preferring to record their own material, the future-Byrds saw themselves doing their own songs, and Dylan was 'just another writer'. Attempts with Gene Clark doing vocals soon stalled, but it took off when McGuinn volunteered to step in, and his voice worked better. He'd recently found Subud – an Indonesian form of Buddhism – and switched his name from Jim to Roger in recognition of its spiritual rejuvenation. It seemed to empower his interpretation. Crosby was still very opposed to doing the song at all and maintained a continued opposition – until it became a hit. The deciding factor was when Dickson contrived to get Dylan himself to visit them in the studio. He turned up with Bobby Neuwirth and Victor Maimudes in tow. Dylan was on good form, he'd just got back from London where he'd hung out with The Beatles, and befriended Lennon. A fortuitous recommendation from Miles Davis provided further momentum in securing the proto-Byrds a CBC deal, and the three core-member signed to the label on 10 November 1964.

All that now remained was to select a more appropriate group name, after which the newly renamed Byrds were assigned CBS's youngest producer, Terry Melcher. McGuinn had first encountered Terry – who was Doris Day's son – some years earlier, during his brief 1963 stint at the New York Brill Building. Melcher recruited Phil Spector and Beach Boys' sessioneers Hal Blaine (drums), Larry Knechtel (bass), and Leon Russell, whose keyboard contribution was ultimately mixed out. Roger, alone of the Byrds, would get to play his twelve-string on the record.

A group called the Rooftop Singers had taken the twelve-string guitar

into the charts eighteen short months earlier with 'Walk Right In' – as
Bruce Channel had pipped The Beatles with harmonica. Recorded
in a three-hour session on 20 January 1965 at Columbia's studios on
Hollywood's Sunset and El Centro, 'Mr Tambourine Man' began with
the brought-in musicians igniting the session with the rhythm they'd
used for the Beach Boys' 'Don't Worry Baby'. Then, in conscious
replication of Beatles harmony-structures – with John backed up
and emphasised at critical moments by Paul and George in various
combinations of voices – Gene provides shadow-harmonies to Roger's
lead vocal, while Crosby adds a contrapuntal third harmony voice,
weaving in and around the melody-line. Curls of needle-sharp harmony
push and pull, challenge and charm, excitingly nape-pricklingly
disorientating. The record is concisely constructed with opening
chorus, a single aching verse, back into the chorus, chiming into the
fade, injecting new energy, character and precision into the former
strum-along demo.

According to Byrds-academic Johnny Rogan, the vocal-line was
precisely targeted to occupy the vacant niche that existed between
John Lennon and Bob Dylan. Beat, with brains. To David Crosby,
'Beatle-music was very close to folk music. The essential elements of
the synthesis that took place with Beatle-music are folk music changes,
much more complex chord changes, put to a rock 'n' roll backbeat
with bass added. You add bass and drums and take those kind of
changes, then you get to where Beatle music started to happen. And,
of course, once they found that place, then they were off and running.
They created a whole new genre...' Supposedly, it was *Billboard*
journalist Eliot Tiegel who first named it 'Folk-rock'. To McGuinn, 'in
the spectrum of music at the time, that was the niche (between Lennon
and Dylan) I saw vacant', he told Rogan, 'I saw this gap, with them
leaning towards each other in concept. That's what we aimed at, and
hit it.' And the 'we', so far as the single was concerned, consisted of just
three Byrds, and as 'Terry mixed out Gene Clark's vocal', according to
Dickson, that reduced it further. Gene, however, took lead voice on his
own 'I Knew I'd Want You' for the B-side.

The limbo between the studio session and the release date form
a void that seemed to extend interminably. Gene Clark and Chris
Hillman had swiftly formed a bond that would outlast their Byrds
association. They – and Michael Clarke – roomed together at Melrose,
while McGuinn and Crosby, in John Phillips' words, holed out in an
'old wino's flophouse' hotel in Cahuenga, just north of Hollywood
Freeway. During March – as Dylan's own debut foray into electricity,

'Subterranean Homesick Blues', was issued, he guested with the Byrds on stage at scene-setting *Ciro's*, bestowing his seal of approval. He also insisted on a series of photographs taken with the group that became an important part of their iconography. From a PR point of view, the photos were pure gold, as Derek points out, 'Dylan didn't go out of his way to do anything that wasn't meaningful to him.' Decades later people still attempt to define the essence of 'cool'. This is cool. The sharp aloof hipness of the Byrds, pitched somewhere between detachment and languour, a nonchalant self-assurance that both insulates and glamorises.

The other significant development was that, into the gap, strolled Derek Taylor whose 'love for the Byrds would shortly be translated into reams of fulsome praise.' And, in McGuinn's words, 'in a week or two, if you make the charts, the girls'll tear you apart.' Such was the galactic impact of 'Mr Tambourine Man' that the album also bearing its name – issued 11 June 1965 and soon up to no.6 – and the follow-up 45rpm, though both excellent in their own way, can't help but fail to equal its quintessential perfection. The strongest original songs on the first three Byrds albums – the finest debut trilogy in rock – were by Harold Eugene Clark. 'In 1965 Gene Clark was the Byrds', writes John Einarson in this excellent rigorously detailed biography. Even decades later, McGuinn seems to agree. Talking at the Leeds City Varieties (24 June 2002) he admits how 'blessed' the group was to have so fine a writer aboard. But Gene's were slow-burn songs, initially relegated to B-sides in favour of Dylan or Pete Seeger covers, because they lack radio immediacy, revealing their beauty only through repeated plays the airwaves couldn't afford. But 'I'll Feel A Whole Lot Better' – later peerlessly covered by the Flamin' Groovies, and by Tom Petty – 'She Don't Care About Time' and the rest, are class compositions.

'All I Really Want to Do' is an altogether looser, more throw-away example of Dylan's approach to songwriting. More a playful exercise in alliterative rhyme, yet zeitgeisty in that sense that it goes away from the usual pop concerns in which gender relationships are defined by romance, attraction, hurt or betrayal. In a modernist rejection of all that, hey, he just wants to be friends. The Byrds re-recorded their album version for singles release and rushed it out in direct competition with the newer enticingly evocative Cher version. Sonny & Cher had apparently visited *Ciro's* where the Byrds performed the number as part of their set, and it impressed the duo to the extent that they promptly appropriated the arrangement for their own use, riding the immense wave of audience goodwill following 'I Got You Babe'.

Derek was not well-pleased, 'I was not only disappointed, I was disgusted. Sonny & Cher went to *Ciro's* and ripped off the Byrds and, being obsessive, I could not get this out of my mind that Sonny & Cher had done this terrible thing. I didn't know that much about the record business, and in my experience with The Beatles, cover versions didn't make any difference. But by covering the Byrds, it seemed that you could knock them off the perch. And Sonny & Cher, in my opinion, stole that song at *Ciro's* and interfered with the Byrd's career and very nearly blew them out of the game.' As it was, both versions sold. But neither of them reached the sales potential they would have were it not for the chart-battle. For the Byrds, Gene Clark's powerful flip 'I'll Feel A Whole Lot Better' might actually have made a stronger side, it's a title that still repays repeated play, but the label preferred to stay with the winning Dylan tag.

According to the CBS PR machine, Dylan was marketed as 'the new cult leader'. But there was a misconceived theory circulating among some sections of the critical press that Dylan's own harsh nasal delivery – 'a voice of sand and glue', according to David Bowie's tribute – was too extreme to ever penetrate beyond a niche audience, and that sweetened cover versions performed by more acceptably musically competent artists would provide his only access to a mass market. That he'd be best-served commercially by 'softer' imitators. Indeed, he'd earned more money, at that stage in his career, as a writer for Peter Paul & Mary than as an artist in his own right. To Derek, 'Dylan was then super-hero, but his impact had yet to be measured in record sales. It looked as if he was bestowing his presence upon them, but the Byrds were doing him a favour as much as he was doing them. I always thought they had a good deal going together'.

The pivotal year 1965 also brought Dylan's Bringing it All Back Home, which has an equally valid claim to be the first Folk-rock album. Perhaps it was, fusing hallucinatory lyricism and, on half its tracks, a powerful raw, ragged rock 'n' roll thrust. On the opening track – 'Subterranean Homesick Blues' – he manages to pay simultaneous homage to Chuck Berry and the Beat poets. Allen Ginsberg can even be seen loitering in the background of the much-imitated promo film-clip. Dylan made the Byrds no.1, but the Byrds also helped Dylan to the top of the charts. The album not only carries advance tremors of his momentous 'Like A rolling Stone', but anticipates the surreal wordplay of Rap too. The Byrds were intellectually out-of-step with a lot of the Bubble-pop going on around them, but they had hit singles, so it didn't matter. Most music-journalists didn't really know how to deal with it.

They were still geared up to teeny-pop fan-level prose. Yet, for those few vital years, the record-buyers were ahead of the music machine, and the charts were wide open to whatever was good.

Throughout the decade, every time pop seemed about to become detached from reality, a re-immersion in roots music – R&B, Blues or Folk – re-energised its relevance, renewing itself by going back to its ethnic origins. And with the scene shifting on a week-by-week, month-by-month basis, the advent of Bob Dylan, accelerated by Dylan's influence on *Beatles for Sale*, and made manifest by 'Mr Tambourine Man', altered the focus away from the previously dominant R&B model toward a new roots resource, the Folk tradition. To Derek, 'the Byrds turned up the cerebral level of music.' Opening up new possibilities by delving back along relatively unexploited song-lines. An arrangement of the nineteenth-century minstrel tune 'Oh! Susannah' for the *Turn! Turn! Turn!* Album. 'Wild Mountain Thyme' and 'John Riley' on *Fifth Dimension*, which all came bearing the 'trad' writer-credit. While the Byrds were by no means the only group to delve into the Dylan songbook.

The Animals first two singles – 'Baby, Let Me Take You Home' and 'House of the Rising Sun' – were both adapted from traditional sources. But the fact that they both also occur on Dylan's first album is far from coincidental. Although there was a reciprocal process taking place too. Dylan was both shocked and impressed by the stark electric dynamics the Newcastle group imposed onto 'House of the Rising Sun', and by its impact on the charts. It provided another catalyst. Nudging him toward a similar direction. But Manfred Mann were also carving out their own catalogue of Dylan covers, including an abbreviated EP version of 'With God on Our Side'. That Dylan once quoted the Manfreds as his favourite covers band might have had something to do with the fact their current royalties-generating single was taking his 'If You Gotta Go, Go Now' towards the no.1.

Two months after 'Mr Tambourine Man', the Turtles took 'It Ain't Me, Babe' into the American Top Ten. So the Byrds uniqueness, although closely associated with their utilisation of Dylan songs, can't be attributed solely to it. As Derek argued, 'anyone ungenerous enough to suggest The Byrds rely on Dylan – and surprisingly, there are one or two mean people in show business – will be disappointed to see that of the eleven numbers within this gorgeous sleeve (of the second Byrds album, *Turn! Turn! Turn!*), six are by Byrd-members, one is by Pete Seeger, one by Stephen Foster, another is an old country standard. Only two are by Dylan. What else is there to say?' Nevertheless, eventually, peeved by continual accusations of the Byrds playing 'Dylan-beat', as the extended electric arm of Dylan, McGuinn came up with a raft of alternative tags, suggesting Raga-rock or Philoso-rock, while claiming that, although undeniably important, Dylan was merely one of a pool of writers contributing to their success.

Even so, there's truth there. The Byrds were the first group to translate the 'British invasion' into a new American vocabulary, defining the transatlantic balance on their own terms. They took from Dylan, but they also took generously from The Beatles, and even the Searchers' rippling twelve-string take on Jackie de Shannon's 'When You Walk in the Room'. The Byrds had already done their version of 'When You Walk in the Room' as part of their *Ciro's* set, and Jackie had been one of the group's earliest advocates. To Dickson, she 'was the first professional person in rock 'n' roll to risk her credibility by saying the Byrds were great and helping them to get work.' Now they return the favour by adding their own 'Bo Diddley-beat' variant of De Shannon's 'Don't Doubt Yourself Babe' to the *Mr Tambourine Man* album (she would go on to score her own hit with 'Put A Little Love in Your Heart' in 1969 and co-write 'Bette Davis Eyes', a monster hit for Kim Carnes in 1981). While for the Byrds, *Mr Tambourine Man* was the first of their suite of pristine albums. The iconic fish-eye lens group-shot by Barry Fienstein established their hipness. There were four Dylan songs, referenced by the liner-photo from *Ciro's* on the reverse. Five of their own compositions reworked from the World Pacific tapes. 'The Bells of Rhymney' which Pete Seeger had adapted from an Idris Davies poem. And their closing take on 'We'll Meet Again', ironically referencing the nuclear paranoia of *Dr Strangelove* (1964). Despite the subsequent messy recriminations, on these tracks the Byrds complement each other remarkably. It was a career-peak, but they had other peaks yet to come.

Soon, there were Byrds-copyists. Writing the sleeve-notes to *Turn! Turn! Turn!* (December 1965), Derek observed that 'the sky around them is heavy and resonant with the predatory wings of imitators. The Byrds merely wince slightly and smile within themselves.' He was also maintaining a hands-on connection with England by contributing a weekly column to *Disc Weekly*. It lasted for around three years – starting out as 'Our Man In America', and later 'Hollywood Calling'. Always playful, with a relaxed attitude to veracity, he invented two relatives for John Lennon – Uncle Stan and Auntie Flo – so he could describe their embarrassing adventures in LA. He also developed the theme, 'one of the great bores this week is the rash of new Byrd imitators – attempting to capture the same high, jangling twelve-string sound, the same chords, the same changes, the same breaks. It's all very tiresome. IMITATION MAY BE THE SINCEREST FORM OF FLATTERY BUT IT'S A BLOODY PEST'. Derek's capitalisation! In fact, this was only the first flush of bands using the template, it would prove durable enough to be regenerated, with merely the slightest of variants, for decades to come.

Back at the Europa Hotel in Grosvenor Square, following the elaborate hoopla of the Byrds London reception, Derek recalls that the chambermaids were saying 'I don't know what they're doing in that room. They've got all these things piled up like children's bricks on the table. And what are they doing with the towels?' The towels in question were pressed in across the bottom of the doors to act like draft-excluders to muffle the distinctive aroma of marijuana, while 'they had crystals and coloured cubes' to amuse themselves when they were ecstatically stoned. 'The dope smoking was chronic' Derek continues, 'and we were taking purple hearts, which I bought from some bloke who came up from W10. He said "what do you want, buddy?" I said "I don't know. What have you got?" He said "these are fifteen-quid a hundred." So I said "give us them." I distributed the purple hearts and generally behaved irresponsibly, I would say.' And – through Derek Taylor's timely intervention – the Byrds get to hang out with The Beatles too. 'I wanted them to meet The Beatles', he pointed out. Roger McGuinn recalls, 'it was my great pleasure to have worked with Derek Taylor, he made touring fun! My favourite memory of touring with him was when he arranged a meeting between the Byrds and The Beatles. We were in London at a small club and Derek booked a hotel room above the venue. Derek arranged for John, Paul and George to meet us in that room after our performance. We were ardent fans of The Beatles, we were ecstatic! It was the wit and charm of Derek Taylor that kept us from being completely overwhelmed by the situation.'

Some regional dates – at the Imperial Ballroom in Nelson, and the Pier Pavilion in Morecambe – more or less lived up to Derek's worst forebodings. They were gigs that left him wondering to himself 'take them out of Hollywood… put them in the real world, and they can't handle it.' They were better playing a set at the trendy Knightsbridge club *Blaises*. The London hiperati turned out in force to see and be seen seeing. It was the Byrds third gig in seven hours. The celebrity-count included John and George, plus Brian Jones and Bill Wyman, Pete Townshend, various members of the Pretty Things were there, Denny Laine, Perry Ford, Adrienne Posta and Dana Gillespie.

'*Blaises* was a place where people wouldn't mind being seen', as Derek observed, 'but it wasn't an ideal gig. The stage was the size of a sofa and the Byrds played extraordinarily loud and appeared both awkward and temperamental. Still, I loved them, and George Harrison and John Lennon were also impressed.' Both Beatles then accompanied the group to Brian Jones' flat where they hung together all night, availing themselves of whatever hedonistic inputs they could lay their collective hands on. Which was a considerable amount. The next day, Friday, they guested on *Ready Steady Go*, then went on to the *Flamingo* where they followed Geno Washington and the Ramjam Band on-stage around two in the morning. 'Paul McCartney came to that', recounts Derek, 'and there were people with blood-stained shirts when we arrived. The *Flamingo Club* was awful. It was quite the wrong place.' Nevertheless, Paul was at his diplomatic best, driving the Byrds back to their hotel afterwards.

The unseasonable chill was also taking its toll. Chris Hillman collapsed with an asthma-related chest infection. McGuinn came down with a temperature of 103F. Then Michael Clarke caught the flu. They pull out of some gigs. Yet at one point during the trip, at a reception for the Byrds at the London *Savoy Hotel*, Derek found himself in conversation with Andrew Loog Oldham. 'You should be very pleased to come back with a hit act', he told Derek, 'this proves you can do it.' That moment, at least, must have been a very sweet one...

Whichever way you read it, it was an eventful trip. It was during the London sojourn, as their flight-path descended into grey-grey London town, that Gene Clark conceived the lyric-images that would germinate the seeds of another classic single – 'Eight Miles High', which would be Gene's last major contribution to the Byrds. And the third of a trilogy of era-defining singles – with 'Mr Tambourine Man' and 'Turn! Turn! Turn!', which are the equal of anything that amazing decade produced. Equal to 'Satisfaction', 'My Generation', 'House of the Rising Sun' or 'I Want to Hold Your Hand'.

Sticking with the proven formula, Dylan's 'Times They Are a-Changin'' was originally intended as the follow-up to 'All I Really Want to Do', but the sessions didn't work out as intended. It was the end of August, 'two of the Fab Four' turn up at Hollywood studio recording sessions from their temporary base in LA's Benedict Canyon following their Shea Stadium triumph – 'when they could have been sprawling beside their Bel Air pool gazing at Joan Baez. Some choice.' They were 'Byrd-watchers'. They watch as the Byrds complete Gene's 'She Don't Care About Time', illuminated by McGuinn inserting a phrase

from Bach's 'Jesu, Joy of Man's Desiring' into the guitar solo. As Derek
recounts, 'down from the hills rode George and Paul because they'd
liked the Byrds' "Mr Tambourine Man", and they know that a record
like that doesn't happen by accident. ("Ho", John had said, "the Byrds
have something" and the others had nodded.) So there they were,
at Columbia – bachelor Beatle two-some, denims and fringes and so
much experience, heads bent to pick up the sound-subtleties of the Los
Angeles Byrds, whom The Beatles publicly named as their fab gear fave
rave American group. Well, that was one glamorous night.'

Despite such endorsement, there was still no viable A-side until, at a
further session on 10 September, McGuinn came up with 'Turn! Turn!
Turn!', extending out into the Pete Seeger repertoire. Roger had already
scored arrangements of 'Turn! Turn! Turn!' and 'The Bells of Rhymney'
for Judy Collins' breakthrough album, *Judy Collins 3* (Elektra, 1964),
before using them for the Byrds. 'Much of the time' recording the
album was a process of 'bark and bite, struggle and re-tape, battle and
reshape, experiment and reject. "Just once more," said famed producer
Terry Melcher a thousand times. The Byrds, you see, are not prepared
to be imprisoned by their music. They know that if material is good,
it can be moulded and fashioned at will. Any material. Any music.
They proved this in their first album ("We'll Meet Again") produced a
wonderfully fresh interpretation. And tasteful, too, for The Byrds are
nothing if not aesthetic. Similarly, in this new album, they reach back to
Stephen Foster for a song. They pluck out "Oh! Susannah" and make it,
suddenly, pure Byrd. Again they add a touch of humour. Faint, but just
enough. The Byrds rarely overdo anything. The album is eclectic. (No,
not electric. Eclectic. Look it up in Webster's.)'

Finally, 'Well, here it is. And about time too…', announces Derek's
original sleeve notes to the second Byrds album. He goes on to pose
the question 'didn't our old grannies wag their wise and weathered
heads and tell us that good things are worth waiting for? This album
was as long in the making as a President. But, as Jim McGuinn trusted
it would, everything's worked out all right. Personally, I think it's a
beautiful piece of work, and maybe the Byrds were right to linger
over it. And with so many once-mores and, we now have this most
splendid album. Why is it so good? Mainly because The Byrds are so
good. The great quality common to all The Byrds is that they really care
about their music. I don't want to be boring about this – though they
will bend your ears for hours on this subject – but the point is worth
making because it is this prolonged, exact attention to detail and this
involvement with the very best way to make music work for you that

set the Byrds ahead, above, beyond and totally out of reach of their competitors. Enjoy this lovely album, and give it to grumpy uncles for Christmas. It will help.' The notes are signed 'Derek Taylor. Press and Public Relations Officer for the Byrds.' It might just constitute his second most widely-read text.

As Derek had already observed, 'though McGuinn is leader, each member of his flock is an adroit, individual musician' and 'the constant artistic conflicts within the group – the striving for a thoroughly argued compromise – ensures that their songs are influenced by the best qualities of each of them. In other words, there is little chance that a song will be recorded without a dozen fistfights and great mouthfuls of awful abuse.' Now, as the power-struggles within the group intensified, with McGuinn and Crosby envious of Clark's songwriting royalties from the first album, McGuinn's position was strengthened by the success of 'Turn! Turn! Turn!'.

With the single's release – on 1 October 1965 – the Byrds were touring the eastern seaboard as part of 'Dick Clark's Caravan of Stars' double-heading with Derek's clients Paul Revere and the Raiders, with Bo Diddley and We Five also on the bill. Derek opined that 'Folk-rock came and went this year, and the mortality rate was high. Protest growled briefly and died in great, wheezing gasps. 1965, too, brought Hair music and no-room-at-the-inn music. That, too, grew inwards and suffocated itself. The Byrds, unfettered, looked the other way. The Byrds whistled "Oh! Susannah" and flew away on their motorcycles – away, away into the night over the Hollywood hills. The Byrds came out of 1965 very well, their dignity unimpaired. They are admirable people, and I never tire of their musical music. They have their disciples all over the world.'

If James Stewart once said that film actors give their audiences 'pieces of time', the same thing is equally true of recording artists. They give little two-and-a-half to three-minute singles-length pieces of time that indelibly freeze the moment, the event, the emotion, and that stay with the listener forever. The Byrds provided more pieces of time than most. 'Eight Miles High' set the advance tremors for psychedelia, and carried all the way into the San Francisco sub-culture.

'"You know how that song really started?", Gene Clark asked me casually. "It was me and Brian Jones sitting in a Hotel room on the road when we – the Byrds that is, were touring with the rolling Stones. And we got to be – me, Michael (Clarke), and Brian, we all got to be real good friends. Brian was always a little more sociable than Mick and Keith, even though I really love Mick, I think he's great – he's

definitely a tough guy, he stays out there and he does it real good. I respect him totally. But Brian was always real friendly. So he and I and Michael started hanging out together. I remember we were up in the Hotel room. We ordered dinner one night and we were all sitting there eating a coupla steaks, talking and having a couple of scotches, and we started talking about William Burroughs. And somehow I just got this idea – it came into my mind, I don't know how the conversation led up to it or anything like that, but all I know is that I started scribbling down the poetry, y'know. And Brian said 'what're you doing?' And I said 'this' (he mimes showing him), and he looks at it, and he reads a little bit of it, and he says 'that's pretty good, you ought to work on that!' So that's how the song started. And then, I think… I worked on it kind-of in private for – gosh, maybe about two weeks or something, almost every night in the Hotel room or something like that. And then we were on the bus – there was all of us travelling across country on a Motor Home, and we were listening to a lot of John Coltrane, and a lot of Ravi Shankar, because we were 'programming' ourselves. And Bach – we were listening to a lot of Bach too. And I played the song on acoustic guitar for McGuinn. I remember our Road Manager turned around – god rest his soul, he's dead now – but he turned around and said 'that's good poetry!' And McGuinn goes 'yeah, I like that.' And then Crosby comes down out of his bunk – all the way down he goes, 'yeah, I like that too', and he says 'I got a line for that one place where the words are kinda shaky', so he threw a line in. And then McGuinn started working on it, he began getting into arranging it. So it ended up, the three of us ended up writing the finished thing. But the original idea came – of course, out of Brian Jones, but he didn't know it. He never even got to know it. At the time he probably didn't halfway remember having the conversation, you know what I'm saying…?"'
The actual line that Crosby contributed where the original words were 'kinda shaky' consisted of 'rain-grey town, known for its sound.'

David Crosby had been spinning against Terry Melcher, so they tried out the new track at the RCA Studios in Hollywood (22 December 1965) with Jim and David Hassinger producing. The sound they achieved is impressive – with the RCA take eventually included as a 'bonus track' on the *Fifth Dimension* CD edition, nevertheless, the version that became the eventual single was re-cut at CBS. Although they always denied it, 'Eight Miles High' was generally assumed to be about drugs. And 'artificial energy' was something that was very much an integral part of their supercool ambience. Derek openly admits that their recording method consisted of 'the Byrds creativity and a capful of other ingredients.' And radio stations were wary of those supposed drug references. The influential tip-sheet *Bill Gavin's Record Report*, from which stations based their playlists, unequivocally banned it. And it's only the fact of its supposed drug-references denying it radio play and proportional over-the-counter sales that determined it never reached the chart heights its innovative quality and longevity deserved. Although it rewrote the rules, transcended the group's reliance on Dylan, and ignited psychedelia, it got no higher than no.14 on the national chart.

And simultaneously, Gene became the first original Byrd to quit, seeking a solo career. The Byrds boarded a New York flight for an end of January 1966 promo trip with an acetate of 'Eight Miles High' and a Murray the K radio-slot lined up. Then Gene got off the plane. In David Crosby's 'Psychodrama City' tale, the Byrds got on a plane, and 'one of my friends got off again', the lyric adding 'to this day I don't know why.' The reasons included rivalries and internal conflicts among what Derek referred to as the 'innovative, turbulent personalities' involved. The only Byrds A-side Gene Clark song – spun off *Turn! Turn! Turn!* As a follow-up to its no.1 title-song – was 'Set You Free This Time', twinned with Roger and Harvey Gerst's old Beefeaters song 'It Won't Be Wrong', but it failed to chart higher than no.79 in February 1966.

The tensions were amplified by their stratospheric celebrity. Gene had become unsettled by the sudden status afforded the Byrds – as the American Beatles. And to some extent by his genuine aversion to flying. Strangely, around the same time-frame, another of Derek's clients, Brian Wilson, had come to a similar decision. To quit touring, but remain a Beach Boy. A course that was not open to Gene. His association with the group would not be officially severed until 2 May, he would step in to temporarily replace an 'ailing' David Crosby for a Filmore Auditorium set in September, and there would be other fleeting reunion's, but effectively, by the time the Byrds' third album, *Fifth Dimension* (July 1966), was closing with the warm engine-roar of '2-4-2 Fox Trot (The Lear Jet Song)', Gene was gone.

All successful long-term bands have a unique chemistry with a shifting hierarchal structure. The Beatles functioned around the Lennon-McCartney axis, a sliding balance that tilted and evolved with the years, while George fought to get album-space for his own compositions, and the group democratically conferred one track per album to Ringo. A later Philip Norman biography (*John Lennon: The Life*, 2009, Harper) even seems to suggest a homoerotic intensity to the duo's relationship. A closeness that equates to platonic marriage, replete with all the hurt,

recrimination and bitterness of eventual betrayal and separation. As
Lennon was to flay their ruptured friendship mercilessly in his 1970
interview with Jan Wenner of *rolling Stone*. Perhaps it was 'Yesterday'
– a title selected for special vitriol on Lennon's 'How Do You Sleep?',
which first intimated to John that McCartney was more than merely a
junior member of the partnership. In the fade of 'All You Need is Love',
it's John who adds the 'Yesterday' retro-refrain, another indication
that he considered the song as something special. Something maybe
irksome in its significance. And later, as John's interest shifted more to
his art-projects with Yoko Ono, Paul's participation expanded to fill the
vacuum, altering the axis around which the group functioned. Even
post-Beatles, they continued to be regarded as partners, equals, until
John's assassination elevated him into an immortality that Paul could
never match.

The incestuous closeness a band confers, compounded by the success
that removes them into a shared exclusivity, can create an intensity
more powerful than family, more powerful than sex. Derek confided
to Lennon's biographer Larry Kane that John and Stu Sutcliffe had
shared a 'physical relationship'. Pauline Sutcliffe confides how 'Derek
Taylor told a friend that John talked in 1968 about a physical thing
with Stuart during a drug tryst', she wonders aloud that 'no-one really
knows, but it was entirely likely because of all the strange things they
were experiencing.' What happened within The Beatles was uniquely
unique, because it was forced to extremes that never existed before, or
since. But was shared in different ways by other bands.

The rolling Stones started out as Brian Jones' R&B covers band. But
as the Jagger and Richards writing partnership began to predominate,
encouraged by Andrew Loog Oldham, Brian became increasingly
marginalised within what had been his own band, until he was
eventually pressured out entirely. The Who, perhaps more than any
other sixties group, functioned as a fully-interlocking four-piece unit
with clearly defined separate roles. Pete Townshend as the writer
who – largely – did not sing. Roger Daltrey as the singer who did not
write. Keith Moon as the most distinctive power-drummer in rock. And
John Entwhistle whose solid presence and bass figures did so much
to define their sound. It was only death that could crack the tightness
of their configuration. As Derek wrote, voiced through Brian Epstein
in *A Cellarful of Noise*, 'balance, in groups as in life, is all.' For the
Byrds that was never the case. When they initially signed to CBS it was
only McGuinn, Crosby and Gene Clark who inked the contract. They
were officially the only real Byrds. And they were all singer-songwriter-

guitarists with undefined overlapping group-roles, all jostling and competing for the centre-ground. In such a light the surprise is not that the line-up fell apart so early, but that it survived as long as it did.

For Gene, ill at ease with stardom, there were to be a series of albums, groups, lost opportunities, and new beginnings. He went on to pioneer ventures into roots and country that would be more lucratively exploited by others. But he would forever be an ex-Byrd, living well on Byrds-royalties. His solo work was varied – from the textured density of *No Other* (1974) to the stripped-down *Two Sides to Every Story* (February 1977), but nothing he did would produce a signature 'Gene Clark sound' strong enough to replace his Byrds identity. Never quite 'in synch with his time', his albums tended to be overlooked, only to be subsequently recognised as influential, and reclaimed by music historians later.

As the *Younger Than Yesterday* (1966) Byrds album emerged – recorded against the backdrop of the Sunset Strip riots – its high-profile launch eclipsed *Gene Clark with the Gosdin Brothers*, including the enchanting 'Echoes', Gene's first solo album with sidemen including Clarence White, Doug Dillard, Leon Russell, Van Dyke Parks, Michael Clarke and Chris Hillman. Largely lost at the time, it was subsequently rediscovered by the hiperati. *The Fantastic Expeditions of Dillard & Clark* (October 1968) with Doug Dillard and Bernie Leadon met a similar fate, even though it premiered 'Train Leaves Here This Morning', which co-writer Leadon would take forward onto the Eagles mega-selling debut LP (Gene's jokey B-side version of Elvis' 'Don't Be Cruel' would be added to the 2001 Edsel-label CD reissue). The second Dillard & Clark album, *Through the Morning, Through the Night* (August 1969), recorded with an expanded line-up of Donna Washburn, Byron Berline, Sneaky Pete Kleinow, Chris Hillman and Michael Clarke, contains no less than two hauntingly beautiful Gene Clark songs which would achieve acclaim as part of Robert Plant and Alison Krauss' *Raising Sand* album in 2008 (it also includes covers of Don Everly's 'So Sad' and John Lennon's 'Don't Let Me Down'), yet at the time, Gene's reluctance to play the industry game, his unwillingness to tour, to do interviews and promo meant that his albums consistently failed to reach the audiences they deserved, and generated little more than critical respect.

By now the Byrds even looked different. Crosby in huge furry Cossack hat. McGuinn bearded. And Chris Hillman had stopped straightening his naturally curly hair into a fringe, allowing it to balloon into a halo. But by then they'd largely moved out of Derek's orbit.

Derek was always intuitively close to George Harrison. But he had what Beatles biographer Ray Coleman called 'a particularly strong intellectual rapport with John' too, enhanced by their shared appreciation for obscure Music Hall comedians. Derek was also an enthusiastic 'early convert to marijuana' and later LSD too… another strong bonding ingredient. During the stormy summer months with the limitations of his marriage preying on his mind, John sought refuge by spending a long drug-heavy weekend staying over at Derek's large Ascot home. Where Joan and the kids added their own kind of therapeutic magic.

'My marriage to Cyn was not unhappy', he explained, 'but it was just a normal marital state where nothing happened and which we continued to sustain.' Joan had always been a little wary of getting on the wrong side of John's unpredictably acid tongue, but this time John was so impressed by the Taylor's seemingly contented domestic bliss that he went home to Cynthia enthused with the idea of starting their own large family. Cynthia confirms the story in her autobiography. Yes, Derek and Joan 'seemed incredibly contented' together. Like many of his instant passions, John's enthusiasm for more kids swiftly turned in other directions. As did the constancy of his friendships. After The Beatles' break-up, with John in New York, he could turn his acid vituperation not only on Paul, but on Derek too, as his mood, and as his pharmacological condition dictated…

Chapter Nine: Fake Tales Of San Francisco

When the stream of changing days
Turns around in so many ways...
('No Other', Gene Clark)

'Derek Taylor: His Life and High Times'

It's now impossible to recapture the inwardness of it all. Caught out
by time, we see and hear only the outscape – the music, the press,
the film-clips, but we can no longer know the innerscape. We catch
glimpses from the impressions of others. To Beach Boys biographer
Steven Gaines '(Derek) Taylor had a great capacity for alcohol and
marijuana, as well as a reputation as a kind of psychedelic visionary.
In a world where publicity was considered so much hot air, Taylor
was extraordinarily talented. He was blessed with charm, wit, and
intelligence. Journalists loved him, and the feeling was mutual. Taylor
was able to convey a message about the groups he handled better than
anyone else.'

To Philip Norman, Derek was the 'Merseysider with the chiselled
good looks and immaculate grooming of an Italian film star.' For Al
Aronowitz, 'I, for one, recognised Derek as a great seducer. To meet
him was to be immediately disarmed, if not just thrown on the bed
and raped. But raped in a pleasurable way which you couldn't help
enjoying. Because, as press officer for The Beatles, the suave and
charming Derek was not merely their grandiloquent spokesman, he
was part of their magic.' With another, more sarcastic intent, Albert
Grossman compares Derek to suave English actor Ronald Colman – 'the
Man Who Broke the Bank at Monte Carlo', with his precise moustache,
his 'beautifully modulated and cultured voice.'

From Los Angeles, city of movie stars and cocktail bars, Derek was
picking up 'gossip, lightning images, and insights from the charts.'
And he was watching The Beatles' progress into 1965. Beginning, on
22 February, with their tidal wave hitting the peaceful, sun-drenched
Caribbean island of Nassau where they were to spend two-and-a-half
weeks filming phase one of their second, as yet unnamed, trip into the
movieverse. Various potential titles were being thrown around. An early
New Musical Express report suggests 'A Talent For Loving'. Meantime,
Brian Epstein was powering a new weekly pop venture, taking
Liverpool's groundbreaking magazine and breaking it nationally – the
fourth issue of *Music Echo and Mersey Beat*, priced at six-old-pence,
dated 27 March 1965, carries the front-page story 'Beatlecrasher' with

reports of the movie-to-come, announcing it as 'Eight Arms to Hold You'. The centrespread consists of Billy Fury – exclusive photographs from his family album. While the title 'Eight Arms to Hold You' is mentioned a number of times in press-reports. And it seemed to work, four Beatles = eight arms, which also ties in with the multi-armed Hindu deity that features in the plot-line.

Marc Behm, a US author of offbeat thrillers, co-scripted *Help!*. Born in Trenton, New Jersey in 1925, among his later novels, *Ice Maiden* (1983) features a vampire as its central character. He died aged eighty-two on 12 July 2007. Eleanor Bron of BBC-TV's satiric *Not So Much A Programme, More A Way of Life* had been signed as female lead. And naturally, radio-stations were alerted to the activity, they were already taking up the challenge of getting whatever exclusives they could from the situation. From New York, lawyer Walter Hofer – American attorney for Epstein and NEMS Enterprises – announced that the filming schedule was so tight that no official tie-in deals were possible. Not that that proved much of an obstacle. Unofficially, wheels were turning, especially from the shores of Miami, just 185-miles west of Nassau.

The two top regional pop stations, WQAM and WFUN, were bitter rivals who had already fought themselves to a standstill over The Beatles' Miami visit the previous year. Now they were both trying to work out a new angle. WFUN had, after all, sent news reporter Larry Kane to tour with The Beatles during the summer of 1964, and had inveigled him a role as part of the tour's entourage. (As well as The Beatles-Derek Taylor interviews, another was included within the eventual album package between Larry Kane and Derek, taped during that 1964 tour.) Now WFUN was attempting to use that slight leverage to make direct personal representations by overseas phone to Epstein, in order to OK some kind of tie-in promotion, possibly involving flying contest-winners out to Nassau to meet The Beatles on-set. WQAM disc jockey and programme director Charlie Murdoch told *Melody Maker* he was also 'working through some sources close to The Beatles and I expect to come up with some surprises' (13 February 1965). There were high expectations that the Fab Four might even take time out to fly into Miami to check out the scene...

But there were other schemes afoot, and as it turned out – for Derek, the Nassau traffic would go in the opposite direction. He was being set up to become KRLA's secret weapon to infiltrate the security and interview The Beatles on the set of their new movie. Wasn't he the perfect choice to do it? Hadn't he been their press officer during the summer 1964 US tour? Didn't he know them more intimately than any other standard reporter? Sure he did. And hadn't KRLA brought Derek out to California, set him up, invested good greenback dollars in promoting him? Weren't they due a little payback? Even if that ended up compromising Derek's friendship with The Beatles?

The Beatles could be devastating to off-message journalists, finishing off anyone who didn't match up to their ready wit and off-the-wall humour with barbed put-downs. Even Kenny Everett had innocently opened a Radio London interview by asking 'How's it going then, John?' Lennon responded with the withering taunt 'You're not a very good interviewer, are you Ken?' But then again, Derek was Liverpool (although, so was Everett). They had history together. He was damned-near 'one of us', despite his sober blue tie, grey shirt, and what Lennon described as 'grey tweedy-thingy trousers'. According to John, he was also wearing 'Beatle'-boots. Derek denies it, but John insists. To begin with, Derek flew out for the Bahamas with Dave Hull, KRLA's 'squarest DJ'. Then, by ferry from Nassau to the beach at Paradise Island.

Conducted onto the beach for The Beatles interviews, there were some sound-problems with the 'gentle swish of the Caribbean' and the wind interfered with the microphone. Leo mckern was standing at the water's edge like a Polynesian High Priest. The colours seem to vibrate with a luminous brightness. The sand is hot beneath Derek's toes. He's come a long long way from Hoylake. But the situation was ill-defined. What was his exact role – a friend who just happened to be carrying a tape-recorder, a journalist, their ex-publicist, or a man on the make intent on building a career on US radio? He wasn't sure himself. He'd been told to do it – to generate some working capital for Prestige Publicity. It had been just three months since they'd last met up, as they would mention more than once during the informal chats – since the last month of the previous year. For the most part, the conversations provide a good-natured glimpse into The Beatles easy-going attitude and offbeat humour. Being friends with Derek made them much more relaxed and at ease with the questions.

The most interesting of the eight 'tracks' that eventually emerge as a record-album, is the second – which has all four Beatles present. 'How's your wife, Derek?' drawls George. 'And the kids?' adds Ringo, 'give them our regards.' Then they go through a playful 'testing, testing, testing' routine using silly voices into Derek's hand-held microphone. Each of the other interviews with separate Beatles have their moments too, especially some of Lennon's jokes. Each of The Beatles seems relaxed and more than happy to talk, to indulge Derek for as long as he wants. Which makes the results even more frustrating. This is not a deeply penetrating insightful interview. Despite Derek's intimacy with The Beatles, his knowledge about and involvement in their developing story, this is not the John Lennon-Jan Wenner interview. Derek seems to be 'winging' the questions, without too much premeditation or plan. He's operating from his journalist default-setting, rather than thinking more long-term. But that's the way he'd always operated since *The Hoylake and West Kirby Advertiser*.

They kick around possible 'laugh-titles' for the movie – 'High-Heeled Knickers' perhaps? No, Derek helpfully suggests a Goldilocks-themed 'Who's Been Sleeping in My Porridge?' – which he attributes to George, he seems particularly pleased with this as he mentions it more than once. Wrong, says John, 'it'll have to be singable, we can't very well' sing that. Alternately he suggests 'He Who Laughs, Laughs, Laughs, Laughs'. So Paul reveals the genuine working title – 'Beatles 2'. Derek's attempts at learning more about the 'little eccentric script' itself are tactfully diverted by Paul who explains that 'Walter Shenson doesn't want the plot to be revealed', other than that the original story is American and 'translated into English'. All of which, with time moving rapidly, would obviously soon be revealed anyway. Then Derek repeatedly asks them what their plans are for the coming months, which ties the interviews to a very narrow time-band, and largely yields the information that the individual Beatles themselves didn't really have much grasp about what was to happen. Tours. Concert dates, of course. But the exact schedule would be arranged by the management structure, not by the 'boys' themselves. So that line of enquiry leads nowhere. He talks to George, who wears straw hat and blue jeans. George reveals that he prefers filming to touring. He talks about his new house, his brother's wedding in Liverpool, and the problems of eating-out in London. Derek talks to John, who wears dark glasses, blue plimsols with black socks, white trousers, and a multi-coloured jacket over a lilac shirt. He talks about problems with 'the usual fat American tourists'. And Derek talks to Paul, in 'deep tan make-up and bare feet' wearing grey trousers and blue check shirt.

Perhaps the most insightful sequence is when Paul volunteers details of his songwriting methodology with John. Which is the one item from the interviews that has passed into Beatles-lore. They write separately? They've always written separately. But they also edit each other's songs. Paul explains the evolution of 'I Saw Her Standing There', which he wrote while driving his car, lifting the bass-line from Chuck Berry's 'I'm Talkin' 'Bout You'. The original opening line 'Well she was just seventeen, and she'd never been a beauty queen' was the only modification John made to the lyric. Although it seemed perfectly fine to Paul, John insisted that the line doesn't work, it contains 'one word which would have made it very wrong', one word, or maybe one phrase. So they come up with the colloquial substitution – 'you know what I mean', 'a Liverpool expression, as it were, Derek' which, as Paul cheerfully admits, actually means nothing. We don't know what he means, beyond the kind of 'nudge-nudge' teen-slang. It works on the same conversational level as when John writes 'baby's good to me, y'know' in 'I Feel Fine' (and as Noel Gallagher writes in the Oasis hit 'You Know What I Mean'). It's a revealing kind of insight, just as when Paul explains how he wrote 'World Without Love', provoking John's derisively ridiculing guffaw when he first heard the opening line – 'Please lock me away'. Ridicule that didn't stop Peter and Gordon taking Paul's song to a global no.1.

Derek also attempts to provoke some rivalry about whose song gets the A-side, and who gets relegated to B-side status. Paul's raucous 'She's A Woman' is a good example of his spontaneous first-thought-is-best no-lyric-revision approach which, like 'I'm Down' – or after the old nonsensical Little Richard hits they're modelled on – works when it's at its sharpest. Even though in Paul's later, more comfortable career, the technique would lapse into a lazy sloppiness. Anyway, 'She's A Woman' was first lined-up for the next single, until John came up with 'I Feel Fine'. Was Paul resentful? Was his song 'less commercial'? Paul seems momentarily thrown by the assertion. Perhaps only Derek was close enough to the process to aim such a barbed point. Which makes it all the more regrettable that there's not more of such questioning.

Instead, they briefly argue over the exact status of the Bahamas – are the islands American, as Derek assumes, or British? Although such banter is time-wastingly amusing, the kind of trivia that passes time between acquaintances, it is hardly the stuff of historic interview-tapes. Of course, this was February 1965 – pop stars were still not expected to voice opinions on politics, hold forth on Vietnam, or preach moral or spiritual issues. As would become the norm a few slight years down the line. But then again – through his interactions with Bob Dylan and the Byrds, as go-between across scenes – Derek could not have been unaware of what was happening. Of what revelations lay on the horizon. And if anyone was ideally placed to initiate such questions it was Derek. Yet it didn't happen. The opportunity was missed. It seems likely that Derek was unsettled by the deception, by the devious nature of the venture he ruefully found himself a participant in, giving him a ticcy nervous edge. As though his own misgivings meant he was subconsciously not giving his best. As though he was reluctant to give his stories legs. He also interviews the 'Beatles hairdresser', Betty Glasow, under the Nassau pine trees. Since the set of *A Hard Day's Night*, she'd been working on Beatle hair, 'keeping it tidy, getting rid of loose ends.' With Derek probing into such controversial areas as 'it's probably invidious to compare their hair' but 'who has the softest hair?' 'Ringo' is her clipped, precise response, then 'John'. And yes, John's hair has an auburn tinge.

In *KRLA Beat* (17 March) Derek describes how perplexed he was by prominent British entertainment journalist Peter Evans, who described The Beatles as 'rude and arrogant'. As an insider, Derek saw it differently. At The Beatles' invitation, he stayed around once the tapes were done. Giving Dave Hull and Murray the K the slip, they spend a pleasant evening meal together. Derek flew back the following day. Once safely handed over, a team of KRLA tape-editors, mailers and sales-people segmented, trailered and packaged the interviews for sale to interested radio stations. He even provides an enticing all-purpose station trailer, announcing brightly 'Hello there, this is Derek Taylor, I used to be Press Officer for the extraordinary Beatles…' voiced over a brash big-band 'All My Loving' background, talking-up the interviews before closing 'this station is very happy to bring them to you, exclusively' – without actually specifying the station name, which could be dubbed on later.

After all, similar industry-only discs had been produced before, Capitol had circulated a *Meet The Beatles* promo to US radio stations during the first 1964 campaign, there was also *The Beatles American Tour with Ed Rudy* that same June. Trouble was, they were authorised, this one wasn't. And the words Derek had worked into *A Cellarful of Noise* where Brian says 'numerous attempts have been made to produce interview long-playing records which are not legal and which our lawyers have dealt with fairly severely', must have echoed in his head throughout the adventure. Dave Hull, whose Bahamas interview with Ringo was run in *KRLA Beat* (31 March), had already fallen out of favour with The Beatles after broadcasting their private addresses on-air. Yet when it came to marketing the tapes, there were very few takers. One of those who were tempted was WFUN of Miami – they knew the value of The Beatles' names and had been frustrated in attempts to get their own exclusives.

But the adventure left a sour taste in Derek's mouth. 'Got the tapes', he mused ruefully, 'lost his soul.' Eventually, the interview-tapes would be used, non-edited and complete, for an album called *Here, There &*

Everywhere (Thunderbolt CDTB221), and to even the casual listener it will be enough to transport minds back to a more innocent and exciting era. But the project earned Derek good-natured rebukes from The Beatles. During the Byrds' first London trip, while he was staying over at the Europa Hotel in Grosvenor Square, Derek attended the *Blaises* gig. Despite his reservation – 'since "These Are Not Merely Interviews: These Are Conversations Between Friends" the last thing I wanted to do was run into The Beatles' – he joined John and George upstairs after the gig. It was the first time they'd been in the same room since the Bahamas. 'Thank you for the tapes', said John, very loud. 'Which tapes?' bluffed Derek, very softly. 'You know which tapes', retorted John, still very loud. 'True', he conceded contritely. And that was it...

In *Help!*, Ringo's ring becomes what Alfred Hitchcock called the 'maguffin', the device around which the plot revolves, the one ring to rule the world. It's a film filled with memorable and much-imitated comic sequences, gentle surreal absurdism, catchy songs... and now-unrecognisable racial stereotypes. With Asians – played by Leo mckern (as 'Clang'), Eleanor Bron ('Ahme') and John Bluthal ('Bhuta') – from the 'mystic East' who sleep on beds-of-nails. It was premiered on Thursday, 29 July 1965, at the London Pavilion in Piccadily Circus. All four Beatles attend. I was also there, and it was astounding. With screaming crowds held back by police-enforced crash-barriers, Beatles album-tracks pumping out of speakers from the corner music store where the iconic semaphore sleeve-image actually displays 'NUJV', and not 'HELP'. Two weeks later they kick off their triumphant US summer tour as the year came to the career-event peak that was Shea Stadium (15 August 1965). An event that drew a 55,600 audience, and decisively elevated pop out of the theatre and into the era of Stadium-rock.

Derek seldom appeared less than garrulous and personable. It came with the territory. A degree of charm and clubability were necessary and essential attributes to his role. His easy presence could alter the atmosphere of a room just by entering it, defusing tensions or awkwardness. In the circles within which he moved, no-one was allowed to be anything but wonderful or feel anything less than fantabulous. As Al Aronowitz recalls, 'Derek knew his way around, and so he got around. He could play any role, and so he played many. Did I already tell you that what I admired most about Derek was his ability to carry on individual conversations with a roomful of people like a chequers or chess champ playing a few dozen challengers at once, and beating them all? In my montage of memories about Derek, he stands out as someone who was always fun to be with.'

Like many of his generation, he was over-compensating, making up
for a youth spent in post-war austerity by flinging himself headlong
into the cultural explosion happening all around him. A circuit that
lived in a haze of late, late nights, marijuana and alcohol. But there
were other, more complex, elements at work that were not so easily
visible. He was wonderfully free with his time, with a strong 'desire
to please', to say 'yes' instead of 'no', to praise rather than denigrate.
Mixed with 'a powerful wish to escape, to run from trouble', to avoid
unpleasant confrontations. It was an uneasy chemistry that had been
there since those first tremulous days on *The Hoylake and West Kirby
Advertiser* when he drank alcohol for the first time and discovered it
gave him greater confidence. 'Heavy drinking is an automatic brake on
maturity', he comments with typically dismissive wit, and it's a defence
mechanism. Drink – and now rituals with other stimulants – smoothed
otherwise intolerable situations, eased sociability. Surmounted
awkwardness. Nothing else ever worked quite as well. It even
functioned as an enabler when 'an inclination to allow anxieties or fear
to overwhelm me' led to an urge to 'blot it all out.' Of course, there
was an element of denying these things were taking place. But taking
place they were. It was not always so easy to conceal it to his family, to
Joan. Behind closed doors, everything was not always well.

Since their Atlantic-crossing he and Joan had 'swung from branch to
branch', frequently 'awfully hard-up'. They'd got a house in Nichols
Canyon with bills to pay, and Derek was compelled to take what work
came his way – 'a dollar is a dollar, however it is earned.' Now, the
Byrds connection was going good, 'paying the rent from our modest
percentage of the very agreeable royalties from "Mr Tambourine Man"'.
Derek was making the most of his new status as part of the high-flying
Byrds package. On 4 July the Byrds played at a private party for the
Hollywood elite – 'Jane Fonda's Independence Day Party' in Malibu,
attended by 'A'-listers Warren Beatty, Sidney Poitier, James Fox, Roger
Vadim, Mia Farrow, John Leyton, Roddy McDowell, Peter Finch, Louis
Jordan, David McCallum, Leslie Caron, Jill Ireland, Steve McQueen,
Ronald Fraser, and Diahann Carroll, with Henry and Peter Fonda also in
attendance. Derek was suitably impressed, but more than a little uneasy.

'I was thinking "this is really something," and hoping that the Byrds
would behave. I still had this rather suburban view of life that when
people came to a party they should be wearing suits. Brian Epstein had
always made sure that if the "boys" had been going to a party where
Henry Fonda was going to be with his friends, then they would be
suitably dressed and well-behaved. Even into 1965, when The Beatles

were going to special evenings they would look nice. But when the
Byrds turned up they were just the Byrds.' At one point in the evening,
when the Byrds' entourage of weirdos also turned up, he'd appealed
despairingly to Jim Dickson and whispered 'Jim, this is terrible. These
people look a mess.' Dickson couldn't see the problem – 'well, they
always look a mess! You don't understand. This is Hollywood. They're
used to this kind of thing. It's been going on for thirty-forty years.' He
was right. Henry Fonda managed to query why the group had to play so
loudly, but 'socially, it was a very successful evening', Derek conceded.
'There was no bad behaviour. I saw Fonda and his wife pinned against
a wall by the writhings of (dancer) Carl Franzoni and company. They
seemed to be saying, "we are the new Americans and we're out of our
heads." They were not going to go there and just have a glass of sherry.
But it was a good night. Jane Fonda was a lovely girl and Roger Vadim
was suitably interested in these new people.'

Shortly afterwards Derek was flying cross-continent as part of the
Byrds delegation to the Columbia Records Convention in Miami, where
the label bigwigs and stuffed shirts were gathered. Goddard Lieberson
was there, who had been label president since 1956 and largely
credited with introducing the concept of the long-playing record to
its repertoire. As was Clive Davis, whose more recent innovations had
resulted in a renewal of the label's fortunes through a series of more
contemporary signings. 'The big cheese was Clive Davis', Derek notes,
'he was more accessible than Lieberson. But he wasn't as interested
in the Byrds as he was in Paul Revere. They were the ones who were
thought to be the item. And, indeed, Chad & Jeremy were thought to
be more important because they were easier to handle, and there were
only two of them. The Byrds were very tough for a record executive to
get a handle on. They were the kind of people who'd wander around
a room. They weren't disciplined. They weren't trained like soldiers.
There'd be three of them on a sofa, one would be somewhere else,
and Crosby would be doing something weird, just to be a nuisance.
Record companies weren't used to this nonsense. And Dickson was
right – Columbia did not know what they had, although certain people
at Columbia – like Billy James, most certainly did. And so did Terry
Melcher. He had clout and skill and was a jolly good asset.'

Mid-summer, the 12 May cover-photo of *KRLA Beat* shows Derek
and Bob Eubanks with Dave Hull beneath the arch of the Hollywood
Bowl, with a headline announcing 'Here Comes The Beatles'. As Mott
the Hoople would later point out, 'it's a mighty long way down rock
'n' roll, from the Liverpool docks to the Hollywood Bowl,' and The

Beatles play the Bowl, 'overlaid with stardust drifting down from the Hollywood Hills'. The newly-signed Mamas & Papas watched the concert from the 'top rim' of LA looking down on the Bowl 'which gleamed in the darkness like a jewel. The roar of the delirious fans carried through the night into the stillness of the hills and canyons.' A week later – and just ten days after Shea Stadium – The Beatles were ensconced in their 'secret' rented Benedict Canyon house in LA where Brian and Carl Wilson came to hang out. Naturally, Derek was there too. Roger McGuinn, David Crosby – into pills and hash before he was into Stills and Nash – and a stoned Peter Fonda partied. John Lennon's lines for 'She Said, She Said' – about 'I know what it's like to be dead' – were lifted from Fonda's LSD-scrambled dialogue.

On Friday 27 August, The Beatles were driven from Benedict Canyon to meet Elvis Presley at his Bel Air home on Perugia Way. Elvis had just returned from Hawaii where he'd been filming the tragically poor *Paradise, Hawaiian Style* (June 1966) following the even worse *Harem Scarum* (UK *Harum Holiday*, September 1965), the absolute nadir of his career. Replaced at rock's focal point by The Beatles, their success had been spectacular enough to make him curl his famous lip. Yet the meeting between the two was, in some ways, what Martin Lewis (of *Variety* magazine) calls 'the denouement of a nine-year love affair.' John is quoted as saying 'before Elvis, there was nothing.'

Elvis was brooding sexuality. Elvis was unspecified rebellion. And from 1956, when the fifteen-year-old John first laid his ears and eyes on Elvis, he wanted more than anything else to be him. He wanted to be that swaggering, incendiary rock 'n' roll star. It was partly to this end that he gathered fellow-travellers Paul – who also recalls that 'when we were kids, growing up in Liverpool, all we ever wanted to be was Elvis Presley' – then George and Ringo, who all shared that passion. Together they synthesised much more than Elvis ever did. They absorbed rock 'n' roll, Rhythm 'n' Blues, Country, rockabilly, Jazz, Swing, Brill Building pop, Calypso, Blues, Dance-band Crooning, English Music-Hall, Vaudeville – and a myriad other shards from the musical universe. But at its heart lay Lennon's passion to be like Elvis. Until the fateful day he met him.

There were already advance tremors of what could be expected. When The Beatles formed the panel of a special edition of BBC-TV's *Juke Box Jury* – filmed at the Liverpool Odeon Cinema on 7 December 1963, immediately following an afternoon concert at the Empire Theatre – they were presented with a range of new singles for their critical assessment. Records by Bobby Vinton, Shirley Ellis ('The Nitty

Gritty'), Paul Anka, the Swinging Blue Jeans ('Hippy Hippy Shake' – 'not as good as the original by Chan Romero', judged Ringo) – and Elvis' 'Kiss Me Quick', a single lifted from his year-old *Pot Luck* (June 1962) album. Predictably, they were less than enthusiastic about it. Paul began by tactfully admitting, 'you know, I love his voice. I used to love all the records like "Blue Suede Shoes" and "Heartbreak Hotel", lovely', before derisively pointing out 'I don't like the songs now. And "Kiss Me Quick"? – it sounds like Blackpool on a sunny day.' There was wild audience laughter, followed by supportive applause. Ringo's contribution was restricted to a terse 'I didn't like it at all, no.' Rather more expansively George explained, 'I must admit I didn't like it very much. Not at all. It's an old track. And I think, seeing as they're releasing old stuff, if they release something like "My Baby Left Me" it'd be number one. Because Elvis is definitely still popular, it's just the song's a load of rubbish. I mean, Elvis is great. He's fine. But it's not for me'. Finally, it was John's turn – first conceding 'well, I think it'll be a hit because it's Elvis, like people said. But I don't think it'll be very great.' Then he comically reverts back to Paul's ridiculing comment about Blackpool – 'I like those hats, though, with "Kiss Me Quick" on it!'

On the other side of the vast cultural divide, much later, in one of the many movies made following Elvis' death, there's a recreated scene – probably apocryphal – in which Pricilla suggests to Elvis that he should comb his hair forward, into a fringe, in the new 'Beatles' fashion. And he angrily explodes that no, at one time every pop star imitated his hair – Ricky Nelson, Fabian, Bobby Vinton. To Elvis, it was he who set fashion, he didn't jealously follow other upstarts. He both resented and was confused by his sudden loss of status.

'Never meet your heroes', the old adage says, 'they always disappoint'. And so it was to be. To Martin Lewis, 'when Lennon finally met Elvis he discovered the tragically empty façade that Presley had become. The physical obesity had not yet manifested – but the sterile, vacant cadaver living in ivory-tower isolation and divorced from musical invention, devoid of any intellectual curiosity and apparently content to be the pawn of a greedy manager – was in Lennon's eyes as corrupt spiritually as Elvis' body became ten years later. He was a redneck, reactionary shell of the old Elvis'. It's fair to say that this summit conference of rock was no great meeting of minds. The Beatles were, despite their bravado, a little in awe, a little wrong-footed by it all. Elvis, despite his telegrammed greetings to The Beatles, was defensive and more than a little jealous of the way they'd usurped his pop supremacy and overnight relegated him to a sideshow. He didn't understand their humour – his own was of a far more earthily physical nature, and he retained a sneaking prejudice against their supposed effeminacy. The divide only came together, briefly, when guitars were produced, and they began to jam.

But for The Beatles, the meeting was more than just a final disillusionment. To Martin Lewis, it provides 'the key to understanding' the immaculate next phase of The Beatles career. Lennon was impressed to find Charlie Rich's 'Mohair Sam' on the King's personal jukebox, but was impressed by little else. 'The fan hit the shit. And the fan resolved that he would not emulate his former idol. There was now something that Lennon wanted even more than his 1956 wish to be like Elvis. He wanted to be not like Elvis. He wanted to be the opposite of Elvis. He didn't want to become enslaved to fame. He didn't wish to stagnate creatively. He wanted to use fame for good purposes – not for indolent self-indulgence.' So now, among their meetings with famous men, The Beatles could number both Bob Dylan and Elvis Presley. Presenting a stark contrast. Elvis represented not only the past but also the horrors that future-fame might hold for The Beatles – if they allowed that to happen. While Bob Dylan represented the future, and what potential that future might hold with a more creative vision of rock 'n' roll. Was it just coincidence that two days after the uneasy Elvis Presley meeting, The Beatles played San Francisco's Candlestick Park? The last time they'd ever play a full concert together. And that later, Lennon would prefer to see The Beatles fall apart at decade's end than subside into some kind of dull predictable complacency?

For Elvis, it was different again. He was not above recording Beatles songs, from George's 'Something' (on *Aloha from Hawaii Via Satellite*, 1973), to Paul's 'Hey Jude (on 1972's *Elvis Now*), to the perennial mor fall-back 'Yesterday' (*On Stage – February 1970*, giving the 'I'm not half the man I used to be' line an added poignancy) he's even caught jamming 'Lady Madonna'. But he retained a suspicious mind about The Beatles themselves. Part of his ludicrous mission to the White House to petition Richard Nixon to give him FBI special-status was his belief that The Beatles well-publicised 'anti-establishment' drug-use was contributing to the moral decline of American youth. When they were eventually released, the FBI files of the visit reveal Elvis' urgency to confide to FBI director J Edgar Hoover his belief 'that The Beatles laid the groundwork for many of the problems we are having with young people by their filthy unkempt appearances and suggestive music while entertaining in this country during the early and middle 1960s.' Ironic views in the light of his own dependency on the over-prescribed pharmaceuticals that brought on his death...

Although Gerry Marsden made a limited impression, and Billy J joined Brian Epstein on his first New York forays, The Beatles-led American breakthrough had happened too late for most of the original Merseybeat wave. The Searchers, oddly, achieved two massive late-hits with singles that didn't even register on the UK charts – 'Love Potion no.9' and 'Bumble Bee'. But the new American chart-frontier was already being defined by the cute toothsome grin of Herman's Hermits, and the Dave Clark Five who became bigger in the US than they ever were at home. Peter & Gordon continued to chart in America long after their limited run of hits here. And then there was the curious case of Chad Stuart & Jeremy Clyde who briefly became significant American chart-stars without ever scoring more than a ripple on the European side of the Atlantic.

English, was cool. Even if it was not cool enough to gift Epstein's latest signings with enduring careers. The Silkie were a folksome student four-piece from Hull University – Sylvia Tatler (voice), Mike Ramsden (guitar), Ivor Aylesbury (guitar) and Kevin Cunningham (double bass) who named themselves after a Hebridean song about a seal. Taken under the auspices of Alistair Taylor they were given the usual NEMS treatment, the PR and photo-opportunities, and the media connections that the Epstein profile took as a given. When a debut Fontana-label single – 'Blood Red River' c/w 'Close the Door Gently' (June 1965) – failed, they were gifted with that crucial Beatles song. In fact, when they went into the IBC Studios on 9 August John was there behind the mixing-desk, Paul helped out on guitar while George beat out time on a tambourine. Lifted from the *Help!* Soundtrack, John's highly Dylanesque 'You've Got to Hide Your Love Away' c/w 'City Winds' emerged in October. To Cathy mcgowan, 'the Silkie look a bit older than most groups on the pop scene. But Brian Epstein is very shrewd and clever to sign them up.'

Despite his spat with Brian, Derek was still considered very much part of the extended NEMS family and was on call to add weight to the campaign. On Friday 17 December, he was at Brian's side as they boarded the flight to New York to assist setting up a promo visit for the Silkie. The Moody Blues – another Epstein signing – flew with them. As a two-way exercise in networking, the trip's input fuelled his journalism, while taking advantage of Derek's unique media-position to add extra push. Derek commented in his *Disc Weekly* column that, 'as I forecast, the Silkie's "You've Got to Hide Your Love Away" has come into the charts. Expect it in the Top 30 here (USA). I don't see it getting into the Top Ten somehow. The influential Beatle-fan element resent "covers" of Beatles songs. This was why Keely Smith's beautiful Beatles album failed in America.'

Against Derek's prediction, 'You've Got to Hide Your Love Away' actually scraped as high as *Billboard*'s no.10 (6 November), but true to form the Silkie stalled at no.28 in the UK (21 October 1965). Their sole album was largely made up of Dylan covers, no less than eight of them! – later reissued by One Way Records (One Way 31441) on an expanded CD that gathered bonus singles tracks. The American tie-in dates to capitalise on the hit failed to materialise, and when two subsequent singles vanished without trace – 'Keys to My Soul' c/w 'Leave Me to Cry' (February 1966) and 'Born to Be with You' c/w 'So Sorry Now' (June 1966) – they discretely broke up. There's a happier appendix to the tale, though; Ramsden and Tatler married in 1966 and continued to perform as Silkie long after the original line-up had split. Another cover of 'You've Got to Hide Your Love Away' – by Dino, Desi & Billy – managed to apply a rippling Byrds guitar figure across the track in an immaculate transatlantic bridge, doing to Lennon-McCartney what the Byrds had done to Dylan.

Soon the Taylor family, with Joan and their four children, were living at 1416 N. La Brea Avenue, Hollywood, California 461-9931. Gerard began his education in 1965 at LA's St Victor's School, under the tutelage of Sister Francesca. Later, during his final semesters at the school, he was 'lucky enough' to find himself in classes conducted by an elderly African-American teacher Mrs Brockman. She banned toy guns from her classes and used the personal history of her slave grandmother to illustrate her lectures on the Civil Rights struggle. She was also an outspoken opponent of the Vietnam War.

Derek was representing and managing publicity for the Byrds, the Beach Boys, and – among others – Paul Revere and the Raiders, the first group he'd signed 'of whom, as follows...'. Like, say, Tommy James and the Shondells, they scored a string of massive American hit singles, while unlike Tommy James, not one of them made the slightest impression in the UK. Fun opportunistic populists with a sure sense of catchy riffs, their first hit 'Like, Long Hair' happened as early as 1961, and they were doing beefcake spreads for teeny-mag *16*, edited by Gloria Stavers who went on to become an early Beatles-champion. But as the English invasion exploded they were perceptive enough to angle their sound accordingly. They supposedly did the original cut of 'Louie, Louie', but lost out to the Kingsmen version on the chart, although both were done in the same Northwest Recorders studio in Portland, Oregon.

The track is included on their third album, *Here They Come*, produced with Terry Melcher in 1964, amid a patchy grab-bag of covers associated with English-invasion bands, some done 'live'. Of course, technically 'Do You Love Me', 'Time is On My Side' and 'Money' were not British at all, but American R&B sides. Only 'Something' is a shameless stand-out, a magnificently cheesy teeny-bop power-ballad as immaculately targeted as it is irresistibly effective. Later, recorded with what is considered their 'classic' line-up, their fifth album, *Midnight Ride* in 1966, up-powers into 'Kicks' which is trash garage-punk at its finest, a Mann & Weil anti-drugs infotainment fuelled on the artificial energies of Byrds guitar-twang, rattling tambourine and driving chorus. They add surf-harmonies to 'Little Girl in the Fourth Row' which stokes romantic audience-fantasies that pony-tailed vocalist Mark Lindsay was serenading directly at them, a ploy as cynical as mcfly or the Jonas Bros would ever get.

Then they set the template of Boyce & Hart's 'I'm Not Your Stepping Stone' for the Monkees, Flies, Sex Pistols – and Ant & Dec – to replicate. Finally tipping the album over into the voice-over kitsch of 'Melody for an Unknown Girl', measure for measure, everything you most love about sixties psych-beat is here. Although they seldom got better than this, the hits went on, as did their regular slapstick antics on Dick Clark's *Where the Action Is* – and its sequels *Happening '68* and *It's Happening*. 'Indian Reservation (The Lament of the Cherokee Indian)' provided their only no.1 as late as May 1971, despite it having started out as a Mark Lindsay solo project and despite it being nicked from an earlier UK hit from Don Fardon. By then, changing tastes and changing personnel had rendered them unfashionable. Even Derek was forced to admit that although they had become 'irrelevancies' there were still 'nervous citizens (who) felt reassured some good safe things never changed.' Paul Revere and the Raiders filled that role as headliners through the rest of the seventies, well into the eighties, and survived comfortably into the decades beyond.

All the while, Derek dutifully continued to file his columns for *Disc Weekly* to deadline – 'Hollywood Calling!' with the by-line 'By Derek Taylor, Hollywood, Tuesday'. Although by no means cutting-edge journalism, more an assembly of diary-jottings, gossip, industry chatter and opinion – inevitably biased towards his clients – his entries provide a fascinating insider's glimpse into exciting times. The issue of *Disc* dated 16 October 1965 is little more than twelve pages of text broken up by black-and-white half-tone photos, the only glimpse of colour provided by the red title-flash. The front-page story announces

Beatles' British tour dates running through December, from
Glasgow Odeon (3), Newcastle City Hall (4), Liverpool Empire (5),
Manchester Apollo (7), Sheffield City Hall (8), Birmingham Odeon
(9), London's Hammersmith Odeon (10), Finsbury Park Odeon (11)
and the Cardiff Capitol (12). Derek's report opens on the lower half
of page two, with inset photos of PJ Proby and Bob Dylan – beside
an advertising panel for 'DENSON FINE POYNTS' elastic-sided ankle-
hugging boots with a 'toe shape that tapers so smoothly to the tip'
(priced as 49s11d). The column was continued and concluded on
page eight. 'The most important news over here is that the BYRDS
have a new single. And about time. With DYLAN'S store of songs now
thoroughly ransacked by countless self-styled "folk-rock" groups, the
BYRDS switched suddenly to PETE SEEGER and "Turn! Turn! Turn!"
With words extracted from the *Book of Ecclesiastes*, Chapter three.
Unquestionably it will be no.1 in America…'

Star-names are capitalised for ease of recognition. He goes on to
comment on the curious state of the British charts as seen from the
Californian perspective, 'strange things are happening on your side
of the pond. KEN DODD at no.1!' Indeed, Knotty Ash's favourite
comedian was well into a five-week run topping the chart with the
sentimental schmaltz of 'Tears', holding off more credible contenders
such as Manfred Mann's Dylan *Basement Tapes* cover 'If You Gotta
Go Go Now', and Barry McGuire's PF Sloane Dylan-pastiche 'Eve of
Destruction'. 'I have a copy of the record here, and it's extremely
pleasant… very 1930-ish. But no.1? Anyway, I'm glad because KEN
DODD is a lovely lad'. While similarly saccharine fare was being
provided by mor veteran Andy Williams closely behind him. As Derek
notes in mildly mocking tones, 'and what of old ANDY WILLIAMS?
Well, well, well. I thought "protest" was the big thing… Is there a
reaction against the young sound, then? Andy himself is delighted
about the success of "Almost There". From Honolulu he tells me: "It's
very gratifying. Every singer is pleased by success in the single charts,
though obviously I don't want to stand or fall by the fate of a single.
Tell them 'Thanks a lot' in England".'

The week's American no.1 was Paul McCartney's original 'Yesterday'
– never a UK single for The Beatles – but, as Derek comments about
the Matt Monro version, it's 'a song for anyone who can sing!' While,
a new American Top Ten entry with 'Just A Little Bit Better', Herman's
Hermits – always bigger in the States than they were in the UK – were
maximising their impish ultra-English-invasion appeal, and proving
a talking point. Graham Nash, then still with the Hollies, jibed 'don't

know what to say about HERMAN's. I like him but I don't like many of his records', adding tartly, 'still, who am I to talk when we can't get hits in America?' Derek had a more gossipy insiders slant on the story. 'HERMAN is still here and expressing himself freely on this and that. If I were a group, I think I'd stop knocking other groups and take a cool, appraising glance at the top of the British chart and wonder where I was going wrong. Little Mr Noone was in *The Trip*, Hollywood's new, hip club, twice this week, gazing in wonderment at the electricity generated by the BYRDS and Barry McGuire. On the second visit he and one of his guitarists – the one who wears glasses – leaned against the bar, sniggered between themselves, attempted a brief impersonation of Byrd-leader JIM MGUINN with the glasses on the end of his nose, and then walked out with an approximation of a swagger. WELL... I SUPPOSE McGuinn CAN TAKE IT'. The capitalisation is all Derek's. And the fact that he was there to witness Herman's prank indicates that Derek was also a *Trip* night-owl of some regularity.

Elsewhere in the same column, Derek provided an advance notice of another new group, 'prepare for the LOVIN' SPOONFUL, a wonderful group all of whose members know exactly what music is about. They, like the BYRDS, refuse to be bracketed in "folk-rock", "folk and roll" or "protest". They call their endeavours "good-time music", a charmingly apt and unpretentious phrase.' The charmingly unpretentious Spoonful were at that moment moving up the *Cashbox* charts with their first single 'Do You Believe in Magic'. Which was important to know, because during this unique period, what was happening there would soon be happening here, just as what was happening here would soon be happening there! The column also found space for approving mentions of Jackie De Shannon's 'A Lifetime of Loneliness', and Billy Joe Royal's 'I Knew You When', while dismissing the Toys' wonderful 'A Lover's Concerto' as 'a dreary, squeaky, scale progression which looks like being a hit. Awful.' Derek also tipped the new rolling Stones single – 'have they ever made a bad record? I doubt it' – and sure enough, 'Get Off of My Cloud' would depose the much-maligned Ken Dodd from the top of the chart by the start of the next month, and rule both sides of the Atlantic. Although Derek scarcely needed psychic predictive powers to anticipate that. He closed the column by posing the capitalised question 'SO OUR CHARTS AREN'T REALLY ANY MORE SETTLED THAN YOURS. WHAT'S HAPPENING I WONDER?'

What was happening, by implication, was the Byrds.

Although essentially playful, the column was capable of provoking controversy. Dave Dee, confused and bewildered by the changes overwhelming pop which were marginalising his own career, launched an 'Amazing Attack' on the 'Hollywood Hippie' scene, singling out 'Mr Taylor' as a target. He defensively claimed his own group – Dave Dee, Dozy, Beaky, Mick and Tich – had pioneered wearing 'silly clothes', incapable of differentiating their contrived Pantomime from the new bohemia. Derek generously concedes that Dave's prose was 'obviously ghost-written'.

David Crosby adds (posted on *America Online*) 'Derek was a good, funny, irreverent and inventive man. He was a good friend to me and to The Byrds.'

Chapter Ten: 1966: It's A New Generation, With A New Explanation, People In Motion, People In Motion…

'Catch A Wave…'
For The Beatles, what Lord Buckley might have called nineteen-hundred-&-sixty-jumpin'-six was to be the watershed year. As 1965 died they'd just completed what turned out to be their last-ever UK tour, lasting from the third to the twelfth of December, a mere nine dates strung out from the Glasgow Odeon Cinema, to the Cardiff Capitol Cinema. The release of their fifth album – *Rubber Soul*, opened an eighteen-month period of amazing growth, above and beyond anything else previously imagined in popular culture. The new year would achieve a career-high with the release of *Revolver*, leading towards *Sgt. Pepper* by June 1967. But also their final disaster-strewn tour with death-threats, vengeful tyrants, organised Beatles record-burning pyres, and sad Ku Klux Klan fatwa intimidation.

It happened in waves. It happened with 'a lot of howsyerfather hitting the fan before you can say Jack Lawsuit.' When John first tossed his 'The Beatles more-popular-than-Jesus' hand-grenade quote, the throwaway quip was made without adverse reaction in an interview-feature written by Maureen Cleave, and published in *The London Evening Standard* (Friday, 4 March 1966). Had he meant 'bigger than Jesus – or just a fleeting higher recognition factor'? Who knows? Who cares? It passed pretty much without comment. Unfortunately, when it was syndicated and reprinted in the US *Datebook* they lift the quote and splash it across the cover. The issue was published Sunday 31 July, but cover-dated September, which meant that – deliberately – it impacted the newsstands as The Beatles were leaving London for their US tour. Sensitive God-fearing Christian souls across the Bible Belt were induced to read 'Christianity will go, it will vanish and shrink. I needn't argue about that, I'm right and I'll be proved right. We're more popular than Jesus now. I don't know which will go first – rock 'n' roll or Christianity.'

To most thinking beings these are statements of the obvious. During the sixties, certainly, old religious certainties had receded along with other superstitious remnants of darker less-enlightened ages, church attendance was healthily down, scepticism, atheism and pan-spiritual acceptance of other belief-systems – or none – was in the ascendant. And yes, for most, The Beatles were a more significant presence in their lives than Jesus. But not to the kind of religious fundamentalists who now insist on shoving creationism in the guise of 'intelligent design' onto the curriculum.

Proving that Islamic fatwas have no monopoly on censorious intolerance, they began organising mainstreet pyres of Beatle-burning, consuming albums, posters, T-shirts and related memorabilia (an orgy of destruction many must have subsequently regretted), whipped up by the same rabble-rousing shock-jock radio harangues that had once denounced the vulgar racial aspects of early Elvis rock 'n' roll. An outrage invisibly backed up and fanned by consortiums of disgruntled American business interests still resentful over losing their dominance of the teen-market to in-comer Anglos, the situation reached critical mass. The Beatles were flying into a different kind of hysteria. John made various convoluted apologies to 'Jesus as a person or god as a thing', in the guise of explanation. But the truth behind it was, as Derek once claimed, 'I'm anti-Christ' – not The Anti-Christ, just anti-christ, but they – meaning The Beatles – 'they're so anti-christ it frightens me!'

Kenny Everett joined the tour in his role as Radio London correspondent, sponsored by Bassett's confectioners who had benefited from George's casual aside that the group enjoyed nibbling jelly-babies. The comment created an instant sales bounce, and resulted in each concert appearance involving a hail of jelly sweets from the audience. The entourage embarked from the UK in awful weather, with one of the aircraft engines emitting a sharp detonation as it taxied across the runway, the sound of some kind of ominous omen. They were joined by tour-support acts the Ronettes and Bobby Hebb, to play a hectic thirty-one dates across thirty-two nights. Listeners to Radio London caught Everett's tour-reports spliced in with excerpts from his crudely-recorded concert tapes, fragments of a Paul McCartney interview, intercut with Bassett's commercials. This was when Everett became The Beatles' court jester, accepted into the tour's inner circle to witness the kind of insanity Derek Taylor had stage-managed for the earlier tour.

Travelling towards Shea Stadium, they were caught up in manoeuvres amounting to some kind of military operation. Security received advance alerts that the limousine-fleet was about to be ambushed by frantic fans. So they halt on a dark highway outside New York and switch the performers into a large army truck, in which they complete the journey. In Philadelphia, fans charged the stage, The Beatles – with Everett in tow – took refuge in a caravan which rocked violently as it was engulfed in a nubile sea of hysterical teenage-flesh. The tour climaxed at San Francisco's Candlestick Park on 29 August 1966. But Epstein missed what would be their last full-length show anywhere in the world. In Beverly Hills the previous day he'd hooked up with Diz Gillespie, a former boyfriend. It was a reunion that held out the promise of reconciliation, and Brian was on an emotional high, only to discover that with morning Gillespie had disappeared taking Brian's briefcase full of confidential documents with him. He was so distraught and fearful he failed to make the concert venue. For George, maybe more aware than the others of the downsides of being 'Fab', the event was less complicated, grinning as they came offstage 'well, that's it, I'm not a Beatle anymore!'

There was more controversy – as Derek recalls, 'when Paul McCartney was asked whether he had taken LSD, he said "yes", and after *Life* had printed it, TV interviewers asked him didn't he think it irresponsible for a man in his public position (oh really?) To influence others to take LSD. Paul asked the TV interviewers didn't they know it would be irresponsible of them to broadcast that he had taken LSD? Oh, wait a moment... Well, the television interviewers did broadcast it, so what with their irresponsibility and Paul's, I guess some people did follow his example. OK.' As Paul points out to his TV interrogator with guileless honesty, 'to say it is only to tell the truth.'

Although both of these high-profile incidents happened after Derek had left their employ, they were events that would be woven into his continuing narrative. Acid was a force for change, as David Crosby said, 'it did sort-of blow us loose from the Fifties' mindset. When Crosby gave a political harangue from the Monterey stage it was at least in part intended as an LSD-gesture of solidarity with Paul over the issue – 'I don't know whether any of you have seen, probably a lot of you have, *Life* magazine this week. In it, there is a statement that affects our times and is gonna cause a lot of trouble. I'd like to quote it to you roughly. "I believe that if we gave LSD to all the statesmen and the politicians in the world we might have a chance at stopping war." That's a quote from Paul McCartney. And I concur – heartily!' The audience-response was explosively positive. Yet Paul had been the most reluctant acid Day-Tripping Beatle. John and George took LSD first. Ringo next. Paul, a rather more reticent fourth.

Meanwhile, Derek Taylor was watching, and commenting on it all from Los Angeles. David Hughes (head of communications at EMI) says, 'I felt I knew Derek Taylor before I actually did. While working on *Disc & Music Echo* in the sixties, Derek's wild weekly column from Los Angeles became the most eagerly-anticipated words of any music-writer of the time. When in recent years, I came to actually know him, it was as if we had been friends for all those years.' *Disc* was edited by long-time Beatles follower and friend Ray Coleman. *Music Echo* – the first British title to publish a short-lived UK Top 100 – had been navigated from its *Mersey Beat* origins by Bill Harry. Brian Epstein acquired a large stake in the combined titles, and for the 23 April 1966 relaunch offered a free cover-mounted spoken-word 'Sound of the Stars' flexi-disc which includes a brief Beatles question-and-answer session with Radio Caroline DJ Tom Lodge. *The Music Paper* followed it with an 'exclusive' cover for the 11 June 1966 issue from The Beatles controversial 'butcher' photo-session. From 1964 The Beatles 'official' photographer had been Robert Whitaker. He lasted until the 'butcher' photo sessions.

Derek's column in the same issue reported 'Epstein's Cyrkle are doing pretty well. That's an understatement – they're doing very well.' An American New York signing, renamed by John Lennon, given national exposure through a supporting slot on The Beatles' 1966 US tour, then gifted with an original Paul Simon song in the shape of 'Red Rubber Ball', followed by another, 'Wish You Could Be Here', the Cyrkle were – very briefly – very big.

From his Sunset Boulevard desk, Derek was front-line witness to the new social ripples that were being galvanised into a cohesive force by, first, opposition to the escalating Vietnam killing fields, and stirred into new psychedelic constellations by hallucinogenics. Hadn't Victorian essayist Thomas Carlyle said something about 'write, write – it's the only thing you're there for'? Derek wrote. And music – the music that mattered beyond the chart fluff – had gone way beyond mere entertainment. It was creating a graph of contemporary sensibilities. It was leaking from the vinyl grooves, into people's lives... and vice versa. It was registering the changes happening in front of their ears. It appeared to stretch out towards its listeners by becoming some kind of shared experience. And in that sense, it had the ability to change lives. Dramatically. The counter-culture, 'The Greening of America', was finding its voice through the ragged proliferation of new 'underground' publications, the most immediately influential being Jann Wenner's *rolling Stone*, because of its insider coverage of the new music.

By mid-1966, the LA hippies hanging out around the Sunset Boulevard clubs were causing serious concern among the 'straight' community. A city councilman accused the strip of being 'a dangerous powder keg, ready to explode.' A curfew was imposed in an attempt to curb it all. After 10pm, anyone under the age of eighteen still on the street was liable to summary arrest. Enforced by cruising LAPD prowl-cars with loud-hailers. The conflagration that erupted immediately became a trash-exploitation – but a fun movie, called *Riot on Sunset Strip* (1967). What was happening was the Cops moving in to close *Pandora's Box*, the club that had inspired Association's 'Pandora's Golden Heebie-Jeebies'. A leather-booted baton-wielding 'flying wedge' of 'the heat' mowing down the protesting hippies who retaliated with flowers, beads and placards 'mostly saying Hooray For Our Side', or 'Cops: Uncouth To Youth!' John Peel – another ex-patriot Englishman trading on his Liverpool origins – described it as 'the first signs of the senseless brutality that we have come to expect from the police in big American cities.'

To Derek, 'I saw how bad things could be, before they got worse.' Jim Dickson's direct response to 'the battle outside raging' that was rattling his windows and shaking his walls, was to form an action group with other musicians, movers and shakers, which they named CAFF – 'Community Action for Fact and Freedom'. It included David 'The Mayor of Hip' Anderle, who had signed Frank Zappa's Mothers of Invention to a startled MGM label. They all took coordinating headquarter-space in Derek Taylor's office. The ideal insider's situation for him to report back on it all for his *Disc & Music Echo* column... and Buffalo Springfield – fronted by both Neil Young and Stephen Stills, scored their only major chart hit with 'For What It's Worth', directly provoked by the incidents, seeing the 'battle-lines being drawn', warning 'something's happening here, what it is ain't exactly clear.' The song would be updated for a new time of conflict for the 2006 Crosby Stills & Nash tour.

John Peel, compering a concert at San Bernadino's Orange Showgrounds for Radio K-MEN, recalls, 'the Byrds played, and the Dillards, but Johnnie Darin and I agreed that the Buffalo Springfield were the best thing there.' More of a promising try-out for future stardom than a hit band in its own right, the Springfied were a group of hugely talented individuals, the problem is that the group never transcended that individualism to achieve a collective identity. It was always Stills' song, or Neil's song. The American and Canadian group-components first met by running into each other in an LA traffic jam. Stephen Stills, who wrote 'For What It's Worth', also wrote 'Sit Down I Think I Love You', a hit for the Mojo Men, and 'Hot Dusty Roads' recorded by Chocolate Watchband. Rhythm-guitarist Richie Furay – who wrote 'Merry-Go-Round' for Buffalo Springfield's *Last Time Around* (August 1968) – and bassist Jim Messina went on to form sweet soft country-rockers Poco. Neil Young, who wrote the melodic 'Do I Have to Come Right Out and Say It' and 'Expecting to Fly' for the flawed *Buffalo Springfield* (February 1967) and *Buffalo Springfield Again* (December 1967), became... well, Neil Young. I clearly remember Peel playing the immaculate fade-in to 'Expecting to Fly' on his Radio 1 *Perfumed Garden* show – the lyrics opening 'there you stood, on the edge of your feather' – surely not? Was it, 'on the edge of forever'?

But before all that, the Springfield played a CAFF benefit concert that scene-maker Alan Pariser helped stage, raising awareness, and funds. The CD insert for *The Notorious Byrd Brothers* reproduces a CAFF poster dated Wednesday 22 February (1967) at the Valley Music Theatre headlining Peter, Paul & Mary with the Doors, Byrds, Hugh Masekela, and Buffalo Springfield. Briefly, Derek was doing PR for them too, since they'd played a six-week stint into June 1966 at the *Whisky a Go Go*. 'Charlie Green and Brian Stone, brilliant delinquent brains behind Sonny & Cher and other Great Adventures of the sixties, hired me to do the Buffalo Springfield, another group I liked front and backstage, and Charlie gave me $100 in green in advance. Very nice, I thought and spent it that day.' The arrangement lasted for maybe 'a coupla months', until Derek wrote to the management duo saying 'let's call the whole thing off', although 'time dims my motives.'

Writing has a lot to do with sitting and staring into space in a cumulus of cigarette smoke. It tends not to be pro-active. Journalism is a form of voyeurism, observing and feeding off other people's lives. Critics watch as others do things, and later, they write about it from the safety-zone of careful consideration and a distancing perspective. The only real hazards come from demanding deadlines and word-limitations. And there's a central paradox involved – the stuff deliberately written with one eye on posterity tends to die on the page. It's the stuff written quickly, with no other purpose than to snag and document the present moment, which seems to endure. Journalists have more in common with zeitgeisty bloggers and magazine columnists than literary fictionalists, and they tend to be neither sentimental nor traditionalist about their writing.

Derek had not freed himself from the newspaper press-room just to exchange it for another desk-bound job. There are investigative reporter-type writers who go out in search of things that are outside everyday experience. And there are journalists who start with the obvious given subjects and find something revelationary to say about it. Derek was the latter. The Beatles might have stopped touring, but hey, other bands continued to do it, with West Coast rock taking music into a quagmire of new definitions. So Derek's PR prose scattered magic dust over Paul Butterfield, the Sir Douglas Quartet (Doug Sahm), Van Dyke Parks, Judy Collins, Chad Stuart & Jeremy Clyde, even The Mamas and the Papas. Andrew Loog Oldham approached him about doing press for the rolling Stones. He did work for Danny Hutton of Three Dog Night, and for a group from Memphis called the Guilloteens. He represented five-per cent of former-Cricket Jerry Naylor. They needed PR too...

In 1965 Derek wrote a biog-sheet for 'the squarest group in the world' – the Sandpipers, and liner-notes for their LP *Guantanemera*, written in twenty minutes for $125. In truth, Derek 'needed the money', so 'I was taking on too much.' During 1965 he 'had a gig working the West Coast' for a magazine called *Record Beat*, until it closed down. He was also contributing a 'really stoned, but tight' occasional column to US trade paper *Cashbox*. He took advantage of his radio-connection to promote his own clients as a listed 'correspondent' for the expanding *KRLA Beat* magazine with the Beau Brummels, Tommy Quickly, Jerry Naylor (Crickets), Mark Lindsay and the Byrds. His Beatles Bahamas adventure featured strongly in the 17 March issue, a Paul interview (21 April), an insider's view of the 'I Feel Fine' studio sessions and a *Help!* Plot-synopsis (5 May). His final three-part contribution (9 to 23 June 1965) retrospected his own Beatles history from that first evening in Manchester.

Although, as Auden famously declared, 'Poetry makes nothing happen', something occasionally happens when a journalist gets things right. It's not entirely that a PR's job is to peddle lies for a living, but it's close, more that his prose gives contour to their cloud. All publicity can do is bring something to the public's attention. Nobody can be forced to buy a record. And, even when carefully considered and anticipated, a record is still very much an impulse-purchase dependent on the precise time-fix, and the amount of disposable income still at hand. But an album's fate can also depend on the amount of print-coverage it receives. The radio and jukebox plays are not the only places where it can be brought to people's attention. A hit can be triggered by a contagious hook, a sound-effect, a catchy lyric, or by the word-of-mouth viral momentum of peer interest, hearing random radio-play at the right moment, snatching a teasing glimpse of the artists on-screen – or by reading an intriguing press write-up in the correct magazine. But quick – get in fast, before the radio plays the next record, or the TV screens an even newer band, or you turn the page.

With the rock industry still very much in its infancy, publicists such as Derek were feeling their way, making it up for the first time as they went along, inventing the vocabulary. There could be tension underlying the sharp interface between journalists and the PR industry. A basic level of mutual mistrust and scepticism – the PR man was only being nice the better to push his client, the journalist only interested in covering established names with circulation-boosting appeal. But Derek had experience of working from both sides of the equation. So there was common ground, with the potential for collusion too. There were interdependences that were ripe for lubrication and cultivation. Where interests were aligned, differences could be conveniently forgotten. And sometimes, a publicist can overcome the industry's inertia, and make a significant difference to an artist's career.

The perfect example is young Harry Nilsson who signed with RCA Victor in 1966 and released an album the following year – *Pandemonium Shadow Show*. It was a critical, if not a wildly commercial West Coast word-of-mouth success. It most impressed music industry insiders who were struck both by the evident songwriting skills and by his pure-toned, softly melancholic, multi-octave vocals. One such insider was Derek Taylor, who heard Nilsson's song '1941' on his car radio, and was so intrigued by this new voice that he bought an entire boxful of twenty-five copies of the album to share with others. At the time there was no financial incentive. Nilsson was not his client. It was simply in recognition of talent that he felt deserved greater exposure. A newly-found pleasure he wanted to communicate. Derek ensured that some of those albums found their way to The Beatles themselves, who soon invited Nilsson to London, and quickly became his most verbal propagandists. John Lennon, in particular, claimed to have listened to the album repeatedly in a 36-hour marathon. This may have had something to do with the track 'You Can't Do That' which not only covers a Beatles song, but manages to weave twenty-two other Beatles titles into its inventively parodying multi-tracked harmony vocals. When John and Paul held a press conference in 1968 to announce the launch of Apple, John was asked to name his favourite American artists, he said 'Nilsson'. Asked the same question Paul also responded 'Nilsson'. The connection led to a long-term relationship, particularly between Nilsson and John Lennon, in which Derek would be a sporadic participant.

Harry Edward Nilsson III, to give him his full title, was born in Brooklyn on 15 June 1941 and had been involved in music through a series of semi-pro projects including an Everly Brothers-style harmony duo – improvising lyrics when he forgot the words – while working at the LA Paramount theatre. When the theatre closed in the final years of the fifties, he applied for a bank job, stating incorrectly on the application that he was a high-school graduate, despite never having made it through ninth grade. Fortunately, he turned out to have an aptitude for their fairly rudimentary computer system, which ensured he was kept on even after his ruse was uncovered. But he continued to sideline by recording demos at $5 a shot for songwriter Scott Turner, tracks that would later turn up in album-form when his name was big enough to exploit!

He also began writing and recording himself, as Bo Pete (for a Crusader label single 'Baa Baa Blacksheep, Pts 1 & 2'), or as Johnny Niles (for Liberty Records, commencing with 'Donna, I Understand'), while collaborating with John Marascalco on a song for Little Richard and writing with Phil Spector and Perry Botkin Jr. Though still holding down the day-job, his songs were being picked up and recorded by Glen Campbell, Fred Astaire, the Yardbirds ('Ten Little Indians'), and most significantly the Monkees. Their recording of his jaunty vaudevillian 'Cuddly Toy' finally enabled Nilsson to go full-time, sign with RCA, and strike up a friendship with Micky Dolenz that would survive through to Nilsson's death on 15 January 1994. With his own office at the RCA building and a number of unsatisfactory TV slots to his credit – he was always more comfortable as writer than performer – Nilsson answered the phone one day to discover John Lennon on the line, full of praises about the album Derek had passed on to him. He invited Nilsson to join The Beatles in London, and possibly to sign for Apple. His life would never be the same again...

By then The Beatles have released *Revolver* (August 1966). Although no-one realised it at the time, it arrived within a month of their last-ever live concert. The first of a trilogy of LP's – along with *Seargent Pepper* and the *White Album* – that are routinely described and voted for in polls as not only the greatest Beatles album ever, but the greatest album of the rock era. It came a mere eight months after the superb *Rubber Soul* – their last with Norman Smith on-team (although he'd later be entrusted with remixing Beatles tracks into stereo). Politely spoken and smartly dressed, to Lennon, Norman Smith was 'Norman Normal'. But if The Beatles relied on George Martin to conjure the sounds they heard in their heads, Norman had applied the technology that enabled George Martin to realise them.

In June 1966, 'Paperback Writer' topped the world charts, written by Paul in response to a challenge to write something other than love-relationship songs. He used a new Rickenbacker bass in preference to his regular Hofner. They added deliberately Beach-Boy harmonies to the mix, and the innovative use of reverse-tapes on the B-side, 'Rain'.

And just three months later, their seventh album proved to be light years ahead of its twelve-inch predecessor, paving the way for the acid and meditation-fuelled psychedelia to come, and pioneering lyrical invention that thrashed the conventions of what had previously been called pop music. It saw the band – with George Martin – utilising technology to take their sound into new, unheralded realms far beyond the live capability of any band of the era. The peak of their internal chemistry, not just between John and Paul, but George Martin as a huge part of it, the production, the use of instrumentation, and the very palette of instruments used. Every track gets exactly what it needs at the precise moment.

George Martin described his approach to production as the creation of 'little sound-pictures', paraphrasing artist Edgar Degas in his intention to contrive 'not what one hears, but what one must make others hear.' Paul's 'Eleanor Rigby' tells a poignant tale of loneliness and despair with all the lyrical dexterity of the Mersey Poets. Martin scored a baroque string arrangement with Bernard Herrmann's movie scores in mind, especially the shower scene from Hitchcock's 1960 *Psycho*. It never tips over into schmaltz. 'Yellow Submarine' blends fantasy lyrics with an infuriatingly catchy tune. George's 'Taxman' riff – later purloined by the Jam – took an acerbic sideways glance at politics, while his 'Love You Too' forms further incursions into Eastern music. It's impossible to exaggerate how well-written and how creative these songs are. In many ways, it represents the perfect vinyl encapsulation of the decade. So far ahead of the opposition as to be out of sight. There's hardly a note out of place.

'Tomorrow Never Knows' is their strangest, most sonically dazzling recording to date, its lyrics inspired by the *Tibetan Book of the Dead* by way of Timothy Leary, and then allied to a startling drum pattern (which, thirty years later, would provide the template for the Chemical Brothers' 'Setting Son'). Although it's routinely interpreted as Lennon's work, evidence of his pre-Yoko art-tendencies, Paul's fascination with newly-devised tape-loops add depth. Jokingly deflecting claims that The Beatles were anti-materialistic, Paul would later laugh over his recollection of their songwriting sessions as 'sitting down to write a swimming pool.' 'Tomorrow Never Knows' could never have been created purely as a money-making vehicle. This is about as far from commercial bubble-pop as it's possible to get. Yet as if to emphasise its implications it's placed as the album's finale, in the place previously occupied by 'Twist and Shout' or 'Money'.

Certainly, testosterone-fuelled competition with other bands was an element, accelerating the ambitions of the vinyl arms-race. There's a story that during the *Revolver* sessions they despatched a minion to go out and buy *Aftermath* (April 1966), the new rolling Stones album of all-original songs and odd instrumentation. But 'Tomorrow Never Knows' is not a pop song. To pose the question, 'could they have performed it at Shea Stadium?' puts it in perspective. It's as much a studio-construct as Spector's 'Wall of Sound'. Part of the evolving separation of 'song' from 'record' which included Les Paul's experiments with dual-tracking and, not to forget, George Martin's use of studio effects to augment the Peter Sellers' record-album lunacy with stylus-guided bombs and the performers dashing from one room to another. 'Tomorrow Never Knows' could only ever exist in the studio, or on record, fulfilling Lennon's desire to 'sound as if I'm singing from the top of a hill, I want to sound like a Buddhist monk, singing from the top of a mountain. Like the Dalai Lama. Distant, but I still want to hear it', with his other-worldly vocals fed through a Leslie speaker.

Even what is routinely dismissed as a relatively minor no.1 single, if such a thing is possible – 'I Feel Fine' opens with that dull gnawing feedback drone, the accidental effect of the kind usually edited out of mixes, which carried repercussions way into the future. In its utilisation of 'found sound' distortion, it reverberates a future-echo of psychedelia to come. The entire career of Pink Floyd has its origins here. And then 'Yellow Submarine' – a novelty sing-along, a kids song, a joke. So how utterly unexpected it was on its first release as an A-side single, how it confounded all expectations. The sampled effects, the 'band began to play' insert, the oddly surreal lyrics, Ringo's droll delivery. As a follow-up to *A Hard Day's Night* it was laugh-out-loud bewildering. For The Beatles, and in more ways than one, for the entire phantasmagoria of rock music itself, there was no going back...

David Mallet, the British assistant-producer of Jack Good's *Shindig*, approached Derek with a bizarre suggestion. Would he like to represent Mae West? Would he – well, he'd certainly check out the situation. After much deliberation, the fading star 'consented' to a sounding-out meeting at her 'old and very baroque apartment block' in old Hollywood. In the meantime, Derek did a little research. Simon Louvish's biography *Mae West: It Ain't No Sin* (2006, Faber) does an admirable job of seeking out the woman behind the aphorisms, dismantling West's self-mythologising while remaining respectful and fond, even through the depressing lows of her post-1940s career. The book is a portrayal of a 'sex personality' with Oscar Wilde's capacity for quips. But Mae West's 'great secret' was that she was a hard-working writer by night, knocking out three novels and twelve plays and more than twenty-thousand finely honed ripostes. Her liberated and candid theatre work agitated censors and police, who feared for public morality. As early as 1927 she faced prosecution and endured a ten-day jailing for 'corrupting the morals of youth' in the Broadway play *Sex* which she both wrote, and starred in. But although her sexual conquests were legion, the apparently debauched West neither smoked nor drank and remained emotionally distant even from her husband, who was never allowed to stay the night.

In the room he was eventually ushered into there was a voluptuous nude painting of a much younger Mae West, set upon a white grand piano. By contrast, a 'sweet old lady' in a 'long white satin gown' and a 'tumbling wig of pale gold' not so much appeared, as made her entrance. Derek and Mallet rose to their feet like a respectful congregation and stood to attention. Technically retired, she was still 'a star in need of recognition, appreciation, love.' As part of a strange strategy to resurrect her career, she'd signed to Capitol Records subsidiary Tower, for an album called *Way Out West* (1966). She smiled secret movie-star flirtatious smiles. It was an impossible situation, fantastic, as if in a dream. Derek was generous enough to consider her outrageous ego 'a very precious jewel' for which modesty would be 'a most unbecoming setting'. They talked. She reminisced. Expressed her distaste for the topless dresses recently launched. Related how she'd discovered Cary Grant walking across a lot, how she'd put him in her movie *I'm No Angel* (1933) and made him a star. The meeting seemed to have gone well. Derek was taken on for a fee of $300 a month.

She recorded eleven tracks with a studio group called Somebody's Children. The standout was her version of Roy Head's hit 'Treat Her Right', retitled 'Treat Him Right'. Her single from the sessions – 'Twist and Shout' c/w 'Day Tripper' (Stateside SS 2021) – was reviewed in *Record Mirror* as 'rather incredible, this. The old-time sex symbol lacerates a couple of big hits – and gets away with it. Modern beat group behind. Nigh on irresistible, this combination. Try it' (13 May 1967). The unnamed reviewer awards it four stars. She goes on to interpret Jerry Lee Lewis with a very anatomical take on 'Great Balls of Fire'. But by then Derek had been informed that their 'useful relationship' was complete, and he was no longer required. A cheque followed. He xeroxed the cheque, cashed it. Then lost the Xerox…

Mae West later features on the top back row of the *Seargent Pepper* cover collage.

It's a long and winding road from Liverpool to the Haight-Ashbury community. And Haight-Ashbury had succeeded Carnaby Street as the vogue place to be. As Derek comments, San Francisco was 'attracting newer and more exotic herbal and metaphysical additives.' Allen Cohen, with financial input from psychedelic entrepreneur Ron Thelin, produce the first issue of *The San Francisco Oracle* in September 1966. Easily recognised by its psychedelic covers, the journal's goal was, according to Cohen, 'to judo the tabloid low-price anguish propaganda and profit-form to confront its readers with a rainbow of beauty and words ringing with truth and transcendence.' No.7 features a cover collage of Timothy Leary, Allen Ginsberg, Allen Watts and Gary Snyder. The four had gathered together for a 'historic' meeting to discuss 'the problem of whether to drop out or take over.'

With a sub-culture escaping into the alternative universes of LSD, the 'Doors of Perception' were open for business. With naïve optimism as its thesis, and moral panic as its antithesis, acid was the sacrament that combined individual hedonism with communal unity. It's easy to ridicule. The fey idiot-dancing. The outlandish costumes. The pretentious rhetoric. What times they were! But to the children who'd grown up through the austerity fifties, the – over-used term – revelation that life could extend beyond the pervasive drabness to include sensual bohemian freedoms that were poetic, beautiful, uninhibited, spontaneous, was something genuinely – over-used term – consciousness-expanding. Ornate detonations of Dada magazine design, tripped-out pre-Raphaelite posters, gatefold album-sleeve explosions of pop Art collage that replaced the old formal group or artist posed photo-shot and solid title lettering. Previously, pleasure was something that had to be earned, a 'Saturday Night and Sunday Morning' weekend reward for a week of hard graft. Not a casual hedonistic right to a libertine's abandon.

The Beatles had played San Francisco in 1964, 1965, and 1966, but hadn't really had free time to explore. So, 1 August 1967, George Harrison with Pattie Boyd, and Neil Aspinall with 'Magic' Alex Mardas in tow, arrived for a highly eventful visit to the West Coast. He was in LA to hear Ravi Shankar at the Hollywood Bowl, and assist the sitar-virtuoso publicise the opening of an American branch of his Indian Music School. George also took the opportunity of investigating the new happening scene, and seeking whatever cosmic enlightenment there was to be had. The visiting party was met at LA International Airport by Nat Weiss, Epstein's friend and business partner, but they were immediately ambushed by the press, and George dismissively answered a question about smoking marijuana with 'Oh, it's the same as drinking Seagrams'. Much to Brian Epstein's chagrin.

Rescued by Derek, the party travel by limousine direct from the airport to meet a DJ. Meanwhile, Weiss, director of New York's Nemperor Artists, rented a Los Angeles house for their stay. Owned by music-business lawyer Robert Fitzpatrick, who was holidaying in Hawaii, it was located in the pretty suburban Blue Jay Way, where George's *Magical Mystery Tour* song of the same name would be conceived that same evening. On the phone, George gave Derek directions how to get there as they arrange to meet up later. But, notoriously difficult to find, separated by a ravine, it was a foggy night and they soon got lost on the way, as Jack Kerouac calls out across the years, so gone and out of sight, 'wither thou goest America, in thy shiny car in the night?' Tired 'after the flight and the time change', waiting for Derek and Joan to come over – as the song relates in George's thick Liverpudlian slur, 'my friends have lost thurr way, "we'll be over soon" they said, now they've lost themselves instead'.

Finding a small electric organ in the house, George worked on the song, sketching out the lyrics on Robert Fitzpatrick Associates headed notepaper, until Derek and Joan finally arrive and 'when I see you at the door, I know your (sic) worth waiting for...' 'By the time we got there, the song was virtually intact', related Derek later, 'of course, at the time I felt very bad. Here were these two wretchedly jet-lagged people and we were about two hours late. But here, indeed, was a song...!' A song that would later be invested with all manner of mystic symbolism, with 'they' who have lost their way interpreted as the entire materialistic generation. In fact, it was simply a narrative of a visit by Derek and Joan Taylor.

On the third of August, Derek took George over to sit in on a Mamas and Papas recording session, after which the entire Taylor family went out for a meal with George and his friends in Alvira Street. To round off the visit, on the seventh, the party hop a Lear-jet – what Derek termed the 'Porsches of the air' – for a flight along the coast to San Francisco. Pattie's sister Jenny was then married to Mick Fleetwood, and living in Frisco, so it seemed a good opportunity for catch-up time. Once there they park the limo a block away from the fabled Haight-Ashbury corner. A sticky-hot day. George, in heart-shaped rose-tinted shades, carefully divides up several bright orange acid-tabs among his guests, and they take a stroll through ornate but dilapidated Haight-Ashbury where word soon got around and they were besieged by startled worshipful hippies, moving like some 'fab Pied Piper' although 'we were so stoned we just waved at anything that moved.' They banter, a guitar is produced and George stumbles through an improvised performance. Expecting some kind of radiant utopian community, George discovered instead what was more 'like the Bowery, a lot of bums and drop-outs', with less love and peace than beggars, panhandlers and souvenir stalls. According to Derek, the whole experience left 'a bad taste in his (George's) mouth.'

'This Is The Worst Trip, I've Ever Been On...'
('Sloop John B', The Beach Boys)

Then Brian Wilson entered the story. Literally. To Derek, he was 'the Giant Beach Boy'. 'He and I met in his Sunset Boulevard office', recalls Brian Wilson himself, after the Beach Boy had purposefully sought out the guy with The Beatles' connections. Nick Grillo, a young industrious Beach Boys personal business manager, had an eighth-floor office directly across the hall from Derek. It was a short walk, hang a left instead of a right turn, and Brian walked in on Derek. They talk. 'The discussion consumed several hours, and several joints.' 'What do you want?' asked Derek. 'To be taken seriously', said Brian without hesitation. He wanted the group to move out beyond their clean wholesome 'striped shirt' image, into something deeper.

Derek took up the challenge, for two years, for $750 a month. His solution was the one-word slogan that a later Guinness advertising think-tank would pay a million for... 'Genius'. As such, Derek was the man who first pinned the 'genius' label on Brian Wilson. The first time the term had been linked to a pop musician since Ray Charles. And the term which Brian has been trying to live down – or live up to – ever since. According to Beach Boys biographer Steven Gaines, '(Derek) Taylor first got to know Brian and the Beach Boys during the preparation of *Pet Sounds*, and many consider Derek Taylor's influential word – or the "many words" he wrote on them, to be the cornerstone for the album's success in England.' 'I lived in Hollywood then', Derek said, 'but my British links were strong, and with *Pet Sounds* out and The Beatles increasingly flattering about the Beach Boys... and with (a new single) on the way, we started to pump information into England about this tremendous band, with their new plateau. Soon everyone was saying "genius", and the beauty of it, as with the beauty of anything, was that it was true.'

Bruce Johnson brought two early *Pet Sounds* pressings to London, where Derek immediately set up twenty back-to-back interviews for him, including one with journalist Keith Altham, while John and Paul Beatles were sitting in the next room listening to the album all the way through – twice!

Brian Wilson himself recalled, 'when I first met Derek in 1966, I was immediately impressed by his great mind and his fantastic wit. I just knew that I had to convince him to come work his magic for us. And he did. Derek Taylor had as much to do with the success of *Pet Sounds* and "Good Vibrations" in England as anybody, including me, and for that alone, I'm forever indebted. But besides all the great publicity he created for our music, during the time we worked together, we had so much fun, so many laughs, munched so many great hamburgers together. And despite what he wrote about me, it was Derek Taylor who was the genius. HE was a genius writer. He had an unerring instinct about what was important, about what people would want to know and a stylish way of saying it that was as classy as the man himself... Derek was the one who came up with the term "pocket symphony" to describe "Good Vibrations". He encapsulated the record perfectly! I admired the way he could express things...'

The 'Dumb Angel' sessions – that became the *Smile* project – have entered rock mythology, as the definitive stories of excess and oddity. Yet there's also a twisted logic at work beneath the surface madness. Recording the 'Fire' sequence in the Gold Star Studios on Santa Monica Boulevard – 10 November 1966 – with whistles, alarms, 'Keystone Cops' effects, woozy vocal and orchestral undulations, Brian had the musicians wear firefighter's helmets. Which is generally interpreted as a 'Gosh-Wow' symptom of his weirdness. Yet – as the Beach Boys themselves were not present, Brian was using the cream of LA session-musicians, who were note-perfect. But also uninvolved. They worked for Phil Spector. They worked across town with any number of producers for innumerable artists. Barely aware of which records they'd actually played on, even when they heard them on the radio. They were immaculate professionals who could play whatever was required of them. Brian's problem was that he wanted more than just technical virtuosity. He wanted involvement. He had to crack through their professional veneer. He needed to make the sessions memorably different from the one they'd done previously, and the one they'd be doing next. Hence the contrived costumes. It served a practical purpose. In much the same way, for much the same motives, The Beatles created a fancy-dress festival atmosphere to record the full orchestral section of 'A Day in the Life', with false noses and festive props.

George was not the only Beatle to find it both congenial, and useful,
to call in on Derek in LA. Even earlier in the Spring of 1967 – 3 to 12
April – Paul, with movie-star girlfriend Jane Asher, and Mal Evans, called
round to 'our house over on Grandview Drive off Laurel Canyon.'
They'd flown in from Denver by Lear Jet, and stayed over. Derek 'made
them listen to Glenn Miller when they settled in.' Then they talked
about taking LSD. 'Paul told me of a "trip" he had taken with John
Lennon in 1966', recalled Derek. About how 'we had this fantastic
thing. We had taken this stuff, incredible really, just looked into each
other's eyes... like, just staring and then saying "I know man" and then
laughing... and it was great, you know.' They'd eaten strange fruits
together, and remained wonderfully intact. Take a reality-check. Yes,
it's all still working as it should. He also related to Derek how they'd
'ambled quietly into San Francisco to check out the scene', and how
he'd traded licks with Jefferson Airplane's Jack Casady.

The following day, Derek took his guests over to visit John and
Michelle Phillips in their Bel Air mansion set in two acres of terraced
landscaped gardens. House-guest Scott McKenzie was in awe and lost
for words. Mal stayed while, inevitably, Derek performed his catalysing
alchemy by taking Paul around to visit his current client, Brian
Wilson, then sat back to observe. There was much wary, but genuine,
exchanging of compliments. Paul praised the wonderfully structured
harmonies, soaring melodic invention, and deeply melancholic beauty
of *Pet Sounds*. Brian praised just about everything The Beatles had ever
done. Both were a little in awe of each other, yet shared something
of an aesthetic. A musical delicacy and attention to detail. Eventually,
prompted by Derek, Paul sat at Brian's piano. He said 'he'd written this
song a few days earlier' and began picking out a rough sketch of 'She's
Leaving Home'. Brian, and his wife Marilyn, were both emotionally
affected by the raw performance. So much so that Brian backed off,
reluctant to contribute one of his own. He mumbled something about
working on a piece called 'Heroes and Villains' that might just top
'Good Vibrations', but 'I just can't get it right, though.' Typically, it was
Derek who playfully defused the situation, gently mocking Brian with
'listen to him, the tormented artist.' Only Derek Taylor would have
the nerve – never mind the ease of familiarity – to get away with such
affectionate teasing.

Finally, Paul and Derek returned west to the Phillips' mansion,
bringing Brian and Marilyn with them. The ensuing jam extended well
into the morning. According to John Phillips' account of the evening,
'Papa' John ran some cartoons on his movie-projector, while Paul

played Michelle's cello 'as if it were a giant bass guitar.' Then Paul
turned his attentions to the piano – playing the keys and plucking
the strings inside, 'simultaneously watching and scoring music for
the cartoons. It was an impressive display of composing genius.' The
meeting led Paul to attend, and according to some accounts, contribute
celery-chewing noises to Brian's recording session for the track 'Vega-
Tables' on 10 April. 'I never liked the song' admits Derek – or the lyrics
'I threw away my candy bar and I ate the wrapper, and when they told
me what I did I burst into laughter', 'it seemed daft.' Eventually, Paul
and Mal return to the Taylor's for breakfast, and to pack. By the twelfth,
they were flying back into Heathrow, with Paul already sketching out
song-ideas for their next project – *Magical Mystery Tour*. Derek wrote
up the hectic incidents compressed into so brief a time-frame in his
'Brian Wilson A Hard Day's Surfin' Safari: When Brian Met Macca'
in *World Countdown News* 1967 (to which he also contributed the
Monkees-related feature 'The Story of Tommy Boyce and Bobby Hart'
the same year).

There was surf music before the Beach Boys, before what Derek
termed 'the all-American fivesome who comprise the most powerful
pop-unit in the USA.' There was Dick Dale and the Deltones, the
Chantays, the Marquettes. But they were strictly restricted to the West
Coast beach-side surfer community. It was Brian Wilson's songs that
took a local phenomenon, and broke it nationwide, to become what
Bob Dylan called 'The Kennedy Family with surf-boards.' As Derek
wrote, among 'the many words on them over the years', that 'none of
the Beach Boys would pretend that when they went into a little studio
to record a song called "Surfin"' they intended to change the entire
course of contemporary music... "Surfin"' was recorded in two hours
in Hollywood, on a single track tape system, with Al Jardine playing
standard double-bass twice as big as himself, fourteen-year-old Carl
Wilson on acoustic guitar, Brian himself standing up using brushes on
drums, and Mike Love singing the vocals with a severe cold.'

In the dying weeks of 1961, the record sold around 40,000 copies
in Southern California alone, and the $300 royalties were ploughed
back into more ambitious studio-time. The result was 'Surfin' USA', a
no.3 US single in March 1963 – a tune stolen from Chuck Berry, but
with a lyric that invited every landlocked fellow-traveller to participate
'if everybody had an ocean.' Then there were songs about cars, school
and girls. And once the hits started the release schedule demanded by
their label was relentless. Brian found himself in a situation where he
was not only responsible for creating the hits but, by doing so, carrying

the financial responsibility of supporting the lifestyles of the group and their growing families. A not-inconsiderable burden for an already fragile individual.

The Beach Boys were always a fissile combination, with an inbuilt psychological instability. Father Murray Wilson was a bullying belittling frustrated songwriter whose sons had to achieve what he'd never been capable of doing. He was living out his aspirations through them. But no matter what they did, no matter what they achieved, it was never good enough for Murray. Brian suffered from partial deafness – with only six-per cent hearing in his right ear. There are apocryphal but unsubstantiated stories that it was due to Murray's abuse. Biographer Steven Gaines makes Dennis Wilson the hero of the story. He was the brother who fought back against Murray's psycho-games and manipulation. But it was Brian who endured treatment that took his fragile and artistic mind and caused extreme damage and psychological problems into adult life. He retreated into himself. Into his music. Into his cocoon. To become, as in the haunting photograph by Annie Leibowitz, the 'sleepwalker by the pool.'

Brian always had an other-worldly quality, a precarious level of self-obsession unique even for an adolescent. 'In My Room' first demonstrated his ability to break out beyond his own self-created genre, and show a hitherto unsuspected introspective sensitivity. He used the B-sides of pop hits to showcase the smoother harmonies of 'Don't Worry Baby' which, uniquely, impossibly, combines a love song with a drag-racing chicken-run challenge. Or 'She Knows Me Too Well', illustrating the double-standards that apply where he's allowed to look at other girls, but it'd be another story if she did the same with other guys. But while the flow of hit singles came unbroken, the albums, which Capitol demanded on a six-monthly basis, were treated with less attention to detail, strung out and bulked-up with covers and fun make-weights. Was he under pressure...? Sure he was. His new wealth meant he only became further insulated from reality.

'Surfer Girl' was the first single Brian recorded on his own, using session musicians. He wrote melodies like other people drink a glass of water, it was so natural for him. But Brian's first psychological breakdown was on a plane trip from LA International Airport to Houston on 23 December 1964, commencing a tour to promote their hit 'Dance, Dance, Dance'. He was hauled off the tour after just one concert and sent home. After some temporary stand-ins – including later hit-ster Glenn Campbell – Bruce Johnson was drafted in as his touring replacement. Already successful in an unopposed field of their own, this cosy arrangement and new status quo was destabilised in the winter of 1964 when Brian was distressed to learn that his own label, Capitol, was about to launch The Beatles onto the American market with one of the biggest publicity blitzes ever mounted. And suddenly 'I Want to Hold Your Hand' was leapfrogging over the Beach Boys latest hit, the breezy classic 'Fun Fun Fun', on its way to a no.1 domination. The sudden competition quickened Brian's ambition. Setting off new accelerations in exactly the same way that the advent of The Beatles was doing for the imaginings of the proto-Byrds.

The Beach Boys had been the undisputed top white American band, 'solidly ahead of every competitor in what is becoming a very hard-fought pop battle' – according to Derek. 'No-one has ever said 'Who's that?' when a new Beach Boys record is launched on the air.' And Brian was capable of springing lyrical surprises. 'When I Grow Up (To Be A Man)' was a strange concept, a look at adolescence from the point of view of adulthood. Written by a still-adolescent. The arrangement matched by inventive production, with harpsichord, tricksy drum-pattern and soaring harmonies. 'Will my kids be proud or think their old man's really a square?' wonders Brian while the group harmonise the advance of years – 18, 19. It became a top ten hit in Autumn 1964.

But now the Beach Boys had their first serious rivals in the battle for pop primacy. Steven Gaines (in his 1986 book *Heroes and Villains*, dacapo Press) quotes Brian saying 'my most compelling motive for writing new songs (is) the urge to overcome an inferiority feeling. I've never written one note or word of music simply because it will make money... I do my best work when I am trying to top other songwriters and music makers.' His first retaliation was evident in the increasing sophistication of 'I Get Around', Brian's revenge on The Beatles which not only gave the Beach Boys their first American no.1 – in time for 4 July 1964 – but made their first serious inroads into the British Top 20. For me, as a troubled dysfunctional teen in Hull, the powerfully seductive image projected by 'I Get Around', of the coolest hippest gang of movers in town, was irresistibly attractive. The irony I was not aware of at the time was that it was created by a neurotically troubled dysfunctional overweight kid, deaf in one ear, in LA, to whom living the 'I Get Around' life-style was just as much a fantasy as it was to me.

The 1965 album *Beach Boys Party* generously includes their versions of three Beatles songs – 'I Should Have Known Better', 'Tell Me Why' and 'You've Got to Hide Your Love Away'. Then, later that same year, Brian heard *Rubber Soul*. He was high at the time, smoking a joint. He was enraptured. It was the first Fab Four album to be written and recorded under the influence of marijuana. As muse-of-choice, the weed certainly worked wonders, as for many it's their greatest, most enduring collection of songs. Great upbeat pop tunes of the calibre of 'Baby You Can Drive My Car' and 'You Won't See Me' contrast with much more folk-influenced compositions such as the Dylanish 'Norwegian Wood'. In its story of an extra-marital encounter, the song is given its surreal twist as a deliberate concealment, yet in doing so it takes Lennon's lyrical facility into new magical-realist terrain. The poignant 'In My Life' saw Lennon reflecting on past friends and lovers with revelationary song-writing skill, while 'Nowhere Man' was a supreme song of dislocation. These are songs that went well beyond what had been previously understood to be the formulaic limitations of the pop song.

Brian Wilson listened. And he rose to what he saw as the challenge it represents. He'd already worked with lyricist Gary Usher, Roger Christian, and Mike Love. Now – having stopped touring with the band two years previously – he pacted with a new partner, Tony Asher. Around the same time, Brian was induced by friend Loren Schwartz to try some of 'Owsley's mind-expanding' LSD... 'on our first trip I tried so hard to rearrange your mind.' And he fell prey to what Derek calls the fixer, the dealer who 'has sweets for the sweet and sugar for his honey.'

Pet Sounds emerged from a series of stoned chaotic song-writing sessions. Yet its controlled beauty resides not just in its compositional genius and instrumental invention, but in the elaborate vocal harmonies that imbue these sad songs with an almost heartbreaking grandeur. Later, commenting on the work they'd created together, Tony described Brian as 'a genius musician, but an amateur human being.' It became the first album on which no Beach Boy plays an instrument. Brian created the tracks. Singing live to orchestral backing tracks and using Asher as lyrical sidekick, to create an album of the most imaginative pop gems of all time. Even the instrumental 'Let's Go Away for Awhile' has an arrangement rarely bettered by Wilson (even though it's been suggested it is merely an 'unfinished' track still awaiting the addition of its intended vocal track), and the choral section of 'You Still Believe in Me' is truly stunning. The Beach Boys, meanwhile, were touring, and came around later to dub the vocals on. Dennis hardly ever bothered to turn up for recording dates anyway, and session drummer Hal Blaine had been handling the majority of the drumming chores for some time. His off-stage wildness was getting wilder, as Brian retreated further inwards. Brian thought of himself as being on a health kick. Derek was less than convinced. He 'used to talk a lot of totter about health food (while he was) digging into a big, fat hamburger. And gymnasiums! I was fitter than he was… going on about vitamins. I thought maybe he was just being amusing, you see. Having a meal with him was like the Mad Hatter's tea party – "Have some tea. There isn't any."'

At first, Capitol was dubious about *Pet Sounds*. It came with a $70,000 production price-tag, and they didn't like it. It was only due to the success against expectation of the single lifted from it, 'Sloop John B', that they were persuaded to even issue it. And when they did so – 16 March 1966 – they hardly bothered promoting it. But Derek can be seen in the black-and-white promo film-clip for 'Sloop John B' – clean-shaven, with white shirt and tie, as the Beach Boys cavort with an inflatable dingy in the swimming pool. The 'wacky japes' unspool as Brian shakes hands with a procession of Beach Boys as they come in through the door, until – he finds himself shaking hands with… Brian! Derek counts them in with a serious authoritative raised finger. There's also a brief sequence of formation cross-moves, like the Monkees. The clip closes with Mike Love reading a copy of *Tiger Beat* as the harmonies swell into the coded 'this is the worst trip, I've ever been on…' (the clip is reprised on the *Top of the pops 2* edition screened on 30 September 2006).

At the time, in the States particularly, *Pet Sounds* was largely regarded as a commercial failure. It was severely dumped-on by US critics more taken by the band's previous obsessions with surfing, cars and girls, their negativity doing little to assuage Brian's creeping paranoia as hinted at in 'I Wasn't Made for These Times'. So poor was its initial reception that Capitol Records rushed out a 'Greatest Hits' compilation to compensate, which easily outsold *Pet Sounds*. Although now, as if to justify the increasingly reclusive Brian's intention, in recent years the album has replaced *Sgt. Pepper* and is regularly voted the critic's choice as 'Greatest Album of All Time'. But Derek had gifted the project with the 'genius' tag, and throughout the LA music-business community, the term had begun to be accepted, despite the album's commercial failure. And Brian became determined to prove the appellation accurate. The next single, and the next album, would vindicate the failure of *Pet Sounds*. Although the seeds had already been sown by this album in terms of sheer quality and unrepressed joy, it was a single he was especially enthusiastic about. Truly a work that lived up to the term 'genius', it was a single that Derek christened 'a pocket symphony'. It was 'Good Vibrations'.

Ironically, given its Beatles inspiration, Paul McCartney later admitted that without *Pet Sounds* there would have been no *Sgt. Pepper's*

Lonely Hearts Club Band. The Beatles formed their own mutual life-support system. Despite their disagreements and falling-outs, they were unfailingly supportive of each other's musical experiments. Goading and encouraging, competing and provoking each other to even more audacious extremes. As Derek observed, 'there was nothing they couldn't do or get in that last great year of unity, harmony and collective happiness.' The Beach Boys were different. Not only were they not supportive of Brian's ambitions, they were directly and vocally opposed to them. With Mike Love, in particular, being derisive and impatient. Mike Love wanted another good-time hit single, a song about surf and sunshine, not pocket symphonies. 'Stick to the old stuff', he insisted, 'don't fuck with the formula.' His opposition was a powerful disincentive to Brian's already fragile sense of his own worth. Brian merely waited until the other group members had left the studio, erased their vocals, and substituted them by re-singing all the parts himself.

Terry Melcher was a record producer for two of Derek's other clients – the Byrds and Paul Revere. And Brian first met the penniless writer and former Hollywood child actor Van Dyke Parks at Terry Melcher's Beverly Hills home – 10050 Cielo Drive. Brian invited Parks' participation in 'Dumb Angel' – his 'teenage symphony to god' and his answer to *Rubber Soul*. *Smile* was created in the face of Mike Love's implacable hostility. And he was particularly scathing about Van Dyke Parks' way with words.

Bob Dylan had liberated the strictly linear pop-lyric into 'wild mercury, metallic and bright gold... with whatever that conjures up.' But his costumed-symbolist flights of Methadrine stream-of-conscious poetry, even while subsuming deliciously satisfying abstract images, nonetheless builds into a staggeringly visual narrative coherence. The Beatles took the freedom he offered, and ran with it, into their own fractured absurdist surrealism, but even the obscurantist 'semolina pilchards climbing up the Eiffel Tower' carries Magritte-esque visual connections. Soon such 'whiter shades of pale' rhyming evocative nonsense and vague opacity would become the rock norm. But what exactly does 'sunny-down snuff it's alright' mean? It even hints at wilfully slapdash onomatopoeia, or elements of some other language entirely. Or 'columnated ruins domino'? To an extent, the lyrics are merely texts woven into the texture of beautifully interacting voices, with returning motifs to link the sound into continuity. The purity of acapella, gospel, white and black close-harmony groups of the forties and fifties, raised to new levels of sophistication empowered by tape multi-layering and sharply-edited production. Brian lacked a convenient 'George

Martin' figure to lubricate the musicality. Instead, he also saw himself in competition with Phil Spector, and took it upon himself to replicate each stage of the production process personally, with as meticulous attention to detail as Spector's finest work. To journalist Jules Siegel, this sprawling aquatic soundscape stitched with mythic and elemental elements, represented 'goodbye surfing, hello god!'

According to writer Jonathan Gould, 'the saga of this record's creation was reported in the music press thanks to the efforts of Derek Taylor… (who) saw to it that by the time "Good Vibrations" came on the radio in the fall of 1966, nearly everyone who followed the pop scene on either side of the Atlantic was aware that this one single had consumed a full six months of Brian Wilson's life' (in his book *Can't Buy Me Love*). 'Good Vibrations' had cost some $50,000 to create, took six months to complete using ninety-hours of tape from twenty different sessions at four studios – Gold Star, Columbia, Western and RCA – but it became the Beach Boys third American no.1 single, and – welcomed by a *Melody Maker* cover-story as a 'mind-blowing' record – their only UK chart-topper from 17 to 24 November 1966. It held the no.1 over contenders as strong as the Four Tops ('Reach Out I'll Be There'), Manfred Mann ('Semi-Detached Suburban Mr James'), Spencer Davis Group ('Gimme Some Lovin'') and Tom Jones ('Green Green Grass of Home').

And Brian was already working on the sequel. By taking something as essentially ephemeral and inconsequential as the culturally-derided pop single, and treating it, not as a marketing device to promote an album, but as a unique stand-alone artefact in its own right, with every second of its strictly-limited duration fine-tuned to maximum effect, Brian Wilson – with The Beatles and the Byrds – had taken the form to its most advanced expression. Within that precise definition, it would never get better. Which is why compilations of sixties hits consistently out-perform compilations drawn from any subsequent decade, and why the period retains its cachet as the 'golden era' of pop. Nevertheless, by autumn 1966 it had become obvious that the new Beach Boys album would not be ready for the lucrative Christmas market. Instead, as Brian worked in the studio, the group toured, arriving to a phenomenal reception in London. Derek's publicity, as well as the escalating expectations created by the records themselves, had achieved what Brian had first requested – 'respect'. John Lennon and George Harrison called to visit the group at the Hilton. Paul phoned to say 'hello'. They got to meet the rolling Stones.

It was Derek, writing for *Disc and Music Echo*, who first broke the story to Britain that *Smile* had been terminated. 'In truth, every beautifully designed, finely wrought, inspirationally welded piece of music made these last months by Brian... has been SCRAPPED. Not destroyed, but scrapped. For what Wilson seals in a can and destroys is scrapped.' Capitol had officially announced the abandonment of the project on 2 May. After it had become obvious that a precipitous sequence of events had killed it off, Brian's inability to replicate the sounds on tape that he'd originally envisaged in his head, complicated by the drug intake, problems with the lyrics, the filial in-fighting, and then the final blow – the release of 'Strawberry Fields Forever' c/w 'Penny Lane' – what Derek termed 'the greatest two-sided single ever released', which upped the ante to what Brian considered an impossibly high level. The perfect record had already been made. The Beatles had beaten him to it. To Brian, *Sgt. Pepper* was 'a frightener and a joy', it 'sent him running to his room practically for a thumbsucking episode.' The game was over. As Greil Marcus points out, from now on 'the Beach Boys' artistic reputation would be forever based on unheard, unreleased music...'

Jann Wenner called the bluff in an article written for the 14 December 1967 issue of what was then still considered a 'cult journal' – *rolling Stone*. In a thinly veiled attack on Derek's promotional wor,k he questioned the very basis of Brian's supposed 'genius'. Stacking up the evidence of The Beatles' phenomenal evolution from *Rubber Soul* to *Sgt. Pepper*, he found the Beach Boys' comparable progress distinctly lacking. 'No-one is John Lennon except John Lennon', he argued, 'and no-one is Paul McCartney except Paul McCartney, and the Beach Boys... are not The Beatles.' A fairly obvious statement. Such direct comparisons between vastly different artists does no-one favours. But when Wenner goes on to call Derek's 'genius' tag 'essentially a promotional shuck', it seemed as though the voice of the counter-culture had delivered its verdict. So was the whole thing just so much hype so expertly contrived by Derek that rock is still entranced by its diminishing echoes? Objectively the credibility gap between Brian's professed pretensions and what he actually achieved – with *Pet Sounds* and such tracks as 'Good Vibrations', 'Surf's Up' and 'Heroes And Villains' – is so slight as to be negligible. Within the contextual use of the term 'genius' when it's applied to Bob Dylan, Phil Spector, or John Lennon, then yes, Brian Wilson more than qualifies for the accolade that Derek Taylor bestowed upon him.

With the touring members of the group back in the States, various fragments of Brian's grand project were salvaged and cobbled together with new light-weight material assembled by the group who had inherited it, and the resulting curate's egg of an album, *Smiley Smile*, finally emerged on 18 September 1967 within its florid naïf sleeve, as a hugely diminished version of what it should have been. 'Heroes and Villains' became the opening track on side one, 'Good Vibrations' opening side two. The resemblance to the original grand concept ends there. There's 'Wind Chimes' and 'Vegetables' (re-titling Brian's 'Vega-Tables'), padded out with the stoned lunacy of 'She's Goin' Bald', the instrumental make-weight 'Fall Breaks and Back to Winter (W. Woodpecker Symphony)', and the throw-away 01:04 of 'Whistle In'.

Further original *Smile* excerpts would continue to emerge over the years that follow.'Cabinessence' was included on *20/20* (February 1969) – their twentieth album and last for Capitol, leaving their career at its lowest point. And the most beautiful of them eventually titles what would become their critical come-back album, *Surf's Up* (August 1971). Meanwhile, Carl assumed production duties for the next album – *Wild Honey* (December 1967). Brian and wife Marilyn moved into a new house in Bel Air's Bellagio Road – a mansion formerly owned by Edgar Rice Burroughs. Daughter Carnie was born there on 29 April 1968. Father Murray Wilson finally achieved his songwriting ambitions, by co-writing 'Break Away' with Brian – as 'Reggie Dunbar' – a minor Beach Boys hit in June 1969. Then, at the band's low point – in November 1969 – in a final act of betrayal, Murray sold off 100% of the rights of 'Sea of Tunes', every song Brian had ever written, to A&M for a single derisory one-off cash payment. Brian retreated to bed, and stayed there… for many years.

The Beach Boys story then devolves into a hideous farce of frittered-away potential, chemical lunacy turning them into a walking pharmacy cabinet, a comic-tragedy cycle of failed and abusive relationships, enlivened by periodic but largely illusory resurgences that turn out to be more wished-for than real. There's no question that a certain degree of liberation from the constraints of rational thinking permits new associations and ideas to flourish. But what a very hazardous place that borderland between creativity and madness can be. Rick Parfitt of Status Quo told me how 'we went to Brian's house in Beverly Hills. And it was one of the most embarrassing moments of my life. You're in HIS house. And his wife – who is very good for him, looks after him, makes sure nothing goes wrong – she invites us in, shows us through into the lounge where he's sort of sitting there playing the piano. And you got the very strong feeling of "what are you people doing in my house?" And we sort of went "Hi Brian". And after "Hello Brian" there's not really a lot to say. He carried on playing the piano and we kind-of…

Hung out. But it was impossible to have a conversation with Brian. Impossible. It was like "Hi Brian". "Hi". And that was it. But knowing what he's written, there's still an incredible aura about the man. Consequently, we've done quite a lot of gigs with the Beach Boys. It's been a good relationship.'

A version of *Smile* finally emerged in 2004 through the sensitive appreciation and active encouragement of younger musicians including Darian Sahanaja, with whom Brian toured and performed his masterwork to great acclaim. His voice may by then have become a little slurred, yet it carries the recognisable purity of intent. And *Smile* remains a curiously impressive work. With the benefit of four decades of hints and suggestions, theories and explanations, it emerged to sympathetic reviews pre-informed and well-versed in its intentions and idiosyncrasies. Had it emerged as originally intended in 1967, its reception may well have not been so positive.

The Beatles had raised expectations with their progression from *Revolver* to *Sgt. Pepper's Lonely Hearts Club Band*. Integrated thematic albums by the Who (*The Who Sell Out*, December 1967) and the Small Faces (*Ogden's Nut Gone Flake*, May 1968) had gained respect and commercial success. The spikes of weirdness in the rolling Stones (*Their Satanic Majesties Request*, December 1967) and the Kinks (*The Village Green Preservation Society*, November 1968) did not fare so well. And *Smile*, divided into three expansive suites linked by recurring leitmotifs, is a strange work even by such standards. Even now it can be confusing, difficult, downright weird. Not that Brian cared. On 'South American' (on his 1998 *Imagination* album), after taking a pop at paparazzi pressure, he sings 'I've been around too long to care what anyone said.'

Within this continuing sixties drama, Derek remained a constant 'supporting actor'. He was with the Beach Boys in Europe for their 'Good Vibrations' tour, during November 1966 when they were at their most fashionable. They toured the provinces heading a bill that included Lulu. I saw the package when it played the Leeds' Odeon. Lulu dropped an earring, bent over to retrieve it, gifting the front rows with a view of her knickers. A vision that has stayed with me across the years. The Beach Boys themselves were tight and exciting, performing a note-perfect stage replication of the labyrinthine 'Good Vibrations'. They were so good I stayed on, missed the last train home and spent the night walking the city centre, the harmonies echoing inside my head. I was in no state of mind to argue with Derek's assertion that 'no group or individual in the US had made so much progress in so short a time as Brian Wilson and his friends...'

With the Beach Boys, as he'd done with the Byrds, Derek 'drank and drugged my way through London to Hollywood.' Yet when he claims to have 'the attitude of a supporting actor', that is not entirely self-effacement. It's also a creative strategy. Like a session musician rather than the star soloist, it's in the supporting roles that you find some of the most interesting work. You're given a licence to have fun, in a way, because the full glare of the spotlights are focussed elsewhere. You have the influence, without the responsibility. And there's something about working within that smaller space to which Derek found himself more temperamentally suited. Perhaps in itself, the 'supporting actor' may seem to lead the less intriguing life. But such an assumption is pretty much to do with interiors. When it came to in-crowd status, Derek's attitude remains more populist than elitist. 'Leave it to the public – to you and me', he asserted, 'look at our own private record collections, watch which concerts we pay to see. That is the only test.'

For Derek – oddly, despite the contentious end of their business relationship – Brian Epstein maintained contact. In his authoritative biography of Epstein, Ray Coleman quotes excerpts from a revealing letter that Brian wrote to Derek during the early months of 1967. Written in his own hand in Stephens' ink on personalised 'From Brian Epstein' Basildon Bond notepaper, rather than dictated, he confided his enthusiasm for new projects – about his plans for a(n ultimately unhappy) merger with Robert Stigwood's stable of artists, and about his ventures into promoting concerts at the Saville Theatre, including one by his favourite Motown group, the Four Tops. And about the imminent release of The Beatles next single, 'Penny Lane' c/w 'Strawberry Fields Forever', with its January 1967 promo-film shot at Knole Park in Sevenoaks. It would prove to be one of the first and most successful music 'videos', incorporating stop motion animation and other innovatory effects. All acrimony seems to be forgotten as Brian speculates about the actual location of Strawberry Fields – between Menlove Avenue and Beaconsfield Road – and he jokily reminisces, 'I used to get the tram (number 46) from Penny Lane to Epstein's, Walton Street, when I overslept and was too late to accompany Daddy to work in his Triumph at 9:00am.' He signs the letter 'Manager and Frequent Looner'.

In his 'Hollywood Calling' column, Derek described the LA reception of the single, reporting that 'Penny Lane' was ahead as regards radio-plays, while 'Strawberry Fields Forever' was more highly rated by musicians. He even found space to remonstrate with Manfred Mann for 'presuming to comment on The Beatles without acknowledging their endless grace' (18 February 1967). Famously spliced together from two distinct separate masters, Bob Dylan claims 'Strawberry Fields Forever' is 'greater than the sum of its parts, and the parts are pretty good.'

Over-familiarity has dulled what we hear. Oh yeah – 'Strawberry Fields Forever' again. It's impossible to listen to it anew. But re-listen anyway, really listen, attempt the impossible and set aside nostalgic distractions and fixed ideas, make the effort, rack its moment-by-moment innovation against what followed, decade-by-decade. Sure, George Martin facilitated much, but he was working with the material John Lennon brought in. George's editing created the smooth mid-point elision, but only after John had listened to the two takes, and his critical itch suggested 'if we could take the first part of this and the end part of that?' His was the art-vision that conjured what we hear.

Very little across the ensuing decades of rock could ever equal this level of intense creativity. Much would be a retreat from it, picking over and extracting strands, re-examining the expanded vocabulary it suggests. And amazingly, it was a pop record. A chart hit. Other musicians took the spark elsewhere, to illuminate discrete niches. Few succeeded in taking it into mass acceptance. Yet even the impossible currents George Martin contrived attracted cover versions, first by Tomorrow, a cult underground group that included future-Yes guitarist Steve Howe and Keith West (of 'Excerpt from A Teenage Opera' fame), they effectively replicate the complex string arrangements with just the group's guitars and rhythms. Theirs was a more impressive achievement than the pointlessly straight recreation attempted by Candy Flip in 1990 – although it charted as high as no.3, which they probably viewed as sufficient justification in itself.

> The following tone is a reference tone,
> Recorded at our operating level...

The insider code, to Derek, was 'is he freak or straight?' He also represented Captain Beefheart. At the time – 1966 – they'd only just begun. Derek first heard about Don Van Vliet through the catalyst of PR gurus Leonard Grant and Associates, whose office was next door in the 9000 Building. When Derek first moved in, Grant loaned him an obsolete mimeograph machine, 'too old and ugly for his (office) but not, he assumed, for mine.' In a strangely mismatched artist portfolio, Grant managed Frank Gorshin – the 'Riddler' from TV's *Batman* – but had an inkling that pop would make a more lucrative return. To this end, he'd 'strayed out of his market' and acquired the Magic Band, but had no idea what to do with them. He shoved Derek in their direction, told him he wanted them 'cleaning up and selling to the fans', which was pretty much the opposite of what Beefheart himself intended.

'It was the middle-period of the new rock 'n' roll and the smooth old world was becoming involved with the newer elements. Foolishly. The men in suits needed to find out what was happening.' But at the time, money was tight, it was 'a very hard year.' So Derek checked the act out at a club on Santa Monica Boulevard, and 'I liked him very much, he was a very funny man, wry and dry and he sang a very hard mean blues, cupping his hand over his right ear.' Between complaints about the 'shit' sound system, they talked. Derek would take them on. Grant had no budget. Beefheart had no money. He'd have to make his price modest. They agreed to $250 a month – 'and most months I got it.' The single 'Diddy Wah Diddy' had been a minor turntable hit, interpreted as a kind of acid-Blues. Derek was attuned to it. But how to market the new property? 'How to get Captain Beefheart's ugly mug in *16 Magazine*, preferably on the cover along with Mark Lindsay and Jim McGuinn.' Even the hair was way too long for what was acceptable, 'nobody with hair down to his shoulders and jeans made the charts, not even the Byrds.'

There were half-hearted attempts at a fashion make-over to go along with Grant's instruction, with big-collared shirts, ties, jackets and boots from *De Voss* and other trendy Hollywood Boulevard boutiques. Even a hairdresser to trim back the excessive fringe. *16 Magazine* still weren't interested. Overnight sensation was obviously not going to be an option. Derek tapped into his industry connections and pulled some strings. There was a press-night at the *Whisky a Go Go* with Beefheart and the Magic Band supported by the then-unknown Doors, 'Leonard Grant and I had rowed for much of the afternoon over which disc jockeys would sit where (such trivia, it makes me wonder sometimes), and it was quite a disappointing evening, press-wise, in that not too many pressmen came.' Nevertheless, Derek had an ongoing arrangement with *Flip* magazine – published 'with some skill and energy' by Stephen Kahn in New York – whereby Derek could 'wreck my health writing about my clients and he would print what I wrote', in effect, promoting his own clients by writing features about them for the magazine. But Kahn was only seriously interested in acts who 'were making it anyway'. As a generous concession to Derek's new acquisition, he grudgingly agreed to publish a collage that a member of the Magic Band had made.

Then, by night, fuelled on 'too many Dexedrines to count, between the whiskies', Derek took the Jack Kerouac route and drafted a ten-page publicity document called 'The Great Gnome Biography'. Not exactly screwing a paper-reel into the typewriter platen, but feeding sheets and typing like a bebop improviser plays, with a direct intuitive connection between subconscious and fingers, conjuring prose almost without the interference of thought, free-associating first takes without correction or revision. Well – maybe a little, pencilled in afterwards, but not too much, and oft-times not at all. The result was 'one of the most impressive and witty and far-out "biographies" I had ever done', which helped introduce the strange collection of misfits to the already freakish scene. 'Strange, hit-record-like noises have been emerging from a group with the highly unlikely name of Captain Beefheart and his Magic Band', he wrote. 'Alex St Clair was generally, and tacitly acknowledged as leader', he explains, 'though it was clear that Don Van Vliet, as lead singer, and therefore front-man, would be Captain Beefheart. And who would have it otherwise?'

The meandering and dislocated script unravels like a future lyric from *Trout Mask Replica* (June 1969), playfully absurdist, effectively surreal, sometimes engagingly silly. An interview sequence, which might be based on a genuine dialogue with the group, or might just as easily have sprung fully-formed from Derek's head, includes the question, 'What is the trend in popular music as Beefheart sees it?' The Answer: 'The Supremes may want to change their name to Ethel Higgenbaum and the Warts if Motown goes out of style.' The 'Higgenbaum' sounds too suspiciously English to be entirely Beefheartian. The invented group-name is located somewhere closer to the tradition of John Lennon's 'Charles Hawtrey and the Deaf-Aids'. Nevertheless, Derek concludes accurately 'Captain Beefheart is a rather ominous-looking huge fellow by the name of Don Van Vliet.' Leonard Grant was not impressed, he 'took hold of a corner of it and waved it as if to shake the germs away and said 'This is not at all what I wanted. You're making fun of my group.' If the insider code was 'is he freak or straight?' it was obvious that Grant fell most definitely into the latter. But it helped establish Beefheart on the agenda.

Soon there would be *Safe as Milk* (June 1967), with Beefheart emerging as an elision of Howlin' Wolf with surrealist Paul Eluard. With Beefheart acting as one of those Native American operatives with uncanny abilities hired by the army to interpret codes, memes and sonic hieroglyphics that only dogs and ghosts can hear. But Derek's relationship with Leonard Grant never recovered. Both Beefheart and Derek severed associations around the same time. The last time they communicated was to dispute damage done to the loaned mimeograph machine. 'A piece of hard plastic cowling had been damaged' when, 'after too many brandies for breakfast, instead of hitting Leonard Grant, I had punched the shit out of the plastic, bashed it, crashed my fist up and down until the skin broke and blood was drawn. "I think it must have fallen", I told Leonard Grant. Fallen? He didn't believe me and sued for damages...'

Chapter Eleven: 1967: 'I Think That Maybe I'm Dreaming...'

(the Byrds) intertwining their excellent voices into groovy harmonies...
(*New Musical Express* review 23 November 1968)

Paperback Writer...

It happed in Monterey, a long time ago.

1967 was – and always will be – the 'Summer of Love'. The 'First Summer of Love' if you like – as if there's been another. George Harrison told Derek that 1967 was a year that took about fifty years to complete. Again, it's a story that's been chewed over so many times, from a multiplicity of perspectives, that it's virtually imbibed with your mother's milk. To Derek, it was 'simply fabulous, bathed in ever-loving sunshine, cooled by light breezes, full of colour and delight... a year to treasure beyond measure', producing a counter-culture 'running counter to any culture I'd known.' In which 'the assumptions saturating Cold War America were challenged with a vigour and headlong insurgency that no-one had predicted', as writer Mike Marqusee observed (*Chimes of Freedom: The Politics of Bob Dylan's Art*, 2003, The New Press). Elsewhere Derek wrote that 'the great sea-change in pop was, after 1967, it became ever so slightly serious... in 1967 pop music lost its innocence and has never recovered.'

The Beatles' *Sgt. Pepper's Lonely Hearts Club Band* marks yet another of the decade's watersheds, and – inevitably – another turning point in twentieth-century music history. A sound-space where 'expanded consciousness meets ancient Abbey Road technology', or a route – to George – to 'new meanings in old equipment.' An album not only colonising virgin musical territory but erecting sparkling cities in a musical wilderness. We know that. *Sgt. Pepper* made a watertight case for pop being regarded as an art-form in itself, and as such it made analysing pop/rock into a valid intellectual pursuit. Music critic William Mann compared Lennon and McCartney to Schubert, and the gap between high culture and pop was closed forever. In that way it defined the age, and the ages since, for good or ill. Peter Blake may have assembled the cover collage, but Lennon insisted on Dylan Thomas being a part of it. He also came up with Albert Stubbins, the red-haired centre-forward who played for Liverpool after the war. 'The idea originally was for all of us to name our heroes', explained Paul, 'of course, being The Beatles this was only taken half-seriously...'.

John protested that – no, it isn't a 'concept' album, the songs have no thematic link beyond the title reprise and the 'Billy Shears' hand-over. It was left to Derek to identify a continuity – that although there isn't a love song on the album, there's love in every groove.

The assumed 'Lonely Hearts Club Band' personas were liberating, allowing The Beatles to step out of and set their old selves aside, as illustrated by the waxwork dummies on the cover. While ironically, the album's pseudo-live fabrication forms a nice juxtaposition to the fact that no-one – apart from those who happen to wander by outside the Apple building one 1969 afternoon – would ever get to see The Beatles perform live ever again. Their final UK appearance had been a fifteen-minute set at the *New Musical Express* Poll-Winners' Concert on Sunday, 1 May 1966. Openings, and closings. Although no longer touring, The Beatles presence was everywhere, buzzing away like background radiation. As essential as oxygen. Despite John's denial of responsibility, there was an immediate rash of other bands using gatefold sleeves with printed lyrics and unifying concepts. The rolling Stones, who had ridden the early waves of change with the charming 'Dandelion' and 'Ruby Tuesday', were wrong-footed by *Sgt. Pepper*, reacting with *Their Satanic Majesties Request*. The Beatles have done freaky. We can do freakier. And although it's an astounding album, it failed to carry the audience with it, it didn't cross over into mass consciousness as '*Pepper* did'.

And over the decades since its release, *Sgt. Pepper's Lonely Hearts Club Band* has become a critical bloodbath. The greatest album of all time. Or the not-so-good sequel to *Revolver*. A convenient establishment target for revisionist attack. Or an unassailable monolith of a golden era, to Ray Coleman – editor of *Disc and Music Echo* – the 'very zenith of rock 'n' roll.' What is beyond argument is that it altered the rules. As *The Times*' music critic William Mann later confided to Derek, pre-*Pepper*, 'it was in those days fairly unconventional for a serious music critic to write about popular music,' adding that post-*Pepper*, 'they do it all the time now.' All of which is ultimately irrelevant. Just listen. In the final hour of pirate station Radio London, as it was forced off-air at midnight, Monday 14 August 1967, it was Ringo who provided a 'Cheerio', taped a fortnight earlier at the station's Curzon Street office. And – banned by the BBC – 'A Day in the Life' was the final record it played...

Of course, where The Beatles were concerned, there would always be stories to spin. But for Derek, the imposition of the 'studio years' only served to emphasise the correctness of his decision to quit NEMS.

He wrote that 'Joan and I grew up in California, found out a few things and took some of the dreaded LSD, and, finding we hadn't jumped out of any windows, we took some more. It felt fine.' Derek could be somewhat playful, somewhat serious, always very compelling. Performance was never in his blood. There was a private aspect to him. When not working you were unlikely to realise he was there, but as soon as he hit his stride, he became the focus of attention, at least partly because of his extraordinary charm.

Derek was a considered creation who quoted Arnold Bennett with approval – at the end of his short novel *The Card* (1911), one of the characters asks of the hero, 'what great cause is he identified with?' The reply was, 'he's identified with the Great Cause of cheering us all up.' To do that through critical journalism entails a degree of anonymity. The subject of the writing will always be the focus of the prose, not the by-line. Writers build reputations for others, and by doing that, their own names and opinions become recognised in a minor way. But the writer always works through their connection with other more visible, more pro-active lives. As with Brian Sommerville, to step out of that protective shadow is to invite vicious censure.

And, although it's true that journalism, advertising, and public relations may all be part of the same big happy family within the communications industry, PR is an even more extreme form of journalism. In pop, image is everything. Pop pivots on lies. And some forms of PR are indistinguishable from lies. Contriving reputations without being seen to be doing it. Promoting and hyping while at the same time endeavouring to show the artist's rise as a natural and unstoppable force of nature. The catchphrases and marketing literature they circulate is quoted without credit, huge chunks of their PR hand-outs for albums, tours, movies, or artists themselves will be seamlessly integrated into mainstream magazine features and passed off as the work of others.

For Derek, the first reason to write was to write something true and interesting. Second, it was to speak to the readers about artists about whom he felt enthusiastic. Unlike his spell of critical journalism, PR would never need 'a little acid' to punch up its prose. A little LSD maybe, but never acidic prose. It did not require the attack-dog mode Derek had never felt happy adopting. It's true that the words must snag the wandering attention. It's true that such comment, like most journalism, is transient. Also that the task might be more difficult now because of the vast array of media and other competitors for time and interest, but that does not mean that commentary then was not among the liveliest and most combative around.

For rock journalism was evolving to match the maturation of the music itself. Writers were becoming celebrity names in their own right. Hunter S Thompson evolved a participatory journalism that put the writer squarely into the story. His 'gonzo' writing adds touches of surrealism while happily stirring fiction, and the techniques of fiction into the brew – some of it extremely mischievous, writing 'to the edge of libel', as Derek's old *Daily Express* editor would have expressed it, as when he wrote about politician Ed Muskie's drug addiction. Ken Kesey, Charles Shaar Murray, Julie Burchill, Nick Kent, and Mick Farren – all to a greater or lesser extent – made themselves the centre of their text. Derek Taylor was never like that. He didn't operate that way. But he hung out with other writers. Watched the way they worked.

Richard Goldstein, of the *Village Voice* and *New York Times*, was a small, earnest man who hated *Sgt. Pepper*. He and Derek talked, Goldstein soliciting his ideas about polling an insider list of industry movers and shakers. Derek was less than impressed with the idea. And Tom Nolan – young, terribly bright and cool, he wrote for *Los Angeles Times*. He had awful acne, wasn't handsome, but his prose was good. Derek took Tom to interview Brian Wilson, as a result of which it was Tom who broke the news that the Beach Boy had experimented with acid. Red-haired Pete Johnson was another well-known critic who wrote for the *LA Times*. Derek met him at the *Whisky a Go Go* Captain Beefheart press-night, Derek bought him a whisky, then he bought Joan and himself a cognac, and they got into conversation. 'Then a wicked man laid a joint on him, then another, and before you could say "Pete Johnson", Pete Johnson had hair down to his elbows and no desire to be a critic of anything, let alone something as nice as music.' He later joined WEA.

Derek was largely content to assume the hack's more traditional backroom role, as a vacuum cleaner sucking up other people's lives. Only very infrequently stepping out blinking into the furious glare. Although any association with artists as luminous as The Beatles, the Byrds or the Beach Boys was bound to involve some kind of reflected visibility – Derek was cool, but with a markedly more grown-up charisma than his charges. So when he did step out, as he did as co-founder of the non-profit Monterey International pop Music Festival of 1967, it proved to be an exceptional event. As far as British readers were concerned, they first hear about the festival through Derek's announcement in his 'Our Man In America' column. And as with the Sunset Strip riots, it was something Derek wrote about from a number of perspectives. Through Michelle Phillips' ghosted autobiography he writes of Monterey as 'the great dream festival that changed the face of rock 'n' roll.'

The idea for what Derek called 'the first great festival in the brief and furious history of pop Music,' had germinated as early as April. With the triumvirate of Derek, with LA hustler, deal-maker, impresario and promoter Ben Shapiro and Alan Pariser – veteran of the CAFF campaign – credited as its originators. 'It was Alan Pariser who thought of having a pop Festival, and came to me and also to Ben Shapiro', Derek recalls, 'and so was launched the Monterey International pop Festival which was going to make a lot of money.' Together, the three of them set up a Sunset Boulevard office to coordinate bands and allocate advertising space in a concert programme booklet, with Derek as press agent.

The office was situated opposite Gene Autrey's Continental Hotel, an establishment that enforced a strict 'no longhairs' policy. Soon, the Festival's original organisational nucleus was expanded to include John Phillips of the Mamas and the Papas, and Dunhill record producer Lou Adler, 'until John Phillips of the Mamas & Papas and Lou Adler came to lead the festival and took it off Pariser and Shapiro and made it non-profitmaking and made Pariser nonproducer and whipping boy.' To Derek, 'we just had to learn that the only thing that mattered was the music, the music.' They brought in Terry Melcher, and retro-rock singer Johnny Rivers, and 'Ben (Shapiro) was emptied out of the Monterey Festival by Adler and Phillips – probably wisely, for neither unit sat comfortably with the other and after making a statement in the trade papers that he left "amicably to press on with many movie commitments" – a statement so full of lies that it made me, who drafted it, reach for another capsuleful of courage (my second by lunchtime) – was given 5,000 dollars, and, as far as I know, bears no grudges and lives in Mexico.' It was a 'sad affair... cruel in its way' and a poor omen for an event designed to promote peace, love and understanding. But – again through Derek's words – 'in Arcadian dreams of other times there was a belief that everything would turn out all right. It was often unspoken, more danced than dramatised. It was simply understood.'

There have been Be-Ins and Love-Ins, Electric Kool-Aid parties and free community concerts. There had been the autumn Monterey Jazz Festival that ran between 1960 and 1965 at the same Fairgrounds. They had attracted audiences of 20,000 – a lot for those days. Jerry Garcia and Robert Hunter were attendees. Later, a spring Monterey Folk Festival was added to the social programme, with Appalachian white blue-grass players. But this was the first such event of its kind. And the root of every rock Festival to come, from Woodstock to Glastonbury. Yet different, in the sense that 'the seekers of Monterey' were assembling not just for the freak-out, but to tune in to progressive evolutionary energies. Monterey is a spectacle, something never before seen anywhere. An amazing constellation of names, all of whom donate their time for free. As did the Frisco Diggers who stepped in to provide free food-stations, medical aid and come-down support for the anticipated drug casualties. Monterey was intended to be a charity event, that's the initial plan. Although, finally the $200,000 profit came largely from the sale of TV rights to ABC, and the subsequent distribution of that money remains… somewhat dubious. Nevertheless, what is undeniably achieved is twenty-five hours of amazing music sprawled across two-and-a-half days. A coming together of unknown, well-known, and soon-to-become legendary bands. The Byrds headlined, with Laura Nyro, and Buffalo Springfield – although with Stills and Young often at each other's throats, Neil failed to appear for this most crucial of engagements. A contentious friction they'd continue into their more high-profile next joint project.

There were chart names present like the Association, Simon & Garfunkel, and Scott McKenzie who topped the charts with his anthemic 'San Francisco (Be Sure to Wear Some Flowers in Your Hair)', composed by and recorded with his fellow ex-Journeyman folkie John Phillips. A hook-up with San Francisco promoter Bill Graham brought Bay Area musicians such as the Grateful Dead, Steve Miller Band, Quicksilver Messenger Service, Country Joe and the Fish, and a nervous Janis Joplin (with Big Brother and the Holding Company) on-board, despite Ralph Gleason's wariness of LA exploiting their 'movement' as a 'Flowerpower Festival'. As Derek phrased it, 'all these and many more were drawn towards each other's tribe in strange ways, as if on threads.'

Jefferson Airplane too – Derek knew them, Crosby had already brought them around to the eighth floor 9000 Building rehearsal room specifically to meet him. Patti Smith later confided that 'after hearing Grace Slick as a teenager, anything seemed possible', about the headlining Airplane's singer/writer. And it did. The SF contingent had been initially dubious. In their immaculate hipness they considered LA scenesters to be phoney breadheads and plastic opportunists. Until the festival's charitable free 'for the people' basis convinced them. Gene Clark confided to Derek, 'I like long hair, but those cats in San Francisco! It's going too far!' They found themselves playing alongside the first major US appearances of the Who and Jimi Hendrix (who slyly drops the 'I Feel Fine' riff into his live 'Hey Joe'), plus Eric Burdon and the Animals, Booker T and the MG's with Otis Redding, with the 'international' element fleshed out by South African trumpeter Hugh Masekela and sitar guru Ravi Shankar.

Only The Beatles were missing, despite rumours that spread like infections. The Monterey 'Board of Governors' did little to dispel the idea, with hints of a 'Group With No Name' on the bill. Derek concedes only that 'The Beatles were there – of course, in spirit'.

Even within the fractal swirl of Monterey, Derek did not always appear to be an exact fit. His cravat. A moustache that looks a little less than hip, and more than a little caddish. Pete Townshend even recalls that 'Derek Taylor was frightened to come out of his little box where he handed out passes'! And, during what was officially billed as 'The First Annual Monterey International pop Music Festival', Joan in her secretary-style spectacles, 'was pregnant with our fifth child (Dominic), but she flew in for the first night with the four we had. I went down to Monterey Airport to meet her. She was on the same flight with the Animals and lots and lots of fine freaks. What a trip it all was.' The children, including six-year-old Gerard, were caught up in all the weirdology, as Derek worked 'in a redoubled frenzy of preparation, discarding sleep like Tom Jones his tie, or Jim Morrison his trousers,' but 'pressing on as if everything were OK, which is the only way to approach anything.' Gerard was in San Francisco where he enjoyed being baby-sat by Janis Joplin, 'who was very good with children.' Throughout the period, he was becoming inured to strangeness, as he 'saw some very interesting things as many of the "grown-ups" were out of their heads much of the time.'

The sun-gods smiled on this syncopated federation, this extraordinary congregation. A gathering of the tribes, 'flying on the ground'. To Hank Harrison, the event was part of an attempt 'to regain the forests and great herds of chanting mantras, the songs of the Hindu Buddhists, and by focusing on the magic centre of energy that was forming there in the backyard of Haight-Ashbury... the meeting was a baptism... a calm and peaceful approbation, a reaffirmation of the lifestyle, a settling of the waters. There in a splendorous array, one could see fans, feathers, plumes and tufts; bells, chimes, incense, pennants, banners, flags and talismans; beaded charms, lettuce-and-tomato sandwiches, balloons, paradise flowers and animal robes, bamboo, fruits and baskets; folded hands, closed eyes, bright brows and smiles, stoned people; prayer cloth and shaman sticks, floating, dancing marijuana flags with peace symbols, and the smell of the divine herb wafting through the void vortex that we created' (*The Dead Book*, Links, 1973). 'Thousands eating of the free food provided by the increasing awareness of the times and cooked by the Diggers. Barefoot girls in tie-dye madras, saris, and corduroy, teen-age braves stripped to the waist... and further, folk-singers charting mountain ranges in their imaginations, shamans and motorcycle cultists, lovers, voyeurs, hippies, magic theatre.' To look with morning eyes. It must have been bliss, as William Wordsworth said of an earlier revolution, to be alive in that dawn.

Monterey. Friday 16, Saturday, and Sunday, 18 June 1967. And A Splendid Time Is Guaranteed For All. 'Music, Love And Flowers', according to Derek's slogan. 'There you go', Grace Slick confides to me, 'a bright beautiful event, that was the MONTEREY POP Festival.' Not as gross-out as Woodstock. Not as violent as Altamont. The event was literally unprecedented. Until that moment, nobody was really sure that the 'love crowd' was even out there. In the weeks of build-up, they anticipated audience-figures of around 15,000. Eventually, the event attracts – well, estimates vary between 50,000 and 200,000 to the County Fairgrounds of Monterey, located in the beautiful setting of a small town on the California Carmel coast south of Frisco, where the emerging sub-culture first discovered the power of its collective 'vibe'. I wasn't there. But Grace recalls 'a three-day list of performers made up of nothing but headliners!' Through her breathless account, through her eyes, walk this 72-hour event. See the audience area located on that large, grassy lawn surrounded by cypress and pine trees. Unlike most summer concerts where the sun beats down mercilessly, here the big tree-branches are breaking the light into soft beams, transforming it into a Disney version of Sherwood Forest. 'A new kind of dawn', as Brian Patten had once phrased it, in another context. Readjusting your consciousness.

The first inaugurating pow-wow of the 'love generation' in a perfectly appropriate pastoral setting, choked with warm music and warm-hearted people. Hippies were roosting in the trees. It was dusk, of course. Behind the trees, around the perimeter of the seating space, you stroll around thirty small booths, individually decorated with coloured silks, cottons and hand-painted banners, showing off every kind of original creation – from one-of-a-kind boots and belts to framed paintings by amateur artists. Even the stalls bartering food and concert items are quaint and uninfected by corporate logos and pitchmen. There were flowers. Kaftans. Long hair. People were 'chock-a-block with acid' in a higher-than-thou sun-shiny stoned-peaceful hippy-happy-groovy oh-wow man mystic-vibe as nude girls idiot-dance gyre and gimble while casting spooky hand-shapes to the music, 'colours surround them, bejewelling their hair, visions astound them...' Here, everyone combines to create a peaceful and extraordinary event, which Eric Burdon hymns on vinyl and the Byrds might have called a 'Renaissance Fair', if they hadn't already done so for another event – even the police cruisers have orchids on their antennas... 'This is our generation, man' announces Mike Bloomfield from the stage, 'all you people, man, all together man. It's groovy. Dig yourselves, 'cos it's really groovy.' And it was.

For the emerging counter-culture, it becomes a test-case for open dope-smoking without fear of provoking arrest. David Crosby – using what Johnny Rogan called his 'insurrectionary tactics' – openly recommends LSD from the Monterey stage. He was guesting with Buffalo Springfield, standing in for the absent Neil Young, co-writing and adding harmonies to 'rock 'n' roll Woman', their tribute to Grace Slick. Crosby also went on-stage to announce Mike Bloomfield's Electric Flag. To McGuinn's chagrin and annoyance, Crosby's generous networking was seen as an 'act of betrayal', and provided yet another catalyst for his eventual expulsion from the high-flying Byrds.

The Byrds own set at Monterey was the last engagement arranged for them by Jim Dickson. Crosby had been scheming the group's severance from him and Tickner, their 'Brian Epstein', as well as Terry Melcher, their 'George Martin'. At first, the group weren't even shortlisted for the event, but John Phillips insisted 'it wouldn't feel right without them', and Dickson finally confirmed the booking. They'd earlier endured a chaotic engagement at the *Whisky* (16 to 24 May) supported by the up-and-coming Doors. Even Derek, in his *Disc* column, had been forced to concede their set there was 'terrible'. Yet against the odds they fought back, prepared solidly in rehearsal rooms adjacent to Derek's suite in the 9000 Building, warmed-up by playing Radio KFRC's Fantasy Faire and Magic Mountain Music Festival at Marin County's Mount Tamalpais amphitheatre (Sunday, 11 June) – joined on-stage by Hugh Masekela, with Captain Beefheart, PF Sloan, the Seeds and the Mojo Men – and managed to turn the situation around by pulling off an impressive set at the festival. 'Hey – the times are a-changin'', jived Crosby mischievously as they ignore yells for the old hits, preferring 'Hey Joe' and new material – Chris Hillman's 'Have You Seen Her Face', Crosby's 'Lady Friend', but retaining 'Chimes of Freedom' and 'He Was a Friend of Mine'. Finally, Masekela rejoined them on trumpet for 'So You Want to Be a rock 'n' roll Star'.

Monterey was a prototype advancement in the acceptance of an alternative lifestyle, helping to create that Yellow Brick Road that unravels all the way to Woodstock, a realignment of tectonic plates in the subcultural topography. Do you think it's possible to change the world? Isn't this the blueprint of a new evolved future world community? Can't this cosmic vibe flow ever-outwards to engulf and transfigure the world...? Actually, no. But for this long three-day moment it seems perfectly reasonable to suspend your disbelief and be buoyed by this beautifully fragrant illusion. 'Cos hey – that's where they're at!

Once again, it seems, the world is tilting on its axis. Two weeks earlier, *Sgt. Pepper's* release had startled and astounded the planet, while The Beatles – still interested in participation despite their withdrawal from the stage – had 'All You Need is Love' satellite-linked across hemispheres live from Abbey Road as part of an *Our World* tele-spectacle (25 June). Networked through the area educational channel, 'Joan and I were watching with the family in Los Angeles around midday. Brian Epstein had telephoned from the studios to make sure we were tuned in' to what Derek called 'a cornerstone of the era, a turning point in communication.' On the festival's first day, Paul McCartney – who was considered 'talent consultant' for Monterey – was on the cover of *Life* magazine, enthusing about the magically transfigurative properties of LSD, for which Crosby voiced his enthusiastic support and solidarity from the Monterey stage. In London, although Mick Jagger and Keith Richard were legally entangled in their drug-bust prosecution, Brian Jones showed up at Monterey to represent the Stones 'in spirit'.

And once again, Derek Taylor was at the epicentre of the global shift... although he got to see very little of the action on stage. Too busy dealing with Diggers and cops. 'I presented a glass-prism necklace to the chief of police at the final press conference... and he took it without embarrassment. Imagine such times... I wonder if you can?' A mighty long way down rock 'n' roll, but in a direct line of evolution from an altogether more modest affair, yet with equally world-shaping consequences, when a sixteen-year-old John Lennon met Paul McCartney at Woolton Village Fete, a slight ten years earlier, 6 July 1957. With Lou Adler, those instrumental in organising things include Michelle Phillips typing and answering phones in the Festival office, as John laces Otis Redding into his corset in preparation for his ground-breaking set fronting Booker T and the MG's plus the Mar-Keys three-part horn-section. And this weekend is one that wafts the first hallucinogenic hints of the Haight-Ashbury sound of the Airplane and Janis Joplin to the world, reciprocating by introducing the Who, Ravi Shankar and the Hendrix Experience to American audiences ('nobody had ever heard anything like Jimi', John Phillips tells Grace).

'Superficially, at least, the atmosphere was not especially competitive', with the exception of the Who and Hendrix – a playful battle of the bands in which the Who's theatrical auto-destruction is powered by basslines powerful enough to pull a train, climaxing in Keith Moon's miscalculated detonations, goading Hendrix's pyrotechnical sense of showmanship into retaliating by igniting his guitar with lighter fluid during 'Wild Thing'. Looking and playing like a brother from another planet, he delivered the most dramatic set of the event. Marrying blues and psychedelia, dexterity and feedback trickery, while redefining the guitar's sonic possibilities, while beyond the fretboard pyrotechnics burnt a fierce artistic vision which made Jimi rock's most convincing cosmonaut.

They can all be seen in the *Monterey pop* (December 1968) docu-movie. DA Pennebaker had previously created the pioneering *Don't Look Back* (May 1967) spin-off film-documentary by following Bob Dylan's 1966 UK electric tour. Now he and his crew use those 16mm hand-held cameras to record a tactile time-capsule of this uniquely significant West Coast event (the original 79-minutes later expanded into a 270-minute three-disc *The Complete Monterey pop Festival* set in December 2002). Watch. Pennebaker restricts himself to just one, maybe two songs per act. He also cuts up and splices the festival's chronology, alternating night and sun-stunned day, light and dark, fury and calm. Sliding into a light-purple sunset. Liquid night. Strangeness and beauty colliding.

'It is to this number that we attribute our enormous wealth', quips Cass before the perfect triple-threat opening voices-attack of 'California Dreamin'' and 'Gotta Feelin'', floating, winging and soaring on rising cadences. Although, as John Phillips perceptively notes, the band wasn't the headline act for the audience, their drugs were. The music merely supplied the soundtrack for the mind-movies playing in their heads. Michelle in red-and-yellow Indian pants and coat. Denny in Indian coat. John – a genial wizard, in long velvet cloak over gold-spangled suit. But for John Phillips, this will be the last party before their ship falls off the edge of the universe. There are brief interviews with fans, and some behind-the-scenes footage of John Phillips organising the event. Monkee Micky Dolenz is there is full native-American war-bonnet.

There's Derek Taylor onscreen too. But mostly the focus stays correctly on the music. Twenty-four-year-old Stephen Despar had built the Beach Boys travelling sound system, one of which they donate and send to Monterey. The victim of a sudden panic-attack of existential

loss of confidence, the Beach Boys themselves – originally scheduled
to close Saturday night – got cold feet, lost their collective nerve and
pulled out of the event at the last possible moment, fearing they'd
appear anachronistic in such hip company. Jan Wenner attacked their
absence in print, and Hendrix announced the 'death of Surf Music'
from the stage at the mid-point of his pyrotechnical set. Despar stayed
on and served as one of the main sound technicians for the festival.

Ravi Shankar performed for an afternoon. A significant proportion
of the marijuana-primed reverence for his extended set was down to
George Harrison's borrowings into Indian scales, a misunderstanding
that becomes even more obvious when they ecstatically applaud what
was Shankar's careful tuning-up session prior to his opening raga. But
even that naivety... that gullibility?, shows their degree of openness,
prepared to listen to – and applaud – Ravi Shankar alongside Otis
Redding's Stax exhortations, the Who's choreographed Mod rage,
Simon & Garfunkel's sweet harmonies... and Tiny Tim's impromptu fey
and camply eccentric ditties captured in the Green Room.

The Festival's success tended to catch everyone by surprise.
Pennebaker's second DVD of bonus features includes two short films
pieced together retrospectively from previously unused footage,
Jimi Plays Monterey (49 minutes) and *Shake! Otis at Monterey* (19
minutes), made up of their entire sets, plus background interviews and
film of Hendrix in London. Derek's own account of the festival – 'The
Bloodless Battle of the Badge: The Press at Monterey pop' – appeared
in the July 1967 *World Countdown News*, recounting his story of
issuing Press badges to all manner of dubious claimants. Among those
he turned away was future Apple 'House Hippie' Richard DiLello!

Unfortunately, the establishment was ill-prepared for the more
excessive manifestations of that counter-culture and drafted a proposal
preventing the State Fair Board from booking any such future event
likely to attract over two-thousand visitors without explicit permission
of the city. Effectively denying a sequel. No more pop Festivals for
Monterey. 'Cold hard bastards', comments Derek, 'they made life hell.'
Yet, although the vibe went elsewhere with the persistence of venereal
disease, and it was left to Woodstock, and its dark twin Altamont (also
filmed by some of the same production crew), to reshape the course
of the live rock experience. While young people with contemporary
faces wearing contemporary spectacles were selling 'Love Love Love'
like some kind of miracle detergent, Monterey remains one of the
three defining events of the US 1960s counter-culture. 'In Arcadian
dreams of other times there was a belief that everything would turn out

alright. It was often unspoken, more danced than dramatised. It was simply understood.' 'Cloud Cuckoo-land?', asks Derek, 'No! An earthly paradise? You bet! Every generation should be so lucky!'

Of the performers present, only the remnants of the Who were to survive long enough to play at Live8, contrary to rumour, growing up and growing old don't necessarily mean selling out. As Derek comments, 'Phew. Wow. Oh, well... there is no punchline to this...'

'So Catch Me If You Can, I'm Goin' Back...'

The cover of the launch issue of *rolling Stone*, dated 9 November 1967, carries two Derek Taylor-related stories. An investigative 'The High Cost of Music and Love: Where's the Money from Monterey?', plus a report on John Lennon's latest movie venture, *How I Won the War*. Then the largely text-composed cover of no.3 (14 December 1967) is made up of two more stories, also with Derek Taylor connections. The lead-in 'New Thing for Beatles: Magical Mystery Tour'. In the bottom right-hand column story there's 'Byrd Flipped: Clark Leaves'.

But there were other adventures. Derek first saw the Doors when they supported Captain Beefheart at the *Whisky a Go Go* press-night, and 'the place was not full', 'hardly anyone had heard of them, hardly anyone except all the people who had always known how good they were which didn't include me, not until that night.' Later – as they were about to peak – Derek was invited to work for them too. Their management called him in 'and said they had heard good things about me and I said I had heard good things about them which was a downright lie because I had heard nothing about them at all, but I loved the Doors.' The arrangement endured for a week, Derek arranged an interview for the group, then spent a day with them wandering around Beverly Hills 'talking about colour transparencies.' He got on OK with the Doors. But managements can be very strange. There was a basic incompatibility. He couldn't make it with them, 'dunno why'. Nevertheless, they paid Derek a $500 fee. Shortly afterwards, the Doors left the management too.

Eventually, 'on 31 December 1966 as part of a New (Cosmic) Year Resolution, I decided to "drop out" – having "turned on" but not quite "tuned in"' – and he scaled down his workload. Just as alcoholics have step-programmes for recovery, he reduced his commitments. 'It was only a matter of time, I thought, before I represented every group in town and went absolutely crazy. I realised something was going wrong when I was picking up famous bands and dropping them a week later.' Then the taxman called. Since arriving two years ago, he'd paid no tax, and was in no position to make up the shortfall. 'I told him so frankly and he betrayed less interest than if I'd been Brigitte Bardot, nude in his kitchen sink, though not much less.' After a detailed six-hour interrogation, Derek was extended twenty-four hours to rectify the situation. 'I thanked him for his enormous courtesy and offered him an album by Chad & Jeremy whom I also represented. He refused to be swayed into showing any humanity and said that it could be construed as a bribe which, he explained, he was not empowered to accept, and also, "I do not have a record player, at this time, Sir".' In the nick of time, the Beach Boys step in with $5000, saving the day. But it represented a wake-up call.

'Times were tough, reader.' Derek fired everyone, 'particularly my clients who were all driving me out of my mind. They all forgave me and they left graciously and almost all of them paid me, some twice over, even Paul Revere, a parsimonious and honest man.' Instead, after 'impersonating a press agent for about two years,' Derek sat beside the pool, and reflected, haunted by the ghosts of idle thinking. Just like the Paul Revere song, 'kicks just keep gettin' harder to find, and all your kicks ain't bringin' you peace of mind.' A biography is more distilled than a life so that much of the faceting and detailed specificity is reduced down to thumbnail approximation. What was Derek like within his own head, behind the ashtray eyes? What were the doubts, deceptions, dreams? He had hurtled through three years of 'freakish leaps, loops and twists and tantalising trickery.' He'd got away with a lot in his life. He must have wondered, how the hell had he arrived here? There must have been a growing suspicion that this might just be as good as it was going to get. The thought must have occasionally stopped him in his tracks.

Derek was one of the few participants on the scene to have a stable, full and fulfilling family life away from showbiz. That was rare. He had an intelligent, loyal, and attractive wife, with an expanding brood to fall back on. Yet the demands of being the consummate PR performer of his generation stretched that connection to the limit. Playing off the conflicting elements of his personality, the Celtic excitement versus the English detachment, the need for family against the urge for the 'Big Time'.

If you live in Los Angeles for too long, you tend to pick up lifestyle habits not compatible with the social norm. There was even an astrologer, Debbi Kempton-Smith, who would later sell lots of copies of her *Secrets from a Stargazer's Notebook* (1982). Along with the Tarot and the I-Ching, the anti-science horoscope absurdities were part of a voguey openness to new forms of mystic future-divination, not yet quirky New Age kitsch – more in an 'I believe in magic, why, because it is so quick' Arthur Lee sort of way. And Derek's kids were picking up American accents, at school they 'used to pledge allegiance to the flag each morning, and practice "duck and cover" drills, rolling under their desks to protect themselves against explosions in the event of a nuclear attack on Los Angeles.' The thought had already occurred, the decision that it was time to return to England. The older he got, the more he rationalised that he was not always going to keep getting away with it, that it would begin to take its toll. Part of the mysterious process called growing up.

Things were getting crazier. And not always in a good way. During the beautiful LA Spring of 1968, Dennis Wilson happened to pick up two nubile hitchhikers, Ella Jo 'Yellerstone' Bailey and Patricia 'Marnie Reeves' Krenwinkle. He took them home, had sex with them both. They enthuse about their 'friend' the wizard – would he like to meet him? Sure he would. As a direct result of that random pick-up, Charles Manson and his murderous 'Family' move into Dennis' 14400 Sunset Boulevard mansion. Initially attracted and ensnared by the free drugs and even more freely available sex, Dennis helped to promote Manson's musical ambitions. The Beach Boys even record one of his songs, 'Cease to Exist' (retitled 'Never Learn Not to Love') on their *20/20* album. They record 'between six and eight' songs in Brian's home studio on Bellagio Road, while Brian himself was in bed upstairs. Dennis was also instrumental in introducing Manson to Terry Melcher, who was not only a high-profile producer but the celebrity son of Doris Day (he wrote her last British chart single, 'Move Over Darling'). Melcher, Manson assumed, could also further his musical career. When he didn't, in Neil Young's breathtaking understatement, 'he didn't take rejection well...'

It was at the rented home Melcher shared with his girlfriend Candice Bergen – 10050 Cielo Drive – where Brian had first met Van Dyke Parks. Derek and Joan went there to one of Melcher's parties. And it was there that the Manson Family would unleash their 'Helter Skelter' agenda by massacring its occupants. Derek had 'admired the mock oak beams, on which the killers would hang the dead, eight-month pregnant body of Sharon Tate, and admired, too, the grounds where they would stretch out three others described by the papers as "fully dressed in hippy-type garb". Pretty nasty.' On that particular night, Melcher himself – their real target – happened to be absent. So it was actress Sharon Tate, wife of director Roman Polanski, her hairdresser friend Jay Sebring, Abigail

Folger and her boyfriend Voityck Frykowski, who became victims of the savage attack, then Steven Parent, Leno and Rosemary Iabianca… And something like thirty-four Lesser Mortals too.

That was a time when a creeping paranoia took collective hold of the residents of Laurel Canyon and the Hollywood Hills, when what Joan Didion calls a 'sinistral inertia' settled on Sunset Boulevard and its environs like a dank fog. In the tapestry of reportage that makes up her book *The White Album*, she moves in strange circles, crossing paths in her reportage with Eldridge Cleaver and Huey Newton of the Black Panthers and Linda Kasabian, the hippie girl who had become a Charles Manson acolyte. The Tate killing brought all that Hollywood paranoia to a head. 'The tension broke that day', wrote Didion. 'The paranoia was fulfilled.' Even following Manson's arrest the fear continued, as rumours persisted that other members of his 'Family' were still roaming free, programmed to fulfil their master's vendettas and murderous grudges.

An intimidating letter was even sent to Derek, for no obvious reason. A crank weirdo? Or something more? Who could say? Was it even worth taking the risk? Terry Melcher took such threats seriously, he was undergoing psychiatric treatment for his strung-out nerves, employed a bodyguard and took to carrying a gun for his own protection. Derek was less directly involved in the grotesque escalation of events, which peaked after he'd left. But they involved people he was involved with, and the shockwaves shuddered their way throughout the LA media community of which he was a part. And he couldn't help but be aware, 'Hollywood was getting very weird by then,' with all manner of bad juju playing its part. He was wondering, in capital letters, What Was Going On!?!?

Derek's morning ritual – an essential routine – began as he 'dressed, took two small yellow Dexedrine tablets, cleaned his teeth, combed his hair and put on a tie.' In that order. Followed by 'brandies for breakfast', light a ciggie, drag the smoke down deep. To Joan, 'I became frightened, nervous and full of denial, but I hung on hoping something would change. I couldn't leave and deny the children the loving relationship they had with their father, and he couldn't support two homes. I was uptight and hurt, and we weren't able to talk about the damage that was being done to our marriage without it ending in a row…' 'Body all aching and racked with bennies', George Harrison's friends had 'lost their way' in more than one sense. It was 'difficult being Derek Taylor, though. Difficult being…'

In December 1967, Derek stayed over in London for the opening of the Apple boutique. 'I took more acid and talked to George about

Apple.' Then they went to the boutique's opening party together. Soon after getting back to LA, he was roused and brought blearily to the phone... his mouth dry from pills, it was Sunday 'at 8:00 o'clock one morning I got a phone call... it was all four of them, rowdy and friendly and sober and calling, I assume, on a whim. "Come back to England and run Apple" one of them said. What did that mean?' To make the call, the four Beatles were crowded into Alistair Taylor's office at Hilley House, Brian Epstein's private suite, 'like a group of kids organising a party.' It was the early hours in LA, they didn't bother about such trivialities. Once Derek was sufficiently coherent, The Beatles took the receiver in turn to sweet-talk him back into the fold. 'Come and joins us, and you can run Apple Records', said John. 'This is George's idea. I've asked Mal but you can do it anyway, with Mal.' 'Bullocks to yer', said Paul, 'pack your bags and come on over.' 'He asked Peter Asher.' 'You can come and drive the big green jobs anyway', added George – referring back to the first run-through of their *Daily Express* column...

The best solution would be to come and talk through the proposal. Derek agreed. It was the motivation he needed, the incentive he was waiting for. He hadn't anticipated it would happen in quite this way, but he was already prepared for change. The Beatles had always been his first love, and with a love like that, you know it can't be bad. Within days of the conversation, he was already making plans to move the family back to England (as recounted by Stefan Granados in his 'unofficial history of Apple', *Those Were the Days*, 2002, Cherry Red Books).

But first, on 28 March 1968, he threw a farewell party for some five-hundred guests – a 'benefit' for himself held, appropriately, at *Ciro's* on the Strip, where his American adventure had begun. And what a swellegant elegant party it was. The glitzy supper club from the golden era of Hollywood had closed down, but was specially re-opened as 'It's Boss' for the occasion. Derek's 'Farewell to Hollywood' party opened at 8:30pm exact, with entertainment provided by the Byrds, Captain Beefheart and Tiny Tim, who all performed for free. Guests contribute $5:50 each. 'I had made quite a lot of money one way or another during our three years in Hollywood, but I didn't seem to have much left when it came to booking an air ticket', hence the fund-raiser. Short of cash perhaps, but never short of friends. The kind of equation he liked. In terms of talent alone, it was a million-dollar bash. However, Derek over-ordered wine, when most of the attendees were 'wiped out by cannabis', and he underestimated gatecrashing. And hence the evening came out showing a $2,000 deficit.

For the occasion, for that one night, Gene Clark – 'a soul adrift' –

unexpectedly rejoined the new Byrds line-up on-stage, 'over-eager to please, stumbling drunk and a little embarrassing' (according to Johnny Rogan). At that point, with Roger McGuinn and Chris Hillman there was Gram Parsons, Kevin Kelley, and temporary steel-guitar player Jay Dee 'JD' Maness, all shorn of their long hair due to their appearance on the *Grand Ole Opry* barely two weeks earlier (15 March). They play 'Chimes of Freedom' and 'He Was a Friend of Mine'. Then Gene proceeded to take to the stage during their set, as musicologist Alec Palao recounted, 'Gene had been drinking heavily and we'd (Gene and Laramy Smith) been driving in his Ferrari 275 and he was nuts. So there's the Byrds on this huge, huge stage. Everybody's there, all the originals, but no Gene Clark. So they start doing "Eight Miles High". There's a Gibson 335 up onstage and Gene decides to get up and play. Gene gets up, picks up this guitar, puts it on, but there's no cord. So he's gonna take Chris Hillman's cord. Chris is like slapping his hand but Gene is pulling on the cord and Chris is holding onto it and playing bass with one hand. And all of a sudden Gene falls right into the drums and everything goes all over the place.' Embarrassed, Gene quickly rose to his feet, with help from a Byrds' roadie, he bid a hasty retreat into the night. 'Gene was drunk', agrees Derek, 'he sang a few songs with them but stayed up there too long. There was mild irritation. The Byrds never really got on. They were always marvellously dangerous.'

To the group's biographer Johnny Rogan, Gene was 'one of rock music's most frustrating underachievers.' But events had happened fast. Some brief time-frame earlier – by the end of 1967 – David Crosby had inevitably become the second member of the original line-up to quit. The chart failure of the Byrds' 'Lady Friend', Crosby's first A-side single, was one reason. But that was just one. For Crosby – who defines the adjective 'mercurial' – there were other incidents. He'd written 'Triad', a seductive lyrical invitation to three-way sex that McGuinn instantly took against, and vetoed. So, in one inspired stroke, Crosby gave the song to Jefferson Airplane. Grace Slick had no moral qualms about singing it. The Byrds' demo eventually turned up on *The Byrds Box Set* to prove just how wrong McGuinn had been. McGuinn might later have denied this version of events, but this is the story that has entered rock history. From another session – for the slight April (1967) single 'Don't Make Waves ' – Crosby can clearly be heard in the run-off groove with a sarcastic 'let's double it, masterpiece,' making his disapproval eloquently apparent.

Subsequently, the sleeve of the April 1968 album *The Notorious Byrd Brothers* shows McGuinn, Hillman and Michael Clarke looking out of the windows of a stable, while a fourth window which contains a horse, is supposed to portray the way McGuinn regarded Crosby! Briefly, Gene Clark stepped back in to add weight to the resulting trio, and it's said that he added harmonies to the album. As if unsettled by this problematic, today it's an album that both looks wistfully back at a simpler past whilst yearning for better future-days yet to come. Gerry Goffin and Carole King's melancholic 'Goin' Back' embodies a yearning for the innocence of childhood. 'Natural Harmony' and 'Tribal Gathering' look back at the naïve optimism of Monterey, confronting it with 'Draft Morning' spiked with Vietnam battle-noises (as used on Eric Burdon and the Animals' 'Sky Pilot', and Sands' 'Listen to the Sky'), escaping out into the *Easy Rider* endless-highway freedom of 'Wasn't Born to Follow'. 'Artificial Energy' uses the 'got my ticket to ride' lyric-reference to illuminate the amphetamine-buzz. Then 'Space Odyssey' looks further out into a more galactic future when 'atomic energy we'd harvested and survived,' with a storyline set in 1996 which so closely approximates Arthur C Clarke that he could have claimed royalties. All its drone-like quality lacks is a melodic hook. Its 'slight return' wash of electronics fades the album out into infinite future-time.

While it's an undeniably strong album with some stand-out tracks – albeit the first Byrds album not to spawn a major hit single – it's only necessary to hear the neglected session out-takes on the expanded CD edition to realise that, with the addition of 'Triad' (and maybe 'Wooden Ships' too, which Crosby also donated to Jefferson Airplane) just how much stronger it could have been. But by then David had departed, pacted with Graham Nash – 'if he'd been a girl I would've kissed him' – and taken his rejected songs across to Crosby Stills & Nash for their immensely more successful first album. 'Truth is real', concludes 'Change is Now' – stay in 'harmony with love's sweet plan.' Yet in truth, 'Old John Robertson' with its folksy country licks looks to the Byrds' real future.

Chris Hillman and new boy Gram Parsons convinced an initially sceptical Roger McGuinn to take the Byrds out of jingle-jangle space-rock territory, conceiving what they termed 'cosmic American music', a mélange of roots forms that would encompass folk, bluegrass, rock 'n' roll and soul music, with a strong country bias. McGuinn was still conscious of competing – if not commercially, at least creatively – with The Beatles. By decomplexifying. Following Dylan's lead, they decamp to Music Row in Nashville and enlist the services of producer Gary Usher and a team of crack session players. The resulting *Sweetheart of the Rodeo* (August 1968) vanquished the cultural divide between acid-munching, peace-preaching long-hairs and beer-swilling flag-waving good ol' boys by creating the enduring hybrid of country-rock. Allying rippling guitars and silky vocal harmonies with a mix of country tradition ('I Am a Pilgrim') and Gram Parsons' originals, the record irrevocably altered the perspective of two previously contradictory streams of Americana. The album's array of songs by Dylan, The Louvin Brothers, Tim Hardin and Woody Guthrie, plus several Parsons originals, would provide a virtual blueprint for the No Depression alt-country movement of the eighties and nineties.

By the end of 1968, Chris Hillman quit the Byrds too. There would be more, but it would never again be what it had been. Despite McGuinn's striving to re-pool associates from the Byrds' 'creative peak' in a last attempt at competing with Crosby's success as part of CSN&Y. As part of that strategy, Derek was induced to contribute sleeve-notes to *(Untitled)*, an album issued on 16 September 1970 by a Byrds made up of Roger McGuinn, Gene Parsons, Skip Battin and Clarence White. The double-set includes a side of live versions of old hits edited by Jim Dickson, to illustrate the group's historical perspective and suggest a sense of continuity, plus a studio-side produced by Terry Melcher including the elegiac half-spoken 'Chestnut Mare' which, spun off as a single, oddly returns the Byrds to the UK chart (no.19 in February 1971). Derek's liner notes also reveal that Gram Parsons guested as harmony vocalist on the song 'All the Things', as a further step towards integrating the various phases of the group history into a cohesive whole. The commercial success of the album did much to temporarily arrest the group's decline. Melcher, meanwhile, had another stab at working as a solo artist, signing to Reprise for the introverted one-off solo album *Terry Melcher* (1973), which managed to recruit the talents of Clarence White, Roger McGuinn, Chris Hillman and Ry Cooder.

While The Beatles' brave and adventurous *White Album* (1968) was changing the rules yet again. There's a sequence in *Lennon Naked* (BBC-TV, June 2010) re-enacting Derek chairing an Apple meeting with the group spaced around the big polished boardroom table. Derek, played by Michael Colgan, opens by expressing unease about the project: 'No-one does double-albums', he asserts. 'Bob Dylan did.' 'But it's not even Beatles' he persists. By the time the thirty-track double-album came to pass, internal relationships within the group were faltering, so most of the songs were individual compositions, regardless of the credits. 'Julia', he points out, is just John. 'That's about my mother', flares John vituperatively, with heavy hands-off overtones. 'The Beatles are four people', retaliates Paul (Andrew Scott). 'The Beatles are not what other people say they are, The Beatles are what the four of us decide it is.' Whether a scene actually happened as it's portrayed, or a composite construction by writer Robert Jones, it captures something of the fissile energies of the time. With Derek's unenviable task of confronting the group with his opposing views, arguing his points, even if ultimately he has to demur to their decision. If their ideas are unrealistic, their power allows them to create their own reality.

Among the faults Derek outlines are its length. There's a lot to take in at a single listen. And its reputation did rather tend to grow over a period of time. But Lennon is at his most reflective on 'Dear Prudence', and in 'Sexy Sadie' he lays into the Maharishi, while McCartney's 'Back in the USSR' is a fine take-off of the Beach Boys, drawing on – and politically inverting – Chuck Berry's 'Back in the USA'. The Soviet Union has since been consigned to history – but Paul still plays 'Back in the USSR, and it still gets radio plays. The slowed-down version of 'Revolution' (previously the B-side of 'Hey Jude') is grittier than the single version, and songs like 'Happiness is a Warm Gun', 'I'm So Tired', 'Blackbird', 'Julia' and George's 'While My Guitar Gently Weeps' show they can still deliver on the song front – and then some! Ringo wrote 'Don't Pass Me By', according to Lennon, 'in a fit of lethargy.' And lest we forget, a little tune by the name of 'Helter Skelter' happened to catch the ear of a struggling singer-songwriter by the name of Charles Manson. But Derek Taylor would not be a part of those trips...

On Friday, 29 March 1968, tired of his three years on the LA/Hollywood scene, Derek returned to Liverpool with just a curious transatlantic mix of UK savvy and LA luvvie to show for it. 'So much living was crammed into the three years we spent in Hollywood. We flew out of Liverpool in 1965 and sailed back into Liverpool in 1968 totally changed, totally. We didn't feel "British" any more and a good thing too. We belonged, we believed, to a brotherhood in rock 'n' roll which had nothing to do with where we were born but which had everything to do with "where our heads were at, man," as the saying went.' Some claim musical life in LA would never be quite the same again without him. With his wife Joan and their children (Dominic – our 'American child' – born October 1967, Vanessa, Victoria and Gerard) – 'without them I would be a decrepit old fool. With them, I am indeed a fortunate young man' – he returned to resume his role as publicist for The Beatles when they asked him to become part of their newly-instituted company, Apple Corps. Casually establishing his legendary press 'salon' at the Apple building, from where he befriends all comers and addresses the world... until the break-up of The Beatles in 1970.

Chapter Twelve: 1968: Get Back To Where You Once Belonged

Then if your hair is right and your pants are tight you're gonna be alright...
(The Byrds)

It Was Twenty Years Ago Today...

Derek Taylor officially returned to England, to be the press officer – in-house publicist – for the newly created Apple Corps, responsible for media relations for all of the artists on the Apple label. And the timeframe had accelerated, a world of societal, cultural and artistic differences had occurred since he'd last officially been in The Beatles' employ. Initially, from April 1968 the family rented 'Laudate', a lavish eleven-acre country house on Dukes Road in Newdigate, Surrey, owned by and leased to them by Peter Asher. This was the first step in a process Derek termed their 'de-immigration' from California. 'I came because I wanted to and I left because I wanted to and I came back because I wanted to.' Derek was commuting from Dorking station to Victoria every day by train. The family moved from 'Laudate' at the end of July after buying a property of their own – 'The Gables', on London Road in Sunningdale, Ascot, Berkshire, off the M3 just south of Virginia Water. Which meant he was taking the train from Sunningdale to Waterloo Station. John, George and Paul came around to visit. Or George sent cryptic postcards from Twickenham about a musical called 'Hey Man'.

The world had changed. The Beatles' world was changing more than most. Today, bands retreat from the scene for two, three years to record their next album safe in the knowledge that when they coordinate the shout for its eventual release little will have significantly altered during their absence. Back then albums were released within nine months of each other, a failed single meant career extinction, and the entire scene would convulse into new configurations within months. Derek Taylor was caught up in an immense entertainment machine that was unique in history. One that could only have happened then, and can never be repeated.

For the first half of the twentieth century, it was the movie studio system. For the second fifty years, it was music, an industry structured in a way that ensured a small elite of 'star' names became disproportionately more massive than could ever be rationally justified. A small cartel of record companies, especially in the UK, controlled the flow of new artists and new music. The complex technology of making records, the distribution and marketing ensured that its monopoly remained unchallenged. Unique talent is a factor, and certainly The Beatles thoroughly shook the industry up root and branch, but that's only one part of the equation. Once they'd overcome the inertia and drag-factor, and broken through massively, they benefited from the concentrated focus that was the industry model. One, two, and then three TV channels concentrate audience-figures in a way unimaginable in any subsequent period, so that a strategic TV-appearance on, say, *Sunday Night at the London Palladium, The Morecambe and Wise Show*, or more routinely *Thank Your Lucky Stars* or *Top of the pops* guarantee instant nationwide visibility. There was one family TV. It was in the front room. The family watch it together. It was a collective experience. Radio was similarly restricted to the BBC strands, there was no commercial alternative beyond distant out-of-phase Radio Luxembourg, and later the off-shore Pirate Stations. The teen-music played on Brian Matthews' Light Programme *Saturday Club* was heard in a saturation-concentration clear across the nation.

The music press – operating through the artist/label PR filter – controlled access to record-news. A small fanzine culture or the growing 'underground press' could never offer the kind of instant global bandwidth of the internet. The advent of digital technology, and the vast diversity of niche markets it spawned, has democratised all of that, placed the means of production, distribution and exchange in the hands of more and more people so that never again can such a monolithic structure enjoy such an unchallenged dominance. Ensuring that no single artist will ever again enjoy such hyperinflated success. No matter how big a star becomes, they can never be an Elvis Presley. No matter how big a band becomes, it can never be a Beatles. Apple was The Beatles' attempt to scheme a way around that artistic totalitarianism.

During May (1968), John and Paul head up a junket numbering Derek, Neil Aspinall, Mal Evans, Ron Kass and others to unleash Apple upon New York, and explain the mission they had chosen to accept. Deplaning at Kennedy, they board a Chinese junk to cruise around Manhattan island, then convene a press conference at the St Regis Hotel with Derek as referee. From there they hit *the Johnny Carson Show* – with an unsympathetic Joe Garagiola sitting in for the holidaying host – to explain to eleven-million viewers how The Beatles were going to use their immense influence and considerable personal fortune to benefit the world's young people. Apple was going to enable an infinite number of artistic ventures to reach fruition. No longer would the young and creative have to put up with unspeakable humiliations to achieve artistic freedom. The Beatles had formed an organisation that would seek to finance and encourage projects of a cinematic, literary, scientific and musical nature. Apple would be the company where you don't have to crawl in on your hands and knees to get what you want. It was going to attempt to end forever the philistine conspiracy of artistic suppression and tyranny that had dominated for far too long.

Asked what he thought about Western civilisation, Mahatma Ghandi quipped that it 'would be a good idea.' Yes, Apple too...

Settling back into the English way of life, Gerard failed his Eleven-plus examination 'with flying colours' at Christchurch School, went on to attend Fancourt (Christian Science) Prep School where he 'spectacularly bombed out of' his public school entrance exams.

Significantly, Brian Epstein was no longer around. Derek's father had a number of imaginative euphemisms for death, the deceased had 'fled this vot (vale of tears)' or 'joined the GM (great majority)' or they had 'gone where they don't play billiards.' With The Beatles' increasing independence and self-determination, Brian had become progressively marginalised. The Beatles never lost respect or affection for him. They never forgot or minimised the immense value of his work on their behalf during those vital early days, months and years. And later, through the astute launching of Northern Songs on the London Stock Exchange in February 1965, those shares had quadrupled in value across the years since. But Paul was purposefully encroaching on managerial responsibilities for the band. While George was openly critical of certain financial decisions and inquisitive about the economics of deals that Epstein had struck. Oddly, it was Lennon who displayed the greatest continuing loyalty to Brian. But their refusal to tour only served to further diminish Brian's role in their affairs.

Increasingly directionless, Brian even proposed an unlikely marriage to Alma Cogan, the big-haired Stepney-born 'girl with the giggle in her voice' who scored some twenty post-war pre-Beatles hits, presented her own TV-shows and had already been romantically linked with some of the biggest stars of her day, including Cary Grant. She recorded a version of 'Eight Days A Week' in a kind of two-part slow-and-fast segue, which gained Brian's approval. Whatever the degree of seriousness of his proposal, she died from cancer on 26 October 1966, aged just thirty-four.

Of course, for Brian, there were other pressures and personal problems that would have figured in the addendum to Derek's

A Cellarful of Noise, if it had extended to cover those years. He
was left distraught by his father's death on 7 July 1967. His early
misunderstandings with father Harry had been healed and reconciled
by Brian's success, which made his death even harder. Brian spent
'therapy'-time at the Priory Hospital in Roehampton Lane in Putney for
his growing pill-popping dependence on amphetamines. At the time,
he was sharing a flat in Chapel Street, off Belgrave Square with Peter
Brown, the lapsed-Catholic from Liverpool name-checked on 'The
Ballad of John and Yoko'. Brown had a six-month intimate relationship
with twenty-two-year-old Kenny Everett, which only ended amid the
confusion of Epstein's death.

Everett was there on Sunday 28 May as a guest when Epstein held a
grand 'house-warming' at his new property in Sussex. Kingsley Hill was
an eighteenth-century country house set in five acres of landscaped
grounds, the place where John's namesake Winston Churchill had
worked out some of his World War II campaigns. Now it was the
unlikely location for a party recalled by participant Pete Brown as
'The Kingsley Hill Acid Party', an enormous LSD trip, with those
present including George (in beads and bells, deeply into his Indian
mystic phase), Klaus Voormann (the Manfred Mann who designed the
Revolver cover-art), Mick Jagger with Marianne Faithful, Lionel Bart,
and numerous other notables of the hiperati. In what seems to have
been a gesture of reconciliation, Brian sent two first-class round-trip air
tickets from LA for Derek and Joan, who was seven months pregnant
at the time. They were welcomed at Heathrow by John, Ringo and
Terry Doran. The old handshake formalities were gone. Instead, they
were greeted with hugs. They stayed over the weekend with John and
Cynthia at Kenwood. When John played them *Sgt. Pepper* it was the
first time Derek and Joan had heard it, but John talked over the album,
'anxious to get to the next place in music.' He was already so used to
the LP he was eager to play them an even newer demo of 'Baby You're
A Rich Man'. Derek and Joan 'weren't concentrating, being rather
"zonked" after the long flight.'

The friends travel down to the party in John's Romany Art Nouveau
psychedelic rolls Royce, to find tripping party-goers wandering around
the house and grounds solemnly declaiming on the meaning of life.
Epstein had bought a grand piano for Paul. But when Paul didn't show,
Derek planted himself at the keyboard instead, playing Ivor Novello
songs, while those around him 'tripped the light fantastic'. Recalling
the celebrations directly, Derek admits he 'would have liked to have
tried it (LSD) earlier, if only we had had the courage.' Now the decision

was taken out of his hands. 'I took LSD with Joan... it was put in our tea, without our demur, by John Lennon and George Harrison. I took a double dose of the chemicals because I drank two cups of tea by mistake.' As in 'I'd love to turn you on'?

The image of LSD combined with the quintessentially English cup of tea in a Sussex country house is ludicrously irresistible. 'After that', Derek continues, 'things changed. Salt-cellars became Chartres Cathedral and the Seven Pillows of Norman Wisdom at least, and barbed wire sprouted leaves in the windows of John's rolls-Royce to the accompaniment of "A Whiter Shade of Pale". I had already been prepared to examine life through a prism of cannabised cigarettes. That had been good, but this new lark was ridiculous. How could a poor man stand such times and live?' (in the introduction to his *It Was Twenty Years Ago Today*). Meanwhile, Terry Doran contrived to fall out of a window, yet remained unscathed.

Derek returned to LA with an advance copy of the album to amaze the Monterey Festival office 'one lunchtime in May'. He also took the Procol Harum single to trailblaze its climb into the American charts. The Kingsley Hill party was the last major Beatles event Brian Epstein attended, and the second of two launch parties for *Sgt. Pepper's Lonely Hearts Club Band*. The first had been a press party in the drawing-room of 24 Chapel Street, the ultra-fashionable Belgravia townhouse that had been Brian's principal London residence since moving there on 20 December 1964, redecorated for him by Ken Partridge. On Friday nineteenth, Derek was there, directing the carefully-orchestrated proceedings, ensuring that each of the twenty-or-so Fleet Street photographers got their fair share of Beatles-time. Among them was Barrie Wentzell from *Melody Maker*... and a certain Linda Eastman. Ironically, it was the same day the BBC announced the air-time banning of 'A Day in the Life' due to its drugs references.

The second event was the Sunday party. On the 23 August Epstein had attended the recording session for 'Your Mother Should Know'. Unusual for Brian, ever since John's acid comment during the recording of 'Till There Was You', that Brian's role should be merely 'counting his percentages'. A retort that 'terribly annoyed and hurt' him. It was an apocryphal story that Derek admits 'Brian told me they'd said that, and it could have been said.' Brian's final act for The Beatles was to set up the tele-networking of 'All You Need Is Love' – with 'Yesterday' and 'She Loves You Yeah-Yeah-Yeah' inserted into the extended fade, as if to illustrate just how far they'd all come in so short a period of time. And just how far Brian had guided his 'boys'.

In *A Cellarful of Noise*, Brian describes The Beatles' internal rules as 'workable', ones that never damage anyone, adding 'which is more than one can say for some of society's rules.' Derek was perhaps recalling the 1951 incident, as a young reporter, when he witnessed the aftermath of a young man's suicide by throwing himself from a railway bridge into the path of an approaching electric train, briefly surviving the amputation of both legs. Facing 'gross indecency' charges he'd tragically tried to 'do the decent thing' by his family. Traumatised, Derek was incapable of writing the story. Upbraided by a reporter colleague, 'Jim told me I wouldn't forget that day, and I never did.' A month before Brian's death, the 'Royal Assent to Sexual Offences Act' altered society's damaging rules concerning homosexuality. Simon Napier-Bell suggests that 'The Beatles' popularity, coupled with their affection for their manager, made it a sure bet that Harold Wilson's government would move forward on legalising homosexuality. Unintentionally, The Beatles were helping force the issue' (to the *Observer Music Monthly*, November 2006).

The last time Derek ever spoke to Brian – 'before we had taken anything' – it seemed that Brian was 'extremely happy'. Brian Epstein died on August Bank Holiday weekend (27 August 1967) from what the coroner described as an 'incautious overdose', aged thirty-two, alone in his Chapel Street bedroom, with bottles of prescribed drugs and a variety of pills strewn around him, Librium, Carbrital and others. Most opinions are that it wasn't suicide. It wasn't deliberate. He left no will, no suicide-note. To Derek, 'his death was sudden, shocking and almost certainly accidental. He drank too much (quite a few of us did) and he took too many drugs (again, so did others among us – in those days), and he died of a combination of both.' At the very least he'd become careless with his own life. And 'The Beatle-Making Prince Of pop', as next morning's *Daily Mirror* front-page described him, was as lonely in death as he had been in life. (His brother Clive, born just twenty-one-months after Brian, died of a heart-attack on 1 February 1988, aged 51.)

Ironically, following Derek's departure, Tony Barrow assumed the 'correspondent' role for *KRLA Beat*, covering Brian's death and a damage-limitation report on *Magical Mystery Tour*. NEMS continued, but now there were new priorities. Intoxicated, high on wealth, largesse and unworkable ideals, The Beatles were already planning a venture way beyond Epstein's reach. Brian's death was the final punctuation in their long-drawn-out separation. As if to emphasise just how far they'd grown up, and grown away from him, The Beatles registered their new Apple Music Ltd company within weeks of Brian's death (on 25 May 1967). The new venture established a temporary first base occupying the fourth floor of 95 Wigmore Street on Monday, 22 January 1968, with Derek assigned a Press office on the floor above. Then, hopelessly overstaffed, they move to luxury offices in the Georgian building no.3 Savile Row on 15 July, although the accounts department stay behind until the lease runs out in January 1969. Their new location would be the site of much legendary mayhem and hedonistic self-indulgence, as well as The Beatles' impromptu live rooftop performance with Billy Preston.

Around lunchtime on 30 January 1969, a din erupts in the sky above the staid garment district. Grey-suited businessmen, with expressions ranging from amused curiosity to disgust, gather alongside miniskirted teenagers to stare up at the Savile Row roof. As camera crews swirl around, whispered conjecture solidified into confirmed fact. The Beatles, who hadn't performed live since August 1966, were playing an unannounced concert on their office roof. Crowds gather on scaffolding, behind windows, and on neighbouring rooftops to watch the band who had revolutionised pop culture play again. But what only the pessimistic among them could have guessed – what The Beatles themselves could not yet even decide for sure – was that this was to be their last public performance ever. The last time The Beatles would ever play to a live audience. A performance brought to a halt when what Derek termed 'the stiff-necked shits of Savile Row called in the law.'

Apple was to be a diversity of things, 'in the early shining summer of 1968 we had Apple Music, Apple Shops, Apple Films and Apple Electronics.' It was The Beatles' declaration of independence. It was to be the nucleus of their increasingly divergent musical experiments, enabling solo albums and production-ventures to take place through the gradually more-fragmented collective group-identity. But if Epstein's control of his NEMS empire had become chaotic, along with its frequently neglected second-tier artists, it was a model of probity and prudent concern compared to Apple. The gatefold double-EP and comic-book, and the TV-movie that was *Magical Mystery Tour* was only the first product to bear the distinctive Apple logo. Gene Mahon had come up with the sliced-apple label concept. The Granny Smith apple itself was then photographed by Paul Castell. Alan Aldridge did the lettering. Derek recruited Alan, initially calling around his INK studios at Litchfield Street, and struck up an instant rapport. 'You fell in love with this guy right away', recalls Alan, 'warm, witty, urbane and full of hilarious repartee. Within minutes we were throwing jokes back and forth like ping-pong.'

Records – singles, eps and albums – are ordinary artefacts that have the potential to set deep currents of feeling flowing. They contain what Wordsworth called 'spots of time'. Records bearing the Apple logo would create more than their fair share of them. Inevitably, music was to be its most commercially viable medium – in fact, ultimately it was to be its only viable product, but it was initially conceived to be much, much more.

Part of it was tax-related, as George had already lamented on his *Revolver* track, the attentions of the Inland Revenue 'Taxman' were looming huge at the time. For every pound their various enterprises generate it was 'one (shilling) for you, nineteen for me.' Advisers foraging through the immense and diverse state of The Beatles' finances, trying to make economic sense of it all, recommended that a splurge of investment spread across new ventures could extricate them from the predatory interests of the taxman. And as partly a tax-avoidance project, Apple worked, instead of paying 19s 6d on the pound, as a company they would pay only 16s. It was a case of spend it, or hand it over to the Government, whether that meant 'taxman Mr Wilson' or 'taxman Mr Heath'. So they determined to spend it. But not even the most blue-sky thinking analyst could have conceived how they would respond to such advice.

It proceeded pretty much in the manner of *Magical Mystery Tour* itself. Although they'd circled around the idea to Brian before his death, it was to be The Beatles' first post-Brian project. And also an escape clause from the 'third movie' conundrum. How to follow *A Hard Day's Night* and *Help!*? – it would have to be something sufficiently collective, but also evolved from what they'd done before. Playwright Joe Orton had been approached, and he'd delivered script-ideas that were way-too sexually-extreme for Brian's idea of what The Beatles represented. The Monkees were already replicating ideas looted from the first two movies on a weekly basis on TV. But technological innovation meant that, just as home-computers now have a greater memory than the equipment NASA used to send Neil Armstrong to the Moon, and just as Indie recording studios have democratised the secret monopolies of the monolithic record labels, the film industry was no longer restricted to just the big players. There was a growing fringe of eccentric obsessives, such as Ed Wood, Russ Meyer and Andy Warhol who were taking the means of movie-production into their own hands. The Beatles could do that too.

Obviously, the hazards that afflicted other pioneers – such as funding and distribution – were not a problem for The Beatles. The project would be funded by record-sales, and the BBC agreed to screen the results on Christmas Day. The Beatles' home-movie retains some thematic trace of their Northern roots. For what could be more Northern than a charabanc trip? Plus the Ken Kesey chemical-additive of spiking the tour with acid, to take it into the realm of psychedelic fantasia. Even the 'Magical Mystery Tour' opening chant 'roll Up' could be read as a metaphor for 'rolling up' a preparatory joint, for those who cared to read it that way. 'Ringo and Auntie Jessie are always quarrelling about one thing or another', relates the comic-strip story-line, 'but they both agree it would be exciting to go on a Mystery Tour. "Your Uncle Jack always liked a Charabanc Trip" says Auntie Jessie. "And this is a MAGIC trip" adds Ringo. So, a few days later, very early in the morning, they set off to start the tour. Auntie Jessie looks at the B-I-G bus and smiles, "It's yellow and blue! My favourite colours!"' Nevertheless, as the tour bus sets off, as 'the other passengers are enjoying the bright sunshine and the green countryside,' Derek Taylor can be seen sitting in the seat immediately behind Paul.

Apple was to be a quixotic venture intent on a kind of benevolent redistribution of all those unspent royalties to deserving causes. A 'Yellow Submarine' that they'd live in, with all their friends on board. To Derek, 'there was a high quotient of sincerity in there, as well as a bit of madness.' To Richard DiLello, 'The Beatles were four individuals who had exceeded their own wildest dreams and who believed it was their obligation to give something back to the world' (in his *The Longest Cocktail Party*, Mojo Books, 1972). To Derek, 'The Beatles had changed a lot from being rather charming but world-weary pop stars into being extremely nice, gentle, huggable souls. They really were very sweet in 1967, and we believed we were going to make everything very beautiful and that it was going to be, now, a wonderful world.'

Wasn't London – and the world beyond – heaving with untapped talent? There were ideas-rich cash-poor artists, poets, designers, songwriters, film-makers, novelists, inventors, musicians, all out there starving in garrets, or busking on street-corners. All that immense resource of talent needed was to be primed with a little enabling finance, and the artistic landscape of the world would be transfigured. All you need is love, after all. The venture would be a determinedly anti-capitalist, deliberately anti-business plan. Eccentrically of its time, rooted in the anarchist philosophy that to liberate creativity of all restraint is to free the human spirit towards its highest aspiration. Given the opportunity, artists will create. Musicians will play. Designers will design new works. Poets will write skipping reels of rhyme. The world will be intensely illuminated by radiating beauty. The smile you send out will be returned ten-fold. It will be the catalyst of a new artistic renaissance guided and powered by the I-Ching randomness of the hippie dream, by the fortuitous accident. Apple will be the centre of excellence for a new dayglo William Morris workshop of inspired invention…

An ad run in *IT: International Times* shows a one-man band, above the copy 'one day he sang his songs to a tape recorder (borrowed from the man next door). In his neatest handwriting he wrote an explanatory note (giving his name and address) and, remembering to enclose a picture of himself, sent the tape, letter and photograph to Apple Music, 94 Baker Street, London W1. If you were thinking of doing the same thing yourself – do it now! This man now owns a Bentley!'

Naturally, it didn't always work out quite that way.

Apple began by assembling personnel. First, there was Neil Aspinall. According to Alistair Taylor, Neil 'had never finished his accountant training', yet now he was appointed Apple's managing director. With Mal Evans, not only another ex-Beatles road-manager but 'one of the greatest roadies the world has ever known.' He found himself working on setting up the day-to-day running of the vague concept the Fabs had dreamed up while staying in India. Peter Brown, 'who, like me', recalls Alistair Taylor, 'had been a shop assistant in Liverpool selling records', found himself 'running a multi-million dollar company.'

Others, including NEMS 'Mr Fixit' Alistair Taylor himself – on his own estimation, 'a glorified accountant with some management experience' – alongside Liverpudlian telephonist Laurie mccaffrey, defected from NEMS to the new enterprise. Alistair recalls, 'after Brian died, Apple started to expand into music publishing, signing new artists, sponsoring inventors, and generally putting into practice the principle of making business fun. Business at NEMS wasn't fun at all, so a phone call from John a few days ago was very welcome. "Hello Alistair. You're looking a bit pissed off at NEMS recently." "I am, really. All the infighting is getting to me." "Well, would you like to come and be General Manager of Apple?" I didn't need a second invitation. I've given my notice to NEMS and I'll transfer to Apple as soon as I can…'

There's a playful photograph taken in the Apple Corp office by the *Observer*'s celebrated Jane Brown, of John Lennon sitting in a swivel chair with the staff ranged out behind him. Denis O'Dell, who had worked on *A Hard Day's Night* and *Magical Mystery Tour*, is perched on the window-ledge, his tie loosely knotted, his hair slicked back into a near-fifties quiff. Alexis 'Magic Alex' Mardas stands with his arms folded, in a fringe of hair and floral shirt. Ron Kass, the American head of Apple Music poached from Liberty Records, wears an efficient business suit. Neil Aspinall, sits a little dishevelled extreme right in the shot, holding a smouldering cigarette. Pete Brown sits largely eclipsed by John. Derek Taylor sits at John's feet, just to his right. John – in his granny glasses and playful smirk – has his hand extended to rest lightly on Derek's forehead. The photo reveals much about what's going on. The general informality of the office arrangement. The mix of 'suits' and 'hip'. John's centrality to it all, and his implied affectionate ownership of his long-suffering press officer, while Derek smiles indulgently, going along with the amusing jape.

So what exactly was Derek's intended function in this spreading organisation? He 'discussed being given the designation "Office Eccentric" with Paul McCartney'. Quite to Derek's surprise, Paul agreed, and even instructed him to have an appropriate sign made for his office door. Sadly, like so many of the promises that were bounced around the Wigmore Street office during that time, it was another open-ended promise to unkeep. Instead, roles evolved haphazardly, 'we each found work to do, and from each other we took work, and to each other we gave work, and thus we found the very work we liked doing best.'

As part of the process, Derek moved into 'a slim shoebox of a room' in Wigmore Street and immediately set to attempting to bring order to the accumulating chaos. He simply 'introduced people to other people, and inside six months we had quite a salon, a self-propagating, self-perpetrating salon of fun and games in the press office.' Throughout his time at Apple, Derek worked with four secretaries, including Carol – 'number one secretary' – who was already there when he arrived, and was still there when he finally left. In November 1968 Derek hired Mavis to help out the press office as his assistant. She later became Mrs Mavis Smith and eventually left for contented domesticity. There was Frankie Hart, who later became Grateful Dead Bob Weir's girlfriend and George's assistant. Plus a former model called Sally, Sylvia, a temp who stayed three years... and the 'House Hippie' – hired as a kind of 'office assistant' for £10 a week, augmented by whatever else he could blag.

The 'House Hippie' turned out to be twenty-two-year-old American Richard DiLello, with 'his hair like a huge hedgehog.' He'd known of Derek Taylor from his 'Hollywood days' when 'everybody knew Derek'. And, arriving in London, he recognised him from a photo at the head of a music paper feature announcing the launch of this thing called 'Apple'. To Richard, it seemed that 'he looked like he was walking right out of the paper.' So, according to his amusing *The Longest Cocktail Party*, he simply went and asked him for a job. A photo in the book shows Derek moustachioed with straggled shoulder-length hair. According to Richard's introduction, Derek not only told him to 'come in next Monday and start work,' but sorted out Home Office work permit problems with a single 'phone call of ingenious obfuscation and convoluted logic. When asked what his job description would be he specified 'House Hippie', a designation becoming fashionable in Beverly Hills.

That also meant, in Apple terms, that Richard was 'a one-man Gallop-Poll' with a direct line to the brand's most lucrative American market. Derek himself admits that 'jumping this generation gap is a very strenuous ordeal.' He, after all, had a wife and five children he went home to every night. More practically, Derek set Richard filing Beatles documents under a variety of sub-categories. For Richard – paraphrasing Charles Dickens' *A Tale of Two Cities*, 1968 'was the best of times and it was the best of times.' To Derek, Richard joined Apple as an office boy, and 'left as an apathetic wreck.' For a while, Richard's friend and co-conspirator Stocky mcmullen was also at Apple. Finally, a girl called Dicken turned up with a donkey intended as a gift, both ended up with Derek and Joan helping out with the children.

'Wigmore Street was really awful', Derek recalls, 'we were forever getting stoned in the evenings and finding ourselves locked in by those people whose delight is in locking and bolting doors.' Instead, he heard of plans to relocate to Savile Row, 'a street which believed itself to be awfully important.' So 'I went over to Savile Row one morning, and never returned to Wigmore Street.' The new property was bigger, it consisted of five floors with lots of nooks, crannies and warrens of lengthy *Shining*-like corridors, replete with well-worn carpets and inappropriate wallpaper, plus a basement where Magic Alex built a studio, then ripped it out and built another. As first in, Derek claimed the main ground-floor office which he occupied before relinquishing it to Ron Kass, who later moved out to make way for John Lennon's inspired madness. By then Derek had moved up to the second floor, with Neil and Peter Brown already established on the first. 'I got the job because old colleagues on the press started to ring me up saying "Come on, we know you're in there." And I'd say "I'm not the Press Officer. He's in the other room." So they'd say "you can't give us that."' George Harrison adds, 'we all benefited when Derek got that position' because before his arrival 'the Press Officer we had was useless.'

Having been a pressman himself, Derek 'knew their needs'. 'I have always believed that offices should be as much fun to visit as to work in. What is this life if, full of files, an office has no time for smiles and lines of friends for miles and miles...?' The Beatles 'trusted his ability not to sacrifice us to them. I think it worked quite well.' Despite the confused designations, Derek's desk had a sign saying simply 'Sgt DW Taylor'. And a phone – Apple tel: 486-1922. The financial arrangements were highly fluid. Derek's experience and his range of clients made him one of the industry's premier publicists, so his £115-a-week was considered pointedly average, even for the time. Although he also received a cannabis-infused birthday cake specially prepared in the Apple kitchen. Writer Hunter Davies happened to visit. A bored John Lennon was slumped in his office. So he called in on Derek, where what he calls 'a Debbie-looking girl' brought in a steaming ginger-cake fresh from the oven, which she'd just baked, saying it was Derek's birthday. It was so delicious Davies had two slices. Then they went out for lunch – and Davies found himself feeling decidedly strange! It was only then he discovered he'd eaten hash-cake, his first and only experience with drugs.

John Kosh, twenty-three-year-old London artist and designer, 'looking back on it, Apple's fees were ridiculously low, but you didn't need much money in those days. We would sometimes get paid in substances, though I don't know how it was channelled. None of the suits and ties ever got an idea of what was going on. But wherever we went, we went first class. Apple sent me to New York for six months and I lived off the fat of the land – all paid by Apple' (in Stefan Granados' book *Those Were the Days*, 2002).

Anachronistically, The Beatles were still officially represented by NEMS. Which meant that Derek's brief as PR related specifically to Apple, its artists and projects. But journalists hunting for exclusive Beatles access soon discovered where the 'boys' interests really lay. A call to Tony Barrow at NEMS, despite his skills and track record, might yield negative results. Whereas a call to Derek Taylor at Apple, supposedly inquiring about the label's latest protégé, usually hit the hot-button. The 'boys' were only too eager to discuss these spin-off projects with the press, rather than delve into whatever The Beatles were, or were not supposed to be doing. Apple became a vehicle for their own more eccentric records – George's sitar-orientated *Wonderwall* soundtrack (November 1968). And John's work with Yoko Ono on *The Wedding Album* (May 1969) or *Unfinished Music, No.1: Two Virgins* (November 1968). Recorded the night John and Yoko consummated their relationship, the latter proved to be almost unlistenable. Rather than rock, or anything to do with the earlier Beatles work, these albums were very much a continuation of Yoko's art. After all, before she became Mrs Lennon, Yoko was already internationally famous as a conceptual artist. That's how the pair had first met, when John visited one of her exhibitions at the Indica gallery.

By now Derek was acting in what he described as an 'action-reaction' role. Never quite knowing what new weirdness awaited as he passed through Apple's massive oak doors. Opening his desk-draw one morning he discovered sets of black-and-white eight-by-ten photo-prints of the naked John and Yoko – taken by John with a delayed-action shutter. When the front cover of *Two Virgins* consists of one of those same glossies of the duo full-frontally nude, EMI refused to even handle it, and it was distributed by Track, the Who's label. Even then it had to be concealed in a tasteful paper bag. Although this had nothing to do with the 'bagism' that John and Yoko later espoused. That began with their first Plastic Ono Band singles, which came through Apple.

During this time Derek assisted John and Yoko in their peace campaign, becoming, in effect, their propaganda minister. 'I was sort-of controlling a big People Theatre' helping to spread their message to the world's media. As John wrote it, he and Yoko were detained at Southampton by immigration and weren't allowed onboard due to visa problems resulting from drug charges. With John and 'Mrs Yoko Ono Cox' having been fined twenty-guineas at Marleybone Magistrates Court for possession of 219 grains (half-an-ounce) of cannabis, just as they'd completed recordings for *The White Album*. So instead, they 'drove from Paris to the Amsterdam Hilton, talking in our beds for a week, the newspaper said, "Say what you doing in bed?" I said, "We're only trying to get us some peace."' Derek was the man standing next to John and Yoko – 'looking like two gurus in drag', at that Amsterdam Hilton part-honeymoon part performance-art event, directing the press conference. It had become Derek's task to deflect the outraged press.

John and Yoko had formed Bag Productions, a joint company intended to funnel their creative energy into the public domain. Packed into tin-trunks, they were accompanied by the incredibly complex material they needed, films, books, records, miles of tape, clothes for a thousand occasions, white tail-coats, white top hats, black leather suits, tennis shoes, boots, fur-coats, acorns for peace, 'anything the everyday traveller would need to cope with the worst extremities of the equator, both poles and Manhattan, a concert at Madison Square Garden and a visit to the White House.' Together it constituted 'the biggest personal equipment consignment since lend-lease.' Derek was also there at the Montreal Queen Elizabeth Hotel during their eight-day stop-over during May 1969. John and Yoko, with her daughter Kyoko Cox, and their new assistant Tony Fawcett.

The story began in Manzi's Seafood Restaurant on Leicester Street. Derek and Joan were there with John and Yoko, George and Patti, Terry Doran, Pete Swettenham from Grapefruit, and Pete Shotton, when John passed a note down the table. Would all present care to travel together to the US aboard the Cunard superliner *Queen Elizabeth II*? Yes they would. There were three weeks to go, with complicated visa applications. Allan Klein, by then their new American business manager, made initial approaches in Washington. Peter Brown made appropriate noises to the US Embassy in Grosvenor Square. *The Daily Express* got wind of the planned expedition, and speculated about it, wrongly suggesting George and Patti would be joining – no, they were busy house-hunting in Gloucestershire. But Ringo and Maureen, with children Zak and Jason, had booked starboard stateroom 2081, one deck below John and Yoko's intended suite 1050.

And there were other recruits. From Ringo's new movie *The Magic Christian* (December 1969), there was the star, Peter Sellers and his daughter Victoria, director and producer Joe McGrath and Denis O'Dell with their respective wives, plus Terry Southern, writer of the original novel on which the movie was based. Tony Palmer, pop journalist and film documentarian would also be on board. All in all, 'a very bright warm scene, old friends and new, free under god's sky for five wondrous twenty-five-hour days (you gain an hour a day on the Atlantic run, westbound)'. Mal was with John and Yoko in Weybridge, rounding up the final bits and pieces while John, optimistically, was invited to the US Embassy for an interview with an official.

Embarcation day arrived. At 10am the Mercedes called to pick up Derek and Joan. They saw the four elder children off to school, said goodbye to Joan's mother, and set off. They linked with Mal, with an Apple van trucking the luggage and film equipment. The A30 London Road convoy was joined by John and Yoko in the white rolls around Camberley. John had an amplification system wired into the car, so he could greet his fellow travellers as they drove. But first, they pulled into a car park near Basingstoke for an update. The visas hadn't arrived, leaving more than a sneaking suspicion that US immigration authorities were deliberately dragging their heels, using the 18 October 1968 drug-charges as a politically motivated pretext to obstruct the Lennon's taking up residence in the States, 'what chance has fun in the face of authority?' John and Yoko stayed over in the tea-shop to make last-minute calls, 'but you go ahead, have a good time.' 'Have another honeymoon' suggested Yoko.

The version of the story that survives in the song, 'standing on the dock at Southampton', was largely reconstructed when they made the promo film. Instead, they returned to Apple. There was talk of maybe joining the ship at Le Havre. From where they headed out to Heathrow instead and boarded a BOAC flight to the Bahamas, then flew to Toronto where, after being detained for two hours at the airport, they were finally admitted. Not the USA, but by default, close enough. Meanwhile, Derek and Joan, with Ringo, Peter Sellers and their wives, sailed at 12:30, lunchtime. The Beatle-spotting crew were disappointed by John's absence, cheered by Ringo's presence, and confused to discover that rooms booked under the Aspinall name were intended for the Taylors. They stopped off at Le Harve, still no Lennon's, 'it didn't seem fair, it didn't seem fair', then they were surrounded by the calm sea of green, Atlantic-crossing within the Hiltonian luxury of a floating pleasure palace, their friends were all aboard – most of them anyway. Designed for two-thousand passengers, there were 620 people aboard, 'alive and well and all at sea.' Ringo was a little inebriated the first evening after enjoying champagne with the lavish meal, so Derek and Joan took advantage of the darkened discotheque where the Applejacks were playing, a group who, as Derek recalled, had made their chart breakthrough with The Beatles song 'Like Dreamers Do'. They also took in the Ronnie Carroll floor-show.

Just seven years since the young *Daily Express* columnist had holidayed on the Isle of Man beach, the splendid floating hotel resort was a highpoint in a decade of highpoints. Derek took photos of John and Yoko's empty beds, anticipating a cover for their next art-concept album consisting of 'nothing but the sound of a heavy sea running.' Heavy seas duly arrived by the weekend. Ringo premiered the new Beatles album in the disco. Fortified by seasickness tablets, Peter Sellers, Tony Palmer, Denis O'Dell, Joe McGrath, Ringo, Maureen, Joan, Derek and Dominic were invited to meet the officers in the Ward Room high in the swaying upper decks. Recovering from his sickness, Ringo met the captain. Peter Sellers toured the engine room. Zak, Jason and Dominic played in one of the best nurseries in the world. The 'gang' discoed and drank too much. They spoke to John on the phone. He asked if Derek had written a feature about it for *The Beatles Book* – 'Yes', he lied. So he wrote about it and telexed it through to Apple's newly installed telex system in Savile Row.

Eventually, with John and Yoko checking in at midnight on 26 May suffering from heat, marijuana and jet-lag, the party reconvened in Suite 1742 on the nineteenth floor of Montreal's elegant Fairmont

Queen Elizabeth Hotel, and the media circus of the week-long 'Bed-Peace 2' commenced. Lying in bed with Kyoko crawling around beneath the covers, John and Yoko spoke to 150 press-people daily, and called in excess of 350 American radio stations to 'talk peace'. Derek, with moustache and neatly knotted tie, is there in the wealth of photographs taken in the hotel bedroom. John and Yoko, in bed, listening as Timothy Leary leans across to stress a point, while Derek sits between them with a bemused expression on his face. He's there in Steve Gebhardt's film *Imagine* (1971) which splices sequences of the event, as sardonic ultra-conservative comics-artist Al Capp – the writer for *Li'l Abner* – continually attacks and insults John and Yoko to their faces. 'I'm a dreadful Neanderthal fascist', he announced, entering the room in a suit and tie, 'how do you do?' Originally a libertarian, Capp was by then using the sarcastic vitriol of his humour to taunt what he saw as the excesses of the counterculture, caricaturing Joan Baez as 'Jonie Phoney', and denouncing the 'famous freaks' for perpetrating nothing more than a publicity stunt gimmick. Brandishing a sheaf of the naked John and Yoko photos while stabbing the air with his finger, he congratulates them 'now the world knows what your private parts looks like' with an air of amused contempt. Until Derek felt it necessary to intervene.

Later, intent on creating his own 'We Shall Overcome' anthem for the peace movement, John used a four-track Ampex tape-recorder in the bedroom. Yoko pounded out the rhythm with her shoe on the wardrobe, with Tim and Rosemary Leary, Tommy Smothers, Petula Clark, Murray the K, Dick Gregory... and Derek, singing along and bashing a tambourine. He's clearly visible in the pre-video promo-clip of the instant audio-verité single that climbs the charts on both sides of the Atlantic. He's forever enshrined in song when John rhymes 'Derek Taylor' with 'Norman Mailer' in 'Give Peace A Chance'. Derek 'was very committed to John and Yoko things', and despite talk about Yoko's intrusion portending the end of The Beatles, he considered their December 1969 *Live Peace in Toronto* album as 'not the end of anything'. Recorded with a pick-up Plastic Ono Band consisting of Eric Clapton, Klaus Voorman and drummer Alan White, the album of old rock 'n' roll songs bears the cryptic Derek Taylor quote, 'Being born in Scotland carried with it certain responsibilities'! Within the charmed Beatles circle, social conscience and individual indulgence go hand-in-hand without any apparent qualms of conscience. It seemed entirely reasonable to have it more than both ways. Pleasure and progress were less contradictions, than a route-map.

The perceived Yoko-induced rift spread beyond the immediate group, and across Apple itself. Derek remarked, 'I know John thinks we hate Yoko and that we're all a bunch of two-faced fuckers running around behind his back snivelling and bad-mouthing her, sticking pins in our home-made Yoko Ono voodoo dolls, but that's not happening at all. No-one in this building hates her. Hate! That's a very strong accusation and an extreme assumption. I can't say as I blame him for thinking that sometimes, but the reason he feels that way is because we don't love her!'. For John – as in the johnandyoko image-sequence of their faces morphing into each other – when it came to Yoko, there could be no neutral position.

And within the Apple organisation, there was a wealth of secrets going back to the earliest days of Beatlemania, what Derek calls 'all of those plays-within-the-play'. Grudges and schisms posed immense risks of exposure. That very little of it ever escaped into the public domain is proof that loyalty was a stronger binding element. Nevertheless, 'I sometimes think the people closest to them are the people The Beatles resent most. We were so adjacent to the truth, to the money, so near the fame and success and all that glamglitzscreamcheer, we got to look like courtiers covered in gold dust. Did they ever think "Goddamn them! Who do they think they are? Who needs them? We are The Beatles, we are the four"!'

To Richard DiLello, The Beatles were sometimes 'out of touch with the universe outside of their own universe.' Yet John was sufficiently in touch to be wary about the release of The Beatles' single 'The Ballad of John and Yoko' – because of potential radio-play problems over its 'Christ, you know it ain't easy' lyric. His fingers had been burned by the 'bigger than Jesus' debacle. He instructed publicist Tony Bramwell to downplay pre-publicity accordingly. As part of another John and Yoko project, the staff and Apple hangers-on were dispatched to scour the parks and gardens for acorns – the 'fifty acorns tied in a sack' to mail out to world leaders. Then Derek gave DiLello a card with the address of the Robert Fraser Gallery on it. It was his assigned task to inflate and release five-hundred white balloons for the opening of Yoko's art exhibition. Each liberated helium-filled balloon carried a tag inviting the finder to write to John. The response was mixed. Some of it racial or obscenely sexual, aimed at Yoko. Until, as Derek concedes, the press just got 'John and Yoko fatigue'.

There was a growing antagonism to the new weirdness in the press, which was high on the drug of outrage, shooting up on the latest revelations. The Beatles were no longer the loveable mop-tops they'd all taken to their hearts. Derek arrived for the *Yellow Submarine* movie-launch party looking killer-diller, he was flamboyantly wearing an Apple boutique frock-coat, black-and-white shoes, a big ruffled shirt and a silk scarf set off by button-badges. In the press-scrum, he noticed a former *Daily Mirror* colleague, crime reporter Eddie Laxton. Not wanting Eddie to think he was being stand-offish he went across, 'Hello Eddie, you know me.' 'No, I don't, I don't know this new guy at all.' The fact that Derek later tells this story against himself shows that there was an awareness that the craziness was out of control.

Released in December 1968, the original *Yellow Submarine* soundtrack album – since reissued on CD with an entirely revised track-listing, includes only four new songs, Paul's catchy singalong 'All Together Now', John's 'Hey, Bulldog', and two from George, the satiric 'Only A Northern Song' remaindered from the *Sgt. Pepper* sessions, and the stunning psychedelic masterpiece 'It's All Too Much'. They would have made a fine EP. But, announced as 'Selections By The Beatles Plus Original Film Music', and repaying their debt to George Martin by granting him equal billing, the rest of the playing-time consists of George's soundtrack incidental music for 'Pepperland', 'Sea of Time' and 'March of the Meanies'.

In much the same pick-up spatchcock spirit, even the sleeve-notes that Derek contrived utilise a review of the *White Album* from *The Observer*, with only the slightest of introductory lines from Derek himself. It served little purpose beyond gifting the journalist – Tony Palmer – with an unexpectedly huge audience, even though his work was reprinted on one of the few Beatles albums not to reach no.1, and even though the notes were replaced by a more creative cartoon-history of the 'Lonely Hearts Club Band' for the US edition. For Derek, you'd imagine, presented with the opportunity to contribute cover-text for a Beatles album, to write yourself into history… but of course, at the time, it was nothing of the sort. It was a big deal. The biggest. But it was for now, not for the historical record. There was no inkling that half-a-century later books would still be delving into the minutiae of liner-notes, or pop records at all. Derek, under relentless day-to-day pressure, was presented with a project. Sleeve-notes. He fulfilled the project. Job done. Next…?

The Beatles were always more than just a musical or sociological phenomenon. They were also an ongoing Soap Opera of media speculation concerning the shifting state of their amorous relationships. There was George, who met Pattie Boyd on the set of *A Hard Day's Night* and married her in 1966. It was at Patti's insistence that they first attended one of the Maharishi's lectures at the London Hilton, the 'Elvis of Enlightenment' igniting George's long-term interest in Indian music and spirituality. It was at their 'Kinfauns' home that Ayana Deva Angadi gave George his first sitar lesson, and provided the link, through the Asian Music Circle, to recruit the musicians for 'Love You To' and 'Within You Without You'. Moments that would cascade down through rock from the celebrity gathering in India to Ravi Shankar playing Monterey, from – possibly – the Byrds raga-scales for 'Eight Miles High' all the way to George's 'Concert For Bangla-Desh', to Live Aid and World Music. While Patti herself would become Eric Clapton's muse for 'Layla'.

The Maharishi – a self-assumed title – was far from the unsophisticated figure he presented himself as. College-educated, he packed a physics degree into his CV, he'd studied Sanskrit and learned scriptures under the guidance of Guru Dev. It was during the late 1950s that he recognised the potential of the gullible west for a mystical eastern sage. Beach Boy Mike Love – a long-term convert to TM (transcendental meditation) – accompanied The Beatles to Rishikesh. Donovan was there too. But to Ringo, the ashram was 'just like Butlins'. And to Lennon, the Yogi became 'Sexy Sadie' who fooled the world. But George's interest in all things Indian – 'musical, smellable, edible and spiritual' (according to Derek) – was long-term. Its philosophies provide the grounding his life-style needed. As Timothy Leary advised – but as few actually heeded – his LSD experiences were later confirmed in meditation.

Sometimes it seems the form of spirituality is less important than the moral structure it provides. For Cliff Richard, at his late-sixties lowest career-ebb, it was Billy Graham. For Bob Dylan, the desolation following his marriage breakdown chronicled on *Desire* (1976), was assuaged when he got God on his side. When Cat Stevens celebrity life-style hurtled dangerously out of control, he found Islam. For George, the Hindu cycle of reincarnation explained the conundrums thrown up by his spectacular and problematic fame, while relieving him of the awkward responsibilities of the suspect celebrity with which he'd never been at ease. Denuding him of the irksome sense of imposed importance so that what remained – glistening like a nugget of gold amid the silt – was a purity of thought and feeling that strengthened him to the end of his life.

And then there was Paul and Jane Asher, the perfect celebrity couple. The beautiful pair photographed together. The pop star and the waif-like mini-skirted English Rose, the auburn-haired Film Star from the

British movie aristocracy. They were there at the Maharishi's ashram together. Snapped together at Paul's brother Mike McGear's wedding in June. It seemed a given that they would also marry. All that was necessary was for them to announce the date.

But Tony Barrow relates an intriguing tale of how Derek Taylor was instrumental in Paul's subterfuge in bringing an end to these speculations (in his fine *John, Paul, George, Ringo & Me*). Paul had met Linda Eastman. A feisty American divorcee with a six-year-old daughter. This was where his destiny lay. But how to diplomatically extricate himself from his involvement with Jane, in a way that would not paint Linda as the temptress villain? Well, there was Francie Schwartz, a twenty-three-year-old American who'd turned up uninvited in London trying to hype Apple's interest in a movie-script she'd written. Paul wasn't interested in the movie and had no intention of supplying her with a soundtrack. But he inveigled Derek Taylor to take her onto the Apple staff anyway, creating a position for her as a publicity assistant in his press office. From there it was logical for her to be noticed at a couple of Abbey Road recording sessions. Until soon she'd graduated from her own Notting Hill pad to move in with Paul at his 7 Cavendish Avenue NW8 residence in St John's Wood. Inevitably, as Paul fully anticipated, Jane returned from an out-of-town theatre date to find Francie already in residence, and she was appropriately devastated. Too discrete to force a confrontation, sell her love-rat story to the tabloids or create an unseemly fuss, Jane simply removed herself to her parents' home. Having served her purpose Paul could now quietly dump Francie, leaving a tactful pause into which Linda could step unsullied by any past Beatles indiscretions.

John's relationships were equally chaotic. And Derek was as equally involved in them. John had met Yoko. The troubled state of his marriage to Cynthia was common knowledge, even before Yoko's arrival. After all, wasn't the strange symbolism of 'Norwegian Wood' about a furtive adulterous encounter? But after being informed of the Yoko 'situation' by Magic Alex, Cynthia realised this infatuation was different to his other infidelities, and filed for divorce on 22 August 1968, to become final on 8 November.

In the midst of it all, John had always nursed a fascination for Brigitte Bardot. Paul shared the infatuation and placed her at the top of his candidate list for the *Sgt. Pepper* cover collage. Brian Epstein had attempted to arrange a meeting between them during an earlier visit to Paris, which had never quite come together. In Alistair Taylor's *With The Beatles*, he recollects how Lennon had confided to him, 'I'd been

thinking about shagging Brigette Bardot ever since I was at school.'
John told a less sympathetic Albert Grossman how he had 'made love to
her countless times with a practised hand, lying on his bed.' John had
collected pin-ups of the actress from *Reveille* magazine as a kid, and
later attempted to re-make Cynthia by encouraging her to dress and
make-up into a Bardot facsimile. Now Bardot was visiting London, and
the opportunity was too good to miss.

John got Derek to organise a meeting. She was interested, and a date
was fixed up at the May Fair Hotel in Stratton Street, where she was
staying, up-market, yet discreet. Derek and John went together. Again
versions of what Goldman terms the 'farcical encounter' differ. In the
back of the cab, the Beatle overcompensates for his nervousness with
a 'dollop of the dreaded heaven-and-hell', washed down with alcohol.
In BBC-TV's *Lennon Naked* (June 2010), writer Robert Jones has a
wearily reluctant Derek – played by Michael Colgan – only grudgingly
doling out the LSD at John's insistence. At the hotel foyer Derek –
who spoke no French – phoned up to her suite. They were invited to
ascend. Bardot was not alone. Anticipating not one Beatle, but all four,
she'd taken the precaution of inviting her girlfriends. Conversation was
stilted. When finally faced by the embodiment of his teenage fantasies,
Lennon found himself uncharacteristically robbed of his usual verbosity.
And if he'd expected any 'shagging' to occur, the chemicals in his
system determined he was unable to 'rise to the occasion'. When she
suggests they adjourn to the swanky Parkes restaurant on Beauchamp
Place, her guests are less than enthusiastic, partially because of the
likelihood of unwanted press attention, so Bardot and her party go
out to eat anyway, leaving John and Derek tripping out of their brains.
Returning some considerable time later, Bardot found Derek still
crashed out on her counterpane. John managed to play guitar and sing
a little before the meeting dissolved.

For George Harrison, the defining crisis took on a different nature.
Derek was there with the 'Quiet Beatle' when George moved into
'Kinfauns', the Esher, Oxfordshire estate home he was to share with
Pattie, taking over 'this great neglected but not ruined Gothic pile, from
a handful of nuns and a segregated priest with a rude twinkle in his eye
and a broken arm. It was February, it was cold, and we had a cup of tea
in the library.' Derek was involved too when, on 12 March 1969 – the
day of Paul and Linda's wedding – the Drug Squad, led by Sergeant
Norman Pilcher, raid 'Kinfauns'.

George happened to be at Apple with Derek when Pattie calmly got
on the hotline and phoned to break the news. Derek immediately

contacted Martin Polden, a lawyer at Release. Soon after, George arrived home, with Derek in the limousine, to find ten Police cars and a Paddy-waggon already there. The couple were charged at Esher Police Station, from where they were released on Derek's surety. For Derek, George's personal indulgences were his own business and no concern of anyone else. 'Why cannabis is still illegal, I just don't know. Even in England, where we have less oppressive laws, there's still a very negative climate against it, and the Labour party, of which I'm a member, it's official policy is that it should remain illegal, though it is a class two drug.' To George, Derek was 'a real friend in need, always willing to share the downside. He was my bail when I got busted for possession of marijuana. A friend in need is the best policy. He's also like the rock of Gibraltar – he's got monkeys running all over him!'

Maybe the raid was part of a coordinated establishment clampdown on the unsettling extremism of the counter-culture? When police acted on an earlier tip-off from a *News of the World* snitch and raided Keith Richard's Sussex mansion, George had been there too. But the narc squad discretely waited for him to leave before making their move. They were out to get rock 'n' roll's bad boys. And the public still loved the Fabs. Now things were changing and the police were ready to go for pop's biggest coups. John's freedom to travel abroad was already compromised by ongoing drug complications.

Meanwhile, whenever the mood took him, Ringo would lean forward on the hard-backed Regency chair in his Apple office and play company director. For a while, he shrugged aside the disgusting realities of the half-eaten steak sandwich in the litterbin, the receptionist rolling a joint of the finest Afghan hash, the typist who counted paperclips while a single letter was spun out all morning – in the house-style of no punctuation marks! Then she popped out, not returning until the next day. A great light dawned. 'We had, like, a thousand people that weren't needed, but they all enjoyed it, they're all getting paid for sitting around. We had a guy there just to read the tarot cards, the I-Ching. It was craziness…' Other employees were charging clothes and food for their own use to Apple. It was a chaotic world populated by messed-up characters.

Derek sat surrounded by unwanted tapes, unwanted freeloaders and occasionally unwanted Hell's Angels. 'There was a general disposition to be nice to anyone who seemed to be on the trip', recalled Derek later, 'so if someone came in off the street with an idea and looked right and felt right and had a nice manner they would get money given to them. It was naïve, it was idealistic, but that's how it was.' Sometimes it worked. Derek answered the phone. It was a young graduate called Tony Palmer who claimed to have met John Lennon three years previous during a visit to the university. John had said to call him. So he was calling. A guesstimated four-hundred people a day used that line. Derek was perceptive enough to recognise that Tony Palmer was genuine, and forwarded the call. The result was Palmer directing The Beatles-centric pop-documentary *All My Loving* for BBC-TV (1968).

In another typically unpredictable incident, a young Richard Branson – then editing his college journal *Student* – walked in off the street to visit Derek in his ganja-filled third-floor office, hoping to solicit Beatles-exclusive material for a free flexi-disc give-away. Helpfully, Derek eventually acquired a tape of the sporadic heartbeat of John and Yoko's miscarried baby – later to be featured on their *Unfinished Music, No.2: Life With the Lyons* album (issued in May, side one consists of a free-form improvised gig recorded live at a March Cambridge concert, with Yoko's keening howls matched to John's feedback. Side two includes the five-minute in utero recording of John Ono Lennon II's heartbeat, with the sleeve-photo showing Yoko in the hospital bed, with John sitting on a mattress on the floor beside her). But the future Virgin entrepreneur was less than pleased with this hard-won exclusive, and threatened to sue Derek for 'breach of contract'! Derek assumed personal responsibility for whatever the financial outcome of the debacle, but the incident fizzled out inconclusively.

A visit from Kenny Everett helped cheer things, 'he used to come around to Apple and hang out on the sofa by my desk', Derek told the DJ's biographer David Lister. 'We smoked. He could rarely remember why he came. We would just prattle on. In that stressful atmosphere it was a great relief. Anyone was welcome for a drink and a smoke, provided they didn't insist on a recording contract. Kenny was particularly easy to get along with because he was unthreatening, and he was a Beatlemaniac. A genuine, unreconstructed Beatlemaniac.'

To the observer, to the informed insider, there was a wealth of such stories ripe for the writing, for the 'over and below-ground newspapers'. *The Guardian* commends Derek's own account of the period in *As Time Goes By*, as 'Taylor recounts his trip through this paradoxically gentle and ruthless empire in a funny, laconic, dignified tone of voice which marks him out as one of its nicer inhabitants.' Yet the book had a long-drawn-out gestation, begun while still at Apple in 1968. There was obviously a story to tell. People were suggesting 'you should write a book'. Derek was not convinced. Nevertheless, he was introduced to a Los Angeles literary agent, Mitchell Hamilburger, who proffered the assistance of Sylva Romano, who fixed a $2,500 advance from publishers Prentice-Hall that locked him into a contract. More later...

John Kosh recalls, 'I wasn't exactly staff, but I had an office. I started out on the ground floor in Ron Kass' old office, then I ended up on the third floor with Derek Taylor. They didn't have an art studio, we just had an office.' He contributed artwork for a projected *Get Back* album-sleeve and book. The projected album cover was to have included The Beatles older, hairier, 1969 recreation of their 1963 *Please Please Me* album-shot, which would instead later adorn their *The Beatles: 1967-1970* compilation. Although mixed, edited and compiled by Glyn Johns, the troublesome tapes were shelved. Some of the sprawling material would later be remixed as the *Let It Be* album, more of it was obviously salvaged from the *Let It Be* movie-sessions, some extracts of which were circulated in bootleg form. They provide a fascinating fly-on-the-wall glimpse into The Beatles' candid unguarded moments, even more so than the edited movie insights, revealing their inspired silliness, aimless strumming, tedium, a tendency to fall back on old fifties rockers to lighten things up, witty badinage and, emerging from it all, familiar tracks taking shape from sketches and scat fills.

There's a line in 'Get Back' about 'living in a Council flat'. Paul counts out the chords for a work-in-progress 'Let It Be' – 'C-G-A-F, it goes C-down-G, C-G-A-F, and again, then Bowm! Bowm!! Bowm!!! You'll get it, dead easy.' He lyric-fills with 'read the *Record Mirror*, let it be', then conducts the harmony-'ahhhs', enquiring 'who wants to take the one above?' There are playful run-throughs of 'She Came in Through the Bathroom Window' – Paul inviting 'once more with Felix!' When he sings the line 'got myself a steady job', John yells 'bloody 'bout time too if you ask me.' When he sings 'she tried her best to help me', John comments 'you bloody need it too.' Finally, Paul notes 'and this is something that happened to me quite recently.' On another take, he adopts a silly voice to add 'Hello, this is Tuesday, is that Paul? I'd like to have a word with you...'

Although, as in the film, Paul seems to be the most focussed guiding voice, it's the good-natured snapback humour that predominates. In the midst of a wordless phonetic 'House of the Rising Sun', Paul sings the line, 'and god, I know I'm one', with John instantly parrying 'he's one alright.' As it peters out John complains 'I don't want to do that any more', roaring 'Why don't you put it on the toast' to the tune of 'Why Don't We Do It in the Road' instead. After a group-harmony 'Across the Universe', with none of its eventual ethereal transcendence, and a raucous 'Don't Let Me Down', he complains 'come on, I've done all mine. Both of mine.' Then 'OK, straight into Boudicca.' Is that an unknown song? Because there's new material too. 'Give Tennessee Credit for Music' is yet another Carl Perkins song, the original B-side of Carl's 1956 single – Sun 235 – 'Sure to Fall', which they perform on The Beatles *Live at the Beeb* CD. In a curious celebration of rockabilly, John points out, via Carl's lyric, 'they made the first atomic bomb in Tennessee.' In a jam called 'Commonwealth', Paul sings it's 'much too wealthy for me', with John retorting 'much too common for me.' 'I would join the Common Market but it's much too common for me', agrees Paul.

There are also offensive in-jokes they could only get away with inside their enclosed world. When Paul reconfigures 'Get Back' into 'Don't dig no Pakistani's taking other people's jobs', it's difficult to accept it as a serious expression of his opinions, before he goes into a slow blues 'Enoch Powell'. In perspective, Britain's entry into the Common Market (European Union) was a contentious issue at the time, with Labour's George Brown and Conservative Shadow Chancellor Iain Macleod both debating the state of entry-negotiations in the press. And Paul's comments seem to be ironically referring, in much the same way, to the news-feed currents of racism stirred up by Enoch Powell's 'Rivers of Blood' speech – televised from the Birmingham Midland Hotel on 20 April 1968. Paul even sings 'Enoch Powell said to the folks, you'd better get back to your commonwealth homes' and 'Enoch Powell has had enough of coloured men.' In other words, he is satirising Powell's views, not expressing his own.

To contemporary sensitivities, such language, even tongue-in-cheek, remains seriously disturbing, inexcusable. There's even an instrumental work-out seemingly titled 'White Power', which surely must be interpreted in the same context. But irony is a dangerous tool, especially when viewed across decades. It's little mitigation to argue that those were different times. Months earlier they'd been in Rishikesh with the Maharishi. Without black American musicians, there would be no Beatles music. Lennon was already into his reforming relationship with Yoko, which would lead in a few short years to them being in New York City agitating support for Black Power. The humour – if such it can be termed – even as irony seems a reversion to the old barbed John who uses 'cripples' and 'Queer Jew' as comedic weapons, the old reconstructed John.

But from a different perspective, at the same time, yes, sensitivities were different. Such caricatures are part of the pervasive culture of comedy Asians caricatured in *Carry On Up the Khyber* (1968)... or

Help! Itself. Part of the Peter Sellers 'goodness gracious me' context of the comedic Indian doctor. Or Spike Milligan blacking-up as Asian immigrant Kevin O'Grady in ITV's 1969 sitcom 'Curry and Chips'. Later, a track titled 'Can You Dig It?' balances names at random that the group is invited to 'dig', both heroes and villains, Paul suggests Wilson Pickett, Cassius Clay (Muhammed Ali), Mary Whitehouse (anti-pornography clean-up campaigner), James Brown, Judy Garland, Dusty Springfield, Russ Conway, James Brown (again), Richard Nixon, Ronnie Corbett, The Incredible String Vest (sic), David Frost, Betty Grable, Clark Kent, Enid Blyton, Emperor Rosko (Radio One DJ), Gerald Nabarro (flamboyant Conservative politician) and Leonard Rossiter. From the extended Beatles family, there are namechecks for Peter Brown and John Junkin, and even listings for *Mersey Beat*'s Bill Harry, Quarryman Eric Griffiths and Tony Sheridan. John punches out an affirmative 'Get Off' at the end of each verse. There's just a chance the run-through of names contains the germ of the idea for Paul's 'Let 'Em In' – 'Martin Luther, Phil and Don, Brother Michael, Auntie Gin' – on his *Wings at the Speed of Sound* album (1976).

It was a massive failure of opportunity that Apple produced nothing of any lasting value, beyond The Beatles' records themselves. The first companies to be set up under its dayglo umbrella – founded in February 1968 – was Apple Films Ltd (under 45-year old Denis O'Dell whose Beatles-connections extends back as far as *A Hard Day's Night* and John's 1967 *How I Won The War*). George Harrison would eventually become involved with former Monty Pythons in the production of some classic Handmade Films. Derek and George watched the first BBC2 *Monty Python's Flying Circus* runs together, laughing until it felt like their heads were coming off, amazed at the visual-Goon invention. George met Eric Idle initially through the fame engendered by the Pythons in 1975, when their struggle with the burden of their respective group legacies – George with the Fabs, Eric with the Python group – formed a clear bond between them, which developed into a close friendship that has since been described as a 'love affair'.

First 'the incomparable larynx of the quiet one of the Fab Four' guested as a surreal Long John Silver on *Rutland Weekend Television*. Then, set up with American businessman Denis O'Brien, George stepped in when EMI failed to honour its support for *Monty Python's Life of Brian* (1979) – 'Sir George of Harrison heard about the project', as Michael Palin described it – which went on to become one of the year's highest grossing box-office attractions. When asked why he was prepared to provide financing, John Cleese relates how George simply responded, because 'I want to see the movie.' George even manages a cameo in the film. Handmade later picked up on another project deemed too excessive for EMI, and scored again with *The Long Good Friday* (1980). Other titles follow, with Derek coining bylines, including the imaginative Python-related fantasy *The Time Bandits* (1981), *Mona Lisa* (1986), *The Missionary* (1982) and *A Private Function* (1984). Derek and George were met in LA by John and Yoko during September 1980, for a collective trip to watch the Monty Python team live at the Hollywood Bowl. But all that would be a decade after the collapse of Apple.

There was Apple Publishing Company, set up to manage the manuscript-mounds that deluged in with each mail delivery. They were poured into 'The Black Room' – a twelve-foot by fifteen-foot adjunct to the 'talk-salon' playground that was the Press Office, where the ragbag scraps of poetry, sub-literary bumf and unread stories… remained. At least Paul Weller's *Riot Stories* produced some *December's Child* fanzine poetry. Apple produced… nothing of worth. All that was necessary was to invite someone in with anthology-experience to edit something together, perhaps with a few attention-grabbing John Lennon and Donovan verse, to draw on the immense freedoms of alternative press graphics and layout techniques. Derek recalls how such an opportunity was deliberately fudged when 'Tambi' arrived at Apple seeking funding for a monthly poetry journal. Meary James Thurairajah Tambituttu was a Tamil poet born in Sri Lanka when it was still called Ceylon. He had a track record of publishing modernist writing, with work by Henry Miller, Lawrence Durrell and Elizabeth Smart emerging through his imprints. Yet Derek avers, purposefully misdirects him. A low-cost high-yield chance of actually producing something of worth was frittered away. The talk of a spoken-word album-series showcasing Allen Ginsberg, William S Burroughs and Lord Buckley – tapping into the *IT*-underground Lit counter-culture, remained only talk. And Michael Horovitz was left to produce his definitive sixties anthology *Children of Albion* (1969) through less sympathetic mainstream publishers. 'It was getting extremely busy', remembers Derek. 'I had taken on too much, and to endeavour to enable people to get recording contracts and bring in paintings. We'll help you to get your paintings hung, we'll get your books and poems published, we'll get music recorded and all the promises that were made, which we were trying to fulfil.'

The first project to fail – as Denis O'Dell (in his book *At the Apple's Core*, 2002, Peter Owen Ltd) recalls, was Apple Electronics Ltd. Blonde, handsome, with a dazzling smile, Greek-born John 'Magic Alex' Mardas had been there during the Indian Maharishi sojourn, and had convinced The Beatles that all kinds of ideas and patents were possible, if only he were fed the financial backing. So a considerable amount of Beatles-revenue was pumped into the whole expensive business. 'If Alex Madras wasn't magic, then why was he called Magic Alex?', reasoned Derek. Yet not one of his fantastical impressively useless inventions were ever patented, or reached the market, despite Alex operating out of his research lab at 34 Boston Place for nearly three years. Contrast that with the genuine start-up pioneers at Stanford Research Institute (now SRI International) who were simultaneously demonstrating Doug Engelbart's network 'mouse'-operated computer system, making 9 December 1968 the 'dawn of interactive computing'. Meanwhile, Magic Alex did manage to fit the electronics to the Perspex columns used for the 'Give Peace A Chance' photo-shoots. And he managed an appearance – as himself – in *Magical Mystery Tour*. Yet it proved to be the shortest-lived and least rewarding of the Apple projects. By 1969, as Derek phrases it, 'Magic Alex was unmagicked'.

Then there was Apple Wholesale and Apple Retail... the boutiques in Baker Street and Chelsea's Kings Road, run by Apple Retail and Apple Tailoring respectively. The Baker Street store lasted a little longer, from December 1967 through to July 1968. It was stocked with weird and wonderful gear designed by 'The Fool'. The Fool had known for some time that The Beatles were looking to diversify, and Simon Posthuma and Marijke Koger, with Josje Leeger and Barry Finch, had previously run a boutique in Amsterdam known as The Trend. The Beatles were receptive to their ideas, and it was agreed that they would be employed to create designs exclusively for the boutique which, alongside garments, would also sell an assortment of Eastern nick-nacks, furniture, posters, and underground books.

But as Derek pointed out, in a different context, 'the thing they do best, the thing people follow best, is their music'. Asked to explain the 'Apple philosophy' in a September 1969 interview, George simply shrugged and passed the question over to Derek, who offered a typically rambling free-association definition. 'It's an organisation which has developed without anyone really planning it that way, as a service which exists to implement the whims of The Beatles, which fortunately often turn out to be very commercial. However, if they didn't, we'd still have to do it, and that's OK as well. That's the gig. The gig is not Apple, the gig is working for The Beatles. You come here and you work for The Beatles... It's nothing else, you know, and that's what it will ever be'.

And predictably, it was only Apple Records that actually generated revenue. Initially run by Ron Kass, alongside Peter Asher, who was given the A&R title. Distributed through Capitol in the Americas and EMI for the rest of the world, Apple Records was also a strangely directionless thing. There was no focus. No centre. The artists who appeared on the label had no unity or cohesion. Unlike, say 'Immediate' – launched by former Epstein-colleague Andrew Loog Oldham (with Tony Calder) on the back of his rolling Stones' percentage, with its nucleus of sharp Mod R&B overlaid with Spector ambience, Jimmy Page as house producer, all contributing towards its coherent identity. Immediate records were cult items then, and much sought-after highly collectable vinyl now, with the Small Faces, Poets, John Mayall's Bluesbreakers, Strangeloves, and the Fleur de Lys' 'Circles'. But for Apple, there was no quality-control filter. No guiding philosophy. Perhaps if Brian Epstein was still around? But even his impeccable instinct had atrophied, as the Michael Haslam project could testify. And the whole point of Apple, if it had a point at all, was to crawl out from under the NEMS security-blanket (even if that meant poaching some of its personnel) and assume complete artistic independence. Search for any unifying Apple Records theme or label philosophy, it's not there.

11 August 1968 was designated 'National Apple Week' for which Derek assembled a promotional press-pack for 'Our First Four' singles, leading off with 'Hey Jude' (which also retained the Parlophone designation R5722) – it effortlessly sold six million copies in its first four months. The record's confidence and ambition is breathtaking, it seemed effortless, its construction deceptively simple, but it's one of the pinnacles, not only of sixties pop, but of twentieth-century music. The other releases were 'Sour Milk Sea', a George Harrison song performed by Jackie Lomax (Apple 3), with George sponsoring his old Liverpool friend and former member of the Undertakers, who Brian Epstein had brought back from the States where he'd been fronting The Lomax Alliance.

Apple 4 was 'Thingumybob' by the Black Dyke Mills Band, with Mary Hopkin's 'Those Were the Days' (Apple 2) – which sold four million copies in its first four months. Mary was a pleasant pop-Folky singer Paul first spotted winning week-after-week on ITV's *Opportunity Knocks* – a kind of forerunner of the *X-Factor* hosted by the oleaginous Hughie Green, where she was competing against comedians, jugglers and the strange contortionist who flexed his muscles in tune to 'Wheels'. To Derek, the Welsh singer appeared to be 'fashioned in dew, freckled and shy and mini.' For her no.1 hit, Paul's commercial fine-tuning had her re-record 'Those Were the Days' in French, Italian, German and Spanish for the lucrative European market, then he selected the Byrds/Pete Seeger hit 'Turn! Turn! Turn!' for its B-side. He wrote her follow-up single, 'Goodbye', then set about recruiting new material for her debut album, which was padded out with contributions specially written by Donovan, plus some of Paul's flimsiest pop trifles. He even indulged his Busby Berkley 'Your Mother Should Know' fantasies by imposing 'There's No Business Like showbusiness' on her.

Then there was the Hari Krishna Temple, bizarrely but successfully elevated off the streets and into the charts with two singles. In Derek's words, 'now the latest whim is to take the world's worst minority religionists' cult in England – the Hare Krishnas, and get then a Top 30 record in ten days!' Issued as Apple 15, the 'Hare Krishna Mantra' climbed to no.12 (13 September 1969). Then an Apple Press Office release announced Apple 25 – 'Govinda'. 'We in the Press Office, as undersigned, are paying for an advertisement ourselves because we believe the record "Govinda" by the devotees of the Radha Krishna Temple, produced by George Harrison, to be the best record ever made! You too?' Well – perhaps not, but at least enough to shove the record as high as no.23 on the charts (28 March 1970). When Apple issued an expanded CD-edition of *The Radha Krishna Temple* album (May 1993), Derek was responsible for the liner notes. When Bhangra archivists trace the growth of music-influences from the Indian sub-continent, they tend to go back as far as Monsoon, or rapper Apache Indian. Few extend any lasting significance to the 'Hari Krishna Mantra'. Yet it is inescapably there. Other record projects were less successful.

The 'House Hippie' also provides tantalising snapshots of the three Taylors – Derek and Alistair with James Taylor, the laconic singer rolling a cigarette with a glass of scotch in front of him, 'oblivious to all the dialogue bouncing off the walls.' In another of the diversionary circularities of which this history abounds, Peter Asher had brought James Taylor into the Apple family. As the bespectacled geek half of the Peter & Gordon duo, which – like Billy J Kramer with the Dakotas before them – had benefited from a stream of fresh Lennon-McCartney songs, something not entirely unconnected to the fact that Peter happened to be the brother of Paul's actress girlfriend, Jane Asher. Paul had written their first global no.1, 'A World Without Love', as early as 1958, nevertheless, the song made the winsome soft-core folkie twosome briefly, if massively, stars.

It was while touring America that Peter established a link-but-one to James Taylor through support-band The King Bees. Once the arc of Peter & Gordon hits ended, and Asher was back in London, James Taylor followed-up on a nudge from King Bee Danny Kortchmar, who had since joined Taylor's Flying Machine, with a phone call. Asher tipped off Paul and, as Apple's first non-British signing, the 'sharp-eyed' American songwriter 'made of bone and wire in North Carolina', was soon benefiting from the full Apple support infrastructure. A series of recordings at Trident Studios with Peter Asher commenced on 20 June 1968, including 'Carolina on My Mind' – with both George and Paul contributing – and 'Something In the Way She Moves' – with George taking lyric notes. Only for Taylor's eponymous album to languish in Apple's follow-through neglect as The Beatles moved on to newer enthusiasms. It was necessary for the heroin-addicted James Taylor to leave London behind before he achieved any level of commercial recognition. He would eventually go to Warners (as would Derek), where he would re-connect with Asher for *Sweet Baby James* (February 1970) and somnambulistic celebrity.

Other signings included the Modern Jazz Quartet. For the MJQ, appearing on Apple must have constituted a curiously eccentric moment amid a long career. Then there were the Iveys, discovered by Mal Evans. There's a story about Derek expressing his disbelief over an Ivey's photo-session – 'what's Mal doing putting them in those fucking suits? Suits!!! It's 1968, man!' Ken Mansfield, US head of Apple, recalls the very high hopes they had for breaking the Iveys in America, 'I believed in "Maybe Tomorrow" so much that I had 450,000 copies pressed up. We came out full blast, had radio play and acceptance from the stations, but we ended probably selling 200,000 copies.'

There was also a group called Trash who – with some contrivance from Derek – acquired a pre-release *Abbey Road* tape. According to group member Fraser Watson, Derek 'sneaked into Neil Aspinall's office, stole his acetate, and gave it to us.' The group selected the 'Golden Slumbers / Carry That Weight' sequence to cover while Derek arranged for them to take advantage of some unused studio-time George had booked but neglected to turn up for, and they cut their own version. Paul initially vetoed its release on Apple, but John was more conciliatory, Yoko reported back to Derek that he said 'yes'. Issued as Apple 17, the record charted for just three weeks and got no higher than no.35, on 8 November 1969. Discouraged, Trash split up soon after. But there were always other bands. Although only signed to Apple through a song-publishing deal, Fire's 'My Father's Name is Dad' received the full weight of Paul's active support. Allegedly, Kenny Everett took a threatening phone call from the Apple press office to the effect that if he didn't give the single radio exposure John Lennon would never speak to him again!

Derek took calls too. He even got one, at five in the morning, from his former client, Captain Beefheart. 'Hey man, will Apple sign me up? I can't stand these people who own us. Their heads are so small man, forget it.' Apple declined to take up the offer.

Whatever, why worry? If the object was – as Derek playfully phrased it – 'to give money away as fast as we could,' new revenue cash-flows deluged in whenever a new Beatles record emerged. The group had withdrawn from day-to-day events at Apple between May to October 1968, during the recording of *The White Album*, leaving Derek to 'ring-master the circus.' Beatles sessions had always been augmented, particularly since *Revolver* with Alan Civil's French Horn added to Paul's 'For No One', and George's 'Love You To', the first song he deliberately wrote for sitar, with Anil Bhagwat's tabla. But never so much as here. 'The Continuing Story of Bungalow Bill' – written by John at Peter Asher's home in Newdigate, Derek's sometime residence – provided Yoko's first contribution to a Beatles track. For 'Happiness Is a Warm Gun' Derek, John, Neil and Pete Shotton were sitting together in Dorking, free-associating surreal images.

The initial spark had come from Charles Schulz' *Peanuts* strip 'Happiness Is a Warm Puppy', which became a much-parodied slogan. George Martin playfully showed John the cover of an American gun-magazine which ran a teasing subheading 'Happiness Is A Warm Gun'. John picked up the implied challenge. During the first song-section, Derek threw in ideas. It was Derek who suggested the line 'she's not a girl who misses much', which was a favourite saying of his mother's. The 'touch of the velvet glove' line also came from Derek's anecdote about the shifty Manxman they'd met while holidaying in the Carrick Bay Hotel, the man who enjoyed wearing moleskin gloves during sex. Then there was a newspaper report about a Manchester City fan arrested by police for wearing mirrors on his shoes enabling him to voyeuristically peek up girl's dresses. The 'lizard on the window-pane' was something Derek had seen during his LA years. Ideas were thrown in, John reworked them into lyrics. 'it was like a whole mess of colour', Derek concludes.

George wrote 'Savoy Shuffle' while sharing a box of 'Good News' chocolates with Eric Clapton, the line 'you'll have to have them all pulled out' refers to Clapton's diseased teeth, a condition exacerbated by his munchie chocolate habit! When George was stuck for words, Derek provided 'you know that what you eat you are', lifting the line from a short film by his Monterey friend Alan Pariser. The finished song was covered by Ella Fitzgerald for her Reprise album *Ella* (1969), recorded during her May 26-29 sessions at the Olympia Studios, while The Beatles were elsewhere recording *Abbey Road*. The overlapping tape collages that make up 'Revolution no.9' includes 'sampled' conservations in which Derek can be heard apologising to George Martin for not having brought a bottle of Chablis. Elsewhere, on an out-take version of 'I'm So Tired', John throws in an improvised aside, 'I'll give you everything I've got, Derek', presumably aimed at the Apple press officer.

John's 'Glass Onion' draws on Paul's lyrical mythology of 'Lady Madonna' and 'The Fool on the Hill'. And if the 'Walrus was Paul' then – as a status report on the Fab Two, 'you know that we're as close as can be.' While, as a reaction to the complexity of what had gone before, reacting away from the surreal-absurdism of 'I Am The Walrus', John strips his lyrics down to their most basic expression for 'Don't Let Me Down'. Ungrammatical, barely literate 'she done me, she done me good', it became his most naked Beatles song, with a pleading that starkly reveals the emotional fragility and fear of desertion behind the hard-man mask. The post-Byrds duo Dillard & Clark did an intriguingly melodic cover of the song, drawing out some of its vulnerability even further. Outside of The Beatles, John was deconstructing his music further, into the wordless primal howl of withdrawal pain on the Plastic Ono Band's 'Cold Turkey', and the avant-garde minimalism of the *Unfinished Music* albums.

This is the origins of what Derek termed his 'hard-hatted post-Beatles myth-demolition mode' that would reach its most direct expression – 'don't believe in Beatles', on the *John Lennon / Plastic Ono Band* (December 1970) album. But within the group, there was a more generalised 'get back to where you once belonged' theme in the air. If Punk was to be a levelling-down counter-revolution to the grandiose pomposity that Prog-rock had become, then The Beatles 'Get Back' records surely anticipate that moment. Reasserting the basic virtues of their simpler pre-*Sgt. Pepper* days, lubricated with added confidence and daring. George came up with an effective rocker 'Old Brown Shoe', while Paul looked back as far as Humphrey Lyttelton's 'Bad Penny Blues' to lift its piano-riff intact for 'Lady Madonna'. There were studios in Apple's Savile Road basement, lashed-up by George Martin. And when there were tensions, Derek was there when Billy Preston was called in, to lighten the atmosphere. He was also there when Phil Spector arrived.

Abbey Road (1969) is officially The Beatles' recorded swansong, reflecting the growing rift between McCartney and Lennon. It proved that The Beatles as a collaborative unit were over. While ironically it made for some of the most beautiful and harmonically accomplished music of their career. Ringo comments that 'as people we weren't that close, but musically we were still very close.' Yes, even with separate ambitions, fragmentations, sulks and grudges, they can still blend their harmonies into the perfect fusion that is 'Because', where individual voices dissolve into the most immaculate synthesis of their career. It carries all the interweaving beauty they'd invested in 'Here, There and Everywhere', with the added poignancy that such moments of closeness were by now becoming so infrequent. Side one is the most varied. Lennon re-asserts his rock 'n' roll credentials with the gritty 'Come Together', and George finally comes into his own as a songwriter with two of the album's highlights, the soulful ballad 'Something' (Frank Sinatra's favourite Beatles song), and the hopeful folk tune 'Here Comes the Sun'.

Even Ringo gets a piece of writer action with the nursery-rhyme tale of 'Octopus's Garden', taking its cue from the whimsical maritime mood of 'Yellow Submarine'. Although he'd felt slighted by Phil Spector's involvement in the *Let It Be* project, George Martin was reluctantly lured back into the producer's chair. But McCartney's influence looms larger than any of them, and he dominates on tracks like 'You Never Give Me Your Money' and the extended suite they call 'the long one' that forms side two of the original vinyl album, introducing characters such as the 'Sun King', 'Mean Mr Mustard' and 'Polythene Pam' – in which Lennon celebrates a polythene-eating 'Pat' from the group's Liverpool days. If Brian Wilson structured 'Good Vibrations' into the failed ambitions of the *Smile* suite with premeditated calculation, the second side of *Abbey Road* gives the impression of being a collage of failed songs, incomplete fragments of choruses without songs, middle-eights without development, strung into continuity – one suspects, by Paul in his determination to complete the final album. Yet if they are fragments – WHAT fragments!

The evocative, melodic 'Golden Slumbers' sets up the glorious finale, 'Carry That Weight' neatly sums up The Beatles' career in a burst of call-and-response guitar solos before wrapping up on the appropriately titled 'The End' (a 'hidden' final track 'Her Majesty', originally intended to be sequenced between 'Mean Mr Mustard' and 'Polythene Pam', was instead tacked on as a teasing after-thought). The iconic cover-shot of the four Beatles walking across the road, away from the studio that gave the album its title, says it all.

Derek had to deal with the 'Paul Is Dead' rumours that came in the wake of that cover-photo. The lavishly-illustrated *The Beatles Anthology* reproduces a telegram dated 13.11.69 addressed 'Derek Taylor' reporting that 'German journalists have picked up rumour from States that Paul McCartney is dead' and requesting clarification. Derek's teasing contrary strategy was to confirm that – yes, the rumour was true, admit it, on the basis that whatever official statement is made, the opposite would be believed!

In this way, almost uniquely among the freeloaders and wasters who accumulated under the Apple auspices, the Press Office had a clearly defined function with precise targets. Derek was there to promote the acts signed to the label, talking 'until his tongue was thick and red and swollen and sore with talking and explaining and setting the record straight.' Irish publicist BP Fallon sat watching Derek work, observing and learning PR techniques he'd later utilise for his role with Led Zeppelin and U2. First Derek was on the phone to *IT* talking about John and Yoko's acorn project, immediately afterwards he would be equally at ease and fluent talking to *Radio Times* about the sweater Mary Hopkin had worn on a TV show. He could relate to all those diverse people warmly and honestly, yet still be himself. Fallon's observation of what he calls this 'wonderful man' captures a truth.

The music industry machine had lost control. It didn't know how to react. When MGM signed the Mothers of Invention they didn't know, and couldn't understand what they were getting. They knew long-hair bands were selling. They needed a slice of that market. Warners signed Grateful Dead but were incapable of marketing them. Unlike today, the musicians were ahead of the game, the labels struggling to keep up with the changes. And there was a gulf of incomprehension between the corporate and hip mindsets. Derek's gift was that it was no effort for him to bridge that gulf, to speak to both mindsets, and translate one to the other.

Alive and well, Paul was only too keen to talk to the press about Mary Hopkin. Or about the Black Dyke Mills Band, who were another of his unlikely projects. Paul wrote 'Thingumybob' as the theme for a London Weekend Television show. It was Derek's suggestion that he acquire the services of the 'best band in the land' to perform it, who just happened to be in Bradford. At the time, Derek and Joan were still living at 'Laudate'. On Saturday morning, 29 June 1968, Derek put on a navy-blue pinstripe he'd bought at Paul's recommendation. He took a 'very modest 250-milligramme hit of LSD' and left in a fine black rolls to pick up Paul at St John's Wood, then collect Peter Asher and Tony Bramwell. Together, they motored north to Yorkshire.

Once checked into a hotel, Derek found time to contact a couple of
local press friends, including Alan Smith of the *New Musical Express*
who'd been working on *The Birkenhead News* at the time Derek had
been with the *Liverpool Daily Post*. Alan was by now married to the
Mavis who worked with Derek at Apple press. They had a few pints
together, before rejoining Paul at Bradford's Victoria Hall where the
Black Dyke Mills Band had assembled in full uniform, 09:00 Sunday
morning. Once the portable recording equipment was set up, they
began playing Paul's 'Thingumybob', conducted by Geoffrey Brand.
The recording completed, after leaving the Saltaire periphery of
Bradford the Apple party returned south. On the way home they
impulsively stopped off in Harrold – a small Bedfordshire village picked
at random from the AA book. After a detour for a meal at the invitation
of the local dentist, where Paul played guitar and sang a new song he'd
written that week – 'Hey Jude', the whole hamlet gathered in the village
pub where Paul entertained the locals at the piano, concluding with
'Fool on the Hill' while Peter and Derek looked on. As the weekend's
magical mystery tour wound down, Derek observed that 'the wizards
were producing this play by now.'

It wasn't always so magical. 'It was very easy sometimes and
sometimes it was very difficult,' in Derek's own words, 'when it was
easy I enjoyed doing it. When it was difficult I didn't enjoy doing it.' In
the psychedelic ambience of his press office, there was a light projector
– a gift from the Hare Krishna's, which cast scintillating coloured fluid-
shapes rippling across the wall and ceiling, creating an aquatic twilight.
Blurring truth and reality. Dilello relates how John Lennon once asked
him for a 'tanner', with Derek having to explain to the American that a
tanner was 'a sixpence, man!' That was a less stressful truth. Trouble is,
'once people know everything, they begin to invent,' and stories about
Apple proliferate, such as 'a man in a frock-coat with a basin full of pills,
and the guests were allowed to choose what stimulant or downer they
wanted.' An exaggeration, rather than a lie. Nevertheless, such tales have
anecdotal resonance. An early convert to LSD – 'Dr Leary's medicine' –
Derek was once reprimanded for holding a press conference at Apple
while tripping on acid. He joked that whereas others found god, he'd
taken LSD and 'found Piglet & Pooh & Mr Toad.'

His writing took on an increasingly tripped-out quality too. Paul
produced the album *McGough & McGear* (Parlophone, 1968)
– featuring the single 'Do You Remember' – alongside excerpt-
adaptations from the books *Summer With Monika* and *Frink: A Life In
the Day Of*. It was launched with a modest lunch party where copies

of Derek's multiply carbon-copied press-release were distributed, and it's a classic of his conversational most inspirationally stoned style. 'HELLOW. Thank you for coming to lunch. It is very nice of you and we are your friends. Now then, what do you want to know about it all? "Oh well of course", you may say, "how do we know what we want to know, surely you would be the best judge of that. After all is said and done, what is there to know?" It is so much a case of guessing, for there's no knowing what anyone would want to know. No. Let us guess. Eyes down. "Our father, all the eights, 88..." We are already confusing the issue. This approach is what the psychiatrists call "maze making" or "problem posing" or "crisis creating" brought about in order to find a solution, or an exit line. Now... some names... Jane and Mrs Asher, William I Bennet (WIB), Spencer Davies(is?). Barry Fantoni, Mike Hart, Jimi Hendrix, Vera Kantrovitch, Gary Leeds (of the Walker Brothers), Dave Mason and Carol, MIKE McGear, ROGER McGough, John Mayall, Paul McCartney, John Mitchell, Zoot (Money), Graham Nash, Viv Prince (yes), Andy Roberts, Prince "Stash" de Rola, Paul Samwell-Smith, Martin Wilkinson... what have they in common? What have they not? They are all beautiful. The two in capital letters are here today. They made the album. You have in your hand or adjacent. They are in the Scaffold. (The capital letters were mine not theirs. McGear & McGough have no egos.) The other people are friends. Friends. Friends who all contributed to the album in one way or many or all or a little. At any rate they all went into the recording session and sang or played or beat some tangible thing or simply waved their arms to create in the air some benign (we mean, of course, benign) turbulence. McGear & McGough are from Liverpool poetic and funny, concerned and open... Well listen, we are all here together now aren't we? In circumstances such as these, who needs a press release? Have we not tongues to speak. You are kind. Thank you. Derek.'

This text forms a document uniquely of its time. One that could never exist in today's focussed bullet-pointed fact-driven promotional bumf. There's no mention of the actual album at all until almost halfway through its chatty non-sequiturs. Then what detail is offered is slight, flip, oblique. Even the alternate spellings offered to Spencer Davis' name indicate that it flowed unbroken without pause for correction or fact-checking. Documentary veracity counts for less than dashing energy.

In a 1984 interview, Alistair Taylor explained that LSD 'came about as an escape. It was fun, they could afford it, and they mixed with people who said "hey, try this".' Just around the corner from the Wigmore Street office there was a pub where John liked to go for lunch, usually in the company of Derek and Alistair. Once there they'd playfully attempt to persuade the more cautious Alistair to experiment, urging him 'hey, try this'. 'Al, it's mind-blowing. It's incredible. You've never experienced anything like this in your life before.' 'We'll be with you, it'll be great.' But Alistair never did. Drugs were a bonding thing. An us-and-them thing. An initiates and outsiders thing. Al Aronowitz recalls 'another time, when Derek was unleashing a torrent of words in his usual manner while we were sharing a joint during a walk on a narrow, busy street in the centre of London near the Apple Records offices. A little old lady interrupted him to ask where the bus stopped or something like that. 'Fuck off!' Derek told her and, pausing only to take another hit, resumed his conversation as we strolled on.' Perhaps it had been a bad day, after all, didn't Derek once write about how 'I regretted being rude, as I always do'? It could be accused that Derek used his famous charm strategically, and because he had nothing to gain from expending charm on the unfortunate 'little old lady', he didn't. Maybe it was the intellectual smugness that shared drug use imbues its users, after all, she was 'straight'. Or maybe Al simply misremembers?

As an Apple VIP, Derek found himself with a major role in the company's ups and downs, making or enforcing many crucial business and personal decisions. While the acid, and the pot, and his period of laid-back Californian independence rendered Derek ill-prepared for the rigours of administrative life in London. His role is well-illustrated in Richard DiLello's memoir and supported by the evidence of other Beatles biographies. During the final days of Apple, DiLello discussed his *The Longest Cocktail Party* as a work-in-progress with Derek. Derek wanted an advance-peek at the typescript – after all, he was preparing his own memoirs of the same events. But Richard self-consciously declined.

The first indication of downsizing was the closure of the Apple boutique at 94 Baker Street, as early as 30 July 1968. A decision rationalised by a communiqué from Paul, but punched into shape by Derek – 'our main business is entertainment, and communication. Apple is mainly concerned with fun, not frocks… we had to zoom in on what we really enjoy, and we enjoy being alive, and we enjoy being Beatles.' On the boutique's final day, everything that had not been stolen by shoplifters was literally given away in a free-for-all that devolved into what Derek considered 'one of the ugliest things I had ever heard of.' But store manager Peter Shotton was simply redeployed elsewhere in Apple, and 'in the end Jeremy Banks was the only employee to be declared redundant, and he was fired in November 1968.' A part of Derek's extended press and publicity department, 'during his less-than-a-year at Apple, Banks did coordinate some successful publicity photo opportunities and he set up several deals that gave Apple a royalty for all Beatles photos that were provided to the press. However, he was most notorious for spending most of his time at Apple in long secretive convoluted phone calls pursuing his own mysterious freelance work and consuming a potent mixture of Möet & Chandon champagne and panadeine codeine-based diet pills.'

Gradually, it all came unglued. Colour tvs had gone missing. The carpet in John's room had gone missing. A typist was phoning Canberra every afternoon. Someone else had arbitrarily awarded themselves a £60-a-week raise. In an interview with Ray Coleman (dated 2 January 1969), John admitted that Apple was squittering away £50,000 a week. And that the sprawling enterprise 'needs a new broom, and a lot of people there will have to go.' Then there was Apple's spend on 'candles and flowers', an accounting euphemism for drugs. These, as Derek's writing eloquently testifies, were 'Apple days of dreaming and screaming for a way out of the confusion.' The Apple that 'passed into dismay and book-keeping'. For a *Melody Maker* investigation – 'Has Apple Gone Rotten?' – Derek was on the defensive. 'We have been criticised for inefficiency and, I agree, if you're looking for a paradox, you'll find it here in abundance... But if you're looking for help, you'll find that too. And if you're looking for sense, truth, and a friendly face, you'll find that too... With the pressures that are on us, it's not that we haven't achieved all our aims, it's a miracle that anything gets done at all.'

Alistair Taylor recalls 'the money was coming in so fast, but there were no controls. I got laughed out of court when I tried to control Derek. That's when I said we needed a "Beeching"' – referring to the Tory minister who had dismembered the rail network. 'The next thing I read was that John and Yoko had gone to see Lord Beeching. They had taken it literally. It evolved from that and, of course, we ended up with Allen Klein.' There had been a vague feeling of unease. There had been approaches by other outsiders with offers of 'straightening-up' Apple's shambolic finances. And although the 'straight'-world and its strained game-playing faces was still the enemy, the dream was under attack, besieged from all sides. Dick James had been a small-time music-publisher who'd also sung the theme tune for ITV's *Robin Hood* series. He lucked into becoming very rich and influential because of The Beatles catalogue... then he sold Northern Songs to the Lew Grade organisation without The Beatles' knowledge. Around the same time, the time of Klein, NEMS – the company that had begun with Brian's shop in Liverpool – was being acquired by Triumph Investments, a necessity precipitated by the tax situation resulting from Brian's death. 'Darker figures were entering our lives.' Even internally there was an awareness that things would have to change.

Allen Klein – 'a short fat man in a seersucker shirt' – was a man with the soul of a supermarket till. On the desk of his New York office was a parody of the 'Twenty-Third Psalm' that read 'Yea, though I walk in the valley of the shadow of evil, I have no fear, as I am the biggest bastard in the valley'. On 28 January 1969, Derek – who had had an inconclusive brush with him in New York two years earlier – located Klein's phone number, and passed it across to John, arguing in Klein's favour. John and Yoko met Klein in the Harlequin Suite of the Dorchester, and were impressed. Lennon, wowed by tales of his early street-fighter background, was convinced that 'our good friend Mr Klein' would ensure that The Beatles got what they were owed, and decided that he would represent 'all his stuff' from that moment on. This provides the entrance to Beatles-world that Klein had long-desired. Tony Bramwell laughs as he relates how 'Allen Klein's all-time ambition was to manage The Beatles' – there's even a story that when Klein heard the news of Brian Epstein's death on his car radio, he gleefully shouted out 'I've got 'em!' Yet 'the day he achieved it, they broke up.'

The only dissenting anti-Klein Beatles voice was Paul's. He preferred a certain Mr Eastman. Meanwhile, Derek was working on the press-kit for Paul's first solo album *McCartney* (April 1970), using a 'Question & Answer' format. Paul was disinclined to do direct interviews, fearing the obvious state-of-the-Beatles questions he'd have to face, so Derek's suggested subterfuge pre-empted that. Peter Brown also worked on the questionnaire. 'Is your break with The Beatles temporary or permanent, due to personal differences or musical ones?' Answer: 'Personal differences, business differences, musical differences, but most of all because I have a better time with my family. Temporary or permanent? I don't really know.' Then 'do you foresee a time when Lennon-McCartney becomes an active songwriting partnership again?' Paul: 'No'. And the media was onto the story in a minute. Particularly the question 'Have The Beatles virtually broken up?' with Paul supplying the answer 'yes, we won't play together again'.

Mrs Mavis Smith, Derek's assistant and head of Apple's public relations office, instantly denied rumours that Paul had quit, with 'this is just not true' (Thursday, 9 April 1970). When asked directly, Derek admits 'they could be dormant for years'. By Friday the *Daily Mirror* front page was devoted to the story 'Paul Is Quitting The Beatles'. Paul, who had tried more than anyone else to keep The Beatles together, had finally reached the conclusion that the group was beyond salvage – and refocused all of his considerable commercial energies on his solo career. Previous Beatle side-projects had been art-indulgences, George's *Wonderwall* soundtrack, Ringo's easy-going pub singalong *Sentimental Journey*, even John's anti-pop Plastic Ono Band – despite 'Instant Karma' and his heroin-withdrawal single 'Cold Turkey' high-charting. By contrast, *McCartney* was the first serious solo album of new post-Beatles songs. But listen to the lyrics of its finest song, Maybe I'm Amazed, and it discloses something of his state of mind: 'Maybe I'm a lonely man who's in the middle of something that he doesn't really understand.'

As DiLello recalls, 'it was impossible to conceive of it ever ending.' Yet it ended, trailing clouds of glory. The 2010 TV-movie *Lennon Naked* shows John – played by Christopher Eccleston – in his furious anger at the *Daily Mirror* cover story, taking a cab to Paul's house. He vaults the garden wall and lobs a stone through Paul's window. Derek – played by Michael Colgan – tries to restrain him, then sits in the cab watching the drama.

George had stated, 'we obviously can't go around as Beatles when we're in our forties' as recently – and as long ago – as his Derek Taylor-ghosted *Daily Express* column. Now Derek misquotes his other famous client, Harry Nilsson – 'a dream is just a wish you hope will come true, and this one didn't.' Press secretaries – otherwise 'spin doctors' – are filtering intermediaries placed between the artist and the hungry journalists who would prefer to hear the message straight. But sometimes the collective message the artists have to deliver is too torturously convoluted, that they need a PR to make sense of it for ordinary mortals. The final Beatles press release was a communiqué written by Derek, typed out by Mavis Smith, and dated 10 April 1970, telling the world – somewhat circuitously – that it was over. It read 'Spring is here and Leeds play Chelsea tomorrow and Ringo and John and George and Paul are alive and well and full of hope. The world is still spinning, and when that stops that will be the time to worry. See you again...' At a press conference, Derek appeared, cigarette in hand, besieged by press interrogators. He was sitting in his white ethnic-style peacock wicker basket-seat – a gift from Herb Alpert – wearing a white shirt patterned in regular red check, attempting to explain the break-up. Why had it happened? 'I don't know, it's probably to do with growing up, and to do with...', he fidgets absently with his collar. Then begins again, 'there was a time when there was just four of them, but now they're married and there are children, and...'

Yes, but there's Allen Klein. One of the interrogators makes the point that in the questionnaire (presumably the Press release) Paul definitely disowns Klein's take-over of Apple. Why is that? Derek's tongue presses up against the inside of his lower lip, making a contemplative bulge. 'By Paul', he clarifies, then looks up directly into the eyes of the questioner, 'because he doesn't like Allen Klein.' They persist, why doesn't Paul like Allen Klein? Derek coming back candidly, 'I don't know, but he doesn't…'

'Why? Because, be-fucking-cause, because…' 'Apple' – the group's self-sacrificial gesture to hippie correctness – had been set up 'to encourage unknown literary, graphic and performing artists', yet had merrily led them to the brink of chaos and bankruptcy. When Allen Klein moved in, to rescue the ailing company on 8 May 1969, he occupied the office directly opposite Derek's. He fired a lot of people, but Derek stayed for another eighteen months. Although the atmosphere had shifted, in many ways, things went on as normal. Derek was initially enthusiastic. He respected Klein's carnivorous abilities, but at a distance. 'By 1969 it was real madness', explained Derek, 'we didn't know where we were… Apple was like Toytown and Paul was Ernest the policeman. We couldn't have gone on and on like that. We had to have a demon king.' But who would compile the hit-lists – 'maybe Adolf Eichman could, but he was dead. Maybe Mengele could, but he was in Paraguay.'

It's tempting to suggest that the necessity for Klein was actually a search for an Epstein-replacement. What they really needed was Brian, in which case the mismanagement situation may never have reached such extremes. But as he was no longer around, the full unravelling Apple extravaganza grew into an essential part of The Beatles' legend, it could have happened no other way. At a point where Apple needed a visionary with a thinking business head, it had four visionaries who were busy growing up, growing apart, painfully and publicly. In the end, it was down to Allen Klein. He compiled the lists. He did the firings. And he increased Beatles US royalties to 25%. Perhaps he was Apple's last best chance? But if Klein was there to protect them from the bigger predators, who would protect them from Klein? As Alistair Taylor recalls, 'so, the man whose head is on the chopping block first is the guy who thought the idea up. Klein fired me…' Alistair was gone. Alistair who had been there from the beginning, his signature as witness appearing on the original Beatles contract signed with Epstein. Did Derek, as one of the facilitators in introducing Klein to Apple, feel at least in part responsible? 'I owe someone, somewhere, something, that's for sure', he concedes.

But normal Beatles-activity continued, from 23 April to 5 May – as the world burned with the Kent State University shootings, with Richard Nixon poised to extend the SE Asia war into Cambodia, Derek flew out from Heathrow to NY with George and Patti, where the 'quiet Beatle' was to produce Billy Preston's Apple album *Encouraging Words* (released September 1970, in fact, he not only produced but contributed guitar and co-wrote 'Sing One for the Lord' with Billy). George found time to meet up with Klein, and sit in with Bob Dylan for his *New Morning* (October 1970) sessions, collaborating on the classic 'If Not For You'. The outtakes from the *Get Back* sessions indicate the influence as George improvises a Dylan-songs medley of 'I Threw It All Away' and 'Mama You Been on My Mind'.

Meanwhile, the *McCartney* (April 1970) album emerged a month before The Beatles' last official twelve-inch collection. A rebranding of the earlier *Get Back* tracks, *Let It Be* (May 1970) came with a lavish full-colour booklet carrying Derek's back-cover flash claiming it as 'a new phase Beatles album', which it obviously wasn't. 'Two of Us' and 'One After 909' reassert the basic merits of simple Merseybeat. John's 'Across the Universe' was remixed from a February 1968 session that had already been gifted to a charity album. Made up of tracks produced by George Martin fifteen months of squabbling earlier, they had then been re-produced by Phil Spector.

There was history. George had gender-reassigned Spector's first hit 'To Know Her Is to Love Her' on their live *Star Club* album from 1962. There was future too. Both George and John would work with Spector on post-Beatle solo albums (although John's 'Steel and Glass' is a vituperative attack on Klein). Dismissively, John considered that Spector's surgery on *Let It Be* salvaged what was 'lousy, and so bad none of us would go near them.' Paul saw it differently. According to Derek's account in his *As Time Goes By*, it was Klein who induced his former associate Spector to remix Paul's 'The Long and Winding Road', an intervention that 'Paul thinks is the shittiest thing anyone has ever done to him.' Klein merely 'laughs up his silk sleeve' and authorised the doctored track's release as an American single anyway. Although it predictably reached no.1 in May 1970, Paul's resentment over Spector's string-and-choir additions continue to burn through until the *Let It Be... Naked* edition emerged many years later. The incident left Paul wondering why, as one of the four founders of Apple, the company formed to enable their total artistic freedom, he couldn't even exert the power of veto over his own work. 'But Klein isn't wondering. He knows, he knows.'

Mavis Smith resigned in June, but Derek stayed on at an Apple that had regressed into 'the most ungroovy place I ever knew.' Into its final stages, when Klein's cuts had reduced it to little more than a management company. Tittenhurst Park was John's new Ascot house – he would later sell it to Ringo after the drummer's separation from wife Maureen. But first, Derek was part of the entourage when The Beatles turned up there to use it as a location for the group's last-ever photo-session together (Friday 22 August 1969). For the occasion, John and George were sporting wide-brimmed hats. Yoko Ono was there, with a heavily pregnant Linda McCartney observing as the shoot began with The Beatles framed among the stone balustrades on the terrace, using the main house as a backdrop, before they move leisurely down the garden path, past a statue of the goddess Diana, pausing for more shots beneath the weeping cedar trees Was there an autumnal feel of end-of-days finality in the air? Could they feel the world turning beneath their feet? If not, there must have been intimations. Derek hung on. He appeared as one of the faces on the final Apple Xmas card, in a group shot taken by Richard DiLello. Then it was time to go, and he went. It was New Year's Eve. On the brink of 1971, and he was drained. That same month, the Apple Press Office officially closed.

Indulged by the sheer profligacy of brilliant music, and the rising trajectory of innovation and novelty, brilliance was almost taken for granted. The earth beneath your feet was in a constant state of movement, culture-shocks and permanent-revolutions were accepted, the way of things, the air you breathe. Amazing. Intoxicating. Surely it must go on forever? It didn't. And it couldn't. What did Apple achieve? Despite the claims of mythology, it never went bust. More, it created a legend. A narrative. A denouement to The Beatles arc. There had been an odd homogeneity to 1960s pop. A time when easy-listening balladeers, R&B Beat-merchants, and earnest protest Folkies lined up alongside each other on *Top of the pops* without any sense of oddness.

Did music change the world? When I ask Graham Nash, he's adamant that it did, 'I still think that. Music is still changing the world. Every positive action that you do results in the world getting better. Y'know? And every kid's head that you reach... every kid that you encourage, everyone you pat on the head, every flower you see, every – just the normal stuff, you can become aware of all of it, it's all holy to me.' With some justification. The world of 1970 was a substantially different place to the world of 1960. A more liberal, more tolerant place, less-judgemental of minorities, more open to social diversity, freer, less repressive, more at ease with itself, more egalitarian, less deferential than it had been. A lot of those messages had been given expression and accelerated by the music of the period. If those changes did not continue further into the years that followed, if some of those gains were even reversed, others were invested in law, with attitudes irreversibly shifted. For the better. The lack of elitism would eventually be deconstructed by focus-group marketing and digital remastering into niche categories and target demographics. Technologically, commercially and culturally transformed into repetition... and nostalgia. But as the decade closed, at least the goonish clowning on the B-side of The Beatles' final official single – 'You Know My Name (Look Up the Number)' – shows that John and Paul were still capable of making good times together.

In Derek's own words, 'and in the end, the equation between the love they took and the love they made was intact into infinity.' All things must pass. Yet in *Variety* magazine, The Beatles topped their '100 Icons of the Century' poll. By then the greatest story in twentieth-century music was over. The Longest Cocktail Party was over. As Joan Baez sang it at the 1970 Isle of Wight Festival, 'Let it be, Let it be...'

Chapter Thirteen: Discs And Music Echoes

We didn't dream it… though it came out of John's dream
Of the 'man on a flaming pie' who said 'you are Beatles with an 'a''.
It did all happen.
(Derek Taylor's notes to *The Beatles Anthology: 1*)

'Some Are Dead, And Some Are Living…'

A story oft-told. The mound of cultural mythology surrounding the
doing-to-death of the sixties. The seventies as a let-down, a non-event,
the long come-down and the thwarted expectations. In asynchronous
parallel evolution, the Space-Race had been gaining cosmic velocity
across exactly the same time-period as rock 'n' roll. From the first
Sputnik-bleep in October 1957, around the time Elvis was going
global, through the Gemini and Apollo missions, until the moon
landing – after which… it stopped. The Beatles split. Altamont replaced
Monterey. Brian Jones, Jimi Hendrix, Jim Morrison, Otis Redding and
Janis Joplin were among the dead. The sixties is a cultural revolution
from which the world was still reeling. There would be new adventures
and new musics in the new decade. But it would be different. Music
more designed to keep consumers in place, rather than creating
new places. Even the idyllic marital bliss of Nina & Frederick, among
Derek's earliest showbusiness interview subjects, ended in divorce.
Worse, caught up in a drug-trafficking crime syndicate, Frederick was
subsequently shot dead in 1994. Allen Klein went on, after presiding
over The Beatles' final days, until his death on 6 July 2009.

And Derek, who had existed on the event horizon of a collapsing
star, and then, passing beyond that point – as relativity predicts –
time slowed down to infinitesimal moments, or 'living through the
events, and arriving in the Now to celebrate them.' He had gone from
being 'press officer of The Beatles' to become 'ex-press officer of
the ex-Beatles'. And the end of Apple formed a kind of Derek Taylor
denouement too. He pulled the vast white ethnic-style chair from the
debris as he finally quit no.3 Savile Row, and he took it home to 'The
Gables'. Looking like a brooding shadow, he could be seen sitting there
typing in an oak-panelled bay. Long and slender, sloping in the cane
basket-chair, contorting around a cloud of aromatic smoke, backlit by
the sun pouring in through the window overlooking the lawn behind
him. The left armrest of the chair bent out of shape through wear. He
beams a smile. Legends cast long shadows. But there's a price to pay.

'The more things change, the more they are not the same any more.'

The sixties quickened the pulse of lives. Although he'd lived through the forties and fifties, which were the build-up to the decade, now he was into the seventies and eighties, the period of come-down and coming to terms with its implications. He'd emerged from the decade drained. 'I guess everything got too big, too bloody vast for human beings, frail, ill-prepared human beings, to cope, whether Beatles... or us, nervous at their feet. We couldn't take it.' Christ, you know it wasn't easy. A 1971 issue of *Melody Maker* called Derek 'eloquent and world-weary', while *The Guardian* found him 'experienced and pragmatic'. The world had not ended. His 'Apple' period lasted little more than a few brief years, and a lifetime. He was suddenly free to be himself again. With the troublesome proviso, of what exactly that should be?

The issue of *Melody Maker* dated 21 February 1970 announced that EMI was raising the price of 'LP records' from 37s 5d to 39s 11d (just short of £2). This increase, it pointed out, was the first since July 1963. An arc of time that roughly approximated The Beatles chart career. In 1971 the Misuse of Drugs Act established the ABC system for classifying illegal substances. The Advisory Council on the Misuse of Drugs (ACMD) was set up to provide the Home Secretary with the best possible expert evidence on potentially harmful substances. LSD was immediately classified 'A' as much for its impact on the street, as much to try and stop the expansion of its use, as to signal genuine evidence of its harm. And it remained sitting in 'A' classification alongside heroin and crack cocaine, despite the fact that it is indubitably less dangerous to the user or to society. While cannabis became a political football in a contest between evidence and passion.

Derek visited Ascot races on 17 June 1970, the year Rosemary Lomax became the first woman trainer to win the Gold Cup with 'Precipice Wood' romping home in first place. It was the day before the General Election. Derek was confident 'Labour is going to win'. He was even press officer for the local Labour Party branch, with 'as much claim to "working class credibility" as Frank Sinatra has to Roman Catholic monogamy'! All the opinion polls indicated a clear Labour victory. Labour didn't win. Harold Wilson, the Prime Minister who proclaimed the 'white heat' of the sixties technological revolution, the Prime Minister who claimed The Beatles as his 'secret weapons', was replaced at no.10 by Edward Heath. The Taylor's held a barbeque anyway.

Derek was loyal. For a *Disc and Music Echo* feature 'The Byrds: Byrds From The Egg' (May 1971), he wrote 'they're back! The American group who soared to success here in 1965 with "Mr Tambourine Man", then quickly "disappeared". Here "Disc" traces the Byrds flight back...'

A kind of 'what came next' memoir, it picks up the story as the then-current Byrds line-up played the legendary Albert Hall. Roger McGuinn – with Clarence White, bassist Skip Battin and drummer Gene Parsons – would eventually contrive to release the concert-soundtrack as a nineteen-song Sundaze-label CD in June 2008. Elsewhere, Gene Clark's initially stabilising marriage to Carlie, and the country-comforts of Mendocino had run aground. There was a damaging relationship with Terri Messina, and roaring lost months of booze and narcotic excess with Doug Dillard and Jerry Jeff Walker. While touring, their bar bills far exceeded their weekly takings.

The next step for them all was a shaky Byrds reformation, reuniting the full original five-piece, with Chris Hillman taking time out from Manassas, and Michael Clarke fresh out of the Flying Burrito Brothers. Poorly rehearsed and with no real blueprint, old grudges, animosities and antagonisms soon resurfaced. David Crosby, as the most commercially successful survivor of the 'Mr Tambourine Man' line-up, was clearly focussed as front and centre of the cover-photo. With his extravagantly-grown hair seemingly about to 'entangle the entire area', he revelled in assuming production duties as 'executioner and kingmaker'. There have been accusations that he deliberately mixed McGuinn's jingle-jangle low and excluded all but two new Gene Clark songs, although one of them is the album's finest, 'Full Circle'.

Simply titled *The Byrds* (1973) and issued on the Asylum label, other stand-outs include Crosby's sensitive vocals on Joni Mitchell's 'For Free', and his own song Laughing' which ironically features McGuinn's finest raga-rock Rickenbacker solo. However, David had already issued his solo version of the song on his *If I Could Only Remember My Name* (1971) album, and its metaphorical lyric-story reportedly relates incidents from CS&N's internal feuding. It was followed by two songs from his occasional CS&N partner, Neil Young. McGuinn contributed 'Born to rock 'n' roll' which he'd already done – and rejected – with the final Byrds line-up, but as an indication of his continuing dissatisfaction with the song, he would record it again on a forthcoming solo album, *Roger McGuinn and Band* (1975). Among the remaining tracks is 'Things Will Be Better', by Chris Hillman and drummer Dallas Taylor, which retains the twelve-string, but allies it to Eagles-style harmonies. With Crosby 'a burning mass of passion, pride, hubris and regret' (to Johnny Rogan), the sessions show the group back to their old bickering ways, with their unfinished business still unfinished, even though the album delivered their first US Top 20 album since *Turn! Turn! Turn!*.

The full line-up immediately fragmented, but there were contentious

McGuinn, Clark and Hillman reunion dates, structured around separate
sets by each ex-Byrd. Performed to mixed receptions, the rigours of
touring itself forced Gene back into chemical dependence. Contracts
lapsed. There was litigation over the rights to the Byrds name itself,
even as Gene was reduced to touring as a kind of Byrds tribute band.
There was stomach surgery, then, when – for the final time – all five
original Byrds found themselves thrown together for their induction
into 'The rock 'n' roll Hall of Fame' – 16 January 1991 – there was
a partial reconciliation, of sorts. Shortly after, during duo recording
sessions with Carla Olson, Gene was finally found dead, aged 46. The
coroner's verdict was a heart attack. But to biographer Einarson, Gene
Clark 'had a fear of success and whenever it came close his self-destruct
mechanism activated.' 'He couldn't handle fame', agrees McGuinn.
But when I saw Gene at the Wakefield *Pussycat Club* shortly before
he died, playing support to Lindisfarne, he did the full version of 'Mr
Tambourine Man'. And it was mesmerising. While the Byrds, through
many fallings-out and reformations, threw off sparks like an arcing
comet, spawning an entire genre of spin-off acts, Dillard and Clark, the
Flying Burrito Brothers, Crosby Stills Nash & Young. Then a second and
third layer of copyist bands indebted to their template.

Meanwhile, since Paul's formal 'resignation' from The Beatles,
followed by the group's final breakup, Neil Aspinall had almost single-
handedly been running the day-to-day worldwide Beatles business. In
truth, the group may have claimed to have been managing themselves
through the vacuum left by Epstein, but the continuing arrangements
of their affairs had fallen by default to Neil. According to *The Sunday
Times: The Culture Section*, Lennon had actually suggested him for
official manager status, but amid the general confusion he'd turned
it down (12 November 1995). Now the situation merely persisted in
the absence of The Beatles themselves, through the litigious period
George christened the 'Sue Me Sue You Blues'. When Allen Klein split
in Summer 1973, Neil – as Managing Director – was left, he 'is Apple'.

American fans had singled Ringo out as 'cute' from the first tour.
'If you had to be in a band', he quipped, 'it might as well be The
Beatles.' His amiable comedic talent first surfaced in the *A Hard Day's
Night* movie-sequence filmed by the river and meandering through
West Ealing. Although his subsequent acting career failed to develop
whatever potential it indicated, he could be seen sleep-walking through
movie-adaptations of Terry Southern's cult novels *Candy* (1967) and
The Magic Christian (1970). Probably the worst track The Beatles
ever recorded was 'Octopus's Garden' – Ringo's second-only writing

contribution. Although afterwards he charted with a number of half-decent solo hits. When they could have had their pick of just about any drummer in the world, it was Ringo who played on John Lennon's first solo *Plastic Ono Band* album (1971) and George's *All Things Must Pass* sessions (1970). He later turned up on the video for George's 'When We Was Fab' (1988), a song that, at Derek's suggestion, was amended from the more grammatical 'when we were fab'.

He also drums on McCartney's *Tug of War* album (1982). So – why Ringo? Ringo's wedding to Barbara Bach at Marylebone Registry Office (27 April 1981) provided the opportunity for a major reunion, of sorts. Derek and Joan, Paul and Linda, George and Olivia, Neil Aspinall and Harry Nilsson were all there, going on to the reception at the *Rags* Mayfair club. Ringo had always functioned as the group's catalyst. The occasion now provides the three ex-Beatles with the excuse for their first group photo since the 22 August 1969 sessions – albeit with their respective spouses.

John and Paul's highly public spat had become the most disturbing split since the Lenin and Trotsky schism. But Paul, alone of the now formerly-Fab, was capable of turning the clock back to year zero and resuming his career from the bottom up. On the spoken-word outtake CD included with the *Let It Be... Naked* (November 2003) edition, he can be heard suggesting that The Beatles stage a surprise gig by just turning up at some arbitrary venue and volunteering to perform. Lennon, in particular, rubbishes the idea. 'We can't do that! We're The Beatles!!!' He expressed the same sentiment when he explained 'they'd be expecting god to perform.' As if to deliberately prove he was correct all along, once established with Wings – wife Linda, former Moody Blues frontman Denny Laine, ex-Spooky Tooth guitarist Henry McCullough, and drummer Denny Seiwell – Paul did precisely that. In the early months of 1972, Wings drove up and down the M1 motorway, turned off at random to arrive at a college unannounced – the first at Nottingham (9 February) – and asked the social secretary if they could play in their hall that evening.

The strongest and most supportive relationship of his life, exactly when he needed it most, 'Lovely Linda' was the daughter of lawyer Lee Eastman and Louise Linder Eastman, heir to the Linder department-store fortune. Already a respected professional photographer, she'd arrived in London with a commission to take pictures of musicians and ended up committing the heinous crime of falling in love with every woman's favourite Beatle. They met at a Georgie Fame concert, going on to see Procol Harum at the *Speakeasy Club* before she flew

back to New York, without even exchanging phone numbers. The
couple met again at the launch party for *Sgt Pepper* and, yet again, in
New York at a party for the Apple label. It was finally Paul who made
the move and phoned to ask her to accompany him on a trip to LA.
And it was Paul who would ask her, several times, to marry him. They
married at Marylebone Registry Office on 12 March 1969, when she
was four months pregnant with their daughter Mary. The same Mary
whom Linda photographed tucked inside Paul's jacket for the cover
of his first solo album. Linda would provide a gravity-wise down-to-
Earthing force, in the wake of the acrimonious end of the other great
relationship in Paul's life.

Derek watched approvingly as Paul set up MPL – McCartney
Productions Ltd – a more focused, more business-like version of Apple.
Then, settling into a simple pop groove with the inanely trite nursery
rhyme 'Mary Had A Little Lamb', Paul returned to appearing on the Top
of the pops treadmill alongside the newer, sillier generation of pop
stars. Although in a sense, despite everything he'd lived through in the
sixties, he was still young and pretty enough – doing what Derek calls
'pulling all those cute chipmunk faces' – to be a direct contemporary
of the decade's 'new' stars. In fact, Paul 'Gary Glitter' Gadd was two
years older than he was. Alvin Stardust, born the same year as Paul,
had even preceded The Beatles into the charts by scoring a 1962 hit
with 'I'm A Moody Guy' under his previous alias 'Shane Fenton'. Both
Noddy Holder and David Bowie – who'd already been written off as
a sixties one-hit-wonder with 'Space Oddity', had been recording to
little commercial effect through most of the sixties. So as Paul initiated
a new career-arc playing lightweight hits alongside Wizzard and Sweet
on TV pop shows, the fit was not as strange as it might have seemed.
Re-building towards *Band on the Run* (1974), to which even John
Peel conceded adult credibility, and *Melody Maker* nominated the
second top LP of 1974 in its annual survey – behind Michael Oldfield's
Tubular Bells. Then *Venus and Mars* (1975) which made Wings a global
phenomenon. Derek, with George Harrison, was there for the celebrity
album-launch party that Paul and Linda held aboard the *Queen Mary*,
which was permanently docked at Long Beach (24 March 1975).

Wings – as distinct from Paul's solo and duo release – eventually log
fifteen chart hits. An entire career which, even removing The Beatles
from his history, still constitutes a considerable lifework in itself. Many
bands still make a good living playing the nostalgia circuit on less. He
achieved the seemingly impossible when 'Mull of Kintyre' even outsold
'I Want to Hold Your Hand', and he went on to appear on the record

which outsold even that – Band Aid's 'Do They Know It's Christmas'. Alone of the four Beatles, Paul carved out a career independent from what they'd achieved together. Particularly during the years when Lennon was 'retired', Paul was selling to a market who, if they even knew he'd once been a Beatle, couldn't have cared less.

There's a dissenting voice that says once a great band dies, their follow-up projects never quite hook up with anyone as strong as their previous partner/rival. Someone who'll argue with, and love them as equals. By necessity, the new group becomes the sound of one star, with support musicians standing around being quietly excited merely to be sharing the same stage. Linda was an irreplaceably powerful influence. Denny Laine a strong musician in his own right. But a Beatle is a Beatle and is forever a Beatle. And in Lennon's continued absence, The Beatles re-issue machine began slanting its product towards this new Wings fan-base, The Beatles compilation *Love Songs* (1977) bears a Richard Avedon cover-photo with Paul placed well to the fore. There's even a suggestion that The Beatles' songwriting credits should be reconfigured to reflect which of the two had the greater input – say, McCartney-Lennon for 'Yesterday'. Yoko stood out against the idea. It was Lennon-McCartney. Just as it was always Leiber and Stoller. Just as it was always Bacharach and David. Paul was much later referred to by no less a figure than former US President Bill Clinton as 'an American icon' and a 'unifying force'. While Bill Gates claimed he'd created work comparable to that of Bach. Yet Paul's deliberate amputation from all of the elements of his earlier life meant that Derek had little input to make.

But John Lennon's death meant that the man Derek called 'John Lennon of the Famous Beatles' would always be taken more seriously than Paul. And Derek's continuing connection with him, if a little more erratic, was never less than supportively loyal. In a *Disc and Music Echo* feature, 'John Lennon. Fighting The Good Fight' (November 1968), he attacks the critics and doubters with 'this is addressed to those who love Lennon, who call him John, and who give thanks for his being alive, hard by, at hand…' Derek uses Roger McGuinn's term 'electronic magazine' to describe a particular kind of album, or record, that John was consciously striving to create. While Paul was in the studio for hours getting the drum-sound right for 'Obladi Oblada', John was advocating a more spontaneous first-instinct method of 'instant art' recording.

Conveniently forgetting his middle-class upbringing in Liverpool, John had been influenced by Robert Tressell's *The Ragged-Trousered Philanthropist* (1914), until he re-envisioned himself as a 'Working-Class Hero'. Or rather, as Derek reveals, he'd been watching BBC2's

TV-dramatisation of the great Socialist novel over-and-over-again on his 'new-fangled machine' – a proto-video recorder. And as a reaction to the over-complexity of what had come earlier, John wanted first-take intuition over technical perfection. For a song to be written, recorded, and in the shops within days. Making it an utterly contemporary reaction to the moment. 'Give Peace A Chance' is an early example of the idea. The double-album *Some Time in New York City* (June 1972) became its flawed ultimate expression. While John sings 'we're all mates with Attica State', in solidarity with the rioting prison inmates, ironically his assassin Mark Chapman would be held in that same Attica Correctional Facility.

As Stuart Sutcliffe had begun to do a decade earlier, Yoko influenced, confronted and seriously fine-tuned John's consciousness. And he was strong enough to accept, and integrate those adjustments. Questioning and affecting changes to the Northern cultural misogyny that had characterised his relationship with Cynthia, and expressed in Beatles songs such as 'Run for Your Life'. By the time of 'Jealous Guy' he was apologising for such deeply-ingrained behaviour patterns, and struggling to amend them. He would emerge from the process a more complete human being, more at ease with himself. Despite the lapse of his 'lost weekend'...

Harry Nilsson was by now known not only as a songwriter but also through his astute choice of cover material, as an interpreter of other people's songs. Derek wrote liner notes for his second album, *Aerial Ballet* (1968), which includes his take on Fred Neil's 'Everybody's Talkin''. It became a major hit when drafted onto the *Midnight Cowboy* (1969) movie soundtrack. The album also includes his own plaintive much-covered song 'One', a major chart hit for Three Dog Night. The pattern was repeated with Harry's wistful chart-topping version of Badfinger's 'Without You', and by his own hit single 'Me and My Arrow' from the movie animation *The Point!* (December 1970).

A 'magic lamp' story printed on the back cover of Nilsson's album *Harry* (1969) was written by Derek's daughter Victoria. So there was a precedent when Derek slipped into the production chair for the next project, studio sessions *for A Little Touch of Schmilsson in the Night* (RCA, 1973). How is it possible to go from publicist to record producer in a single bound? Derek had been around music and musicians for long enough to know how the thing worked. There's the studio engineer to sort out the technical details. Some producers are more hands-on than others. It can simply be to act as a sounding-board, to choose the best between three takes, to call edit when things get too indulgent, to offer an intermediary perspective. The album was an exercise in cribbed songs, a deft theft of standards by the likes of Irving Berlin and Kalmar and Ruby, given an immaculate sheen by veteran conductor Gordon Jenkins' full orchestration. Despite his voyages into psychedelic excess, Derek always retained an affection for this music of an earlier age – which made him Nilsson's perfect foil. Derek even recalled the 'infinite beauty' of the Gordon Jenkins Orchestra playing 'Again' on a 78rpm record he'd heard as a teenager on a trip to Hilbre Island. Yet, although a shot at the 'Great American Songbook' a decade before the revival of such vanities by others, displaying evidence of Nilsson's enduring respect for the songwriter's craft, the album proved to be a less than commercial proposition. Derek's dual involvement in the project meant he received producer credits on an album for which he was also acting as publicist! With the added special significance that he took the title for his book *As Time Goes By* not only from the classic Herman Hupfield song but more specifically from Nilsson's version included on this album.

Prankster Nilsson's eccentric career proved to be never less than erratically self-sabotaging. Supposedly talking-up the album, Nilsson was programme guest on Kenny Everett's Capital Radio show. Everett fired questions for nearly two hours, to absolutely no on-air response, except for a final 'thanks, it's been great to be on the show.' He just didn't fancy participating in the interview. Although he was certainly talking as the records played, delighting the madcap DJ with a story of how he'd been on rival station LBC radio the previous night, where he'd become fascinated by the 'delay button', the device that enabled swearing to be deleted. Nilsson tested it out by swearing every other sentence, resulting in listeners hearing the announcer say 'LBC, where news comes first' every few seconds, obliterating the unbroadcastable bits of Nilsson. During this period, Nilsson owned a central-London flat. Distressingly, it was in this flat that Mama Cass Elliot died in July 1974. Later – in September 1978 – Keith Moon also died there, not only in the same flat, but on the same bed.

During the last few months of 1973, Nilsson found himself back in California, where he was soon rekindling his hero-worship friendship with John Lennon in roaring style, stumbling through chaotic sessions for what would become his *rock 'n' roll* covers LP (eventually issued February 1975). After completing the *Mind Games* (1973) album, John embarked on his painful split from Yoko Ono. But it was a complex interdependence, when he had his affair, Yoko even controlled who he had it with, and when he relocated to Beverly Hills, John was accompanied by personal assistant May Pang. Dated 2 December 1973, he mailed Derek a postcard update: 'I'm in Lost Arseholes for no real reason... Yoko and me are in hell, but I'm gonna change it... probably this very day. Anyway, I'm still famous. He who laffs last is often hard of hearing.' Lennon was an inveterate sender of postcards, most likely self-decorated with doodles. Derek was the recipient of more than most.

The pretext for further extended debauches started out with Lennon's intention to produce Nilsson's next album – *Pussy Cats* (August 1974). But instead, their time together became more renowned for heavy drinking and narcotic indulgences than it was for the album that resulted. Fueled on cocaine and Brandy Alexanders – a potent fusion of milk, brandy and crème de cacao – Nilsson managed to rupture a vocal chord and was spitting blood, leaving tissue-traces from throat-polyps on the microphone after they'd duetted on Jimmy Cliff's 'Many Rivers to Cross', a fact he failed to mention to his 'producer', but which added a new rawness to his voice. Time out from the session also involved the widely publicised incident in March that saw the duo thrown out of the West Hollywood *Troubadour* club for drunkenly heckling the Smothers Brothers.

By then, Lennon's 'Lost Weekend' was in free fall. Drained by crazy-wild LA excess, John and May Pang, with a bearded and overweight Nilsson in tow, returned to the east coast on 27 April, to hole up in Rooms 1604 to 1606 of the Fifth Avenue *Hotel Pierre* – across the New York plaza from the Plaza Hotel where The Beatles had made their first US landfall. In the evenings they'd cross over to the Record Plant at 321 West 44th Street to attempt more work on Nilsson's album. Derek happened to be staying at the Algonquin Hotel with jazz-singer George Melly, on a promotional jag, and they called around the studio where Lennon was producing the LP, and listened in as they recorded 'Save the Last Dance for Me'. Ringo was on drums, Klaus Voorman playing bass.

On another evening, a drunken Lennon accompanied by an equally drunken Nilsson returned the visit, turning up at Derek's New York Algonquin Hotel suite where the former-Beatle immediately sought to smash the chandelier, and almost came to blows with a hapless Melly. Despite the strained situation, Derek later joined the hell-raising duo as a drinking companion for further over-the-top forays in Los Angeles. Calling them 'madmen in tandem', he conceded that John (Lennon) and Harry (Nilsson) 'have been living a vampire timetable recently but have sucked no blood except each others.' Derek contributed sleeve-notes to the disappointing *Pussy Cats* album that eventually emerged from the chaos – 'these are written at 78rpm and should be read at

33rpm. I have one hour to catch the plane. You have all your lives. Lucky bastards.' Peter Skellern suggested a revision, substituting one word 'snapping' for 'breaking', which Derek pragmatically accepted. Mal Evans was also credited as 'OUR PAL' on the liner notes. Through declining record sales, John continued to champion Nilsson, using his not-inconsiderable influence to get RCA to renew Nilsson's contract. But despite further fine albums there were to be no more hits.

Meanwhile, with Yoko temporarily out of the picture, and the more conciliatory May Pang taking her place, there was time for some reconciliations too. Cynthia found she could relate to May Pang in ways she was never able to do with Yoko, leading to John spending quality time with Julian. And then Paul turned up at the Burbank recording sessions. The only post-Beatles occasion that John and Paul played together, jamming on 'Stand By Me'. There is confused bootleg evidence of the occasion. May Pang, who had previously worked as Yoko's production co-ordinator, later wrote a book – *Loving John* (Warner, 1983) – detailing the period. She mentions that John sent another postcard to Derek, addressed to Ascot, revealing that John 'was thinking about visiting the Macs down in New Orleans' – Paul and Linda were there to record their *Venus and Mars* album. Even Paul was initially dubious about the rumour, until Derek began selling off Beatles memorabilia, and the postcard found its way back to Paul himself. The Plastic Ono Band could call on musicians as powerful as Eric Clapton and Klaus Voorman, but the central nucleus was always John and Yoko. The one equally powerful association Yoko feared she could not control was the Lennon-McCartney one. Perhaps the rumour was enough...?

The extended mid-life crisis was brought to a close when John returned to Yoko, commemorated by the release of John's *Walls and Bridges* (September-October 1974) album – also produced at the Record Plant, while Capitol re-acquired the earlier *rock 'n' roll* tapes from Phil Spector. The sessions had been interrupted when Spector was seriously auto-wrecked and the tapes proved 'difficult to retrieve'. Following his rapprochement with Yoko, a more grounded Lennon wrote to Derek in Autumn 1975, telling him he was enjoying Yoko's pregnancy, and about his new state of domesticity. 'I meself have decided to be or not to be for a coupla years... I ain't in a hurry to sign with anyone or do anything. Am enjoying my pregnancy – thinking time, what's it all about, time...?' he asks, 'I'll outlive the bastards in more ways than one.' For the time being, he's just sitting there watching the wheels go round. 'My head and body are as clear as a bell,' with just a suggestion of occasional recreational tripping on 'incredibly Legal Mushrooms' or 'nice window pane' (LSD). Sean Ono Lennon was born on 9 October.

Although fragmentary, the Derek Taylor-John Lennon correspondence never lapsed. John sent Derek a postcard while he and Yoko were in Japan (dated 13 August 1977), 'hellow Taylors, am in Alan Watts country, hi mountains. John Yoko & Sean.' Elvis died while John was in Japan. 'Nothing really affected me until Elvis', he admits, later adding 'Elvis died when he went into the army.' He taped a demo-cassette of 'Free as a Bird' in their Dakota building apartment around the same time, the track that Paul, George and Ringo would overdub and extend into a 'new' Beatles single in December 1995. Joe Pytka's evocative tie-in video was personally approved and encouraged by Derek in a two-page letter.

If Derek had not been there at the beginning of The Beatles, he was there at its end. Filmed during the famous bed-ins with Yoko, John reads out a message sent to them, a warning of a planned assassination attempt, a message purportedly communicated from Brian Epstein through a ouija-board. The pair laugh in bemused amusement, then turn to the next letter. Photographer Annie Leibovitz took her celebrated photograph of Lennon at his most vulnerable – naked, foetally curled in upon himself, clinging to a clothed Yoko – for the cover of *rolling Stone*. It was taken just hours before his fatal slaying on 8 December 1980. And looking out over Central Park, the thought might have occurred, the fact that American designer FL Olmsted designed Manhattan's Central Park with Birkenhead as his inspiration. The ambitious municipal worthies of the Wirral had invited the creator of Chatsworth, Joseph Paxton, to design an idealised country landscape in the centre of an urban sprawl, a park suitable for the great Mersey entrepot with carriage drives, pedestrian walkways, meadows and water ornaments. 'Strawberry Fields' is now a landscaped area of Central Park, adjacent to the Dakota building, dedicated to John's memory.

In London, immediately after hearing of Lennon's shooting, Derek wandered over to Apple's final incarnation on St James Street to sit with Neil Aspinal and await the inevitable calls. They part after a couple of hours of painful reminiscence, and Derek took a cab over to George's London office. From there he steeled himself to phone George, who was asleep at Friar Park when the phone rang. Derek gave good phone. 'After a decade spent on the phone, this was one call he dreaded' making, writes George's biographer Geoffrey Guiliano. When George stumbled to the phone, with a presentiment of bad news, Derek suggested 'George, maybe you should make some sort of statement, just to get the bastards off your back.' George responded 'I can't, later maybe' and the line went dead, the receiver only making agitated noises for ears beyond hearing. Derek hung up, lit a cigarette, and waited. After an hour he phoned again. This time George was more together and agreed to work with Derek on preparing a press statement, in a sad reflection of the way Derek had once ghosted his *Daily Express* column. 'After all we went through together I still have great love and respect for him. I am shocked and stunned. To rob life is the ultimate robbery, to the limit with the use of a gun. It is an outrage that people can take other people's lives when they obviously haven't got their own lives in order.' Derek phoned the release through to the major London news agencies. The job done, and nothing more left to do, he caught the train back home. Watching the suburbs spin by from the window, but not seeing any of it...

Events had accelerated. In 1977 David Geffen had been diagnosed with cancer and given four years to live. He reacted by leaving California for New York, to spend three years in the company of Calvin Klein, Ian Schrager and the Studio 54 crew, befriending John Lennon and, in the process, securing rights to his last album – *Double Fantasy*, released in November 1980, just before the fatal shooting. Profoundly affected by Lennon's death, and the victim of financial embezzlement that robbed him of his royalties, Nilsson suffered the first of two massive heart attacks in 1993. A year later, the second one killed him. Derek Taylor wrote his obituary 'Harry Nilsson: Singer, Songwriter, Fab-Across-The-Water 1941-1994' for *Mojo* magazine. Geffen, meanwhile, learned that he didn't have – and never had had – cancer. He returned west in 1980 to establish Geffen records, scoring platinum after platinum – Aerosmith, Nirvana, Guns 'n' Roses, Whitesnake, along the way falling out with both Joni Mitchell and Neil Young, suing the latter for producing work below expectations.

7 May 1972 was Derek's fortieth birthday. What becomes of the wunderkind once he hits forty? Other issues were coming to a head. There was to be a reckoning. There was collateral Damage. Throughout their arc of adventures together, Joan writes, 'there were lovely times, but the drinking confused us both, and in the confusion we lost our precious intimacy and trust. Our closeness was eroded by alcoholic thinking.' What had begun as drinking with his father in the *Ring O'Bells*, or the five-session weekend pub-crawls with the 'Badgers', what had been a social convention to lubricate conversation and ease nerves in his early newspaper days, had escalated out of control. The

American years passed in a blur of partying, which Derek could joke about – 'coke makes you feel like a new man. Then the new man wants a line!' And back in London, 'I was taking loads of LSD, pills, coke, pot and poppers, and drinking all day and all night... I really lost touch with my marriage and misplaced all sense of reason. I was pouring whisky, brandy, gin, beer and wine into my body non-stop.' It had to stop. For many, the new decade was to be one of drying out, detox, and rehab from past excess. There were indications. In the depths of a vile hangover, Derek was out walking to clear his head after a ten-day Hogmanay bender at the very beginning of 1973, when his friend Jonathan suggested that just maybe he had a problem. A problem with drink? – yes, but an alcoholic? – surely not. Nevertheless, 'that January, I did stop, and then I started again and cut down and cut back and then occasionally broke out on sprees and benders. For all that year, I was in and out of cutting down, back, out and back in again...' But although 'alcoholism is cunning, baffling and powerful', as Derek admits, 'it is not irremediable.' There were periods of 'contentment and self-congratulation' then 'black-out and wild remorse.'

One day he arrived home drunk while Joan was giving a dinner party for two of the children's teachers. Derek behaved badly. There was nothing Joan could do to cover up for him. Derek recalls it as 'one night of abusing everyone once too often with relentless resentment and sarcasm, and extravagant physical falling about, into the river, on the stairs, into bed.' The next day there was a final Saturday morning family confrontation, with the oldest child gathering Joan and all six children together. 'The game is up.' Derek promised he'd go without drinking for the rest of the weekend, and seek help on Monday. No, that was only to procrastinate. It must be now. So he phoned AA. There he found the help and support he needed.

It wasn't easy, although he describes the process with typical humour and charm. About attending a meeting of two dozen strangers, and standing up to shakily declare 'my name is Derek, and I am an alcoholic.' Normally garrulous and clubbable, he said nothing else for the rest of the evening. But step-by-step, day-by-day, from that decisive moment, his life 'almost immediately' got a whole lot better. He did not drink, from the day of leaving that meeting, and has not resumed – 'not since Ted Heath was leader of the Tory party.' There was a family self-help group through which Joan was able to learn about co-dependence and 'the nature of addictive illness'. She visited an alcoholism and drug dependency treatment centre run by Clouds House in Warminster, East Knoyle, Wiltshire, where they were running family therapy groups. In

1976 – there was a period of 'AA Recovery' through SHARP (Self-Help Addiction Recovery Programme) started by Medical Director Dr Brian Wells, Consultant Psychiatrist, and himself a former victim of 'addiction to alcohol as well as other substances'. In Derek's words, 'call it Recovery. The news is good for all who have got sober. We all love it a lot more than the alternative'.

Derek was a writer. So Derek wrote in *Getting Sober... And Loving It!* (1992), a book collecting interviews with 'fellow-travellers in the vale of tears', with special gratitude to Ringo 'Richard and Barbara Starkey' for 'putting us up to it in the first place.' The book was intended as both a fund-raising benefit for SHARP and 'we, Derek and Joan, speaking for ourselves have decided that we might as well "out" ourselves and trust the higher power to see us through.' Dependency is also a social thing, a sharing bonding thing. So it implies lifestyle change to a degree, altering social habits, even severing friendships where those friendships are based around a mutual taste for oblivion. 'There comes a point where either you go crazy or you die, or else you join Alcoholics Anonymous', Derek admitted to Al Aronowitz, 'AA becomes your only alternative. There is no other alternative.' Al was one of those he found it necessary to sacrifice. 'In the years since I gave up', wrote Derek, 'Joan never reproached me for the drinking days. It had often been great fun to pub-crawl together and we had some fabulous parties before things got really out of control. Many of our friends were heavy social drinkers and a few were practising alcoholics. None were ever teetotallers. In recent years, we have recreated our marriage to become remarkably better than the one it replaced and it is so evident to all of our family and friends. We are all enriched by the recovery.'

Coming out the other side clean and serene - 'one hell of a lifetime older and wiser' – Derek was soon enjoying a period of rapid – and sober – career acceleration. He was appointed Director of Special Projects at WEA Records (UK) who, in a foretaste of the corporatisation of rock, had bought up Warner-Reprise, Elektra and Atlantic Records. As the only employee aged over thirty-five, he found himself responsible for the marketing and publicity of a handful of select artists such as Alice Cooper, Rod McKuen, Fanny, America and Carly Simon. Rising to Joint Managing Director at WEA, Derek was still a trendy guy with a moustache, although his slightly greying hair was now worn over his collar. He operated out of a plush office in Soho Square, with gold records on the wall and hot-and-cold running secretaries in every room. He'd audition possible signings, sometimes in a room upstairs at Ronnie Scott's Club, and was courteous and charming even when declining to extend a contract.

During this period Derek also independently produced albums for John Le Mesurier and Jimmy Webb, as well as 'light music' albums for Peter Skellern and the eccentric George Melly – 'another proud and eloquent son of Liverpool.' Skellern, born in Bury, had played in a few low-profile sixties bands – the March Hares and the Country-pop Harlan County – before breaking through with his 1972 hit single 'You're A Lady', powered by The Hanwell Brass Band. His subsequent album, *Hard Times* (1975), includes George Harrison playing guitar on a track called 'Make Love, Not War'. Melly was a dapper surrealist 'flecked with the foam of a tidal wave of fifties jazz' with its cultural roots in New Orleans. He had initially been dubious about the rise of The Beatles, viewing them as a trivial passing fad, until it became obvious to him that he was wrong, that they were, in fact, the advance guard of immense liberating social changes. Once he'd arrived at that decision he became fascinated, at first by the cultural phenomenon they represented, and only later by the music itself. He chronicled the process in his *Revolt Into Style* (Penguin, 1970), which Derek acknowledges as one of many inputs for his *It Was Twenty Years Ago Today*. By the time he was brought to Derek's attention, he was performing as unlikely vocalist with John Chilton's original Feetwarmers, including jazzer and cartoonist Wally Fawkes on clarinet, and Bruce Turner. Derek signed the ensemble to EMI, and an album, *Nuts*, was recorded live at Ronnie Scott's club in 1972, 'a night to remember for those who can. Some can't', as the sleeve-notes recall. The album's unexpected success encouraged Melly to leave his job as *Observer* critic and hit the road for a thirty-year career as a not entirely well-behaved entertainer with a penchant for earthy Bessie Smith blues, and the album's title-song which is, to Dave Gelly, 'a masterpiece of single entendre.' It even spawned a sequel – *Son of Nuts* (1973, both issued together as a double-pack by Warners in August 2004).

There were other intriguing encounters. When Adam Faith started managing Leo Sayer, he visited Derek's office and said 'Derek, I want you to sell Leo like a slab of meat hanging in a butchers window.' Then, towards the end of his eighteen-month tenure, Derek was party to the final demise of the Faces. Their vocalist, Rod Stewart, was already enjoying huge success as a solo artist and had announced to the *Daily Mirror* that his relationship with the band was over. Ronnie Wood was due to join the rolling Stones, although it hadn't yet been officially announced. The remaining group members, drummer Kenny Jones and keyboardist Ian

'Mac' mclagan, were invited to Warner Brothers' East End office 'for a little chat' with Derek and American record executive Mo Ostin. 'Derek had only recently become the head of Warner Bros in England, had worked closely with The Beatles for years.' Nevertheless, the proposition on offer wasn't promising. Why not reform a group with Steve Marriott? 'We looked at each other in disbelief and I told him it was the last thing I wanted to do, and left the office in a black mood' (quoted from Ian's book *All the Rage*, Sidgwick & Jackson, 1998). 'He was a lovely man', recalls Ian now. Although they saw each other infrequently 'he was a gentleman'.

But perhaps Derek was right? Steve Marriott was by some considerable distance a better interpretive singer than Rod Stewart. It's only necessary to compare and contrast their versions of 'My Way of Giving', by the Small Faces, and then by the Faces to realise that. And, despite Ian mclagan's denial, the Small Faces did indeed reform, with Steve Marriott in June 1976 around the time the reissued 'Itchycoo Park' returned them to the Top Ten. While for Derek, older connections were continued, he was on hand when George Harrison launched his *Dark Horse* label distribution deal with Warners (17 November 1976). And he was there in November 1980 when he conducted the launch of John and Yoko's comeback *Double Fantasy* through Geffen Records, then presented the first version of George's *Somewhere in England* (June 1981) album to WB the afternoon of the same day. It was rejected, went back for edits, only to be accepted seven months later! The spin-off single, 'All Those Years Ago' – with Ringo on drums, and Wings supplying background vocals – was not only reflections on Lennon's death, 'living with good and bad, I always looked up to you', but proved to be his biggest commercial success in some time.

At fifteen, Gerard Taylor was 'excluded' and then expelled from Frensham High School when his chances of getting any GCE qualifications were deemed by Headmaster Mr Alan Pattenson as 'zero'. He nevertheless subsequently gained 'O' and 'A's in 1975 through the encouragement of a devoutly Christian Mrs Moore. Then, in 1977, the family finally left Sunningdale for good, as Derek was transferred to Burbank as senior Vice President of the label's American parent company. Announced in March, in an echo back to his 'Farewell to Hollywood' party, Derek hosted three-hundred guests at the Savoy Hotel for a 'Farewell to Britain' luncheon (Tuesday 28 July). George Melly acted as hos, while providing music with the Feetwarmers. Kenny Everett spoke, Ringo paid tribute to Derek via a TV link from LA. Peter Asher also tributed Derek. George Harrison was there, with Joan and the six Taylor children.

Immediately afterwards, the full family headed back to Hollywood, where his A&M Records office was a stroll down Sunset Boulevard from the *Gaiety Delicatessen* and the 9000 Building. 'I was doing Ronald Colman impersonations at Warner Brothers Records at Burbank. I played the English Director of Creative Services, and as Vice-President.' Was there a flirtation with Stevie Nicks? She claims there was, and that her tender song 'Beautiful Child' on the Fleetwood Mac album *Tusk* (1979) was written about Derek; 'your eyes say "yes", but you don't say "yes", I wish that you were mine... I'm old enough to love you from afar.' It was during his LA tenure that he devoted a lot of time and creativity to the marketing of the Rutles first album, Eric Idle and Neil Innes cunningly accurate Beatles-pastiche. He was with A&M 'for a year, near enough a year', around the time Punk was administering a hefty adrenaline shot to the heart of rock, with Gerard becoming lead singer with Punk band The Wildcats, and then the Brothel Creepers. The group even played Derek's old stomping ground, the *Whisky a Go Go*.

Derek was instrumental in signing Liverpool Art School band Deaf School to Warner Brothers, after seeing them playing at Mathew Street, where 'he cried his eyes out', according to vocalist Enrico Cadillac Jr. He's credited as 'executive producer' on their launch album *Second Honeymoon* (August 1976), and on *Don't Stop the World* (1977), although their theatrical cabaret-style suffered by being at odds with the hard angry Punk mood prevalent at the time. Almost all former Deaf School members reunited for a live 1988 Liverpool date, the performance released as a live album, *Second Coming* (1988), produced by Clive Langer and Julian Wheatley, revisiting versions of their best songs from earlier albums, with guests including Tin Machine's Reeves Gabrels, Nick Lowe and Lee Thompson from Madness. Derek made the trip up to Liverpool to attend.

First in 1977, then in rapid succession again in 1978, Gerard had very close brushes with death. A near-fatal accident while 'out partying too enthusiastically' left him in a coma in intensive care. Soon afterwards he was involved in a 100-mph auto-wreck in a Ford Pinto on Firestone Steel radial tyres – both models were subsequently taken out of commission due to their unreliability. He comments ruefully, 'I wish I'd have known about the exploding Pinto, and sued, I could have lived off the proceeds ever since.' The incidents were seen as omens. Derek and Joan saw that if they stayed in LA, their family would suffer. So he traded one of the most powerful jobs in the music industry for the tranquil life of Brundon Mill in the rural 'old Suffolk' countryside as painted by Constable and Gainsborough. 'Joan and the children preceded me', as he proceeded 'to walk in the barley-fields… trying to avoid writing for a living.' Valued at £67,000, George Harrison bought the white seventeenth-century mill-conversion from a Mrs Beresford-Jones on the Taylor family's behalf (Friday, 15 September 1978), with its gabled roof overlooking the swans gliding on the river. The house is situated a short walk across common land from the market town of Sudbury which lies in a loop of the River Stour. Despite winning his AA battle against alcohol, it's said that Derek cultivated a few marijuana plants in his newly acquired garden-space.

'On the terrifying edge of the 1980s', he was not so much retiring to 'spend more time with his money,' as to concentrate more on writing. He'd had a steady job, now he wanted to be a paperback writer. He acquired a literary agent – Reg Davis-Poynter – and set out to endure the 'batterings of deadlines, rewrites, special pleadings, time compressions and self-doubts.' After all, hadn't his present state of prosperity been 'bought by a lifetime of carefully chosen words'? It had. Didn't he have the ability to write on any number of levels, and to switch from one mode to another with apparent ease? Sure he did, he had the ability to write all the way from the functional fact-based no-frills reportage of his earliest journalism, through to his light-hearted contributions to *Punch*.

There was even the most curious addition to his canon when he wrote the movie spin-off book *The Making of the Lost Ark* for Ballantine Books (1981) about his experience of the Steven Spielberg-Harrison Ford 'Indiana Jones' blockbuster. Derek travelled to George Lucas' film-sets in Tunisia, enjoying his vacation there as he interviewed those involved. 'Harrison (Ford) was so crucial to the film and so rarely off-screen that had he been unpleasant, things could have been really miserable', he recalled. But Derek writes well about the technical aspects of filming on location, devoting as much space to character backstories as to the movie itself. For Derek, there was always the playful spontaneity of his press-releases, but there was also the efficient deadline-tight high-readability prose of *A Cellarful of Noise*.

And with its new tone of seriousness, rock 'n' roll was discovering a sense of its own history. From now on, rock would be less concerned with the future, and more preoccupied with its past. A new academic heavyweight celebration of fast-times-past nostalgia-for-the-sixties industry was hitting its stride. *Melody Maker* (dated 7 September 1974) carried a three-page spread asking 'Do We Still Need The Beatles?' in which Derek is quoted as saying 'I'm not interested in them getting together again.' Yet he agreed to participate in a sixty-minute *David*

Frost Salutes The Beatles retrospective screened on US ABC-TV on 21 May 1975. And Derek persuaded George to go and see the London West End premiere of the Lyric Theatre stage presentation of Willy Russell's play *John, Paul, George, Ringo – And Bert*. George left at the interval, watching the re-enactment of his life during The Beatles years proved too painful an experience. But others were voracious for it. Yesterday – and 'Yesterday' – were the new tomorrow. Tony Palmer's *All You Need is Love* London Weekend TV-documentary series kicked off the process, screening its Beatles-years episode 'Mighty Good' on ITV on 14 May 1977 between 22:32-23:28. And for Derek, looking-back books were to be the profitable way forward.

During his west-coast adventure, Derek had been approached to ghost Nancy Sinatra's autobiography. Her Boots Productions – linked with Lee Hazelwood – had a red-white-and-blue 9000 Building office. They'd checked each other out warily. In the end, someone else assumed the task. Nevertheless, the ghosted autobiography has always been a financially rewarding, if anonymous occupation for a writer between projects. And this was still a time when a memoir, an autobiography, was something of a mark of social achievement. In later decades it would merely devolve into a career-move in itself. Today's ghosts, such as Jemima Hunt, give style and grace to Charlotte Church's *My Life So Far* (Time Warner, 2001), coolly lifting an £800,000 advance in the process. 'I was born, so Mum tells me, on February 21 1986... I believe her, since she was there' may come over as a cute Charlotte Church witticism, in fact, it's Jemima Hunt. Or Rebecca Farnworth selling over a million copies in the well-upholstered guise of Katie Price's *Being Jordan* (John Blake, 2004), mouthing 'I've never been one for the "natural" look'. Or respected music-writer Hunter Davies ghosting the five-million advance figures quoted for a five-book Wayne Rooney deal with Harper Collins in 2006. None of the shallow vapid celebrity names on the cover are much-involved in the writing of these autobiographies. It's said that Wayne Rooney's contribution extended no further than signing the contract, adding 'when I was younger I didn't really read books, I was playing football instead.' To efficiently and profitably ghostwrite, it's essential only to suppress the ego. Take a few guidelines. Tape a few hours of interview with the subjects. As Derek had done with Brian Epstein. Then get down to the actual work of elaborating it into marketable prose.

If, as John Updike once said, celebrity is a mask that eats into the face, then it is surely the duty of the serious biographer – or ghostwriter – to lift that mask and provide a glimpse, metaphorically speaking, of what lies beneath. As I have attempted to do in this book. Problem is, no celebrity wants the world to see that face, the one they abandoned once they started reading the hagiographical press about themselves. So the picture must somehow flatter those delicate, powerful subjects even as it attempts to tell the reader something – anything, piercing and true. It's a difficult balance, or at least it is if you are going to take it seriously. Those who don't can content themselves with playing around all those charity shows, premieres and clever lighting, all the way to the fat royalty cheque.

Derek had always stayed on good terms with The Beatles – particularly George, moving on to become closely involved with him at Handmade Films, and collaborating with George on his autobiography *I, Me, Mine*. George, the 'quiet Beatle', had matured into a living conundrum. His meditative explorations of the 'Great Beyond' balanced against his ongoing annoyance with the Taxman, and a very physical passion for earthly delights. Or, to Ringo in the Martin Scorsese *Living in the Material World* documentary (2011), a 'half love-bag of beads, half bag of anger.' To George's wife Olivia, Derek and George 'exchanged a special banter' and a 'verbal shorthand' that 'often left others in the room completely bewildered.' They shared a long complex history, and by now 'Derek's interviews were second nature to both of them, yet they always managed to produce fresh recollections.'

As with Brian Epstein's autobiography, *I, Me, Mine* began with long taped conversations, first in California, then continued back in England after Derek's return. And like 'George's Column', it was massaged into shape together, Derek adding his own italicised passages between George's own recollections. There are Roy Williams illustrations, copies of George's scrawled song-lyric sheet, and a photo-section including Plate XLVIII – Derek with George in the 'Friar Park' gardens taken by Brian Roylance in 1974. There are trees behind them, flowers between, a cat looks up at George, Derek responds with a crooked grin, the breeze lifting his shoulder-length hair. It's a strangely affecting photo documenting one of rock's more creative and enduring partnerships. Joan and the children also knew those gardens. The Taylor children played and explored around those caves and fountains during visits to Friar Park. The book-title, borrowed from George's *Let It Be* track, was composed of what Olivia Harrison calls 'a slightly cynical trinity of pronouns' – I, Me and Mine, which to Derek was 'a sly paradox of a title'. George adds to the reader, 'I have suffered for this book, now it's your turn!'

Derek was also writing about his own life, his involvement with The Beatles, and the phenomenon of the sixties in his own words, in a project called As Time Goes By. In 1970, the deal he'd finalised with publishers Prentice-Hall had begun to become an issue. They were getting impatient. George Harrison even sent Derek home from Apple for six months with instructions to complete the overdue manuscript that Derek had taken to calling 'Foul Stories of Necrophilia'. The publishers weren't impressed with the work-in-progress samples, the deal collapsed and they demanded a return of the advance. Derek was almost relieved, 'it became a real drag and I stopped. Lazy. Idle. Can do better if he tries.' In the meantime, he was commissioned by Tony Calder to prepare a satiric screenplay about a thinly-disguised fictitious northern band called The Myce. It remained unproduced. Then the script was stolen. All the while, Joan hadn't given up on the book project. Neither had Sylva Romano, who hooked it into Straight Arrow Books, publishers of *rolling Stone*. A new advance, a new commitment. So Derek sat at his desk by the window in Berkshire and began again. By 1972 'it is still not completed, and yet it is, because I am not going to write anymore.' The book begins, 'In the sixties somewhere, as random notes', and continues as 'As Time Goes By: Living In The Sixties' which *The Guardian* described as 'intriguing frontline report from the mass-music universe.' The cover of the British Abacus paperback edition shows Derek's head with a suitably psychedelic arc of Beatles faces exploding out of it, obviously attuned to what the publishers saw as the potential market. The contents, too, tend to stick closely to the Apple years, with forays beyond into the Byrds, Mae West and the *Daily Express* years.

For a more intimately personal insight into Derek himself, it's necessary to turn to *Fifty Years Adrift (In An Open-Necked Shirt)* – nicknamed 'The Big Leather Job' or 'The Fat Book' – which was published in December 1983 by Genesis Publications. An early working title had been 'And We All Shine On', but its eventual replacement was lifted from a Liverpudlian expression. Written by Derek, edited and annotated by George Harrison, packed with glorious pieces of memorabilia from his early days as a journalist, to his term as Beatles publicist and great friend, and beyond, it forms a lasting testament to the genius, wit and insight of two unique individuals. With George returning a series of long-standing favours by providing a glowing introduction to the signed, limited-edition volume.

In his introduction, George recalls how 'Harry Nilsson once asked me "what's Derek really like? I mean, I know him, but you really know him. So what's he like?" Well, what could I say? What can I say? He's my friend – that's why I'm writing this introduction – but of course he's much more than that. For me, it's an instinctive thing. I can see in Derek a hint of perfection I'm constantly seeking in everything and everybody. I've known him for years and I'll always know him. A lot of dialogue and scenes we've gone through together over the years have had little to do with the essence of our relationship. Well that went on for years which was why Harry said to me "Well he never really says anything to me"; and so I said "well he never says anything to me either," but somehow it didn't matter. I told Harry I didn't really know what Derek was like because we'd never talked about anything serious, and that was true, we hadn't. Yet somehow it never mattered, we shared our experiences from a broader base and I always knew he was OK. The day-to-day script represents only one level of a kinship that transcends the limitations of the physical body. We are all born many times and in many different forms, but even in the astral world – or any other kind of world we may end up in, I believe friends (like Derek and I) will always recognise each other. "Hello, vicar" he'll say, "fancy meeting you here!" Although there are things that I don't understand – some of the detail, there's something in him that's like a part of me. Derek is very British, even if he does like to dance the Flamenco. But he's OK. He's not what he looks or appears to be. I like Derek because he's clever, funny and honest. He'll say things that are true and it doesn't matter whether people like it or not as long as it's the truth. Ringo does that too. It's not your truth, it's the truth. Armed with that, nobody can get you. Derek is also bold. Derek is a little piece of astral rock I met someplace before and will meet someplace again. Enough of this frontier gibberish… on with the show…'

The text had to be edited down from the 400,000 words that Derek had penned to around a still-impressive 250,000 words. The volume comes in brown half-calf binding with gilt devices and boards, embellished with beautiful engraving-type illustrations throughout, mainly created by Roy Williams. The book incorporating a wealth of reproduced memorabilia, painstakingly excavated from a batch of large steamer trunks containing Derek's assorted possessions which 'one day mysteriously presented itself at our offices having been shipped from Warner Bros Records in Burbank.' These include letters sent to Derek, scribbled notes, photos, songwriting sheets, concert bookings, handbills, concert posters and tickets. Derek and Brian Roylance work through long nights against the punishing deadline pasting-up the complex layout sheets in Genesis Publishing's old cramped Pilgrim House office enabling the publication deadline to be met. 'Legs' Larry Smith creates the end-papers and Harry Nilsson

contributes an 'Afterword'. Although only two-thousand copies
were ever printed, there was a high-profile promotional schedule
commencing with a twenty-minute Radio 4 documentary profile of
Derek presented by Peter Marshall (Friday, 4 November 1983). The
book was launched in New Zealand, where George joined Derek
and Brian Roylance in Auckland (28 November 1984). After a literary
luncheon, they conduct a joint 45-minute press conference at the
Hyatt Kingsgate Hotel, fielding answers to an audience of three-
hundred reporters, photographers and TV-news crews. It must have
constituted a weird turn-around for Derek, who was more used to
arranging such events on behalf of others. They're able to watch
excerpts screened on the evening's TV-NZ news, before travelling on
to Australia for further promotion.

On 30 November, the duo front the first of two conferences at Sydney
Opera House – the second on 2 December – talking about The Beatles,
about each other, and about George's continuing interest in Eastern
music and religion. In many ways, suggests Derek, he and George were
'very dissimilar' people. He liked Opera, George 'can't stand people
making those noises.' George likes fast cars, Derek never even held a
driving license. Talking about Derek, George responds, 'I happened to
like his style of writing anyway, whether it's a postcard or a book.' *Fifty
Years Adrift* was the subject of glowing reviews including a fabulous
one in *The New York Times*, while *The Beatles Book Monthly* described
it as 'probably the best Beatles-related volume ever...' It immediately
sold-out, and subsequently became the most sought-after grail to
Beatles collectors – with rare copies changing hands through auction
rooms and on ebay for £3,750. Derek was interviewed on the Radio
Two *John Dunne Show* (Thursday, 22 August 1985), a conversation
largely based around the book. In Derek's own words, admittedly
within another context, 'there's a seamless, wistfully evocative piece of
history within these covers.' And there is.

Despite their denials, George and Derek did share interests. Some of
them well-authenticated. When George appeared at the 'George Formby
Fan Convention' at the Blackpool Winter Gardens (3 March 1991), Derek
and Joan, along with Olivia, Dhani and Brian Roylance were there to
watch him perform Formby's 'In My Little Snapshot Album'. And there
were claims of other odder, more contentious interests. 'Legs' Larry Smith
designed the cover-collage for George's *Gone Troppo* (1982) album. Larry,
with Keith Moon, then arch-peacenik George, had developed an interest
in Nazi memorabilia. There are claims that Derek went along with that
too. Despite his long-standing membership of the Labour Party.

The source of the story can be found in *Dark Horse: The Life and Art of George Harrison* (1989) by Geoffrey Guiliano, in which the author not only asserts the 'Nazi memorabilia' story but details what he claims to have been a lengthy fifteen-minute telephone conversation with Derek about his disputed 'interest' in Hitler photography. In fact, a closer family contact confirms that 'the only piece of "Nazi Memorabilia" Derek ever owned was a chamber-pot with Hitler's face on the bottom of it. Derek had a very ironic sense of humour, and having lived in Liverpool during the Second World War, at the time of the Blitz, he found the idea of somebody being as extremely awful as Adolf Hitler, somewhat amusing. It was the very fact of his being that evil that was absurd. In terms of collecting memorabilia, he wouldn't have been interested and would also have found Nazi Memorabilia collectors a source of amusement, kind of sinister trainspotters, "overcouts", if you see what I mean? In fact it was English Royal Family memorabilia that he liked. Kitch stuff like Royal Wedding tea-cups and that kind of thing.' Not that Derek wasn't given to regaling family and friends with informed history lessons on both world wars, or commenting on current events and politics, because he was, 'as those obsessives who have not been murdered by close relatives will know.'

In 1985 Derek began working with Granada Television in the capacity of freelance consultant for a documentary film project titled *It Was Twenty Years Ago Today*, with director John Sheppard. Mid-summer 1986 saw his research for the programme taking him back to both American coasts with a production team and an interview list of some fifty people, forty of whom made it to the camera. The film's final edit includes significant participation from Paul and George, Allen Ginsberg, Timothy Leary, Abbie Hoffman, Paul Kantner, Peter Coyote, Ron Thelin, George Martin, Barry Miles, Chet Helms, Allen Cohen, and Derek credited as 'consultant', Malcolm McDowell voice-over's the narration. Derek's book of the same name, from Fireside for Simon & Schuster (1987), grew from the process of re-immersion in that heady era.

It seems that sometimes, people live their lives forwards, but only understand it backwards. It remains probably Derek's strongest work. The book includes archive interviews and photographs as well as extensive transcripts from the documentary celebration of 1967 – but it isn't really about *Sgt. Pepper's Lonely Hearts Club Band*. Although providing a detailed documentary of the people and events that shaped the album, Derek uses the album release as a springboard to talk around the wider events of the Summer of Love, and its experiments in alternative living. 'How starry-eyed and foolish we were.' He

explores the Netherlands counterculture scene, 'Hoppy' Hopkins'
arrest for marijuana, the Diggers, the underground press, pot and LSD,
Happenings, the influx of eastern religions, psychedelic art, and...
inevitably, Monterey. But as an indication of his new-found sobriety,
retrospecting the events that 'brought me to this typewriter tonight,
in the thick of an English winter' (January 1987), he makes a point of
stressing that he now 'neither smokes nor drinks' and emphasises that
'while this book has to deal fairly and squarely with the enthusiastic
ingestion of illegal drugs of an explorative nature during the period
covered in the mid-sixties, there is no intention to encourage anyone
to follow suit.' Unequivocally he punches home the message that 'as
Proust might have said, "all drugs is dodgy."'

John Sheppard – who Derek calls 'the lofty cosmonaut of inner
space' – went on to greater celebrity as co-producer of the TV-movie
macgyver: Lost Treasure of Atlantis (1991). While Derek rekindled
another association from what he terms 'that exotic decade' to ghost
Michelle Phillips' autobiography *California Dreamin': The True Story
of The Mamas and the Papas*. The result is more a competent and
highly readable travelogue through the flirtatious persona of the
engagingly naïf Michelle than a penetrating or analytical critique of
the events she describes. Like the Epstein 'autobiography', it is more
taste and decorum than most academics and rock historians would
have liked, with much of John Phillips eventual narcotic excess excised.
Derek's part in the project is credited as 'hundreds of hours spent
helping me sort out the events of these confusing and tempestuous
years.' His qualification – 'having known Cass (Elliot) and most of the
people involved in this tale', at the very least through their Monterey
interactions, made him 'the obvious choice'. A smooth and finely
crafted piece of work catching her gossipy conversational tone to
perfection, the book describes Michelle's 'old bohemian' father who
was a production assistant on the Gary Cooper/ Paulette Goddard
movie *Northwest Mounted Police* (1940), and her early friendship with
Sue ('*Lolita*') Lyon.

From the start, Michelle lived nomadically, brought up in the chaotic
environment of her father's serial monogamy which eventually involved
five stepmothers – one of them younger than she was! A committed
traveller, constantly adjusting without realising, it became a way of life
that was to prove useful training for the years ahead. She lived through
June 1951 in Mexico in the Colonia Quatemoc with her father's friend
Farian Andres (composer of the Mama Cass hit 'Dream a Little Dream
of Me'). Later she modelled for a 'Lucky Lager' beer billboard, for

Dell Publications *True Romance* magazine and a cover-shot for their *True Detective* title. But inevitably the pace accelerates when she hits seventeen and goes to see folk trio The Journeymen at the San Francisco *Hungry I*, and meets John Phillips. In the line-up with Scott McKenzie and banjoist Dick Weissman, John was twenty-five and already married to a ballerina, with two kids, son Jeffrey (4) and daughter Laura (2). Not that she allows that inconvenience to stand in her way.

John and Michelle marry in rockville, Maryland on the last day of 1962, soon after his divorce from Susie. But by the time of Kennedy's assassination she was already enjoying her first extramarital intrigue. John wrote 'Go Where You Wanna Go' about the affair. Although the book insists on using an annoyingly coy disguise of aliases, her lover is 'Steve', a Phil Spector-connected Los Angeles record producer – it's left to John's own autobiography *Papa John* (1986) to supply the correct identity, Russ Teitelman. Later there's draft-dodging folkie 'Sheldon', whose real identity must also remain open to speculation. By 1964 the group had become the New Journeymen, John (baritone) and Michelle (soprano) with banjo-player Marshall Brickman (who would later become a staff writer for TV's *The Dick Cavett Show*)... later joined by Canadian Denny Doherty from rival folk-group the Halifax Three. Soon, according to 'Creeque Alley', their autobiographical hit single, 'California Dreamin'' was becoming a reality, and 'it was fun becoming famous'. To outsiders 'they're strange and wild', claims Michelle, 'and liberated progressive left-wing feelings spring from them. For all that, we didn't look dangerous. We were young, up with the times, and very commercial. That was it. We were real cool, man.'

Derek's input and influence is keenly felt in certain dialogue exchanges – 'I said "You must be Cass", and she agreed that she was', which is delivered with all the concise wit of a John Lennon lyric. Other phrasing must surely come directly from her – Michelle's self-description as 'a good little ass and no tits'? At one point she calls herself the original flower-child, and – like the Byrds song 'Child Of The Universe' – she gave love to everyone who needs her! 'I was much more relaxed about relationships than the others', is the way she phrases it. To John, 'Michelle wasn't real big on guilt or remorse.' First Denny – their dalliance provides the source material for the hit 'I Saw Her Again Last Night' – then she spills the beans on her relationship with newly ex-Byrd Gene Clark, which resulted in John firing her from the Mamas and the Papas on her twenty-second birthday (4 June 1966), which causes a glitch in their otherwise seamless ascent as hippiedom's golden family. All things must pass...

Her earnest endeavours to renew her marriage to John had less
to do with him, and more about recapturing the wacky celebrity her
membership of the group had bestowed upon her – 'we were certainly
in our element. The Mamas and the Papas sometimes felt as if they
were all the elements.' Yet their vocal blend was unique, something
that temporary stand-in Jill Gibson was unable to replicate – Cass
(forceful contralto), John (knowing baritone), Denny (musky tenor)...
and Michelle (lyric soprano). To John, 'she knew that (sex) was one
area where she always retained control – and considerable power over
me.' Back in the fold, the hits continued. When she claims 'we were
loved across the universe', perhaps there's evidence of Derek's hand
in its partial quoting of a Beatles song-title? The book follows Michelle
only through to the group's eventual breakup which, as she predicts,
precipitates the end of her life with John. There's a brief 'Epilogue'
updating the character's lives, but although she's quite open about their
soft-drug use, there's a tactful skirting of John's years of debilitating
addiction – during which, he comments 'I would have disgraced myself
to go out onstage straight' – and ends instead with his reforming a
version of the group with an amended line-up (with Denny, Mackenzie
Phillips and Spanky McFarlane) for the sad Golden Oldies circuit.

The early fans of The Beatles and the Byrds were now married,
Derek muses, or living like married. And they're carrying their record-
buying habits over into adulthood. 'Are they not the protesters, the
draft-resisters, the emancipated, the alienated and if they are not, how
come they heard the words of the songs and didn't heed them, for as
John Lennon said, "our songs were always about peace and freedom
and love, there was never any other message." Is it possible to march
to war singing "All You Need is Love"? I mean is it physically possible,
emotionally possible?' By way of contrast, to Derek, Johnny Speight's
Alf Garnett comic-rants 'misfired' because they 'gave millions a racist
vocabulary to be proud of.' Although seldom overtly political, Derek's
instincts were libertarian soft-left. When Kenny Everett – The Beatles'
sometime court-jester – grotesquely overplayed his role at the Wembley
Conference Centre Conservative rally during the high tide of Margaret
Thatcher's reign, urging the delegates to 'BOMB RUSSIA' and 'kick
Michael Foot's walking stick away', Derek was quick to respond. An
admirer of the leader of the Labour opposition, he was one of Everett's
friends unafraid to rebuke the wayward DJ, expressing his amazement
at the sight of Kenny joining the Thatcher camp and ridiculing the
tireless and idealistic campaigner Michael Foot. Into the nineties, Derek
saw consciousness being 'directed largely to people doing the very best

they can for themselves. Lining their own pockets, paying hardly any tax, and generally being selfish.'

Liverpool sporadically re-emerged from The Beatles vast shadow. Derek once quoted Allen Ginsberg to the effect that it was the 'centre of the universe,' adding that it was where they were all from – and that they couldn't have come from anywhere else and been so good! Of course, talent in the city hadn't just dried up, it just had an immense legacy to fight against, and a renewed isolation imposed as the south regained and tightened its grip on the music industry. From out of the Folk scene the Spinners remained a top attraction across three decades. In the early 1970s, the Real Thing spearheaded an upsurge of home-grown black music, although group-member Eddie Amoo had been a Merseybeat contemporary with vocal group the Chants fifteen years earlier. Yet new decades were spawning new generations of revolutionary and audaciously gifted bands, from Echo and the Bunnymen, Deaf School, the Teardrop Explodes, through Frankie Goes to Hollywood, China Crisis and Orchestral Manoeuvres in the Dark, the La's, the Coral, the Zutons. But the sixties cast a huge shadow. Subsequent musicians had to deliberately reject or kick against The Beatles in order to establish some kind of separate identity of their own. In the first month of 2008, it was ambassador Ringo who helped open Liverpool's year as 'European Capital of Culture'.

The skyline of what George had called 'Liverpool, the Holy City in the North of England', was irrevocably changed by what Derek termed 'developers with unusual handshakes'. The *Basnett Bar* where he and Joan would meet, where Brian Epstein, George Melly and Peter Brown would arrive on their separate orbits, all unbeknown to each other, is gone, fallen under the hammer of profit maximisation. Now Marks & Spencer faces John Lewis across the same street-space. Liverpool Airport became the 'John Lennon Airport'. With curious irony, during the eighties NEMS signed the Bootleg Beatles, because to many of us, The Beatles are still 'bigger than Jesus'. With son Dhani's blessing, the Wu-Tang Clan sampled George for their 'The Heart Gently Weeps' track on their December 2007 re-formation CD *Eight Diagrams*.

But the repercussions from the sixties were still reverberating and were still to extract yet another price. Fourteen years after Derek had attended his first AA meeting, Joan had a breakdown that was later diagnosed as post-traumatic stress disorder. 'All the pain of the drinking years and the strain of the children's problems had been buried, and now came to the surface and seemed to explode.' Now it was Derek's turn to support her through two years of recovery, rediscovering 'the enduring love and trust and intimacy I had thought would never be.'

Derek is remembered as being never less than a 'good cove'. He was more than that. When history became pastiche in the form of *The Rutles: All You Need is Cash*, he was there too. 'Derek Manchester' is a character played by Eric Idle, interviewed by a nosey reporter in the form of a barely-disguised George Harrison, as Press Officer 'Derek' lied and denied the decline of 'Rutle Corps', as the Rutle Corps offices were being ransacked behind them. The character was deliberately modelled on Derek Taylor. But increasingly, activities were more to do with marking past-events than initiating new ones. Returning to base at Apple's Soho headquarters in London's East End, the real Derek was interviewed on TV-AM about the CD release of *Sgt. Pepper* (1 June 1987). There was a thirtieth-anniversary reception to commemorate the release of 'Love Me Do' (5 October 1992), an evening held at Abbey Road's Studio Two with Derek, Neil Aspinall and photographer Mark Lewisohn (of *The Complete Beatles Chronicles* book). Neil and Derek were back there a year later for the launch of *The Beatles 1962-1966* and *The Beatles 1967-1970* anthologies on CD (9 September 1993).

Hits come and go. That's part of their charm. Two or three brief minutes of sonic escapism that spins at 78, 45 or 33 rpm, and then back into the real world. For the most part, they're as instantly gratifying and insubstantial as bubblegum. Or a snog with a stranger. But every so often, that brief snog develops into a lifelong affair. Loved over and over again, every time a new generation discovers them, to rechew that same bubblegum. Until they become hits beyond reproach, insulated against changing taste and the riptides of fashion. Independent of the context in which they were made. The Beatles back-catalogue defines that process.

Into the mid-nineties, Derek was lured back to Apple Corps, to where he'd orchestrated and controlled the massively-successful launches of *The Beatles Live at the BBC* (1994), to devise and execute the publicity and marketing strategy for perhaps the eras ultimate expression. To work on rock 'n' roll's greatest multi-media project of all, *The Beatles Anthology*. He also wrote the liner notes for all the CDs and videos, the success of the campaigns showing that he'd lost none of his skills over the years. But once he'd been part of what was happening, now he was reflecting on what had happened, he'd become a 'keeper of archives', a historian of the 'vanished moptops', an expert on 'something which no longer exists.' John Lennon was dead. The anthologies were a way of tidying up and tying off loose strands of their collective story. Derek was very much a part of that story. For him, it was also a slightly eerie revisit to his own personal history. The sounds and locations that he'd shared directly, or indirectly with the evolving story the cds told.

If it was an exercise in barrel-scraping – what a barrel, and what scrapings! – then it was also reclaiming an academic archive as valuable to rock as Leonardo Da Vinci's preparatory sketches are to the history of representational art. The distant adolescent harmonies of 'That'll Be the Day', the first attempts at songwriting with 'Cry For A Shadow', the studio debut with 'Ain't She Sweet', the failed demo of 'How Do You Do It', the surprising variant alternate takes of songs we'd considered beat-for-beat familiar, previously unheard original demos of songs they'd written for other artists, and the Everly Brothers harmonies of 'Lend Me Your Comb' lifted from their weekly BBC radio show *pop Go The Beatles*. The experiment in creating 'new' Beatles records by dubbing Paul, George and Ringo's contributions onto Lennon demos that was curtailed after a mere two tracks – 'Free as a Bird' and 'Real Love' – after their failure to equal industry sales expectations. But even they yield rewardingly creative videos drawing on early Beatles-styles cast into new perspectives.

And, of course, 'Strawberry Fields' is an amazing piece of work, but it's just as intriguing to be given some glimpse into the creative process that went into its creation. That working process is part of the work's wonder. The final record is a fluid fusion – the superimposition of an untraceable number of alternative versions. George Martin was the enabler. No matter how vague or extravagant the ideas they brought to him, he had both the musical expertise and the technical dexterity to realise it, from scoring a string quartet for 'Eleanor Rigby' or the French horn solo for 'For No-One', or John's concept for 'Tomorrow Never Knows'. Or the time-shift at the centre of 'Strawberry Fields', achieved by merging tapes from two separate takes into the finished whole. Here, we can watch that happen. Derek arrived with a box of videos, rough-cuts of the programme, for George's initially sceptical approval. Irresistibly, George was drawn into re-experiencing the events as they unravelled on the screen.

Derek and Neil were at Apple Corp's West London HQ in Ovington Square when Klaus Voorman brought in the original sketch-ideas for the series' cover-designs (10 July 1995). Then the same duo attended *The Beatles Anthology* launch-party at the ITV London Television Centre on the South Bank (12 September 1995). And for the promotions at the BAFTA Awards in Piccadilly (10 November). They took delivery of the final edit of the 'Free as a Bird' video, giving it their blessing (18 November), then Derek and Neil were there at the Savoy Hotel for the

Anthology press conference, with George Martin and Jeff Lynne (20 November). Asked where The Beatles were, Derek poignantly admitted 'they are all at home... everywhere else but here.' Neil and Derek were there for a Q&A session at the Apple press conference to announce the eventual eight-volume video *Beatles Anthology* box-set (July 1996). Derek also video-interviewed The Beatles themselves during August for the *Anthology: 3* video press-kit, Paul at his Sussex farmhouse, George at home in Henley, and Ringo in the Ovington Square office.

Returning to that time-period, reimmersing in what George Melly derided as 'the whimpering dog of nostalgia', was a way of bringing it all full circle, as with *It Was Twenty Years Ago Today*, it was a process of 're-living' and 're-learning' the period. Bringing it to a form of closure. Reconciling the past. Tony Sheridan and Pete Best both benefit from their inclusion on the first volume, in terms of royalties on those tracks that had never before been officially drawn into the canon. For Pete, even though the front-cover collage is artfully ripped to excise his face, and almost accidentally reveal Ringo's beneath, it also meant tie-in appearances on chat shows to endlessly recycle the increasingly distant memories of those teenage months, decades ago, when he'd actually been a Beatle. How did he feel about Epstein firing him? Did he hold a grudge? Had he seen *Backbeat* – and how accurately did it portray his youthful self? What's it like now, looking back, knowing what could have been...? He answers the same questions over and over again with patient amusement.

Derek adds that 'Pete will earn a decent amount of money (from *Anthology: 1*), which is only right. He is a good man, and he deserves it. This is a new chapter for Pete.' Indeed, Pete also resumes playing live, taking advantage of the new ripples of celebrity. He'd had a life before The Beatles. He had a brief spell as a Beatle. And the connection sporadically punctuated the rest of his life.

Meanwhile, Aunt Mimi died in 1991 in Poole, Dorset, in a bungalow bought for her by John. She'd had a life before John. She had a life with John. Then she also had a life after John.

Derek had a rich life and career before The Beatles. He had a life with The Beatles. And the connections proved impossible to shake off. He managed an appearance in his own right as special guest on the Jools Holland *Later* TV-show (25 November 1995). Confusingly, in 1995 Bois Books (UK) published *What You Cannot Finish* and *Take a Sad Song*, written by a different 'Derek Taylor' – briefly confusing the accuracy of, for example, Derek's Wikipedia entry. While Gerard Taylor was discovering his own writing niche – outside music, devoted to an African-Brazilian Dance-Fight-Game know as Capoeira. Abigal was living in Salford. Timothy in London. Joan was working with the Citizen's Advice Bureau. With the arrival of two grandsons, Derek and Joan found themselves happily settled. They had 'dealt with the insecurities within our relationship and "re-started" our marriage in the mode in which we would have liked to pursue it all those years ago.' They caught up. It was never too late. He gave thanks to Joan for her 'thirty years of intelligence, encouragement and love.' Derek's father had retired at sixty-five. At eighty he took up painting and joined an art club. He'd been eighty-six at the time he died, in 1975. Derek regarded that as a positive omen for himself. Looking backwards with a sense of strange amazement, 'even now, as I type, I wonder how anything has gone right with me when I have been, for so long, in such a muddle… it is to me a daily miracle that I can tie my own shoelaces.' He looked forward to the year 2000, to living in 2012. It was not to be. Posthumous volumes include *Beatles* (Ebury Press, 1999), plus an audio CD *Here There And Everywhere: Derek Taylor Interviews The Beatles*, released through the Thunderbolt label in 2001. So here are 'a few daft memories to pass to grandchildren to soften the hard twenty-first century…'

Rupert Perry (chairman of the EMI Records Group, UK and Ireland) said 'the untimely death of Derek Taylor is a sad loss for our industry and especially for those of us at EMI privileged to have known him. During his years holding the outside world together during the crazy days of Apple at 3 Saville Row, and more recently as the constant voice of sanity and reason amidst the furore of The Beatles "new" recordings and reunions, Derek's calmness and infinite charm and wisdom cooled many a hot head. Despite his illness, Derek continued to provide support to The Beatles, Apple and EMI, and we will remember him with great affection and gratitude.'

In an interview to the Associated Press a few years before his death, Derek talked of The Beatles, 'I knew they were wonderful. What I didn't know was there were four of them and they could hide away, whereas there was only one of me… nobody ever escapes The Beatles. Unless they behave dishonourably, they never get away. It is for life… I always had a romantic view that the thing should, if possible, be able to continue. There should always be a Beatles.'

Chapter Fourteen: And In The End, The Love You Make Is Equal...

A working-class hero is something to be...

Endpeace...

Fifty Years Adrift...

Back then, no-one remotely imagined that during the twenty-first century, people would still be listening to this stuff. It was great. Of course it was. But it was great for 'now'. Not forever. Pop records operate on short-term time-horizons and impulsive passions. Each single replaced and superseded the one that had come before. Each album was a giant step forward rendering everything that preceded it obsolete. By those distant future years, things would have moved on, music would have evolved into even more fantastic and exciting forms. Other shapes would have emerged to eclipse rock just as rock had eclipsed Jazz. Something we couldn't even imagine, something amazing and absolutely unpredictable, as we picnic on Saturn bathed in our radioactive glow. Sure, some spoke of The Beatles and their ilk as the new classical music of its day. Which it might have been. McCartney was compared to Schubert. And we knew about the Stockhausen and John Cage cross-overs. And if that had been so, you might've assumed that pop would have wound up preserved in conservatories and performed in museums. Not that Paul McCartney would still be filling stadiums doing 'Back in the USSR' or 'Sgt. Pepper's Lonely Hearts Club Band'. No-one imagined that it would still be a vital force endlessly replicated and reformatted. That we'd still be obsessing over it, analysing it, writing books about it. Like this one.

I certainly never imagined this. I don't believe Derek Taylor did either. The twenty-first was never destined to be his century. 'One day at a time, the years have slipped away' and 'it didn't strike me till later, as I wondered how any of it had happened, wondering if any of it had happened', he mused. Derek's relationship with Al Aronowitz – ruptured due to the latter's 'cocaine craziness' – was never fully restored, but for Christmas 1996 Al received a card with a brief message, 'sorry to be late responding. I am a poor correspondent these days, but in other respects I am making good progress with cancer, as I hope are you with your bodily challenges. All a great surprise. I expected to sail on to eighty-five. All's well here, will write more, but very good wishes meanwhile. Happy Holidays to Al from Joan & Derek in 1996.' He was never able to follow up on that promise to 'write more'. At Derek's funeral a statement from Brian Wilson was read out, 'we've all lost a great friend of music…' Derek 'was a jovial type-person, a happy person. I know I'll never forget him.'

Some are born to be spectators. Others are born to be watched. Derek was more of the first, but something of the second too. 'The more I'm ignored, the better', he told interviewer Bob Hieronimus. A life well-lived isn't a succession of career advances, but one of experiment and optimism, with its failures and its reversals, conducted in a spirit of generosity. In a photo taken just two years before his death, Derek's hair is greying, but still styled extravagantly long. Deep mauve shirt set off by paisley tie. His family are protective of his memory, 'a situation built largely on values that were instilled in us from an early age by Derek.' Wary of the rifts and disputes that have consumed other close relatives of celebrities, in family-wars over their legacy, 'the family have made a collective decision not to give interviews about Derek, this is no reflection at all on the interviewer, just something that avoids any potential misunderstandings for us.' Derek's lifetime indulgence in cigarettes, drink and other stimulants may well have contributed to his extended battle with cancer of the oesophagus, but during those same final months, he was working on his real passion, the long-planned official *Beatles Anthology* book.

Derek Taylor died in his sleep at Brundon Mill, his Sudbury home, in the early hours of Monday, 8 September 1997, at sixty-five years old. He was buried at a private funeral in Suffolk the same Friday (12). By family request, all donations went to the Macmillan Cancer Relief Fund. Although George was the only Beatle to attend – wearing a baseball cap, Mike McCartney, Neil Aspinall, Neil Innes, Michael Palin and Jools Holland were there, with life-partner Joan, and children Timothy, Gerard, Abigail (born in Didsbury, Manchester, December 1961), Vanessa, Dominic (born October 1967) and Annabel Lucie (22 March 1969). Paul, who had visited Derek at home on the Friday before his death, made a web-announcement (dated Monday 8 September 2:34 PM EDT) that said, 'he was a beautiful man. It's a time for tears. Words may come later.'

Geoff Baker (Paul's publicist and Derek's *Anthology* press-assistant) added, 'Derek leaves a thousand friends. Derek was not only the World's Greatest Press Officer, he was also one of the funniest, kindest and most decent men you could have met. All who did meet him, loved him. In 1969, The Beatles sang "and in the end, the love you take is equal to the love you make" – Derek Taylor was the proof of that equation.'

In a 5 November 1999 interview with Bob Hieronimus, Derek summed up his attitude as 'the constant battle is the ugly against the beautiful. And the ugly part of it is that which seeks to line our pockets and adorn ourselves and our lives with our own possessions, to the exclusion of our fellow man. It's always been the same, that's why we have to have some kind of a belief in a higher power or attempt to manifest some kind of divinity within ourselves or at least try to be decent human beings. And it's tough because selfishness is such a raging instinct...'

Chapter Fifteen: Post-Flyte

My back pages…

Works By Derek Taylor Himself

A Cellarful of Noise, by Brian Epstein – 'The Autobiography of the Man who made The Beatles' (June 1998, Byron Preiss Multimedia/ Rhino Retrospective distributed by Pocket Books), with new foreword by George Martin and a 45-page introduction by Music Historian Martin Lewis.

As Time Goes By, by Derek Taylor (Davis-Poynter Ltd 1973, Abacus edition 1974, ISBN 0-349-13381-6). It was republished as *rock & roll Remembrances Series No.3* through popular Culture Ink in the USA in June 1990.

The Making of Raiders of the Lost Ark, by Derek Taylor (August 1981, Ballentine ISBN 0345297253).

California Dreamin': The True Story of The Mamas and the Papas, by MICHELLE PHILLIPS (1986 – Warner Books, ISBN 0-446-34430-3).

It Was Twenty Years Ago Today, by DEREK TAYLOR 'An Anniversary Celebration of 1967' (1987 – A Fireside Book/ Simon & Schuster Inc, ISBN 0-671-64201-4).

I Me Mine, by George Harrison with Derek Taylor (Genesis Publications, Extended Edition February 2017, ISBN-10 1905662408).

Parents For Safe Food: The Safe Food Handbook, edited by Derek And Joan Taylor (Ebury Press, 1990, ISBN 085223823), Produced 'in association with the London Food Commission', Geoffrey Cannon, and Pamela Stephenson (introduction).

Twenty-Four Nights, by Eric Clapton, Peter Blake, with commentary by Derek Taylor (Genesis Publications, 1991, ISBN 0904351408). Limited Edition 'scrapbook' souvenir of Eric Clapton's 24-night Royal Albert Hall concerts during 1991.

Getting Sober… And Loving It: Hope and Help From Recovering Alcoholics, by Derek And Joan Taylor with foreword by Ringo Starr (August 1992, Vermilion Paperback/ Ebury Press, ISBN 009175187X). Includes the stories of alcoholics from all walks of life – including 'fellow-travellers in the vale of tears' such as Gary Glitter and Jimmy Greaves. Their personal experiences combined with practical information make this a helpful book for addict and relative alike. The author, Derek Taylor, is himself a recovering alcoholic. He is married to Joan who co-authored *The Parents Safe Food Handbook* (1990) with him. SHARP is a registered charity running courses for addicts from the crypt of a London church. Its patrons include Ringo Starr, Eric Clapton and Anthony Hopkins. A percentage of the royalties from the sale of the book goes to Sharp.

Fifty Years Adrift (In An Open-Necked Shirt), by Derek Taylor (Genesis Books ISBN 0-904351-22-X). Limited edition of 2,000 copies only.

Beatles, by Derek Taylor (1999, Ebury Books, ISBN 0091783798).

Audio-Visual Work Including Derek Taylor

All My Loving (1968) TV documentary mini-series directed by Tony Palmer.

Let It Be (1970) 81-minute film directed by Michael Lindsay-Hogg.

It Was 20 Years Ago Today (1987) 81-minute VHS USA Music Documentary. An examination of *Sgt. Pepper's Lonely Hearts Club Band* and the year of its debut, 1967. The Merry Pranksters, The Beatles, The Diggers. With original footage of Peter Coyote, Allen Ginsberg, George Harrison, Abbie Hoffman, Timothy Leary, George Martin, Paul McCartney, Derek Taylor, and Malcolm McDowell (narrator).

Imagine: John Lennon (1988) Biographical retrospective directed by Andrew Solt, featuring archive footage of Derek Taylor.

The Beatles Anthology (1995) TV mini-series crediting Derek Taylor with 'special assistance'.

rock & roll (1995) Ten-part TV documentary mini-series relating the story of music from post-war Elvis Presley to urban Grandmaster Flash, written and directed by David Espar.

The Abbey Road Story (1998) 65-minute TV documentary directed by Scotty Meade.

Wingspan (2001) TV-documentary charting Paul McCartney's 1970s career, produced by Alistair Donald and Paul's daughter Mary McCartney, featuring archive footage of Derek Taylor.

Here, There, and Everywhere: Derek Taylor Interviews The Beatles (30 November 2001, Thunderbolt CD CDTB221) includes (1) Derek Taylor introduction – 0.49 (2) Derek with John, Paul, George and Ringo – 3.25 (3) Derek with Paul McCartney – 8.05 (4) Derek with John Lennon – 3.43 (5) Derek with The Beatles' hairdresser – 2.54 (6) Derek with George Harrison – 9.50 (7) Derek with Ringo Starr – 7.10, all dated 1965 (8) Larry Kane interviews Derek in 1964 – 4.23 (Produced by Bob Shaw).

The Complete Monterey pop Festival: The Criterior Collection, Atmospheric film Directed by D.A Pennebaker of the historic event (2002, 3CD plus book) includes Derek Taylor interview.

With thanks for additional biographical information to:

The Beatles Anthology (Weidenfeld & Nicolson, 2000, ISBN 0304356050).

John, Paul, George, Ringo and Me: The Real Beatles Story, by TONY BARROW (Andre Deutsch, 2005) by the first 'Press Officer to the Fab Four'.

Brian Epstein: The Man Who Made The Beatles, by RAY COLEMAN (Viking, 1989).

The Beatles, by HUNTER DAVIES (WW Norton & Co., revised edition December 1996, ISBN 039-331-5711).

The Longest Cocktail Party: An Insider's Diary of The Beatles, Their Million-Dollar Apple Empire and its Wild Rise and Fall, by RICHARD DILELLO (First published by Playboy Press, 1972, Mojo Books – an imprint of Canongate Books, 2000. ISBN 1-84195-089-0)

Heroes and Villains: The True Story of The Beach Boys, by STEVEN GAINES (macmillan London 1986, ISBN 0-333-43495-1).

Can't Buy Me Love, by JONATHAN GOULD (Portrait Books, 2007, ISBN 0749-951664-10).

The Lives of John Lennon, by ALBERT GROSSMAN (Chicago Press, 2001, ISBN 155-6523998).

Dark Horse: The Life and Art of George Harrison, by GEOFFREY GUILIANO (Da Capo Press, 1997, ISBN-10 030-6807-475)

Revolver: The Secret History of The Beatles, by GEOFFREY GIULIANO (John Blake Publishing, New Edition April 2006, ISBN 1844541606).

The Encyclopaedia of Beatles People, by BILL HARRY plus his highly informative 'Birth of Mersey Beat' website: http://www.triumphpc.com/mersey-beat/birth/

We All Want to Change the World: The Life of John Lennon, by JOHN WYSE JACKSON (Haus Publ, 2005, ISBN 190495037X).

Lennon Revealed, by LARRY KANE (Running Press, 2005, ISBN 0762423641).

Everybody's Talkin' 'Bout… Derek Taylor, by MARTIN LEWIS, from the revised edition of *A Cellarful of Noise* by Brian Epstein, and the forward of *As Time Goes By* by Derek Taylor.

The Beatles: A Diary and *The Beatles Diary Vol.2: After The Break-Up 1970-2001*, by BARRY MILES (Omnibus Press, 1998, ISBN-10 0711963150).

Shout!, by PHILIP NORMAN (1981, revised edition Pan Books 2004, ISBN 0-330-48768-X).

The Byrds: Timeless Flight Revisited (The Sequel), by JOHNNY ROGAN (Rogan House, 2001).

The Beatles' London, by PIET SCHREUDERS, MARK LEWISOHN AND ADAM SMITH Foreword by Derek Taylor (Pyramid Books, April 1994 – 192pp – ISBN 0600581020).

With The Beatles, by ALISTAIR TAYLOR (John Blake Publishing, June 2003, ISBN 190-403-473X).

On Track series
Queen – Andrew Wild 978-1-78952-003-3
Emerson Lake and Palmer – Mike Goode 978-1-78952-000-2
Deep Purple and Rainbow 1968-79 – Steve Pilkington 978-1-78952-002-6
Yes – Stephen Lambe 978-1-78952-001-9
Blue Oyster Cult – Jacob Holm-Lupo 978-1-78952-007-1
The Beatles – Andrew Wild 978-1-78952-009-5
Roy Wood and the Move – James R Turner 978-1-78952-008-8
Genesis – Stuart MacFarlane 978-1-78952-005-7
JethroTull – Jordan Blum 978-1-78952-016-3
The rolling Stones 1963-80 – Steve Pilkington 978-1-78952-017-0
Judas Priest – John Tucker 978-1-78952-018-7
Toto – Jacob Holm-Lupo 978-1-78952-019-4
Van Der Graaf Generator – Dan Coffey 978-1-78952-031-6
Frank Zappa 1966 to 1979 – Eric Benac 978-1-78952-033-0
Elton John in the 1970s – Peter Kearns 978-1-78952-034-7
The Moody Blues – Geoffrey Feakes 978-1-78952-042-2
The Beatles Solo 1969-1980 – Andrew Wild 978-1-78952-030-9
Steely Dan – Jez Rowden 978-1-78952-043-9
Hawkwind – Duncan Harris 978-1-78952-052-1
Fairport Convention – Kevan Furbank 978-1-78952-051-4
Iron Maiden – Steve Pilkington 978-1-78952-061-3
Dream Theater – Jordan Blum 978-1-78952-050-7
10CC – Peter Kearns 978-1-78952-054-5
Gentle Giant – Gary Steel 978-1-78952-058-3
Kansas – Kevin Cummings 978-1-78952-057-6
Mike Oldfield – Ryan Yard 978-1-78952-060-6
The Who – Geoffrey Feakes 978-1-78952-076-7

On Screen series
Carry On... – Stephen Lambe 978-1-78952-004-0
Powell and Pressburger – Sam Proctor 978-1-78952-013-2
Seinfeld Seasons 1 to 5 – Stephen Lambe 978-1-78952-012-5
Francis Ford Coppola – Cam Cobb and Stephen Lambe 978-1-78952-022-4
Monty Python – Steve Pilkington 978-1-78952-047-7
Doctor Who: The David Tennant Years – Jamie Hailstone 978-1-78952-066-8
James Bond – Andrew Wild 978-1-78952-010-1

Other Books
Not As Good As The Book – Andy Tillison 978-1-78952-021-7
The Voice. Frank Sinatra in the 1940s – Stephen Lambe 978-1-78952-032-3
Maximum Darkness – Deke Leonard 978-1-78952-048-4
The Twang Dynasty – Deke Leonard 978-1-78952-049-1
Maybe I Should've Stayed In Bed – Deke Leonard 978-1-78952-053-8
Tommy Bolin: In and Out of Deep Purple – Laura Shenton 978-1-78952-070-5
Jon Anderson and the Warriors – David Watkinson 978-1-78952-059-0

and many more to come!

Would you like to write for Sonicbond Publishing?

We are mainly a music publisher, but we also occasionally
publish in other genres including film and television.
At Sonicbond Publishing we are always on the look-out for
authors, particularly for our two main series,
On Track and Decades.

Mixing fact with in depth analysis, the On Track series examines
the entire recorded work of a particular musical artist or group.
All genres are considered from easy listening and jazz to 60s soul
to 90s pop, via rock and metal.

The Decades series singles out a particular decade in an artist or
group's history and focuses on that decade in more detail than
may be allowed in the On Track series.

While professional writing experience would, of course, be
an advantage, the most important qualification is to have real
enthusiasm and knowledge of your subject. First-time authors
are welcomed, but the ability to write well in English is essential.

Sonicbond Publishing has distribution throughout Europe and
North America, and all our books are also published in E-book
form. Authors will be paid a royalty based on sales of their book.

Further details about our books are available from
www.sonicbondpublishing.com. To contact us, complete the
contact form there or email info@sonicbondpublishing.co.uk